CISSY

By Paul F. Healy
YANKEE FROM THE WEST,
with Burton K. Wheeler

CISSY

THE BIOGRAPHY OF
ELEANOR M. "CISSY" PATTERSON
BY PAUL F. HEALY

DOUBLEDAY & COMPANY, INC., GARDEN CITY, NEW YORK, 1966

To Kathy, Jane, Monica,
Julie and Kevin

AUTHOR'S ACKNOWLEDGMENTS

Cissy could not have been written without the generous co-operation with this writer of hundreds of her friends, relatives and employees. For information, insights, documents and encouragement I am especially indebted to the following: Felicia Gizycka Magruder, Mrs. Joseph M. Patterson, Rose Crabtree, Frank Waldrop, Mason Peters III, Ellen Pearson Arnold, George De Witt, F. M. (Jack) Flynn and William C. Shelton.

Among others who assisted me through invaluable interviews are: Adela Rogers St. Johns, Mr. and Mrs. Arthur Krock, H. A. (Happy) Robinson, Mr. and Mrs. William Randolph Hearst, Jr., Mrs. Robert R. McCormick, Alice Roosevelt Longworth, Burton K. and Edward K. Wheeler, Mrs. Michael W. Flynn, Jackie Martin, Drew Pearson, Mrs. Eugene Meyer, Mrs. Lawrence Wood (Evie) Robert, Robert Considine, Mrs. Carolyn Hagner Shaw, Walter Trohan, Ruth Montgomery, Joseph Miller, Margaret Barney, Mrs. Ray Brennan (Betty Nowell), Bernie Harrison, Mr. and Mrs. Emile P. Bouchard, Richard Hollander and the late Pat Frank.

For both suggesting and locating sources I also wish to thank Gustav J. Miller, William P. Flythe, Jr., John J. McPhaul and Miss Lina Hoffman. For permitting me the use of their indispensable reference libraries I am indebted to the New York *News*, New York *Times*, New York *Herald Tribune*, New York *Journal-American*, Chicago *Tribune*, Chicago's *American*, Chicago *Sun-Times*, *Time* and *Newsweek*.

Special thanks go to Mrs. Harold Ickes for permission to quote extensively from *The Secret Diary of Harold Ickes* and to the editors of *Field & Stream* for permission to quote from "Diary on the Salmon River."

PAUL F. HEALY

CONTENTS

CISSY

ONE

Herald Angel

This item, boxed in black lines, appeared on the front page of the Washington *Herald* on August 1, 1930. When the staff members saw it, they were baffled and worried. Mrs. Eleanor Patterson was taking over that morning as their new editor and publisher. What did the zany manner in which she chose to introduce herself to *Herald* readers portend? It was bad enough that the new boss was a woman, and a society woman at that. She also apparently was addicted to expressing herself whimsically, if not enigmatically.

See pp 35

Late that morning the staff got its first physical view of Mrs. Patterson. Suddenly there she was, standing in the center of the city room. At her side was Frank Knox, general manager of all the Hearst newspapers, of which the *Herald* was one. She was tall and elegantly tailored, with red hair that glistened like copper, pulled straight back on her head, a snub nose, and a mouth set wide and straight in an oval face.

Knox introduced the glamorous stranger, and she spoke briefly, in a tone of quiet command. Her voice was throaty, like that of an actress, with a languidly imperious drawl.

"All right," she said, as the reporters and subeditors gathered around, "they say this is a stunt—a joke! Well, if that's their idea, let's show them—let's go to work and put it over!"

The men had begun to slip into their coats—reluctantly, for it was a torrid summer day. The new boss added with a smile: "And you don't have to wear your coats when I'm around either."

Then she turned and drifted from the room, trailing an exotic perfume. Most of the staff members shrugged and turned back to their desks. Others grinned at one another: Perhaps the hapless *Herald* had not, after all, seen everything yet.

Early in the afternoon there was another incident, but whether it was a good or bad omen remained to be seen. The new boss had been offered the plush office suite reserved for Hearst executives at the front of the *Herald* building and had turned it down. Instead she chose the relatively small space just off the city room which had been used by the sports department. A wall running only three quarters to the ceiling separated it from the bustle of the reporters, copyboys and editors.

"I intend to learn this business and run the paper," Mrs. Patterson explained to Knox. "And I want to know what's going on."

Knox kept his amusement to himself. He knew she wanted to be taken seriously as an editor. He had been rushed here from New York two days before to cope with possible hostility.

Arthur Brisbane, the Grand Panjandrum of the Hearst organization, had dispatched him with this observation: While veteran
Hearst men should long since have accustomed themselves to
surprises, they might resent having to take orders from a woman.
The appointment was to be regarded as an experiment. Never
before had a female been editor of an American metropolitan
daily. Knox had called together the top men of the *Herald* and
implored them to be patient. After all, they had suffered through
Hearstian innovations before.

"You know she won't be around long," Knox had said to them,
puffing smugly on his cigar. "She won't last six months."

Six months was a good deal longer than some publishers had
lasted at the *Herald*. In the paper's nearly three decades of existence, an average of almost one publisher a year had come and
gone in an effort to rejuvenate the money-losing paper. Some of
them had survived less than a week, and one had thrown up his
hands after only one night and departed in disgust.

The *Herald* was one of the livelier papers in Washington, but
it was undistinguished journalistically and considered not quite
respectable. Now, in mid-1930, its circulation was down to an
anemic 61,000, so who could argue that an offbeat editor and
publisher was not worth trying?

But, ran the counterargument, granting that Mrs. Patterson
was an offbeat choice, what was there about her that suggested
she might bloom into a successful newspaper executive? When
she was sized up, only the wildest of prophets could have foreseen that within a few years she would emerge as a hellcat who
could stand the capital on its ear and command national attention. Or that in fifteen years her executive success would splash
her into *Collier's* magazine as "the most powerful woman in
America."

Who *was* Eleanor Patterson? To be sure, nothing about her
was ordinary. She was a middle-aged millionairess, one of Washington's three so-called "whip-cracking hostesses"—whose parties
were said to have an "Arabian Nights flavor." She was a true

American aristocrat, authentic and dignified, whose lack of inhibitions provoked a restless, damn-the-torpedoes way of life.

This much was known to informed Washingtonians. Those who took the trouble to inquire further were rewarded, for her earlier past was sheer storybook melodrama. A belle in the *fin-de-siècle* European diplomatic set, she had married a Polish-Austrian count and had gone to live with him in a "castle" deep in Russian-held Poland. Within a few years she had fled from him with their baby girl over the midnight snows. The Count had pursued her, kidnaped the child and hidden her in a convent. Only through the intercession of President Taft with Czar Nicholas was the baby restored to her mother.

Divorced, and still known as "The Countess," she had married Elmer Schlesinger, a prominent lawyer, in 1925. When Schlesinger died in 1929, she had legally reclaimed her maiden name. Her close friends called her "Cissy," a family nickname dating from childhood.

To the *Herald* staff it was encouraging that the new boss was the offspring of a distinguished American newspaper dynasty. Mrs. Patterson's maternal grandfather, Joseph Medill, had established the powerful Chicago *Tribune;* her cousin, Robert R. McCormick, was carrying the *Tribune* to new successes; and her brother, Joseph Patterson, was founder and editor of the New York *Daily News*, which boasted the largest circulation of any newspaper in the country.

Cissy Patterson herself was almost totally devoid of newspaper experience. Back in 1920 she had written some articles about the Republican National Convention and about her big-game hunting for the Chicago *Herald and Examiner*. Better known, and much more to her credit, were two novels she had written during the twenties. One, *Glass Houses*, was a cutting commentary on Washington's sociopolitical life. The other was *Fall Flight*, a fictionalized version of her own hair-raising life with the Count. Both books had been well received by the critics.

On one point there was unanimity: Cissy was no sissy. She

had spirit and courage. She was a superb horsewoman, and there were people in Wyoming who claimed she was the best woman rifle shot ever seen in the state. As for conflict and controversy, the lifeblood of exciting newspapers, Cissy obviously thrived on it.

Gusto and imagination were what the *Herald* sorely needed. In 1930 there were five daily newspapers in Washington, and only one of them, the venerable *Evening Star*, was a financial success. And the outlook for an economic boom was nil. The country felt in its bones the economy was in a state of transition —but to what? The people were waiting impatiently for the promised end to the recession which had followed the stock market crash of the previous October. During the late winter and all spring, President Hoover and Secretary of the Treasury Andrew Mellon had soothingly forecast a business revival. But in midsummer it certainly was not in sight.

While the business analysts were worried, the average newspaper reader was looking for distraction. With the 1929 crash still on his mind, he was in search of novelty and excitement. *Earl Carroll's Vanities* and *The Green Pastures* were packing theaters on Broadway, and the new "talkies" were packing rococo movie palaces. The popular songs were "Star Dust," "I Got Rhythm," and "The Peanut Vendor." Vast, invisible radio audiences huddled nightly around sets to catch the rackety sounds of Major Bowes and his amateurs.

If ever there was a time to hand over the fate of a newspaper in the national capital to a frivolous society hostess, perhaps this was it. The Hearst organization sought to capitalize on Mrs. Patterson's name value. Two days before she was to take over, Knox inserted a front-page, boxed announcement composed by Brisbane. Noting that she was the granddaughter of Joseph Medill, it stated: "The Washington *Herald* feels sure that Mrs. Patterson, who in accordance with Galton's Law, inherits the genius of her grandfather, and will be very successful and INTERESTING as editor of a Washington daily newspaper."

Privately, Brisbane had advised his protégé in New York that the way to be interesting in Washington was to attack a sacred cow. The notion appealed to Cissy; she had always enjoyed ridiculing sacred cows, and now she had a megaphone to do it with. In her third day on the job, she saw her chance. Sitting cross-legged on the third floor of her Washington mansion, she was scanning the other Washington newspapers when an item brought a gleam to her eye. It announced that Mrs. Alice Roosevelt Longworth would serve as "adviser and campaign manager" for Ruth Hanna McCormick in Mrs. McCormick's race for a United States Senate seat for Illinois.

Ruth was the widow of Cissy's first cousin, former United States Senator Medill McCormick, and the daughter of Mark Hanna, the shrewd Republican boss who had engineered William McKinley's election to the Presidency. Alice Longworth, the celebrated "Princess Alice," was daughter of the late President Theodore Roosevelt and wife of Representative Nicholas Longworth, the Ohio Republican who was currently Speaker of the House. No one could wish for a cow more sacred than Alice.

Since nearly the turn of the century, Cissy and Alice had been friends—most of the time. Cissy liked to needle Alice, for Alice had the reputation of being one of the wittiest women in America. Like Dorothy Parker, her reputation was so great that she was sometimes credited with bon mots she had not coined. The description of President Calvin Coolidge as looking "as if he had been weaned on a pickle" was widely attributed to Alice; she admitted to having gleefully circulated the barb but disclaimed its authorship.

As a teen-ager in the White House, Alice had been America's hoydenish darling. She had shocked the post-Victorians by smoking cigarettes, betting on horse races, and diving into the ship's swimming pool, fully clothed, during a voyage to the Orient. Lovely, sparkling, photogenic, Alice had been simultaneously loved and criticized. (President "TR" once was asked why he didn't control his daughter. "My dear fellow," he had replied, "I can either try to run the country or try to control Alice. I cannot possibly do both.") Now, as the Second Lady of the land, Alice was more dignified—in other words, a fine target for a Cissy shaft.

Alice later insisted to friends she "knew it was coming." Five years before, she had been unflatteringly fictionalized as a Washington hostess in Cissy's first novel *Glass Houses*. When Cissy had a newspaper to play with she doubtless would strike again, if for no other purpose than to increase readership.

Sitting on the floor, Cissy pondered the item about Alice and Ruth McCormick's campaign, then looked around for note paper. Finding none, she tore a blank page from a book and began writing rapidly in pencil. Making some quick editing changes, she telephoned Mike Flynn, managing editor of the *Herald*. After dictating the item to Flynn, she said: "Put it on the first page, Mike. Mr. Hearst says people don't read anything anywhere else."

The "box" appearing the next day read:

Interesting but Not True

The news is that Mrs. Alice Longworth will not only be a confidential adviser to Mrs. Ruth Hanna McCormick, but that she will campaign publicly for her lifelong friend. Interesting but not true.

Mrs. McCormick takes no advice, political or otherwise, from Mrs. Longworth.

Mrs. Longworth gives no interviews to the press.

Mrs. Longworth cannot utter in public.

Her assistance will, therefore, resolve itself as usual into posing for photographs.

(*signed*) ELEANOR PATTERSON

Washington bought the *Herald* as never before. The question was: What would Alice do?

The next morning Cissy looked at the New York *Times* and

discovered that she was national news. The *Times* quoted the slap at Alice and reported that friends of Mrs. Longworth were "amused" by it. But from Alice herself came no comment.

Cissy continued to use her front page to titillate her readers. In October, she went after Alice again. Recalling that she had said previously that Alice had "no real gifts" to contribute to Mrs. McCormick's campaign, Cissy now observed in a box:

I was in error. I spoke hastily. In ignorance.

Senator Borah, another close friend of Alice Longworth's, has said that if Mrs. McCormick is elected he will vote to unseat her because of her excessive campaign expenditures. Mrs. Longworth may now present her real gifts. She may use her political influence, of which the country has for so long heard so much. She may soften the decision of the frugal gentleman from Idaho.

Senator Borah is also a close friend of Mrs. Ruth McCormick. They are all close friends.

But it is for Alice to come now bearing gifts.

Will she? Can she?

(*signed*) ELEANOR PATTERSON

To those tuned in on Washington gossip, this was an inside joke. Like Alice, Borah had been the model for a protagonist in Cissy's *Glass Houses*—a western senator who attracted the predatory eye of both of the hostesses, thinly disguised as Alice and Cissy herself. The fictional triangle was based on fact.

Once again Cissy's public musings made the New York *Times*. It gave an account of the blast in its usual sober fashion but, in addition, its Washington correspondent, Arthur Krock, devoted a long paragraph to the item in his Sunday column. Noting that Cissy, Alice and Ruth had been chums since girlhood, Krock asked, with proper *Times* dignity, whether Editor Patterson's "cutting disparagement of Alice [between whom he said there had been a sharp estrangement] represents a woman colleague's idea of what is of first importance of comment." In time, Krock was to drop his disdain of Cissy Patterson's news judgments; he also became a good friend and married one of the *Herald's* stable of society columnists.

In Washington, a story was being gleefully circulated which added spice to the feud between the capital's leading ladies. During one of Alice's dinner parties in the twenties, so the story ran, she had placed a distinguished European nobleman at her right. But after dinner Cissy had monopolized the handsome fellow in the upstairs library. The next day Cissy received a hand-delivered note from her hostess. It read:

Dear Cissy,
Upon sweeping up in the library this morning, the maid found several hairpins which I thought you might need and which I am returning.

Alice

To which Cissy replied, also by hand-delivered note:

Dear Alice,
Many thanks for the hairpins. If you had looked on the chandelier, you might also have sent back my shoes and panties.

Love,
Cissy

Alice later maintained the incident never happened. But Cissy told it herself. It sounded completely in character, and it was still being retold years later as an example of what Washington talked about before the big war and the big bomb. In the thirties, the incident became so well known that any reference to it was good for a laugh. In 1933, in a skit during a Women's National Press Club stunt show, playing the role of a newspaper editor modeled on herself, Cissy ad-libbed: "Stop the presses! Stop the presses! My drawers are caught in the presses!"

It brought the house down. Now it spiced the Longworth-Patterson feud, which was to continue for nearly ten years, and

fed the growing legend of "Editress" Patterson, the swashbuckling lady journalist—something new on the American scene and,
perhaps, something that would happen only in America. Un-
daunted, undisciplined, unwilling to knuckle under to man, nature, tradition or government, she cut an increasingly broad
swath. It coincided with the coming of the New Deal, which
changed Washington from a slow-paced town into an exciting
city.

Mrs. Patterson's mercurial attitude toward her employees alone
both flabbergasted and amused the capital. It ranged from an
almost sadistic cruelty to outlandish kindness. Firings were frequent, impulsive, and sometimes bizarre. They were never dull,
and a discharged editor could dine out for a week on his story of
his last day at the *Herald*. By that time he was probably hired
back.

Another conversation piece in Washington was Cissy's wardrobe. It hung from racks filling two rooms of the top floor of her
mansion at Du Pont Circle—gowns, slippers, floppy hats, bathing
suits and other items running into the hundreds. The ensembles
were numbered, photographed and indexed in a catalogue. When
Cissy was planning an evening out, she thumbed through the
catalogue and gave her maid the number of her evening's choice.

Sartorially, if nothing else, she was the most startling newspaper editor in the country. She was likely to turn up at the
Herald office at any hour of the day or night, and her "working
clothes" varied with the hour. In the morning or early afternoon,
she was usually in riding habit, and late at night, coming straight
from a party, she would glide through the office wearing a dinner dress and dragging a mink coat. If she was wearing the coat,
and it hung open, one could glimpse dazzling Oriental brocade
pajamas, her favorite, and a daringly avant-garde, evening costume. The final touches of glamor were her long cigarette holder
—longer even than FDR's—and red-painted toenails.

In the raffish city room of the *Herald*, Cissy was a shimmering
vision. With it, however, came discordant sounds. Mrs. Patterson

was always accompanied by a pack of French poodles. Before she entered the doorway, the poodles' commotion signaled the arrival. They yapped—drowning out her low, awe-inspiring remarks to the editors—and they nipped. Deskmen endured the attentions of the poodles, between silent curses, as occupational hazards. The dogs snooted the editors and reporters and were contemptuous of copyboys. They might tolerate a scratching of their ears for a time, but soon they stalked off, flaunting their snobbery.

To the men of the *Herald*, Mrs. Patterson was "The Lady," and to the women she was "Madame," a term of irony mixed with respect. On first meeting, no one was immune to her impact; it was remembered and discussed for a long time afterward. She had "presence" to such a degree that all eyes riveted on her when she made an entrance. This was not only because she was strikingly dressed. There was a confidence, a slowness, a deliberateness about her which suggested a tigress. Like a tigress, she had seldom-blinking eyes. When they fixed on you, they exercised a potency of will. Yet the strong will was cloaked in an outward femininity and charm that was irresistible.

Cissy's most envied physical characteristic was her carriage. Well into middle age, her figure retained the suppleness of an athlete. She was five feet, seven and a half inches tall, with a narrow waist and small, pretty feet—on which she was wearing ballet slippers years before they became the vogue, and she seemed to glide along like a ballet dancer. President and Mrs. Theodore Roosevelt were fascinated by the fluidity of her movement. They told their daughter Alice repeatedly: "Watch that Patterson girl when she walks—such grace, such beauty in motion!"

It was the grace of a feline animal. As one Washington columnist put it, "Cissy panthered across the room."

Cissy's glamor had nothing in common with the motion-picture-queen style of the twenties and thirties. Her face lacked classic lines and she did not indulge in lacquered makeup. Her

turned-up nose, huge eyes and puglike contours carried more
than a suggestion of Irish pugnacity—which she came by
naturally. Yet the total effect was bewitching. One young Washington matron, blessed with more conventional good looks, complained enviously: "Cissy simply hypnotizes people into thinking she's a great beauty."

Cissy's voice had a cello-like richness. She spoke slowly and
deliberately, every syllable articulated carefully. The pitch was
low, and to some men the tone seemed caressing. Late in her life
the tone became almost as husky as a man's.

Altogether, she could be summed up in the French phrase
"*belle laide*." It was this paradoxical quality which had caught
the eye of Baron von Rothschild, a member of the European
banking family whose pleasant hobby it was to photograph
beautiful women. He met Cissy in 1902, when she was making
her debut in Continental society on the arm of her uncle, Robert
Sanderson McCormick, then United States ambassador to Austria-Hungary. The Baron, immediately impressed, drew the girl
aside.

"You are not beautiful," he said bluntly. "In fact, you are
ugly. But there is *something*. Will you sit for me?"

Cissy's incandescence glowed against a succession of glittering
backdrops. She lived as the *hoi polloi* thinks rich aristocrats
ought to live. In the early thirties, when the rich were just beginning to feel guilty, no American woman lived on a more independent or extravagant scale. Loving movement, she needed
many places to alight, and over the years she acquired many.
Her principal house was a marble mansion at 15 Du Pont Circle
in Washington, D.C. Built by the famous architect, Stanford
White, it had thirty rooms and ten bathrooms and was manned
by a staff of eighteen servants, including a green-liveried footman and a butler actually named Philpotts.

In nearby Marlboro, Maryland, Cissy kept an English-style
house and country estate. In Sarasota, Florida, she maintained a
winter residence on the Gulf, and at Port Washington, Long

Island, she owned the estate formerly owned by Vincent Astor. In New York City she rented a year-round apartment at the plush Carlton House. She had another place at Nassau. And at Jackson Hole, Wyoming, there was the ranch where she hunted elk and bear.

Between some of these residences—and to many other places —Cissy traveled with casual grandeur, like a maharani, in her private railroad car, "The Ranger," christened after one of her favorite horses. The fact that private railroad cars were already obsolescent luxuries in America did not bother her. Cissy was fond of hers. Mrs. Carolyn Hagner Shaw, her secretary at that time, was reminded of a French chateau when she entered the car. It was furnished daintily in chintz, had guests' bedrooms and baths, a cozy living room and a well-stocked kitchen.

Hooked onto the end of a regularly scheduled train and ready to roll across the country, "The Ranger" was a kind of barge-on-wheels for an American Cleopatra. The full complement included butler, chef, French maid, personal secretary, food, liquor, changes of slipcovers, and more than a dozen trunks just for Cissy. Sometimes she decided late at night to leave town on the car in the morning. The staff was immediately galvanized into furious activity to get everything ready to roll at dawn. Even the personal secretary did not always know the ultimate destination or how long they would be gone.

Once, Mrs. Shaw was told to ride the car to New York just to retrieve the poodles—who had unaccountably been left at the Port Washington house—and bring them back to Washington. Probably en route, the secretary speculated that she must be conducting the most extravagant canine escort service in history.

Cissy played each of her roles for all it was worth. In the office, surrounded by editors who vied like courtiers for her favor, she reigned like Queen Elizabeth. On horseback, she rode as easily as a circus rider. At her Wyoming ranch she roughed it and shot like an elegant Annie Oakley. Skillfully guiding the conversation at one of her evening salons, she was Madame de

Staël. Composing her thoughts for publication, she was George Sand.

When necessary, Cissy used her charm, as one friend put it, "like a horsewhip." Sometimes she was prepared to use the horsewhip itself. During her first years in charge of the *Herald*, nothing lit her explosive temper more quickly than innuendos that she was a dilettante editor. One morning, fresh from a ride along the trails around Dower House, she left her Cadillac at the door of the *Herald* building and hurried to the city room with fire in her eye. Under her arm was an early edition of the rival afternoon *News*. In the city room, she strode up and down in her riding clothes, slashing her crop at the desks.

"If I ever get my hands on that ——," she snapped, "I'll horsewhip him!"

The object of her fury was George Abell, the *News*' satiric, mischievous gossip columnist. Abell had noticed a report in the New York *Herald Tribune* to the effect that Mrs. Patterson would spend the winter at her Long Island estate. In his column, "Capital Capers," syndicated by Scripps-Howard, Abell had quipped that Cissy doubtless would edit the *Herald* by "remote control."

Abruptly, she left the building as fast as she had entered, and told her chauffeur to take her to the nearby *News* building. Majestically sweeping into its offices, Mrs. Patterson demanded to see the editor, Ralph (Polly) Palmer. An office boy led her toward Palmer's office, and every typewriter in the city room fell silent as the distinguished visitor stalked through the room.

Palmer, whose manner was nothing if not ingratiating, met his rival editor at the door. With a hopeful smile, he invited her to sit down. Instead, Cissy launched into a lecture about the lack of accuracy in Palmer's best columnist. Her language was not ladylike. Then she asked where she could find Abell, so she could get on with the horsewhipping. The nervous editor, who could scarcely take his eyes off the crop in her hand, replied that, unfortunately, it was Abell's day off. (Fortunately, it really was.)

"We apologize for any implied insult—certainly none was intended," Palmer ran on soothingly. "You know how it is with these columnists, Mrs. Patterson. Pretty hard to control sometimes, I'm afraid. I hope you have better luck with yours than I do. . . ."

Cissy sighed. She sat down. The two editors did have common problems. They fell to discussing them. Palmer asked her advice on how to handle women writers, with which Cissy was well supplied. Cissy, in turn, asked Palmer about some of the technical problems of circulating an ailing newspaper in Washington.

Cissy left the *News* building nearly an hour later. By that time she and Palmer were friends, and Abell no longer need fear a horsewhipping. He had indeed caught the eccentric lady editor's eye, but in a way that was ultimately to his benefit. Cissy not only forgave him for his *gaffe;* she eventually hired him. She rather liked his impudence.

Cissy had established herself as an occasionally frivolous, always flamboyant editor. This is what Washington talked about, but it concealed her basic seriousness about being a successful publisher. She wanted desperately for the *Herald* to succeed; her uncertainty lay in how it could be done. The fate of the *Herald* gave point to her life. She was determined to prove that a woman could be as worthy of the Patterson newspaper dynasty as a man. If she could earn the respect of brother Joe in New York and cousin Bertie in Chicago—and do it the hard way—she would no longer be treated as a feminine ornament in a family of male doers.

And, besides, she felt journalism in her bones.

TWO

Chicago Princess

Cissy Patterson liked growing old even less than most people. But, characteristically, she tried to do something about it; twice she adjusted the year of her birth. In her divorce papers in 1917, she set it down as 1882. Later on, she shaved off two more years, and this caused her obituary to report that she had been born in 1884.

Late in her life Cissy made wry references to her age, but she always managed to leave the impression that she was several years younger than she was.

Cissy's close friend, Rose Crabtree, an outspoken westerner, finally asked her bluntly how old she really was.

"God, Rose, I don't know," Cissy sighed with a laugh. "I've lied about it so much I'm not sure any more."

Eleanor Medill Patterson was born in Chicago on November 7, 1881. Considering her later impact, one might expect that her arrival in this world was signaled by a flash of lightning or a clap of thunder. No such heavenly portents are recorded, but a student of eugenics would have been justified in speculating that no ordinary woman was in the making. On both sides, the child sprang from clans which were bold, imaginative, wealthy and powerful. And basic to their personalities was a distaste for normal, humdrum existence.

The Medills, the Pattersons and the McCormicks were among the first families of Chicago during its period of big-shouldered growth. Cissy's maternal grandfather was Joseph Medill, a self-

made man and a success story in the American tradition. Medill
had been born on a farm in New Brunswick, Canada, in 1823, of
a family of Presbyterians which had emigrated from the north of
Ireland. The family trade originally was shipbuilding, but Medill
was drawn to the written word. He would walk miles for a book.
When the family moved to Ohio, Medill sold subscriptions to
Horace Greeley's weekly New York *Tribune*, taught school and
was admitted to the bar. He saved enough to buy the Coshocton,
Ohio, *Whig*, a strongly antislavery paper. In 1852 Medill married Katharine Patrick, of North Philadelphia. On her maternal
side, she was of Dutch ancestry, and her ancestors had distinguished themselves in George Washington's army. Her father,
too, owned and edited an Ohio newspaper, and, appropriately
enough, she met young Medill while she was setting type.

Medill was one of those to whom Greeley actually said: "Go
West, young man!" In 1855 Medill followed the advice as far
as Chicago, where he sidetracked himself by buying an interest
in the eight-year-old *Tribune*. Its circulation was uninspiring:
2500 subscribers. But Medill was aggressive, and under his
direction the paper grew rapidly in popularity and influence,
though not until 1874 did he own the controlling interest.

One faithful subscriber was Abraham Lincoln. Renewing his
subscription in a letter from Springfield, Illinois, on June 15, 1859,
Lincoln wrote that he would take the *Tribune* as long as he lived
—or, rather, as he put it, as long as he could afford it.

"In its devotion to our cause always, and to me personally last
year, I owe it a debt of gratitude which I fear I shall never be
able to repay," Lincoln wrote. He was a frequent visitor at the
Medill home.

Medill created more than a better newspaper. Disgusted with
the Whigs, he became one of the most enthusiastic founders of
the Republican party. The *Tribune* was violently antislavery and
backed Lincoln in his unsuccessful race for the Senate against
Stephen A. Douglas. In 1860, delegate Medill played a key role

in swinging the Ohio delegation to Lincoln at a crucial moment in the Republican presidential nominating convention in Chicago.

The *Tribune* became the dominant paper in the Midwest, and second only to the New York *Tribune* in national influence. Medill and his family often visited President Grant in the White House. He served twice as mayor of Chicago.

The Medills built a $100,000 brownstone mansion in the heart of Chicago's Gold Coast bordering Lake Michigan. They had three daughters: Elinor, Katharine and Josephine. In 1878, Elinor married Robert Wilson Patterson, Jr., an editor of the *Tribune*. The Pattersons were descendants of John Patterson, who had moved from Scotland to Londonderry, Ireland, in 1640 with his wife and two children to escape the Stuarts' persecution of the Presbyterians. William Patterson, one of his ten sons, moved to America and had two sons who fought in the Revolution. One of these, Alexander, married Sarah Stevenson, and they had a son, Robert, born in Tennessee in 1814.

Since the family was vocally antislavery, it became expedient to move to Illinois. There Robert became an outspoken antislavery clergyman and the distinguished pastor of Chicago's First Presbyterian Church for thirty-two years. The Reverend Patterson's fire-and-brimstone style in the pulpit shook up his congregation. He was a fine figure of a man, standing six feet, four inches. Once, at a public reception in downstate Illinois, the reverend measured his height against Lincoln's. They stood back to back, with a book placed on their heads. Impartial observers swore it did not slant in either direction.

Patterson married Julie Ann Quigley, of Alton, Illinois. They had eight children, including a son, Robert, Jr., born in 1850. Robert attended Lake Forest University, which his father had helped found, and was graduated from Williams College. He began to study law but soon gave it up and, after a stint as a reporter on the Chicago *Times*, he became assistant night editor of the Chicago *Tribune* in 1873. He moved up rapidly, serving successively as Washington correspondent, editorial writer and managing editor.

It was after he became managing editor that Patterson and the boss's daughter, Elinor, were married. Their first child, born January 6, 1879, was christened for his red-whiskered grandfather, Joseph Medill, and a daughter, born less than three years later, was named after her mother (but took the more conventional spelling).

Both were to recall their father as the beau ideal of a newspaperman. Joe Patterson indeed was of the opinion that his father was a better newspaperman than Medill. The reserved Robert W. Patterson, Jr., tall, square-jawed and black-mustached, was not colorful like his father and father-in-law, but he had as much character as either man. It was at his insistence that the *Tribune* steadily modernized itself as new equipment was invented, regardless of the expense.

Once, when his father-in-law was away, Patterson ordered the installation of linotype machines to replace the old handset operation. When Medill returned to the office, he countermanded the order. Patterson promptly wrote out his resignation, but Medill countermanded that too. The machines were installed.

After she became an editor, Eleanor Patterson often reminded herself and others of her father's integrity. She told how he always insisted on playing the news "straight," without distortion or innuendo. Once he came home from the office and told her mother he had resigned from the Chicago Club in disgust.

"Every time I go in there," he explained, "somebody wants me to put something in the paper, or to keep something out. To hell with it!"

When Joe Patterson tried to speak to his baby sister, it always came out "Sissy," and it clung to her as a nickname among her friends. Their grandfather Medill spelled the name with an "S" in letters to her, but Cissy herself spelled it with a "C." Medill had even more than a normal grandfatherly pride in Cissy, Joe and their two first cousins of approximately the same age—

Medill McCormick, and his brother, Robert, called "Bertie." They were the sons of Katharine Medill and Robert Sanderson McCormick, who was a nephew of Cyrus Hall McCormick, the "reaper king." Their union linked two aristocratic families which had feuded as fiercely as the Montagues and the Capulets. During the Civil War, Cyrus McCormick had owned the Chicago *Times* and had screamed his antiwar attitude in its pages. Medill, pro-Civil War, was infuriated. In his effort to ridicule McCormick, he went so far as to charge in an editorial that Cyrus's father, who had invented the reaper, had stolen one of the key components of his harvesting machine from an impoverished inventor!

As a child, Cissy was not as robust as her brother and two male cousins, and was not with them as much as she would like to have been. She felt lonely in her sheltered life in a mansion on Chicago's Gold Coast. Also, she became increasingly nervous in the presence of her watchful mother. The beautiful Mrs. Patterson was domineering and explosive, and her daughter's relations with her were usually turbulent.

When things became too strained with her mother, she slipped off on her own for a delicious taste of adventure. Often it was no more than perching on a stool in the drug store on the nearby corner of Chicago Avenue and Clark Street and buying an ice cream soda. Shabby Clark Street was an exciting contrast to Astor Street, and sometimes after the soda Cissy would skip along a block of this forbidden district. Men might wink or call out to her from doorways, and once she saw a drunken woman reel from the "family entrance" of a saloon.

In such moments, Cissy visualized herself as a primitive little savage on the warpath, flaunting her revolt. When she was ten, she amazed even herself by trying to climb the steeple of St. James Episcopal Church. It was a warm Sunday afternoon, and strollers whose attention was called to the little girl were scandalized. Aroused by their shouts, the church janitor raced to the belfry and pulled Cissy back before she could wiggle out of reach. Her white dress with embroidered ruffles was soiled, and the pale-blue satin sash, white straw hat and blue ribbon were slightly disarranged. She resented her rescue. If she had made it all the way to the top, she felt, she would have gotten even with her mother. Mrs. Patterson, of course, was too horrified by the escapade to speak. She merely boxed her daughter's ears.

Once, Cissy's loneliness inspired her to defy her mother by setting up a lemonade stand directly in front of the Patterson residence on Superior Street. She sold several glasses at five cents apiece before her mother came home.

"That is direct disobedience, and so *common,*" her mother said coldly.

Many years later, Cissy wrote wryly: "My mother didn't like me to sell lemonade, because she was trying to bring me up to be a lady."

Mrs. Patterson also felt a growing concern because Cissy sometimes indulged in the adolescent warfare staged by the tough Irish kids living only a few blocks away. She told her daughter that she was acquiring an ugly accent from playing with the Irish.

Mrs. Patterson packed Cissy off to the same finishing schools she had attended—Miss Porter's in Farmington, Connecticut, and, later, Miss Hersey's in Boston. Mrs. Patterson also had attended Miss Valett's school in Paris. Joe Patterson and Medill and Bertie McCormick had also been dispatched to the eastern seaboard for Ivy League polish—to Groton and then Yale.

Joseph Medill doted on his red-haired granddaughter and occasionally offered her somewhat more useful advice than her mother did. While she was away at school, Medill wrote her letters in the spirit—if not the literary style—of Lord Chesterfield. He was concerned about every phase of Cissy's development. On May 4, 1896, he wrote to her at Miss Hersey's and complimented her on her last letter.

"There was a freedom and swing in the sentences indicating study and advancement on your part," he said. "Your mother always wrote well since she was your age, better than her sister, your aunt. I am glad that your school and teacher please you. I look for more rapid progress in your studies and a fine polish in your manners, because, like rosewood and sugar maple, you have a grain that is susceptible of taking on an elegant tone."

In forecasting elegance for Cissy, Medill was being more accurate than he probably realized. He proved to be less of a prophet in continuing the letter:

"Those little domestic habits you are being taught will always be useful to you. Such as promptitude; dressing quickly; rising at an early hour; coming to your meals punctually and on time; learning to do a little sewing. 'A stitch in time saves nine.' There is nothing better than order and punctuality in all things. It is said to be nature's first law."

As an adult, Cissy seldom was to obey nature's first law.

Medill was impressed that Cissy was the tallest as well as the youngest girl at the school.

"Yankeeland is noted for tall, slim girls," he wrote. "But you do not look very tall, as you carry it off with a light step and an erect figure."

Cissy's natural grace was perfected as a result of her mother's determination that she walk like a princess; she had regularly practiced walking with a book balanced on her head.

In one letter Medill reported with childlike joy to Cissy: "I went last week to a great circus—five rings all going at once, fine performance, wonderful elephants, trick dogs, cute monkeys, astonishing acrobats, 10,000 spectators."

All her life Cissy felt the same way about animals and circuses.

At 17, Cissy was a popular girl at formal dances in Chicago and Lake Forest, a fashionable suburb north of Chicago. Among her many beaus was Frederic McLaughlin, scion of a prominent local industrial family who was always to hold a special place in Cissy's affections. At Miss Hersey's finishing school in Boston she acquired many more admirers, for her red hair and princess-like grace were a magnetic combination. One of them was Blair Fairchild, a Harvard undergraduate.

At least once, Fairchild was handicapped in arranging a meeting with Cissy because of her handwriting. At that time, young men and women customarily communicated a great deal through handwritten, hand-delivered notes. And teas, rather than cocktail parties, were their meeting grounds. Fairchild had met Cissy during a weekend gathering at Harvard. A week later he wrote her this note:

> My dear Miss Patterson—
> Did you think me rude on Friday? Or will you believe me when I assure you that I wanted very much to come to your tea, but I was tutored all that day, hard, for an important exam. . . . I hear I am having the pleasure of lunching with you next Sunday at the Dexters. I saw Catherine at the Apthorpe's last night and she kindly asked me. Hoping to see you there and that you will be forgiving.
>
> I remain sincerely,
Blair Fairchild

Back came a reply from Cissy asking Fairchild to call on her on a specified date. Cissy wrote a script in which elegance was sometimes achieved at the expense of legibility. Thus, Fairchild was obliged to answer her:

> My dear Miss Patterson,
> Thank you very much for your kind note. It will give me the greatest pleasure to avail myself of the opportunity of calling—but when? Shall I be very rude if I say I can't read that word?—But I hasten to add, *that* is the only one.
>
> Yours sincerely,
Blair Fairchild

Medill died in 1899, and Patterson succeeded him as editor and head of the *Tribune*. Mrs. Patterson seized the opportunity to persuade her husband to move to Washington. Running a Chicago newspaper from the national capital may not seem logical, but as top boss, Patterson no longer had to personally put the paper to bed every night. In any event, his wife thought it was high time

they forsook the stockyard city for the glittering social life of
Washington, where Cissy could meet diplomats and nobility.

So Cissy made her debut in Washington after having already
made it in Chicago. And her parents commissioned Stanford
White to build them a fine mansion on Du Pont Circle, alongside some of the capital's most distinguished residences.

While the mansion was being built, Cissy went off to Europe
to join her aunt and uncle. She had been to Europe several times
before, but now, as a debutante, she would play a role at the
court balls of the most dazzling capitals on the Continent. In
July 1902, her uncle, Robert Sanderson McCormick, became the
first United States ambassador to Austria-Hungary. In December
1902, McCormick was assigned to St. Petersburg, and remained
in that post until 1905.

For Cissy, her first court ball attended by Czar Nicholas and
Czarina Alexandra was a memory that remained vivid all her life.
First, there was the long drive in a carriage along the lifeless
Neva River in the piercingly cold winter night. Then, suddenly,
the brilliance of the palace lighting up the blackness. Next, the
long wait as the carriages and sleighs emptied the smartly dressed
diplomatic corps at the four entrances to the palace. Guarding
the entrances were dozens of servants in gorgeous red capes, long
staffs in their hands, and hundreds of soldiers in dress uniform.

And finally, they were inside a room dominated by a vast,
white-marble stairway, shimmering with its bright lights and mir-
rored reflections, flashing jewels and bright feathers, velvets, bro-
cades, and gold-laced, gaudily colored uniforms.

Everywhere Cissy could see magnificent guardsmen, some
with their hair and mustaches dyed for the occasion, lining the
walls in costumes of red and white, with helmets of silver, crested
by silver winged eagles. Stationed at the entrance of the grand
ballroom were bearded Cossacks, immense in red caftans and
black astrakhan caps, their unwinking eyes hinting of their semi-
savage origins.

One of the masters of ceremonies, stiff with the gold embroidery of his black uniform and carrying a slender ivory-handled stick, approached the American ambassador, Mrs. McCormick, and their niece as they stood with a group of diplomats. He bowed low and, murmuring in French, guided them through to their proper places in the ballroom, in the line of diplomats forming on either side of the doors which led to the Czar's private apartments.

The Grand Master of Ceremonies tapped three times with his wand on the floor, and the light tapping of his aides echoed here and there down the hall. A tense hush fell. Mrs. McCormick managed to turn her head to Cissy, standing just at her elbow, and whisper, "Don't forget to curtsy and smile! . . . and, for God's sake, can't you keep off my train?"

The gold door opened, and there stood Czar Nicholas and Czarina Alexandra. Behind them could be seen a group of aides and lesser royalty.

Like a wheatfield before a gust of storm, it seemed to Cissy, the huge assemblage of diplomats now bowed their heads in silent unison. The Czar and Czarina, followed by their train of dukes and grand duchesses, inclined their heads gravely and separated before the gilded doors. The Czar started down the line of diplomats while the Czarina proceeded along the line of their wives.

Cissy was spellbound, although a little disappointed that the Czar proved to be only an average-looking man of middle height, with short legs accentuated by the blue, baggy trousers tucked into high boots. He was bearded, with Slavic cheekbones, and had a short nose and full-lidded, kind and faithful eyes.

In contrast, the Czarina, taller than her husband, was a vision of flashing jewels, swathed in silver and white. Her face, Cissy saw, was a mask from which every vestige of human expression had been stricken, as if frozen out, but pale and beautiful beneath a dazzling diamond crown.

As Alexandra loomed before her, Cissy had to be reminded by a nudge from her aunt Kate that it was time to curtsy. She sank, as if tardily, to the very ground, so that her pink tulle skirt billowed and foamed about her.

"And so you like St. Petersburg?" inquired a slow voice, in English, without a trace of accent. Cissy dared not lift her eyes, but her aunt answered for her in a monosyllable. The Empress held tightly, in her white-gloved arm, an ivory-and-white ostrich fan. Cissy was not too awed to notice that the long tips of the feathers seemed to be trembling somewhat desperately.

Ambassador McCormick, with the frankness typical of the McCormicks and Pattersons, had gotten off on the wrong foot in St. Petersburg. Shortly after his arrival, a crowd of peasants had marched on the palace and asked to see the Czar to protest the harshness with which an uprising of Polish peasantry had been put down by the Czar's men. The leader of the mob was a Father Gapon, a Russian Orthodox priest. The royal family happened to be away at their country estate that day, and nothing came of the attempted appeal. However, the boldness of the priest was much discussed at dinner parties in St. Petersburg. When a dinner companion of McCormick asked him what he thought of Father Gapon, the ambassador, ever the exponent of democracy, replied bluntly that he thought the priest was the greatest man in Russia and that a statue should be erected in his honor. An embarrassed silence fell over the table. The ambassador should, of course, have made an equivocal reply or said nothing at all about a political event in the country to which he was accredited. McCormick's lack of diplomatic tact made the capital buzz.

His niece, however, was immediately popular with the younger diplomatic set. At that time it was the custom for each Russian Guard (cavalry) regiment to hold an evening party regularly in its hall. Highlight of the evening was a carrousel, which was akin to dancing the quadrille on horseback. The officers invited their girls to participate in the stylized riding, and sometimes the Czar came to watch. Cissy was always invited, and she showed herself off as a superb horsewoman. She was attired in a scarlet jacket, with a tricorne cocked over one eye.

At dances in St. Petersburg, Cissy was usually the center of an admiring group of young officers. At one, she found herself face to face with an officer who had courted her in Vienna. He was tall, dark, handsome and strongly built, with the black Guardsman's mustache then in fashion. This was Count Josef Gizycki. His father was of the Polish nobility but had spent most of his time in Austria, and Josef had been raised there. His mother was Lulu Zamoyska, who had been lady-in-waiting to the mother of the Emperor of Austria. She also had studied under the pianist Franz Liszt and had become acquainted with the famous composers of the time, including Schumann and Schubert.

The Gizycki estate was in the Polish Ukraine, at that time occupied by Russia. By birth, the Count was a citizen of both Austria and Russia, but a Russian law enacted in 1900 decreed that proprietors of Russian estates must be citizens of Russia only, so Gizycki had to move from the Austro-Hungarian monarchy to his estate, at Narvosielica, to protect it. An expert horseman, for ten years he had been an officer in the Austrian Uhlans, and he preferred the gay life in Vienna to the somber Ukraine.

Like Cissy, the Count was fond of horses, made a graceful figure on horseback and loved to race horses. In fact, he loved all forms of gambling and was fairly typical of the free-living, free-loving Russian and Austrian cavalry officers of that time. He was also nearly forty years old, but a bachelor, and, to a young American girl, a highly romantic figure.

Cissy and Josef had made a handsome couple when he had squired her about in Vienna—in a carriage behind spanking bays in the Prater, at the opera festival in Salzburg, and in the snowy hills hunting stag and deer.

The Count made no secret of the fact that he had followed Cissy to St. Petersburg to woo her, and he made good progress. When she had to return to Washington the following May, Gizycki pressed his pursuit through a series of ardent letters. He saluted her as "My dear little filly," and signed off with, "Yours,

Gizy." One letter concluded: "Now goodnight, Cissy darling, I kiss you ever so nice (have not smoked cigars)." There was also a P.S.: "Do write me something nice."

The Pattersons had serious doubts about Gizycki, and the Count showed his anxiety about this in his love letters. Nonetheless, by the late fall of 1903 they were informally engaged. In February, Cissy was back in Europe, resting at Baden-Baden, and the Count was writing her from the Élysée Palace Hotel in Paris. He was having trouble with Mrs. Patterson about setting a date for the wedding.

"I just saw Mama," he wrote. "I suppose she just had some letters, etc., as she told me the marriage in any case ought to be in two months and not now in one month. . . . If there was a real reason for doing so, you know very well, my little filly, I not only should await one month more but even walk to Siberia and back again if necessary, but I don't see the reason. . . ."

Gizycki goes on to explain to Cissy that the old European idea of delaying weddings was to keep each party in a separate convent "studying the character" of the intended spouse, and pondering the decision to engage in solemn matrimony.

"There is nothing more idiotic," he complained, "as it is rather easy to be a charming husband from a far distance—and very hard to study the character of a man 7000 miles away. Now, of course, as Mama is very sensible after all, and as I explained [to] her all that (several hours) I had the pleasure to leave her in a rather good mood—only one must keep her in that good mood. Then, I think, it is rather necessary to make the acquaintance of your father—who arrives about Monday. And I will on that purpose run back from Vienna especially."

Robert W. Patterson—with very good cause, as it turned out —insisted that Gizycki supply documents proving that his estate at Narvosielica was unencumbered by mortgages. The estate was in a remote, desolate region of Poland, and Gizycki hastened to inform Cissy in one letter that he hoped to have a railway pass through Narvosielica and likewise have a post office installed there ("then Mama can wire easily every day").

In the year 1904, American heiresses were rushing to marry titled foreigners in record numbers. But, perhaps even more than most shrewd American fathers, Robert Patterson was skeptical about a smooth-talking count from remote eastern Europe.

By March, Gizycki was back in New York City, champing to pin down the marriage plans. Impatiently he wrote Cissy from his suite at the Waldorf-Astoria:

"Didn't they do everything possible and impossible since we parted in Paris to poison your mind? If at the present moment we still stick together, it proves that we were born to do so—of course, you have been perfect all the time through, and if I failed perhaps lately in some details, you must forgive me, Cissy, because I am going through the worst crisis of my life—and one is only human."

At the end of March the Pattersons, sensing the possibility of an elopement, gave in to Cissy's entreaties. They formally announced the engagement and agreed to a wedding on April 14. Gossipy Washington buzzed like a beehive over the news. Gizycki had made several previous trips to the United States and had acquired a reputation. His fondness for horse races, wine and women was no secret. Once, at a formal dance in Newport, he had drunk not too wisely and ended up showering the orchestra with a fistful of ten-dollar bills. Stability, obviously, was not his strong point.

The dashing Count was charming to Cissy's friends. Alice Roosevelt, daughter of the President, was fascinated by his black Guardsman's mustache, which reminded her of an illustration from Tolstoy's *Anna Karenina*. Gizycki went out of his way to be friendly to "Princess Alice" and presented her with a silver cigarette case because she would be in the wedding party.

But if Cissy's closest friends were dazzled by the handsome Count, they were sensible enough to realize he would hardly make the ideal husband for Cissy Patterson. Some of them tried to talk her out of the marriage. Up until the very night before the wedding, Cissy's cousin, Ruth Hanna McCormick, sought to persuade her to change her mind. But to Ruth and Alice, Cissy stubbornly replied: "I know he's had mistresses, and probably illegitimate children, but I don't care. I'm going to marry him."

Alice suspected that Cissy's attitude was less pure romanticism than it was defiance of her parents. Her mother had no objections to her marrying a titled foreigner, but she shared her husband's misgivings about the kind of man Gizycki obviously was. Cissy had battled her mother on a whole series of important decisions ever since childhood. They seldom saw eye to eye on anything, and headstrong Cissy had been always reluctant to yield.

Cissy was in her twenty-third year and, by turn of the century standards, she was not a young bride. One Chicago newspaper announced the engagement with the comment that Cissy had "vanquished the old proverb, 'three times a bridesmaid, never a bride.'" According to this story, one of her friends had laughingly said, "It really isn't good form to get married unless Eleanor is a bridesmaid."

Actually, Cissy had been bridesmaid four times in the preceding year. One of the weddings had united her brother, Joe, with Miss Alice Higinbotham of Chicago. In May 1903, Cissy had raced home from Europe on steamship and special train in order to reach Chicago in time to act as maid of honor at the wedding of Miss Helen Johnson, niece to Mrs. George M. Pullman.

The Gizycki-Patterson marriage took place in the library of the Pattersons' thirty-room Du Pont Circle mansion. Because Gizycki was a Catholic, the ceremony was performed by a Catholic priest; but at that time a mixed marriage could not be performed in a Catholic church. The Washington *Times* reported that the event was "one of the most brilliant and perfectly arranged weddings ever seen in Washington."

Some of those who attended recalled years later that Cissy
and "Gigi," as he was called, made the handsomest bridal couple
they ever saw. Cissy wore a white net dress, made over chiffon
and silk. She wore a tulle veil and carried a small bunch of white
roses.

Ruth McCormick was maid of honor. Alice Roosevelt looked
stunningly pretty in a biscuit-colored crepe and a large, black
picture hat. The Russian and Austrian ambassadors were present
with their wives, as were a delegation of McCormicks and Pattersons who came out from Chicago. At the wedding breakfast,
groups of six and eight were seated at flower-decked tables. The
entire room was decorated with white flowers.

The Chicago newspapers, as well as those in Washington, carried complete accounts of the wedding. The Chicago *Inter-
Ocean* gushed: "The bride was gowned in her going-away
gown of tan cloth, an imported tailor-made creation, that set off
to rare advantage the wealth of red-golden hair and pink-and-
white complexion for which she is famed. She wore a large
picture hat, garnished with plumes. The new Countess is much
admired in Vienna . . . for several seasons she has been counted
one of the most beautiful girls in Chicago society. She is tall
and slender, and most gracious, a type of femininity that seems to
be considered purely American."

While Cissy was changing to her going-away clothes, Countess
Marguerite Cassini, daughter of the Russian ambassador, tied a
bunch of orange blossoms with white ribbons to the wheel
spokes of the shiny Patterson carriage waiting outside. Alice
Roosevelt hurried home to the White House to change to street
attire in time to return and see the bridal couple leave the
mansion on their honeymoon. But when Alice got back, she was
surprised. The Count was missing. When Alice inquired, Cissy
told her that her new husband had gone to his hotel to change
and didn't think it worthwhile to come back to the Patterson
home. He said he would meet his bride at the railroad station.

So Cissy drove off in the carriage, with her mother to keep her company, to the station.

Alice and her friends considered the situation odd, to say the least. It was the first hint to Cissy that she might have married someone as independent as she was, but she could scarcely have imagined what sort of marriage was in store for her.

THREE

The Sad Countess

See P P 2

As the ocean liner *Kaiser Wilhelm der Grosse* docked in New York harbor on August 18, 1909, the newspaper reporters beat a path to one elegant suite. In it sat the Countess Eleanor Gizycka; her daughter, Felicia; her cousin, Joseph Medill McCormick; and his wife, Ruth Hanna McCormick.

The Countess' small, firm mouth was tight-lipped.

"I am weary," she told the newsmen. "I do not wish to talk of the past. I wish to forget it. Now that I have my baby I am satisfied."

The former Cissy Patterson put her arms around little Felicia and hugged her. During the rest of the brief interview most of the talking was done by Medill McCormick.

The next day the New York *World* carried a picture of Cissy, attired in a smart traveling gown and an elegant hat trimmed with a stuffed bird, holding Felicia's hand. The caption read: "Woman who married Russian Count just home with daughter long stolen."

The story reported that "the little Countess was in olive-green with a large sailor hat set jauntily on her yellow curls. She is a beautiful child with perfect complexion, fine features and large blue eyes. She clung to her mother and would not consent to release her hand for a moment." The reporter further noted that "the Countess is tall and girlish in appearance, though her eyes bear a look of sadness that is relieved only when she smiles."

When the stories of her arrival hit the New York newsstands

that evening, Cissy and Felicia were a long way from the city. With the McCormicks they had been whisked from the ship to the Holland House for lunch, and immediately afterward they had caught the afternoon train for Chicago. As the train jolted through the dark toward her native land, Cissy felt as if she were floating out of a dream which had turned into a five-year nightmare. Since she had sailed from New York as a bride in 1904, she had lived an entire lifetime. Flooding her mind were a succession of scenes which she wanted to blot out forever.

Scene One was her wedding night in a suite at the Waldorf-Astoria. Nothing had gone right after the confusion, bewilderment and shame of that night. Suddenly, the charming and ardent Count had seemed a stranger. When they had finished their after-dinner coffee, he had virtually banished her to their bedroom like a child, with the casual comment that "perhaps" he would see his "little filly" later. This was not the eagerness or understanding she had expected from her bridegroom, and it only increased her natural nervousness.

It was three hours before the Count joined her. Then he took her roughly and routinely, without a word or a caress, like, it seemed to her, a panther rutting in the dark. She had cried out in fright and pain.

Scene Two was their arrival at Narvosielica, in a remote part of the Russian Ukraine that once was Poland. During their courtship, the Count had spoken of his ancestral "castle," with seventy servants, and she had imagined drawbridges, moats and turrets. Now, after a five-mile drive from the depot in an old carriage, they abruptly came upon his estate. Through an avenue of beautiful poplar trees and enormous blooming lilac, she saw the "castle." Ramshackle and wooden, it stood gauntly and with a certain dignity, boasting two ungainly wings, a large, sheet-iron front door, and uncurtained, unshuttered windows. Bowing and scraping before them were a dozen servants, who, she was to learn, comprised the estate's entire staff.

The Count murmured that Cissy undoubtedly would find it

"amusing" to fix up the place. He led her inside to the shabby living room, with a fireplace, two large leather chairs cracked through to the canvas underneath, and massive mahogany tables, and then, quickly, upstairs to her bedroom. An even bigger shock awaited her there—a sagging bed with a shabby cotton counterpane, a plain wooden washstand, a copper pitcher filled with steaming water.

So this was the bridal chamber, Cissy numbly told herself. As her husband left her, without making any comment, she moved toward the dressing table below a window through which she could see a small park, with fields and stables beyond. Idly curious, she pulled open the drawer. Inside it lay the photograph of a rather pretty young woman, and beside the picture was a solitary black wire hairpin. She flushed, and touched it with the tip of her finger, as if it were a live thing. She felt a little sick at the realization that the Count's last mistress had used this room, this dressing table and the bed she would sleep in.

When she confronted Gizycki* about his other women, he blandly told her he had no intention of playing the role of a faithful husband. As the months went on, he would make love to her, suddenly and violently, then tell her coldly it was only for the purpose of begetting a child. He made it equally clear he had only one other interest in her: her $30,000-a-year income. Her husband not only was broke but in debt. Despite previous assurances to her father, his estate proved to be heavily mortgaged.

Scene Three occurred on a night in September 1905. A week before, the Count had said he had to make a trip, and Cissy, reminding him that their child was due to be born very soon, had begged him not to go. He had gone anyway. She had sent for a doctor, but he had never arrived. Now, on September 3, giving birth to Felicia, she went through five hours of labor, attended only by a clumsy midwife. Whenever she groaned in agony, the

* Ed. note: In Polish the name ends with an "i" to denote a man, with an "a" to denote a woman.

peasant woman muttered gypsy-like incantations, which frightened her even more. She had sent for her husband, but he had
not even replied.

The numerous female Gizycka relatives treated Cissy little
better than her husband did. They discouraged her from even
giving her opinions. They were aristocratic Poles, they told her,
and young American girls, however wealthy, were still boors.
Once she was bluntly informed that it was condescending for
the distinguished Count to have married her at all, but that he
had wanted his estates restored, and the Pattersons had money.
She had been at the mercy of the Gizyckas; there were no telephones and no telegraph station.

Scene Four came a little more than two years later. It was a
freezing winter midnight. Outside the Gizycki house the snow
was deep. A trusted servant helped Cissy bundle herself and her
daughter to their eyebrows in furs; a horse-drawn sled was
waiting, manned by two other servants. Some of the Count's
peasants hated him. Among other things, they had to endure occasional savage beatings from him—and Cissy had talked three of
them into helping her escape with Felicia. Now, carrying the
child, she stole from the house and slipped into the waiting sleigh.
Soon they were racing over the icy slopes toward the Russian
border. Cissy was afraid but exhilarated. Wolves were known to
prowl the area; but, luckily, she was not pursued that night by
man or beast. Once before, in desperation, she had fled from the
Count and stayed for a time with the Potocki family, which was
more aristocratic but kinder and less snobbish than the Gizyckis.
But now she knew this was the only thing left for her to do—
escape from the place of her great unhappiness and head for
Paris, which she could reach by train. If the Count wanted to
follow her there, let him.

Scene Five took place several weeks later in Pau, a resort town
in France. Gizycki had gone to Paris and talked Cissy into taking
a villa in Pau and attempting a reconciliation there. She agreed,

feeling an obligation to give their marriage one more chance, away from the grim atmosphere of the so-called castle. But things had not gone well. Again, he had mistreated her physically. He was obsessed with gambling for high stakes, which bored Cissy. One night, after heavy losses, her husband came home in a furious temper and complained that her mother had refused to pay his debts.

"I am dining out with 'Madame R,'" he announced defiantly. Cissy warned that he had better not, if he expected their marriage to continue. Her ultimatum had sent him into a frenzy. He had beaten her on the face and breast with his fists, then dragged her out of the bedroom by her hair. Finally, he stormed from the house, and she decided that this time she had had enough. Quickly she packed their bags, dressed Felicia, and set out for London.

Scene Six occurred in March at Camden Hill, a rather obscure part of London, where Cissy was living with Felicia and the girl's governess, Mary Gernat. One day, while Miss Gernat was watching Felicia play in a park, a large touring car halted at the sidewalk. Three men got out. Two of them approached the governess and engaged her attention by asking directions. Meanwhile, the third man, who was wearing motoring goggles and a fur coat, scooped up Felicia and carried her swiftly to the car. Miss Gernat rushed to the car and saw that it was the Count. He informed her curtly that he had a right to his daughter and was taking her to Paris. The car sped away.

Through her connections in St. Petersburg, Cissy discovered that the Count had taken Felicia to Russia. Now, on the train rushing toward Chicago, the kidnaping loomed as the final incredible humiliation she had suffered at her husband's hands. But, as a Patterson, she was not accustomed to take trouble lying down, and she had resolved that she would get her daughter back if she had to move the earth to accomplish it.

The obstacles were formidable. She did not know exactly

where her husband had taken Felicia, although she heard that he had subsequently hidden the child in a convent. Her baby was a Russian subject, so she had no legal right to take Felicia out of the country even if she could find her. Divorce was not then recognized in Europe, and Cissy realized that it would take an order from the Czar to force Gizycki to release the child to her. She wrote to a friend, Princess Cantacuzene, the granddaughter of President Grant who had married a Russian prince and was living in St. Petersburg. Her husband was a member of a distinguished regiment which had been formed by Catherine the Great and was aide-de-camp to the Czar's brother, the Grand Duke Nicholas. Cissy asked the Princess if she could get the Grand Duke's wife to intercede with the Czar. The princess replied that nothing could be done. Any intervention would have to be at an official level, and protocol forbade a wife to make an official representation.

Desperate, Cissy traveled to St. Petersburg with her aunt Kate, who knew her way around there because of her husband. The McCormicks got her a private audience with the aged Dowager Empress, the widow of the late Czar Alexander III, who suggested that she could arrange to have Gizycki jailed for six months, or until he changed his attitude. Cissy replied that she had not had quite such an extreme measure in mind. The answer chilled her.

"Child," the old lady remarked with a smile, "I have had people beheaded for absolutely nothing."

Cissy stressed that she wanted no harm to come to her husband; she had hoped for a court order from the Czar.

"I'll speak to my son about it in the morning" was the final reply.

(In later years Cissy could always enthrall friends with this account of the Dowager Empress' casual attitude toward violence, given ironic point by the massacre of the Imperial Family—save for the Dowager herself—at the hands of the Bolsheviks nine years after the interview.)

Nothing came of the interview, and Cissy's mother decided to pull some strings on her own. In December 1908, she wrote about her daughter's plight to an acquaintance, William Howard Taft, who had just been elected President of the United States, though he would not be inaugurated until March. Taft, then vacationing in Georgia, responded. On December 21, he wrote Czar Nicholas this letter in longhand:

Your Imperial Majesty,

Miss Elinor [sic] Patterson, the daughter of Mr. and Mrs. Robert W. Patterson, was married in Washington by a Roman Catholic priest to Count Joseph Gizycki and thus has become Countess Gizycki of Russian Poland.

One child, a daughter, has been born of that marriage. Since that time, in a quarrel, the Count struck the Countess. She left him, taking her baby daughter with her. He followed her and succeeded in securing the possession of the baby against the mother's will. The Countess has now been deprived of even the sight of the child for many months. The child has been placed by its father in a convent in Russia. Both the Countess and her mother are in danger of a nervous breakdown because of the strain and worry attending these circumstances, unless some arrangement can be made by which the baby will be restored to its mother at least for a period of time each year. There is no question of divorce proceedings whatever.

I am advised that the only recourse of the Countess is to appeal to the sovereign will of Your Imperial Majesty, and I write on behalf of the mother and grandmother to appeal to Your Majesty to direct an investigation into the circumstances and to make such order to Count Gizycki as shall seem to Your Majesty equitable and merciful.

I retain the pleasantest recollection of the audience which Your Majesty was good enough to accord me, and of the feast of the Second Regiment of the Guard and of the luncheon to the officers of the regiment given by Your Majesty, at which, by your gracious courtesy, I was a guest.

Hoping that I do not trespass upon the proprieties in thus addressing Your Majesty personally, I beg to subscribe myself,

Your Majesty's obedient servant,
Wm. H. Taft

P.S. Mr. and Mrs. Patterson are prominent residents of Chicago and Washington, and Mr. Patterson is the proprietor of the Chicago *Tribune*, one of the greatest newspapers in the United States.

Mrs. Patterson thanked him for writing the letter, and he replied to her on January 18, 1909, that he was happy to have done so, but that "I am not at all certain it will be effective."

The President-elect of the United States had more influence with the Czar than he realized. The Czar signed an order which overrode Russian law and directed the Count to release the baby to the custody of her mother. However, the paper could not be served for six months. Gizycki was staying out of reach, in Austria. It was not until summer that Gizycki found it was necessary to visit his estate. He was promptly arrested and served with the order of the Czar, and had no recourse but to comply. He sent someone to procure Felicia from the convent where she was hidden.

A few days later Cissy and cousin Medill waited nervously in a hotel room in Vienna. There was a knock at the door, and when it was opened Felicia toddled in, followed by the Count's emissary. Cissy swept the child into her arms. They caught the first train for Germany and from there took the first steamship to America.

In the New York *World* account of the arrival, McCormick flatly denied a report that the family had paid out $500,000 to the Count in ransom money.

"Not one cent was paid," McCormick said, "not one cent. It is true that influence was brought to bear upon the Russian

Government to have the child restored to her mother. That is all I care to say."

McCormick gave no hint to the ship reporters that the "influence" came from no less than President Taft, and his role in the negotiations did not leak out for some years.

There was no basis in fact for the shipboard rumor, reported in the *World* story, that a reconciliation was possible. More than a year before, Cissy's parents had passed the word through lawyers that a divorce seemed desirable, and the Count had agreed. During these preliminaries, he had haggled only over some furniture-storage costs, which he insisted his wife should share.

Yet Cissy herself, despite all she had suffered in a few brief years, balked at the thought of going into court and abruptly ending her marriage of only five years. She was disillusioned, yes, but she could not shake the spell of her love for the Count.

In 1910 she was further shaken up by the death of her father, at only sixty years old, after a long illness. Cissy had loved and admired her father more than she could tell.

On September 13, 1910, Gizycki secured from the Austrian courts what was, in effect, a decree of separation. The archaic court order declared that he need no longer throw his protecting arm around the Countess, inasmuch as she had left him without his consent, taking their child and refusing entreaties to return.

Angered, Cissy went him one better. On January 28, 1911, she filed for absolute divorce in the Cook County Circuit courthouse in Chicago. The suit charged the Count with three specific acts of infidelity, as well as many more apparent ones, and alleged he was unworthy to have the child.

The reaction to the suit from the Gizycki side carried a whiff of Continental comic opera. His Viennese counsel, Emil Frischauer, wrote to the Patterson attorneys in March complaining in stiffly polite language that the Countess had not warned the Count that she was about to initiate a divorce action. In even more pained tones, Frischauer said that it was

deplorable to have hired two "vagabond detectives" to shadow
the Count and secure evidence against him. It was particularly
impertinent for these two "scamps" to have spied on Gizycki
while he was in St. Petersburg!

Pompously, the Austrian attorney continued:

I beg to bring to the knowledge of the Countess Gizycka
that I have taken the necessary precautions that this rascally
attempt upon the honor of Count Gizycki, supported by
bribes and perjured witnesses, will have no success.

He explained that he would advise the Count—even though
the marriage was legally dissolved in the Austrian courts—to
go to America, appear before the judge in Chicago, and present "the material he has collected from honorable people."

Frischauer's parting shot was unchivalrous. He wrote: "I have
advised the Count with regard to the fact that this lady bears
the name of Count Gizycki, to show the greatest consideration
in Europe, but for America this consideration may be entirely
disregarded."

Cissy's counsel, Levy Mayer, laughed off these quaintly
phrased threats, pointing out that Frischauer had conveniently
ignored the fact that the Count himself had employed detectives
to shadow Cissy all over Europe after she had fled from him.
Cissy's friends also were sardonically amused. They quipped
that, if the Count did indeed choose to drop his "consideration" for the Countess while in America, he might find that in
Chicago there was no "divine right of counts" corresponding to
the ancient "divine right of kings."

But whether or not Frischauer seriously meant to persuade
the Count to go to America to defend his honor in court, he
would have had little time to act on it. War broke out in Europe
in 1914, and Gizycki never returned to the United States. Cissy's
divorce case was not heard until June 1917.

Preceding Cissy on the stand for supporting testimony were
Medill McCormick and the governess, Miss Gernat. The governess not only described the abduction of Felicia, but gave the

court a vivid account of the married life of the Gizyckis. She testified that one night in February 1908, at Pau, "they were in a room in their villa and I heard sounds of slapping and heard the Countess scream. When she came out of the room her face was very white and her hair was in disorder. Shortly after that they separated. . . ."

The next day Cissy was questioned for two hours. As the Chicago *Herald* reported it: "She enacted the part of the patient, long-suffering wife of Count Gizycki of Austria-Hungary, described by her as a cruel, dissolute and eccentric nobleman . . . in terse, epigrammatic sentences, she sketched her unhappy married life . . . her testimony was emphasized by many little gestures. She was dressed in a simple but modest suit of dark material."

"Money was always the source of our differences," Cissy told the court. "He married me for my money and he didn't get it. That's the whole story."

But there was much more the court wanted to hear, and Cissy did not spare her husband in recounting the details. Led by Levy Mayer, she continued:

My husband had always talked about his castle in Russia, his wonderful place in Russia, and how enormous it was. And he always made the bluff that he did not marry me for money.

Q—That he did not marry you for money?

A—Yes. He always said he did not want money. When I got there, I found the house almost tumbling down. It was not finished. The wallpaper was hanging off the wall in strips.

The Count had told me a great many stories about his ancestral estate and the seventy servants required to keep up the place. It looked as if at one time it might have been a place of considerable pretensions. Now it was old and ramshackle and stood in the middle of a little village full of peasants' huts. It was five miles from a railroad and almost entirely without modern improvements of any kind.

The seventy servants existed only in his imagination.

(Here and at other times Cissy left the implication that the Count had carefully kept the true conditions of his estate from her eyes until after they were married. This was misleading. In December 1902, a year before they were engaged, Gizycki had written her while she was with her uncle and aunt in Russia: "How long do you stay still in St. Petersburg? When are you going to Vienna? Going there you should visit Narvosielica, which is only 24 hours from Vienna. I just bought 20 first-class . . . mares, but besides the horses I am sure you will enjoy the place, especially in spring.")

The worst thing of all was, it soon appeared, that he had a woman living there with him for five years before I married him, by whom he had a child. When I got to the castle I was shown to her rooms and they were exactly as she had left them, with her bed the same way, with all her little objects lying around. Photographs were everywhere, and in his room there were photographs—not very decent photographs—of actresses. And quite a number of photographs bore signatures—signatures of Viennese women.

Of course, I was terribly upset that he hadn't taken the trouble to clean out the house before we went into it. That was the first real trouble; the fact of his not having money I didn't mind. But the revelations about these women I minded very much.

Cissy testified that six weeks after their marriage, when they were staying for a time in Vienna, her husband returned home at 5 A.M. to inform her that he had been gambling and had lost "a serious amount of money."

"He said he could get it, of course," she continued, "but I knew what he wanted. I gave him $11,000 on his promise to repay it, in a few days, but I never saw the money again."

Cissy then recalled the circumstances of the birth of her daughter, when the Count stayed away and she was in the hands of "a rather ignorant woman." During this absence, Cissy related, she found a diary in his desk.

"Did it contain entries regarding his friendship with other women?" inquired Mayer. Attorney Adolf Kraus, representing Gizycki, objected, and was sustained, but not before Cissy replied with a smile: "Well, you can guess what it contained."

The questioning continued by Mayer:

Q—Tell the court what were his habits, and what was his temper; how did he treat you?

A—Well, I could not describe it better than by saying that he was really an Oriental in his nature. He did not like me to read. He would take books out of my hand. He did not like me to think. I could not order the carriage; I could not order the servants; he did not want me to learn Polish; I was nothing at all in the house. He drank always, every day, a great deal. He drank a quart of champagne at dinner, or a quart of Burgundy. He was a sensualist, living simply for his senses, exercising, and drinking, and women. That is all he cared for. His friends will tell you that he is an eccentric, his enemies that he is crazy.

Q—What as to his temper?

A—He is a man who is subject to violent outbursts of temper. I have seen him take the coachman off the box and hold him with one hand—he was very powerful, very strong—hold him up and punch him in the face. And he used to whip the stable boys.

Cissy related the incident in which the Count knocked her down at their villa in Pau, and also a night in Paris when he burst into their apartment in the Élysée Palace and set upon her:

He put his knee on my chest as I lay in bed and started to choke me. Then he apparently changed his mind and said, "Why should I hang for a thing like you?" Then he stamped out of the room.

A letter from Gizycki to his wife, written from Vienna in March 1908, was introduced as evidence. It began, "My dear Cissy," and ended, "Yours, Gizy."

"It is impossible for me to live with you any longer," he wrote. "I do not want Felicia to have the sort of education of which you are the victim. Last love, last time."

Cissy explained to the court the reference to her education. "He had a contempt for everything American," she said, adding: "The Count never loved me. He always said I bored him."

Immediately after Cissy testified, June 18, 1917, Judge Charles M. Thomson granted the divorce and gave her custody of her daughter, now eleven years old.

Cissy's portrayal of the Count as a dime-novel villain must be viewed both in the light of her desire to win a divorce and her tendency to milk every scene for its last ounce of melodrama. While the Count was obviously not a model husband, a less one-sided picture presents him as "an absolute gentleman in the old Middle-European style, very popular, and respected for his impulsive kindness." An Austrian cousin, Miss Marguerite Freudenthal, recalls that when her brother needed two good horses for his cavalry service at the outbreak of World War I, "nobody among our acquaintances pretended to have any to sell, except Count Gizycki, who sacrificed his two best hunters."

Gizycki had no need of a horse in the war, because he had had to give up riding in races or anything strenuous. He had fallen from his horse a few years earlier and the horse had trod on his head. Ever after, he was subject to violent headaches.

Whatever hostility Cissy had suffered from the Gizycki side of his family, she was treated warmly by her Austrian relatives. Madame Marie E. de Steiger, a first cousin of the Count, recalls that the European aristocracy was opposed to their men marrying American heiresses to solve their financial problems. The main reason was that their wives and children, lacking the requirement of sixteen aristocratic ancestors, would not be received at court.

Thus, there was "great agitation" when Gizycki's family learned that he was returning with an American bride, even though that was exactly what his economic plight called for. But it was a pleasant surprise, says Mme. de Steiger, when "Josef brought us a beautiful and charming young cousin. I liked Cissy very much."

For a time after the war, the Count lived in a hotel on the French Riviera and then on the estate of Count Rudolf Kinsky in Matzen near Vienna, where he kept a smart apartment. He died of a sudden illness in Vienna in 1925. He had never remarried.

In reporting Cissy's performance on the witness stand, the Chicago *Herald* pointed out that she had "taken leading parts in many private theatricals in Chicago and Lake Forest" for several years. With her arresting "presence" and her sense of the dramatic, it was natural for Cissy to have turned to the amateur stage while marking time before the divorce.

In Lake Forest, where she rented a house, she performed occasionally in plays presented by Mrs. Arthur T. Aldis at Mrs. Aldis' Lake Forest estate and in charity benefits at Jane Addams' Hull House in Chicago.

Cissy was a good actress—Joe insisted she was the best amateur actress he ever saw. Mrs. Aldis' son, Graham, said of Cissy years later: "I recall her in a short play by her brother Joe in which she was an attractive but honest working girl pursued by the forces of evil. I also recall her in another—I think a translation from the French—in which she was delightfully enigmatic (both to her husband and to the audience) as to the existence of a lover." This was *The Pocket Book*, with Cissy in the role of Flourette Tambour, a French girl.

Cissy was occupied with several beaux. The one she saw most often was Frederic McLaughlin, a wealthy, young Chicago coffee merchant, clubman and sportsman. Freddy was an outstanding horseman and a six-goal polo player. She often rode with him. Women were just beginning to ride in Lake Forest, but Cissy was no beginner. She had fox-hunted in France and stag-hunted in Poland and England, and was a daring jumper. Nothing more elegant than drag hunting was then available to her in Lake Forest, and she made the most of it. In drag hunting, the hounds chased an odoriferous object which had been dragged over the area before they were unleashed, and the riders chased the hounds over an obstacle course of wire, hedges, fences, etc.

Cissy and Freddy frequently made up a foursome with Prentice Coonley, a local manufacturer, and Mrs. Coonley. One night Cissy invited the Coonleys and Freddy to dinner. When they arrived at her house, a servant let them in, and Cissy did not make an appearance. After forty-five minutes, Mrs. Coonley went upstairs and discovered that Cissy was having trouble getting into a new dress. Finally, in disgust, she cast the dress aside, grabbed up a piece of green silk, wrapped it around her and tucked it under her shoulder. When Cissy descended the stairs, the effect she had impulsively created was one of great style and classic grace; to Coonley she looked like a character in a Greek play.

Cissy occasionally went out with Count von Bernstorff, the handsome German ambassador, and Freddy didn't like it. Bernstorff knew the Pattersons in Washington, and was popular generally with Americans who knew him during the tense period after war broke out in Europe in 1914. Cissy was not alone in being swayed, however briefly, by the German's charm, for Bernstorff found time, while being a correct and conscientious diplomat, to be a successful ladies' man. (Barbara Tuchman, discussing prewar espionage in her book *The Zimmermann Telegram*, indicates that the ambassador's foreign affairs offered some diversion for the Secret Service agents who listened in on his telephone conversations—and to the State Department officers who read the transcripts. In one conversation, according to the book, Bernstorff "modestly protested to one caller, he really should not be compared to the title character of a play called *The Great Lover* because, unlike the play's hero, he 'stopped.'

'Perhaps you have taken a rest, but not stopped,' a female voice replied. 'You *needed* a rest.'")

Bernstorff paid court to Cissy on his trips to Chicago. Once, he took her driving in an automobile along the lonely North Shore road, much favored by the amorous, between Chicago and Lake Forest. No sooner were they parked and locked in embrace than the jealous Freddy swung alongside in his roadster. He had followed them, armed with his riding crop. Now he leaned over and furiously beat the ambassador with the whip. Cissy had nervously jumped from the car at sight of McLaughlin, and as soon as Bernstorff could start his engine he roared off into the night alone. After that incident, it was said, the German confined his dalliances to the more diplomatic atmosphere of Washington's Embassy Row.

Such episodes embellished the growing picture of Cissy in Chicago as the Countess with a romantic past, to whom melodramatic things often happened. Gradually, tales of her life with the Count became more and more lurid. According to one story, she had trapped him in a bordello by wangling a job as an inmate of the house and confronting him as he was actively engaged on the premises. In another, after learning the time and place of rendezvous with his mistress, she disguised herself as a woman of pleasure, ousted the mistress, and offered herself to her surprised husband when he arrived.

The stories are doubtless sheer fabrication. Cissy did not have to resort to elaborate tricks to get evidence of her husband's philandering; he practiced it openly. But, nonetheless, such tales were often believed because of Cissy's reputation for doing exactly what she wanted to do.

Once she had her divorce, she was ready for a completely new life. She was supercharged with energy, and restless. Like many another American in this circumstance, she decided to "go West."

FOUR

Cissy, Get Your Gun

Have you ever heard the love call of a bull elk? It's an eerie, high-flung note—a silvery whistle. If you are near enough, you can hear the animal grunt at the close of it.

This was the lead paragraph of an article in the Sunday Chicago *Herald and Examiner* on November 21, 1920, "by Countess Gizycka, formerly Eleanor Patterson." Cissy had now won such a reputation as a big-game hunter in the West that she could write about it with authority. Her article was one of a series she wrote in the Blackstone Hotel in Chicago in early November after returning from a two-month, big-game hunting trip in Wyoming and Idaho. It was a good trip; she had bagged a bear, two deer, an elk, "a goat and a half," as she put it (her guide had helped on this one), and scores of pheasant.

Her article continued:

We jumped off without a word, tied up our ponies, pulled out our rifles and started down the canyon, Indian fashion, avoiding brittle twigs and dried leaves as best we could.

Bull elk in love have some of the characteristics of a man in love. They mope along a little to the side of the herd, half-hidden in the brush, engrossed in their own emotions. It devolves upon one old cow or two to shoulder the responsibilities of life. Watch a bull herd feeding, all noses to the ground. First one old cow, then another, stops picking and, head up, holds a rigid guard. Bulls don't

trouble themselves with details. They turn the housekeeping over to the ladies.

We crept up unseen to within a few hundred yards of
this particular herd. And then, round the corner of some
brush we came face to face with an indignant, elderly
matron. We looked at each other as if all three had turned
to stone. Then with a warning snort she dashed up the
opposite side of the canyon, a bunch of cows and calves
at her heels.

The love-struck bull began to follow the herd, but then,
"more curious and courageous than the cows," turned, as Cissy
put it, "like Lot's wife—for a fatal look behind."

He paused. I shot, and he shied to one side like a horse
shying at a scrap of paper. He plunged on. I knew he
was hit, but I knew too that if he were not struck in a
vital spot he might run and die in the forest, where we
would not find him.

But the worry was of short duration. Within a minute
the air shook with a great roar of agony and rage. Down
he came, rolling over and over to the bottom of the steep
incline. We could not see him distinctly, for he was hidden
in the brush, and he thrashed and raged and fought for
his splendid life till the last breath left his body.

He was a magnificent creature, bigger than a western
horse, stronger, heavier. He had 14 points, and the horns
were heavy, wide and long. He was fat and sleek, in the
very prime of life—the most beautiful specimen shot in
Jackson Hole last year.

This was Cissy's fifth year in Jackson Hole, that exquisite
little valley cupped high in the backbone of the Rockies. Forty
miles long and from eight to fifteen miles wide, it is famous today
for the breathtaking Grand Tetons National Park, its 1500-acre
wildlife preserve, its dude ranches, its big game and its ski runs.
The Continental Divide is a gentle swell to the east, the Snake
River range is to the south, and the Grand Tetons' great gray
peaks form a wall between Idaho and Wyoming to the west.

Strung along the feet of the Tetons are a series of shimmering mountain lakes. Two million tourists now pour through the cool valley every summer.

When Cissy first went to Jackson Hole, in 1916, there were no tourists, no cars, no telephones, no plumbing, and there was electricity only in the town of Jackson. She thought of it as an isolated Eden. Desperately restless, and in the long-drawn-out process of getting divorced, she tried it at the suggestion of a Chicago friend, George Porter, who was one of the first "dudes" —a word newly coined. Porter recommended spending a summer at the Bar-B-C ranch and going hunting with a guide named Cal Carrington.

Cissy's arrival was long remembered. Besides Felicia, then eleven, she brought along seven trunks and her French maid, just as she had traveled in her millionaire manner to Newport during the two previous summers. They immediately found that Jackson Hole and Newport had nothing whatever in common.

After taking the long train ride to Salt Lake City, they took another train north to Victor, Idaho, and discovered that the worst part of the trip was still ahead: the long ride over Teton Pass into "the Hole." The Bar-B-C had sent a driver with a homemade ranch wagon to fetch them. When the grade on the dusty mountain road grew steep, the driver made them get out and walk to ease the strain on the horses. Cissy struck out ahead of the procession in her long-skirted tweeds from Paris and custom-made walking boots. Felicia recalls: "She looked like a big wildcat and her red hair flamed in the mountain sunlight." Felicia herself was in a state of ecstasy at the profusion of wild-flowers, the tall pines covering the slopes and the clear topaz-colored streams.

The wagon rumbled into the Bar-B-C, seventeen miles north of Jackson, after dark and in the rain. A strangely attired woman came to the door of the main cabin and said, "Hello, I'm a cavewoman."

It was Katherine Burt, who with her husband, Struthers Burt, a writer, owned the ranch. At the moment, the Bar-B-C's annual fancy-dress party—to which the Hole residents came from miles around in homemade costumes—was in full swing.

The Gizycka party faced one more climb, over a trail to a guest cabin, and it was a little too much for the French maid. She sat down on the trunks and wept; Paris was never like this. She vowed she would not go another step, but she finally got up when Cissy announced that she was returning East the very next day, and sounded like she meant it. She had not realized until now the meaning of "roughing it."

The next day, Cissy sent her maid and six of the seven trunks back to Chicago, but she and Felicia stayed. They set out on a hunting trip, with a boy to cook and help with the horses, and Cal Carrington, who worked out of the Bar-B-C.

In Cal, Cissy felt she was seeing the real thing—an authentic nonfiction cowboy. He was a little over six feet tall, with a narrow waist, a great chest, enormous hands and the bowed legs of a rider. A wide-peaked hat shadowed a truculent nose and a face that was seamed and lined like a walnut. In his fringed leather chaps, molded to his legs by years of wear, he moved with the slow grace of a horseman, flashing a single Mexican silver spur. When he was dressed up, Cal wore silver-studded leather cuffs and a black-and-yellow neckerchief tossed airily over one shoulder.

His language could be cuttingly laconic. Obviously, he knew all there was to know about animals, and liked them. But he acted as if he hated all boys, most men and quite a few women. His first impression of Cissy was that she would be helpless, and probably obnoxious, on the trail. He was amused when she informed him that she had done quite a bit of fox hunting. But he discovered as soon as she sat a horse that she really could ride. This was no ordinary rich easterner. There was something special about her above and beyond the fact that she was determined to prove her endurance.

Once, after riding for three days to their camp at the Soda Fork on the Buffalo River northeast of Jackson Hole, they ran short of food and it began to snow. Cissy showed no signs of distress. She produced a volume of Tolstoy, one of her favorite writers, and read to Cal and Felicia as they huddled around the stove in the tent and the snow hissed on the warm canvas. Cal and Felicia were enchanted.

Cal did not try to hide the fact that he was taking a shine to Cissy. In the manner of Jackson Hole, he referred to het as "my dude." The fact that this hard-bitten guide was showing solicitude for a client was unprecedented; it was even more remarkable that the client was called "the Countess" and stood out even among the highly picturesque guests at the Bar-B-C. Grumblingly, Cal explained himself to Struthers and Katherine Burt: "She don't know nothin'. She's a mighty nice woman, and someone might get the better of her."

To Cissy, Cal was a romantic figure, the fabled White Hunter straight out of Victorian novels about African safaris. She was not only in awe of his expertise. She was curious about what everyone called his orneriness—particularly toward camp boys —and she needled him about it.

When he once complained to Cissy, "I can't find my knife," she quipped, "You stuck it in the new hired boy and forgot to take it out."

Always attracted by rascals, Cissy was delighted with Cal's reputation for stealing horses. She was even more delighted when he blandly explained that he merely "helped himself" to horses.

Cal owned a homestead ranch in Flat Creek Canyon on the south side of Sheep Mountain, east of Jackson Hole, which he admitted was ideal for hiding his "borrowed" horses. The canyon is narrow, and, as he put it, "I can see the sheriff a-comin' either way."

Cissy fell in love with the unspoiled beauty and the sheer

inaccessibility of this meadow directly below the mountain that looked like a sheep. When she first visited it, and for a number of years after, the last four miles of the primitive road leading to the ranch from the mouth of the canyon were impassable to automobiles; one had to hoof it or ride a lumber wagon.

In 1917, for her second summer in Jackson Hole, Cissy leased the White Grass ranch, but once she saw Cal's place she was determined to buy it, and she never let him rest until she did. In the Hole it was said that "Cal always gets ornerier when he finds he's doing someone a favor," so he resisted her offers as long as he could. But Cissy was learning how to get around him. When she found out that Cal kept the deed to the place in another cabin on the other side of the mountain, she sent another guide, George Ross, to get it. Then she confronted Cal with the deed, and he complainingly sold to her. She was dreaming of fixing up her own ranch in this valley, whose spirit seemed so remote from Chicago, Washington, New York and Europe.

Cissy collected offbeat "characters," and Jackson Hole offered a refreshing assortment. She went into Jackson and mingled with the cowboys and the gamblers. A feminist at heart, she was thrilled when Jackson, in 1920, elected a good-looking girl, Pearl Williams, as sheriff, and women to its other five municipal offices. The all-male city council had been thrown out of office because it had run the town $750 into debt and its citizens were outraged. The petticoated politicians inspired Cissy to write her first newspaper story, which appeared in the Omaha *World-Herald* as well as her family newspaper, the Chicago *Tribune*.

The news dispatch gave her a chance to plug her adopted town. She reported that Jackson "is the commercial hub of the Jackson's Hole [as it was then called] region, once notorious as the stronghold of outlaws, but now, and for years past, one of the most peaceful and prosperous localities of the country. Owen Wister in *The Virginian* made Jackson's Hole famous as a rustlers' rendezvous, but cattle raising, undeterred by rustling or any other forms of outlawry, has made it wealthy."

The *World-Herald* ran a picture of the five new city mothers; its caption hinted that the town was as inaccessible as darkest Africa:

> This photograph was taken from the isolated city of Jackson, Wyo., via automobile, boat, wagon and sled to the nearest railroad, 75 miles away in Idaho. Between this railroad and Jackson is the swollen Snake River that has taken out all bridges, and the Teton range, almost impassable from soft snow.

One of the five women elected was Mrs. Rose Crabtree. She was the bravest of the five, for her opponent was her husband, Henry, a carpenter. Rose was a cook for Ma Reed, who ran the Reed Hotel in Jackson. A short, broadly built Amazon who carried brass knuckles and used them effectively when cowboys became too obstreperous in her hotel, Ma Reed would have made Calamity Jane look like a Sunday-school teacher.

One day she said she was going on a two weeks' trip and asked Rose to run the place in her absence. She was gone seven years; she had good reason, since she had been stealing from the grocery store next door. Rose legally inherited the hotel and operated it as the Crabtree Inn. Still operating in 1965, it is a small, unpretentious place with a large, combined sitting room and old-fashioned kitchen. Cissy stayed there frequently.

Rose and Cissy were approximately the same age and, in the beginning, that was all they had in common. Rose hailed from Weeping Water, Nebraska, and they were as far apart in heritage, upbringing, education, and social prestige as any two people could be.

Rose was what Cissy needed. Cissy never tried to impress Rose and never wanted to. Conversely, Cissy was what Rose needed. While Rose did not play the humble companion to Cissy, she had a whole new world opened to her by this glamorous heiress who had waltzed in the palaces of European capitals and had been married to a rake-hell count. When Cissy unburdened herself about her early life, Rose grew to know, and like, the real person that was revealed.

To Cissy, Rose was the prototype of the self-reliant, yet pretty and feminine western woman, a counterpart of Cal. In contrast to many aristocrats Cissy knew, Rose could be utterly charming just being completely herself. Her plain-spokenness, both to Cissy and to others, was irresistible. One summer, after telephones had been installed in Jackson Hole, an impatient beau of Cissy's telephoned Rose at the Inn, asking her to get a message to Cissy at the ranch. Rose explained that Cissy was on a hunting trip, but the man kept telephoning to ask if she was back.

Rose finally sent him a three-word telegram: "OH SHUT UP."

Cissy knew she could trust Rose. In long talks and in the stream of letters covering more than forty years, Cissy unloosed her secret thoughts to her as to no other person. In one letter she wrote: "I've laughed with you and cried with you more than any other person in the world." They never quarreled.

After Cissy died, Rose told Felicia that, without Cissy, her life would not have been worth a damn. Conversely, Rose loomed large in Cissy's life; among other things, she was a port where Cissy could always return in an emotional storm.

According to Felicia, "Rose Crabtree was the greatest influence in my mother's life. It was her friendship that showed mother what she could do—that she could do anything, that there was nothing she *couldn't* be. Mother occasionally used to feel sickly or fragile—she was used to being waited on hand and foot by servants—but Rose told her she couldn't be that way out West.

"Mother had never seen life as it is lived by everyday people before. She had always had a passionate interest in stories and people, and now she was meeting them close up. Sometimes it was a shock. Once, when Mother and I stopped off to change trains at Salt Lake City, an old woman collapsed. Mother, who always took pains with people in distress, came to her rescue and we brought her into the hotel. She gave her smelling salts, and I got water. When the woman came to, Mother asked, 'Are you a Mormon?' 'Yes,' answered the woman. 'Has your husband more than one wife?' Mother asked. The woman said no. Mother wanted to know how she would feel if he did have other wives. 'We'd be just like sisters,' the woman replied. Mother felt hurt."

In an article in *Vogue* magazine ("Jackson Hole, 1916–65: A Reminiscence," April 1, 1965) Felicia explained:

> Back East my mother was considered a fascinating lawless creature, a charmer and a menace. Nobody could oppose her without getting hurt. Out here she was a source of constant entertainment. People weren't afraid of her. Jackson Hole used to be full of characters, who could be themselves without benefit of psychiatry or interference from the law.

Felicia feels that the time her mother spent in Jackson Hole was the happiest and most tranquil of her life. After she became a newspaper editor, and hardly visited her ranch at all, Cissy tried to preserve some of that joy by keeping in touch with Cal and Rose and painting their virtues in bright verbal colors for the edification of her friends and employees. In the twenties she started bringing Cal and Rose to Washington and showing them off at her parties.

The first time Rose arrived at the Union depot in Washington, she attracted attention by wearing her customary wide-brimmed hat and high-laced boots.

"When do I meet President Coolidge?" she asked immediately after Cissy greeted her there. "Right away," Cissy told her. She had anticipated that Rose would expect nothing but a straight path to the White House, and so, by prearrangement, Cissy was able to whisk her there to be presented to the President, whom Cissy knew quite well.

Cissy was not embarrassed by Rose's preference for wearing the same western regalia in Washington that she wore in Jackson. After all, nobody had a more solid reputation than Cissy for wearing what she pleased. There was the night that she and

Felicia were expected at the engagement party given by the
Ogden Armours at the Blackstone Hotel for the richest little
girl in Chicago, their debutante daughter Lolita. The most elegant ladies of the city were dressed to the elbows in long, white
kid gloves, and to the heels in sweeping trains. The Gizyckas
arrived late, both dressed in their riding clothes. The guests
stopped talking and simply stared, but Ogden Armour took
Cissy on one arm and Felicia on the other and graciously introduced them all around. Cissy explained that they had just stepped
off the train from the West and had not wanted to waste time by
changing clothes.

If "the Countess" was at first an object of amused curiosity in
Jackson Hole, she quickly proved to those who accompanied
her on the trail that she needed no pampering or special protection. Exulting in her freedom from the dandified atmosphere of
counts, diplomats and Chicago socialites, she plunged into the
wilderness like a reincarnated Diana.

Rex Ross, who worked for Cissy on the ranch with his father,
guide George Ross, recalls admiringly: "I don't think I know
of any other woman who came out here and did what she did."

Cissy even won respect by the swashbuckling way she drove
a team of horses. Considering the mountain roads in Jackson
Hole at that time, this was no ordinary skill. Donald Hough, in
his book *Cocktail Hour at Jackson Hole* (Norton, 1951), recalls that one Clay Seaton was "the greatest driver of them all,
and that the secret of keeping his teams moving was profanity
('the things Clay can say to a horse shouldn't be said to a dog')."

However, when it came to swearing, Hough wrote, "the only
person Clay Seaton ever acknowledged as matching him was
Countess Gizycka. She was the only one he ever turned over
the reins to on the [Teton] Pass, and the only one he ever let
talk to his horses. 'I owe her much,' Clay still admits. 'She didn't
teach me all I knew in talking to horses, but she sure as hell
gave me a few wonderful ideas.' "

One of the characteristics much admired in Cissy, according

to Rex Ross, was that she "would say anything for the hell of it."
One night in Jackson, the Countess was eating dinner in a combination restaurant and pool hall (a roulette wheel and poker
and dice games were available in the back room). A local
gambler, Pat Patterson (no relation), tried a number of stratagems to attract her attention, including some squeaky sawing
on his violin. Short, pudgy and dark-complexioned Pat was
obviously not sweeping Cissy off her feet. Rex Ross, then in his
late teens and employed as roustabout at Cissy's ranch, saw Patterson sit down at her table for a short time, then get up abruptly
and sidle over to him. To Ross's puzzlement, the gambler was
attempting to butter him up. Only later did he find out that
Cissy had told Patterson, with a straight face, that the Ross boy
was her son.

Cissy cared little for gamblers, but she studied cowpunchers
with a keen eye, and described their appearance this way:

> Cowpunchers care a great deal for a smart appearance
> . . . theirs is our only national costume, and it is one to be
> proud of. We borrowed it from the Spanish, of course,
> but we have made it our own. Picturesque though it is,
> each part is based on practical reason—from the air-cham-
> bered, waterproofed Stetson hat to the high-heel boots,
> which provide sound anchorage when roping. Cowpunchers
> are finicky creatures. They will not milk, for instance.
> Right in the middle of a cow camp, they use canned milk
> or go without, rather than sit down with a tin bucket to
> the ancient and honorable task.
> There is snobbery in all things.

She also noticed that many cowboys wore soft gloves, and
that their hands were so nimble in cooking, sewing or untying
complicated string knots that she felt as if her own ten fingers
were "made of cotton flannel."

Cissy made Cal foreman of her ranch. Fortunately, it was a
very small one, for Cal was lazy. Nonetheless, he maintained a
proprietary air and resented other men being around his boss.

He even became jealous when she asked young Rex Ross to
drive her to Jackson in the Model-T Ford (after autos could
negotiate the road, she also kept a Model-T Ford truck and her
Pierce-Arrow at the ranch). Cal insisted he would drive her
there. In that case, Cissy decided, she and Rex would sit in
the back seat.

This further annoyed the foreman; in a fury, he drove them
down the mountain road, rough, steep and winding, at twenty-
five miles an hour, four or five times the safe speed. At several
turns, the Ford came dangerously close to leaving the road
entirely, and the passengers narrowly escaped being hurled from
the car. Cissy continually shouted at Cal to slow up, but he kept
on his headlong course, luckily without incident.

As Rex Ross recalls him: "Cal spoke soft and slow, and didn't
look like a real tough guy—which he was. He was not scared of
anybody in the world. And he was a good guide, a real pro."

On hunting trips Cal soliloquized about his life, mostly to himself, but Cissy listened. He said he didn't know who his parents
were. Probably this was because he wanted to forget them.
Felicia learned years later that his real name was Enoch Julin,
and that his father had been a shoemaker in Sweden. His parents
had been converted by the Mormons and had shipped the boy
when he was five years old—despite his tearful protests—on
ahead to the promised land of Utah. He never saw them again.

Cal himself said his earliest memory was that he was an orphan
in an Arizona cow camp. When he was about eight, he said, he
was adopted by a couple who had a small ranch in Idaho. His
foster father was a hard man, so Cal, big and strong at sixteen,
beat him with his fists and ran away.

For the next twenty years he roamed the Far West from
Mexico to Canada as a top cowhand. When he was twenty-one,
he taught himself, painfully, to read and write. But he never got
to like the written word, and regarded it with suspicion. As an
orphan he had no name, so he chose one for himself—"California," because it was the name of a cowboy he liked. Later, he

changed that to "Calvin," and added the last name in honor of an
Englishman who had befriended him. The middle initial was
simply because other people had one.

On one hunting trip with Cal, Cissy excitedly thought she
had sighted a goat in the distance—until she remembered that
they were on Sheep Mountain and that there were no goats in
Jackson Hole (they were across the mountains, in Idaho).
Through field glasses, Cal saw a bushy tail and identified the
snowy-white animal as a wolf. They took off on their horses to
cut off the wolf, who had quickly melted into the mountain mist.
As they drew closer and sighted the wolf again, Cissy sat
down on the trail and took aim, but, between the fast beating of
her heart and the violent wind, she could not hold the gun
steady. Just then the wolf sighted them, and began to move
swiftly away. Cissy had no choice but to shoot. She fired two
shots, paused, then fired a third. The animal fell and rolled over.
Cal said he saw him turn around and, wolf-fashion, bite at his
wound. Before Cissy could fire again, the wolf had dissolved
into the murky plain. They never saw him again. Presumably,
he was crawling home to his den to heal, or die. Cissy felt terrible. She told Cal it was a miserable thing to cripple an animal
and let it get away—for humane if no other reasons.

The plateau on top of Sheep Mountain has sheer rocky walls
on almost every side. On the edge of one wall, Cissy and Cal
spied three ewes and a young ram who had gotten the hunters'
wind and were scrambling wildly along a rim of rock which
led within a few feet around a bend and out of sight. One misstep
by these sure-footed sheep would have meant a fall of a
thousand yards. On her first try, Cissy overshot the ram, who
promptly turned and wheeled back, driving the ewes before him.
They vanished beneath a ledge of rock.

"Shoot right in front of the ledge," Cal told her. "That'll drive
'em out!"

Cissy obeyed orders and out came the sheep, back again over
the same runway. Now she shot the ram through the shoulders

and killed him. He was just about to spring across a narrow chasm when he was hit. He hesitated on the brink, then pitched down, headfirst into the abyss below. They saw his body roll over and over, and could still hear it fall after it was lost to sight.

"Well, come on," Cal said. "He's gone."

"Gone?" Cissy protested. "But I want the head!"

"How you gonna get it?" Cal inquired. "I ain't noticed no airplane round here yet."

"Can't you make it down?"

"I ain't a-goin' to risk my legs for that little head."

"It isn't little," Cissy argued, pleading. "And maybe I'll never get another."

"The horns'll be broke," Cal pointed out.

"I don't care," she pouted. "I'll glue some on."

The sharp wind had stung tears in her eyes, and she added a feminine sniff or two. She pulled at his sleeve and forced him to turn and glance at her. In white-lipped anger, Cal stooped and unbuckled his great silver spur and flung it aside, sent his wide hat skimming after, and strode off, growling, to get his lariat from the saddle. He skirted along the brim of the precipice in search of an opening, then let himself down over the edge and into the rock.

For the next four hours there was only silence. Cissy felt like a tiny, lonely speck beneath the big sky, the gloomy rocks and the brooding plain. She began to regret sending Cal into the abyss. He always did as she wanted, in the end, but just now she felt a little ashamed of herself. She longed to sneak back home, to her familiar things in the cabin at the ranch. But she knew she would have lost her way in ten minutes.

She found a little hole in the rocks, perilously near the jumping-off place. By drawing her knees up, she could lie on her back out of the wind—in comparative shelter. Every once in a while she would poke her head up and look down for Cal. At last she spied Cal's stringy figure, bent beneath a great hump on his back, and coming around a point in the slide rock. After another hour's struggle, Cal came suddenly from under a ledge into plain sight. Triumphantly, he held up the head of the ram, an unbroken horn in each hand—as radiant, Cissy told herself, as Salome proudly balancing John the Baptist's head on a platter.

Cissy generally used a 6.5-mm., Italian-made Mannlicher rifle with an eighteen-inch barrel, some six to eight inches shorter than the barrel preferred by men.

George Ross regarded Cissy as "the best shot of all the women I've ever seen." Al Johnson, another guide who sometimes accompanied her, said she could take the head off a grouse at 50–75 feet and hit an elk at 375–400 yards.

"She would go anywhere an elk went," Johnson recalled years later. "She would ride all day, never want to quit or pitch camp early. And there was no fuss or bother."

Cissy carried on one packhorse a twelve-foot-high teepee, about fourteen feet in diameter. She got a fire going in its center and slept rolled in a blanket, like an Indian. The teepee was an awkward shelter, compared to a tent, and proved a tricky chore for one man to put up. Once Johnson got it into place slightly askew. Shaking his head, he chuckled, "Sitting Bull would never go into *that!*"

"Not if I saw him coming, he wouldn't!" Cissy quipped back.

Sometimes Cissy had an itchy trigger finger. On one pack trip to Turquoise Lake, which was twenty miles from the ranch, they were rounding a mountain trail when Johnson looked up and saw a black bear above them. Cissy saw it too, and the guide yelled back at her, "Wait till I get the horses out of here!"

Cissy acted as if she hadn't heard the warning. She jumped to the ground, aimed her rifle—a Winchester .06—and fired. The bullet struck the bear right under the heart. He squealed like a stuck pig, rolled down the hillside toward them and scattered the horses but did not hit them. There, on the trail, the bear died while they watched.

Nothing offered more excitement for Cissy out West than bear hunts. Bears were always fair game, for they killed a lot of cattle in Jackson Hole. One October day in 1922, Cissy and Cal drove a crippled cow 400 yards from the ranch to a narrow, rocky gorge and left her there as bait for bear. Next day they returned. Immediately, through the willows, Cissy spotted a square black head and two ears pricked at attention. Quickly she and Cal plunged into the muddy creek and waded upstream until they were below the bear, and hidden from view by the brush.

As soon as the head came into view again, Cissy began to raise her rifle.

"No! No!" Cal whispered. "Step out this way."

"Oh, shut up," Cissy muttered, flinging the gun to her shoulder and firing at what should have been the center of the bear's chest. The animal was apparently struck, but instantly vanished. Cal told Cissy testily that she should have moved a yard or two to one side, where she could have had a clearer view. She disagreed, and they argued.

Two days later they came back for another look at the bait scene. There, feasting on the cow, was the bear. He was a soft charcoal color, and to Cissy, as she aimed, he seemed to have a solitary, wistful expression. A second or two afterward, Cal fired too. Then the bear charged. Cissy aimed and fired again. The bear swerved and went past them like a black cannonball. Cal shot again, and they rushed out of the brush to catch him as he went up the mountainside. As they raised their rifles for a final shot, the animal fell dead.

As a novelty, they next decided to trap a bear. Assisted by George Ross and Tony, they used pine needles to conceal the trap and its bait, the hindquarters of a fat, young bull elk. On the following day they found a bear caught by one leg. Cissy was horrified; the poor beast looked humble—bitter and broken-hearted, like the men she had once seen in the Joliet, Illinois, prison. Noticing her compassion, Cal scoffed, warning that the bear was strong enough to drag the loose log he was chained to. He recalled that a trapped bear had chewed a man to death a year before. Cal took a hard-nosed bullet from his pocket and silently handed it to Cissy, as the animal growled. She slipped the bullet into place and then, resting her elbow on her knee and holding her breath, she shot the bear neatly through the forehead.

On a hunting trip, Cissy wore either a five-gallon hat or a bandana, tying back her abundant red hair; a man's shirt covered by her ancient, fringed-buckskin waistcoat; levis, or a pair of Cal's black sheepskin chaps.

From time to time during her first years in Wyoming, Cissy heard tales about the wild and mighty Salmon River across the Tetons in Idaho. The Salmon has its source on the Continental Divide and flows westerly through the center of the state until it empties into the Snake River, where Idaho, Washington and Oregon meet. It has cut a trench across Idaho which for nearly 200 miles is a mile deep, creating a series of some of the most picturesque and awe-inspiring canyons on the North American continent.

The Salmon is called the "River of No Return" because it is, for all practical purposes, impossible to go upstream its entire length by boat. When Lewis and Clark first gazed on it, they decided it was impossible to go downstream either, so turbulent were its rapids, and so they made the heartbreaking trip overland. Not until after 1900 was the Salmon navigated downstream. But in 1921 no woman had ever navigated it, and that was enough of a challenge for Cissy. She determined to be the first woman to go down the "River of No Return."

She trusted herself to the longtime victor over the Salmon, one "Captain Gulike," who used a unique flat-bottom wooden boat. Also aboard was Cal Carrington and the boat's "mate." The object was to traverse the dangerous 163-mile stretch of water from Salmon City to Riggins, Idaho. Cissy kept a diary, which subsequently was published as a two-part series in the magazine *Field & Stream* under the by-line "Countess Eleanor Gizycka." The first article opens with this boxed precede:

"How scary will it be, Captain Gulike?"

"How scary are you?"

"Oh—I'm scary."

"Well, you'll get a kick out of it, all right."

In the first diary entry, dated July 9, 1921, Cissy described the boat: thirty feet by eight, sawed off square at both ends. Two clumsy-looking sweeps, front and back, were constructed out of a three-foot square of boards riveted onto a straight young pine tree.

"This unlovely but capable scow draws only six inches of water," Cissy noted in her diary. "It swims unresistingly along like a cork over the rocks and through the monstrous swirling rapids, shooting sometimes clear out of the river as it drops down the bigger falls."

In the next sentence, she revealed her mood and motivation:

We scrambled in and put off at 9:30 this morning. A moment of exaltation as we faced the morning breeze and began to float rapidly from the very start; a feeling of relief and sudden unleashing. Five days' hard travel and miserable fatigue for the reward of moments like these. We poor humans so mess up our lives and everything we touch that we must escape from each other, and from the cities and towns, our own creations, to find a little peace. Strange, when you stop to think about it.

But Cissy's ecstasy was short-lived. By 11 A.M. the roasting heat nearly drove her crazy. Her hair came down. She lost her gloves and had to hide her blistering hands in the pockets of her khaki breeches. The sun scorched through her heavy woolen stockings.

Suddenly, a brilliant, tossing current knocked the sweep out of the captain's hands and landed the boat high and dry on some rocks in midstream. Pried loose, it soon struck deeper water, and Cissy notes:

The rapids are wilder, more brilliant, more bewildering. The boat slaps down on the white-crested waves, amazingly steady, and the spray slashes mockingly over us, soaking us all to the skin. We stand at the bow and laugh and shout, excited but not really afraid.

They are sobered when they come upon an empty boat, with sides caved in and paddle missing, further down; its occupant, it turns out, had been knocked overboard going over the big rapids. Gulike tells Cissy at this time of three other men said to have drowned here.

She notes wryly that it is a joke for a woman to find herself in a spot where she can't change her mind. "For there is no turning back on the Salmon River," she adds dramatically. " 'Forbidden River' the Indians call it."

On the second day, the boat headed into the feared Pine Creek Rapids, a three-mile stretch of eerily white water. Over the centuries, huge blocks of rock, some of them as large as a house, had fallen into the river from the towering granite cliffs looming above. Cissy wrote:

The whole scare, if scare there is, comes in avoiding the rocks. Sometimes in the narrows there's not six inches leeway on either side. Of course, smaller boats than ours have another problem to face; the treacherous undercurrent and swirling eddies pounce sometimes upon them catlike, spin them around, turn them over at one stroke, and suck them under and out of sight.

One night, after they had camped, the mate announced there was a deer lick nearby and that they might see some game if they got there before dark. Cissy, still in her bathing suit, could find no underwear or other clothing in her duffel bag, so she simply drew on a brand-new pair of English field boots over her bare feet, grabbed up her gun and scrambled her way through the brush. Only then did she realize that she was still wearing a pair of diamond earrings she had forgotten to remove before leaving the East.

She saw no deer, but returned after dark and sighted the silhouettes of two doe on the very crest of the hill against the skyline ("big ears, long, slim neck, round bodies, they look as big as elephants up there"). But she would rather look than shoot.

Cissy was fascinated with the delicacy of deer. One night, she reported, "after we've made camp at dusk, a doe and fawn come down the mountainside opposite to water, in the wistful, silent way of deer; she fragile, finicky-stepping, the little fawn docilely limping along behind."

Another time, at a salt lick, Cissy lay in wait for hours and then saw four doe and two young buck come to the water to drink. She philosophizes:

> There is always something mystic, remote, yet infinitely appealing about animals, unsuspecting and undisturbed in the wild. I laid my rifle on the ground and sat down to watch, a lump in my throat. For the passion for the chase lies deep beneath the conscious lust to kill. To the natural-born hunter the mere sight of game stirs to the roots an ancient, fundamental instinct, inherited through the ages, probably from the days when a fight between man and beast was a fight on both sides of deadly consequence. It is the same animal instinct which throws a setter dog, for instance, into a trembling ecstasy at sight or scent of a grouse.

The river journey took thirteen days, and near its end Cissy was getting sick of it. She no longer could find anything in her duffel bags, the food was poor and monotonous, and the boat "smells of bilge water and many more, equally unpleasant things."

"Today," she reports dolefully, "I sat at the bottom of the boat for an hour, listless, dejected, a broken comb on one side and a forgotten sock floating in the sump at the other."

Still, the Salmon River adventure was one of the high points of Cissy's active life in the West. She was forty years old and she never tried anything quite so strenuous again. She continued to hunt big game for years, but more and more she was feeling guilty about killing. She vividly described her growing problem in an article in *Liberty* magazine in October 1925. During a prolonged hunting trip in Alberta, Canada, she woke up one morning in her teepee feeling fatigue, discomfort, bad temper, dirt, boredom, and—despair.

Yet, she still wanted to shoot goat—bigger ones than the two she had shot in Idaho. She decided not to go back to Banff without one. That day her party pursued some elusive rams for hours, trying to get a good shot. Finally, they got close enough, and Cissy shot and killed the one with the finest head. The head measured sixteen and a half inches at the base, and the guides agreed that it was one of the ten finest ever brought into Banff.

They continued to hunt goat that day, and when they spotted the next one, Cissy felt depressed the moment she laid eyes on him. But from force of habit she jumped from the horse and pulled her rifle from the saddle scabbard. From a game trail along a ridge, well above the goat yet only seventy yards away, she shot him.

Cissy related:

His white body lay prone, directly below us, but his head was still up. That was the sickening thing: the broken body and the head still up. The jet-black horns pointed our way, and the intense eyes gazed straight into ours.

Distaste for the whole proceedings welled up in me, a feeling almost of nausea. I had never really wanted that goat.

. . . As we took our first few steps down, he staggered to his feet, lowered his horns, and made one mighty plunge forward up the trail, then sank back again onto the ground.

"I think this is perfectly horrid," I said. "Why doesn't he die?"

. . . I could bear it no longer and raised my rifle: but I remembered: a shot through the back might paralyze but would not kill. Only a head or neck shot would kill instantly, and both were hidden.

. . . the animal stirred a little and began to moan—sobbing choked sounds. He was fighting for breath. I felt very sick indeed.

"Life was intended to destroy life; all nature is cruel," I argued with myself. "Big fish eat little fish; hawks kill sparrows; even in this country bears, wolves, wolverines, coyotes kill when they can. Wild animals die a tragic death anyway. They die of starvation and cold when they are old and weak, the prey of others. Wolves even eat wolves."

But reasoning did not help much. He took so very long to die.

. . . three or four of my acquaintances I remembered—African hunters, hunters in our own north countries—who one day, without adequate explanation, had laid down their rifles, never to take them up again.

Satiety—I thought to myself—the thrill has suddenly quite all gone. It lasted ten years. That's a very long time.

Cissy did not immediately hang up her rifle for good, but the hunt was never the same again. Before the end of the twenties she gave it up entirely. Her love of animals suppressed the hunter's instinct, which was also a basic part of her character. Besides, as the twenties progressed, Cissy's restlessness was turned back in the direction of the East, of Europe, and of another man.

FIVE

Wandering

Although she sometimes lived as strenuously as a man out West, Cissy Patterson had neither the stamina of a man nor even the robustness of a hardy woman. She was no hypochondriac, but she had her share of illnesses, some of them hard to diagnose.

On February 8, 1921, she wrote Rose Crabtree after being in bed for four weeks in the studio apartment she then kept at 6 East 61st Street in New York:

> Dear Rose, I was so happy to get your dear letter and all the news from Jackson Hole. It was just like a big breath of that wonderful, fresh mountain air. . . . When I came East I seemed to toboggan right downhill. That hunting trip was too much for an old lady nearly forty! Sleeping in the dirt and *snow* and dragging around those mountain peaks when I had scarcely the strength to put one foot in front of the other . . .
>
> So that charming boy Tony is working for you. Teach him please all you can, and then if he comes West this summer, perhaps he will cook for us? Where is unfortunate Emma? She was really in love with him—but he just let himself be loved. Perhaps that wasn't quite all. They both used to look a little pale at breakfast. I know those Poles. But Tony is a sweet boy.

(Tony was a youth of Polish descent, from Texas, who cooked for Cissy on the ranch.)

"If you and sweet, grouchy Cal, and Tony . . . would come in

[East] together," she continued, "I believe I'd get right up out of bed and be well again." Cissy told Rose that "they've fastened tuberculosis on me, but I don't believe it somehow." (She was right in being skeptical.) She added:

> In fact, I rather enjoy the role of *Camille*. Did you ever read *Camille?* I'll send it to you. You'll have to lock the doors while reading it.
> Leaving here Thursday and going back to Washington. Not with any particular joy, though. But I've gained ten pounds—quite a bust now! Which is what I always wanted.

Washington in 1922 bored Cissy, as she had anticipated, and she restlessly yearned to see Europe again. She decided to combine it with a sentimental journey to Poland. She was fond of the Polish nobility; Russian Poland had cast a spell on her. She arrived in Paris in November, accompanied by her mother and Cal Carrington (presenting him with his first trip abroad). On December 15, 1921, Cissy wrote Rose that she hadn't seen the sun once since arriving in France. "Each day is like the last—chilly, raw and gray," she explained. "It's awfully good for the nerves. I never slept so well in my life."

"Paris has changed, but very much," she rambled on. "No one wears anything but dead black. Sometimes one seeks a discreet, dull brown—never in all Paris a dark blue, red, or any other color."

She reported that she and Cal had visited Napoleon's tomb and that both of them had cried—"just from the majesty and beauty of the thing." (Rose raised an eyebrow at the thought of Cal Carrington weeping at Napoleon's tomb.)

Cissy wrote:

> Dear old Cal went off to Italy over three weeks ago. He wrote me a cute letter from Rome—and that was over two weeks ago, and not a word since. I really have begun to worry for fear something terrible has happened—although I'm sure the old simp is having the time of his life and is too busy to write.

Cissy complained that it was a problem getting away from her mother during the day. Mrs. Robert W. Patterson had begun to fail, and would continue to do so until she died in 1933. Cissy told Rose her mother "is worse than I expected—mind and memory quite gone. Without exaggeration, she asks the same question ten times over in ten minutes. But I think she is physically better than when I came."

Her mother had sent to Austria for one of their "poor relations" to take her home, after which Cissy would proceed to Warsaw.

Cissy, who always rued the signs of age, was meeting old friends whom she had not seen for years. She told Rose they reminded her of "characters in a play—twenty years after—second act. Physically so much changed—much fatter—much thinner—wrinkled, puffy-eyed. They seem to think and talk and act the same—their personalities appear to be unchanged. But this queer, ghastly change of the body. Indication of old age and death. Of course, it's just the same with me. I (once) had a silly, fat, perfectly round face. And now I'm all wrinkled up and skinny."

Cissy was not doing herself justice. As long as she lived, she was never wrinkled up, and she was never skinny. At the time of her letter to Rose, photographs in *Harper's Bazaar* show her (even allowing for possible retouching) as girlishly slender and glamorous. The pictures illustrated "Polonaise," her short story about pre-World War I Polish aristocracy, in the December 1921 issue, and "Sentimental Journey From Fifth Avenue to Warsaw," an account of her trip to Poland, in the August 1922 issue.

Cissy's memory of prewar Poland was exotically nostalgic. In later years she often talked about the style of life at Antoniny, the estate (adjacent to the Gizyckis') where the Potocki family reigned like feudal princes in a Louis XV palace. Aristocrats came from all over the world to stay with them during the hunting season. Cissy herself had experienced some narrow es-

capes hunting stag in that land of dark forests, yawning ditches
and muddy banks.

The way Cissy told it, upper-class life in the Polish Ukraine
just before 1910 was as indolent as life in a Russian novel—
except that the Poles seemed to have a busier sex life. In her
article in *Harper's Bazaar*, she reminisced:

> Tea time in the library; like the rest of the house, a
> combination of barbaric splendor and sophisticated modern
> comfort. And the rivalry in tea gowns! Some of the men
> lounged about, still in their muddy boots and splashed hunt-
> ing coats; others changed into dark-green or black or wine-
> colored velvet smoking suits. It was the most delicious
> moment of the day; relaxed and languid, safe out of the
> cold. Soft lights, low voices; someone among the multi-
> talented Poles on the piano. Sometimes a pretty lady would
> rise and, her chiffon draperies drifting about her, float by
> small stages out of the room. One of the velvet jackets
> might yawn, then stretch a little, pick up a bibelot, put it
> down askew, peer into a book, yawn again, and so, gradually
> fade away. And when this interesting double maneuver had
> definitely been accomplished, everybody smiles at every-
> body else, perfectly delighted. Many a romance had begun
> and ended at Antoniny.

Somewhat guiltily, she also remembered the peasants—"rough-
bearded sheep-coated, a dim-living kind of serf, I thought then in
my reckless youth—rooted, along with the potatoes and the
carrots, deeply in the soil." When a peasant couple wanted to be
married, the barefooted girl bride, a wreath of flowers on her
head, and her lover would go down on their knees before the
Potockis to ask permission. Now these same Ruthenian peasants,
thanks to the war and the Russian Revolution, were master of
Antoniny and other estates. Many of the Polish landlords Cissy
had known so well had been massacred when the Bolshevik
hordes came down from the north, their homes burned and
their farms pillaged.

When Cissy visited Count Joseph Potocki, he assured her that the peasants of the original kingdom of Poland—who lived in the Ukraine side by side with the Russia-oriented Ruthenians—had not fallen for Bolshevism. Perhaps this was so, but to Cissy the Polish aristocrats were living in the past. She felt they should face reality and make some concessions to the wave of the present and the future. At afternoon teas, she went as far as she dared in urging the most influential Polish leaders not to resist the peasants' demands for a bigger share of the land and a stronger voice in the representative form of government then emerging. She urged it on the practical ground that it would bring prosperity to their impoverished land. In the United States, she pointed out, the strength of our country is the farmer and the small property owner. But Poland is not America, they answered, revealing their fears of being outvoted by illiterate peasants. "I left pretty soon after that," she wrote, "feeling conscious of having made myself unpleasant with my new democratic idea which, from my friends' point of view, spells Socialism, which is on the road to Communism, which inevitably leads to Bolshevism, which is Hell."

The article from Poland did not go unnoticed. *Labor*, a magazine published by sixteen railroad labor organizations, said in an editorial:

> Anyone who wants to know why the people of Russia and adjacent territories embraced the doctrines of Lenin and Trotzky would do well to read Countess Eleanor Gizycka's story, "A Sentimental Journey From Fifth Avenue to Warsaw," in the current *Harper's Bazaar* . . . the brilliant Polish woman is no "red" but she has eyes and understanding.

Hearst columnist Arthur Brisbane, commenting on the *Labor* editorial, snorted:

> She is indeed not "red," also not a "Polish woman," and no "Bolshevik." Her name before she married the Polish count that didn't amount to much was Eleanor Patterson.

Her grandfather was Joseph Medill of Chicago; her mother, Mrs. Patterson, gets at least a million a year from the newspaper that Joe Medill started. There is no antidote for Bolshevism like a mother with a million a year.

Feeling rootless, Cissy kept on the move. During the next two years she went from one resort location to another—from Colorado Springs, Colorado; to Santa Barbara, California; to Banff, Canada; and to Jackson Hole, with in-between retreats to Chicago and Washington. She had a good time at the Broadmoor Hotel in Colorado Springs. On May 26, 1922, she wrote Rose Crabtree:

It's quite gay here. Lots of people I know. All of them have some illness, etc., or scandal or tragedy of one kind or another to keep them here.

But she was concerned about Felicia, then seventeen years old. She decided she would return to Chicago to collect Felicia when she was finished with school (Felicia was attending Foxcroft in Virginia) and take her to Santa Barbara. She told Rose that her daughter "should see more young people—particularly make friends with some boys of her own age. It's time for her to learn how to hold her own with them and not be so shy. She looked lovely in Chicago by the time she went back to school. But had the awfullest clothes when I came home, poor child."

Santa Barbara turned out to be what Cissy was not looking for. "I am not counting the days but the minutes to get away from this damn place," she wrote Rose in July, after being there a month. "There are some nice people, I suppose, because there are some nice people everywhere—but I never see them. The nice ones have beautiful places hidden in the hills and hardly ever come out—I only imagine this because a place as big as this should have a few agreeable people in it, and I haven't met any yet. I love vulgar people if they have just a little charm. But the Santa Barbarians are vulgar alright, and pinheaded besides. That's a poor combination."

On the other hand, Felicia and her cousin, Elinor Patterson, who had come out to stay with her, were "much more attractive" and "having the most heavenly time." Cissy wrote Rose:

They both have passionate beaux, which of course makes me feel rather pleased and satisfied and also scared to death. Never on earth can I persuade them to go to the Sierra Nevadas with me—and it wouldn't ever do to leave them here alone. They howl and yell at the bare mention of leaving even for a day. Well—that's youth. A dance to them is as important as the Battle of Waterloo to Napoleon.

To further complicate matters, Cal Carrington had shown up at Santa Barbara, though Cissy had telegraphed him not to come:

Of course I am perfectly delighted to have some one to speak to—Felicia's friends look on me as a kind and consumptive old party easily disposed of—and he will get mad and run off before we have a chance to get tired of him.

Cissy announced that they would be in Jackson in two weeks and asked Rose meanwhile to find someone to build one more cabin at Flat Creek like her own—plus an addition on hers. She said she also wanted to put up a big living room and a kitchen on the little point across the Creek.

(When Cissy got through with her building program, her ranch consisted of a barn, where she kept as many as fifteen horses, the main cabin, and seven other cabins for guests and ranch hands.)

In another letter to Rose, Cissy had announced she was bringing a Jew with her to the ranch.

The Jew was Elmer Schlesinger, the son of a Chicago department-store owner and a nephew of Levy Mayer, the attorney who had represented Cissy in her divorce and had since died. Schlesinger had taken his bachelor of arts and his law degrees at Harvard and had quickly and solidly established himself as an up-and-coming lawyer. As counsel for the Chicago

Tribune, he had participated in the expulsion of William Lorimer from the United States Senate. And he also represented William Wrigley, the chewing-gum king.

In 1921, Schlesinger had become general counsel and vice president of the War Shipping Board at the request of its chairman, and his friend, advertising magnate Albert D. Lasker.

Schlesinger's path had inevitably crossed Cissy's because he was a friend of her cousin, Medill McCormick, who had been elected to the United States Senate from Illinois in 1918. Figuratively, Elmer and Medill regarded themselves as twins, Alice Roosevelt Longworth later recalled; once, they literally bounced into her living room, arm in arm, with Medill announcing: "Mike and Ike, they look alike"—borrowing a popular phrase of the time.

Cissy invited Schlesinger to the ranch during the period in which he was being divorced by his wife, Halle, who was a daughter of Joseph Schaffner, of Hart, Schaffner and Marx. Mrs. Schlesinger charged desertion and won custody of their two children—Halle, 10, and Elmer, Jr., 4. They had been separated since 1920.

In letters to Rose, Cissy described Elmer as ugly, a typically disparaging remark about someone she liked. A prominent nose spoiled his face and he was not handsome, but Schlesinger made an impressive appearance—the epitome of the self-confident, successful lawyer. He was well-mannered, and with Cissy he was gentle, kind and protective. To be cherished and looked after was something Cissy needed in those footloose years.

It was a mistake for Schlesinger to go to Jackson Hole. He arrived with his English valet. Since the valet was in charge of a case of whisky brought by Schlesinger, and was generous with it among the ranch hands, he managed to make himself tolerated, but his master was regarded with more than the usual amusement reserved for "dudes." Though somewhat athletic—a fine tennis player—he did not take to this type of outdoor exercise. Poor Elmer hated horses and he hated roughing it. Sitting around the ranch house, Cissy kidded him about it so much that he was obliged, occasionally, to take a plunge into the brush.

Once, the guide, George Ross, took Cissy and Elmer to a lake straight up—so it seemed to Elmer—the side of Sheep Mountain. The trail was clogged with jack pine, and Elmer's legs got badly scratched. He complained to Cissy that Ross must be a "crazy man" to take them over such a route, but Cissy laughed and called him a "big sissy." Privately, she remarked to Ross's son, Rex: "Just think—I had thought of marrying that man!"

Some of Cissy's closest friends and associates in future years were Jewish, but Schlesinger was the first she knew well, and, somewhat to her surprise, she was becoming involved with him romantically. To begin with, she was not sure that he really appealed to her romantically; all she knew was that, more and more, she was depending on him.

Cissy continued to write to Rose about once a month, from wherever she happened to be living. Her letters showed that she was at odds with herself and impatient with others, but her writing was also chatty and included some teasing of strait-laced Rose about men.

On February 9 she wired Rose from New York, after another European trip:

> Landed last night. More dead than alive. Please express bear skins at once to 1601 R Street, Washington, D.C. Must show them off. Certainly was stung over the victrola. Will send check for express. Feel very badly. Your letter about Flat Creek made me very happy. Would not have a brick house in Jackson for a present. Whoever heard such nonsense. Who does your typewriting? Is it that nice, good-looking young man in the land office? I hear he is quite rambunctious. Stop. Stop. Stop.

She kept sending Rose directions for the improvement of the ranch. On March 2 she wrote:

> Yes—yes—yes, I want a good dance floor in the living room. I want a big brick fireplace in it too—a *big*, huge

one—I want a barn painted red. I want the road to go up the creek on the *left* side, going up to avoid the swampy places. I also want a little cabin for myself to write in— all about how you had a baby by my brother, and Nick McCoy (your husband) never found it out. (I don't know where I'll hide this yet.) Fox knows better than I do where to put the other cabins. Anyhow, I wouldn't dast to say, for fear you wouldn't approve, and the whole thing would have to come down again.

Also, I want a nice big cabin in Jackson and a shed for some horses! So tell Fox he is *mine* for the summer.

Will write as soon as I can get someone to dictate to. Would that charming Mr. Ellis like to be my secretary this summer?

(The joke about Cissy writing a short story in which her brother Joe would be cast as Rose's lover, and Nick McCoy—a disreputable Jackson saloonkeeper—as Rose's husband, was typical of Cissy when she was in a broadly spoofing mood. Charles Fox was a Jackson building contractor who put up her extra ranch cabins.)

When Cissy wrote Rose again in April, her mood was depressed:

I'm so sorry you are ill—you're discouraged by the long winter, I suppose. Well, I'm discouraged too. Just by life. I can't find my way through. Anytime you want to change places—Henry and all—just let me know. I could give him nice pictures to look at, if not much else.

Will take Dr. Huff's house for any price you think reasonable from May 15 on—for—I don't know. Two or three months.

If I get the house, you see, I can come out early.

Love to darling old Cal. Tell him I miss him almost as much as when I went away.

Ever your devoted
C.

The summer of 1923 passed uneventfully for Cissy in Jackson Hole, as she concentrated on making the ranch at Flat Creek more comfortable. The town of Jackson was fifteen miles away and the nearest ranch was ten miles, and most guests from the East still regarded it as the end of the earth. There was no central heating and no water, except what you fetched yourself.

But even Jackson Hole palled on Cissy after three months. She decided to climax her summer with some big-game hunting in Alberta, Canada, and she took Cal with her. At Banff she hired a well-known guide, Bill Potts.

From Banff she wrote Rose:

I really think this will be my last hunt with Cal. We all know he's been a little treacherous and light-fingered all his life, but I was so conceited I never thought he'd be either with me. Well, he has been *both*—and I never will get over it.

She then directed Rose to have her horses taken care of for the winter—but, specifically, not in Cal's care.

She wound up on her usual note of mental fidgeting:

My dear—I'm so damn lonesome I think I shall be sick. You hang on to Henry, for you don't know (judging by your foolishness) a *real* good thing when you've got it.

Have no plans for the winter. I had thought of going abroad, but these last two days all alone have cured me of that idea, unless Felicia or Mama go with me.

Cissy went from Canada to Chicago and lived for a time at the Lake Shore Drive Hotel. On December 4 she wrote Rose that Schlesinger had turned up and was "looking perfectly terrible —he is thin and grey, and killed by work. I tell him what is the use of making so much money when he never has time to enjoy it, or anything else. I must say he is the cleverest man in some ways that I have ever known."

At this point in her letter Cissy swung into a report on another important man in her life, Freddy McLaughlin. She wrote Rose:

> Did you hear that our friend—Frederic McLaughlin—was secretly married to the dancer, Mrs. Vernon Castle? He is her third husband, and everybody predicts a near calamity, but as a matter of fact, it may work out all right, as they both have reached the normal age of discretion; but whether they really have acquired a little sense or not remains to be seen. She gave her age as 29, but she is really 34 or 35, and he (so coquettish of him) clipped off a year or two too. They were married in his apartment —the apartment you saw, and skipped out of town before anyone got hold of the story, and are now on their way to the Philippines, Hawaii, China and Japan. But whether it turns out all right in the future or not, I am sure they will have a most *interesting* and pleasant honeymoon.

The letter closed with thoughts on still a third man:

> I had a sweet letter from the man who took me out hunting—Bill Potts, in Canada. Cal told me that he was the toughest man he had ever met in all his life, but you know how we women are—we always fall for that.

Rose was surprised at how well Cissy apparently was taking the news of McLaughlin's sudden marriage. Several years before, on a visit to Chicago, Rose had been taken by Cissy to meet McLaughlin. Cissy had previously told her they had had an off-again, on-again romance. When they left the apartment, Cissy had hung back, wanting to say goodnight to Freddy in private. A year later, when Cissy was telling Rose how fond she was of Freddy, Rose asked her if he had kissed her that night as she left the apartment.

"No, he just hugged me close," Cissy replied. Rose understood. Cissy had conveyed the impression that the silent embrace was more expressive of their feelings than a kiss.

Rose felt that Cissy must be sad that McLaughlin was out of her future. Rose was right. Three years after McLaughlin's

1

Eleanor Medill Patterson played a part in a dynasty. Her grandfather was Joseph Medill, founder of the Chicago *Tribune*. Her cousin, Robert R. McCormick (seated left) became publisher of the Chicago *Tribune* and her brother, Joseph M. Patterson, founded the New York *Daily News*. Cousin Medill McCormick (on her left) became a U.S. Senator from Illinois.

2

Cissy's mother, Elinor Medill Patterson, was beautiful and domineering. Her father, Robert W. Patterson, succeeded Medill as head of the *Tribune*.

3

6

4

Cissy was a rambunctious little rich girl who once tried to climb a Chicago church steeple, a demure adolescent, and a sought-after American heiress in European capitals. This is the court gown in which she was presented to the Emperor Franz Joseph in Vienna in 1906. The picture was taken by Baron von Rothschild, who photographed nothing but beautiful women.

5

7

Cissy married Count Josef Gizycki, an Austrian-Polish count, in 1904 and went to live in his "castle" in Russian Poland.

8

marriage to Irene Castle, Cissy confided to Rose that she thought Freddy was the only man she ever really cared about. Strangely, they had never come close to being married, even though they had obviously been in love. Cissy once told Rose something that summed up the depth of their feelings. Some time after his marriage, Cissy watched Freddy arrive at a party and walk right past her without speaking. Later on in the evening Cissy asked Freddy why he had cut her.

"I couldn't speak," he told her.

"I understand," she had replied. "I feel the same way."

"I love you, Cissy," Freddy said softly.

"And I love you," she replied.

Cissy and McLaughlin were to remain close friends until his death in 1944. She was accurate in her letter in predicting that his marriage might very well work out. Irene Castle McLaughlin sued her husband for divorce in 1937, but later withdrew the suit. At the time of his death, "Maj. McLaughlin" (he had been an army major in the 333d machine-gun battalion in World War I) was chiefly known as a millionaire sportsman and owner of the Chicago Blackhawks hockey team.

Cissy could not quite accept the fact that there was only one man in Rose's life, her husband Henry. Indeed, she was slightly suspicious that Rose might not have told her the whole truth about her love life. Once, Cissy said: "Rose, don't ever lie to me. Don't answer, if necessary, but don't *lie* to me. I don't think you ever have—except that I'm a little doubtful about your saying Henry was the only man in your life." Cissy greatly admired and liked Henry Crabtree, but the idea of a woman having only one man in a lifetime seemed monotonous.

Rose thought it strange that such a close-knit friendship had developed between herself and a multimillionaire society woman. She once remarked to Cissy: "When I was running barefoot in Nebraska, you were a princess in Paris."

"The hell I was," Cissy had replied. "I was being spanked, and pulled by the hair, kicking and screaming, all over Europe."

On February 26, 1924, Cissy wrote Rose a typically winter-lonesome letter from her mother's town house at Du Pont Circle. Her mother was then spending most of her time in the Lake Shore Drive apartment in Chicago.

What can I tell you about my winter. I had a perfectly vile time in Chicago between my poor, sick mother and Felicia, who is about as easy to drive as a team of young bull moose. However, on the whole I must say she has improved. I let her have her way because I couldn't very well help it, and she has found out for herself that she is only human after all and capable of making quite a few mistakes.* She and Elinor went to Bermuda with an old-maid cousin for chaperone. I expect Felicia back in about 10 days now—or rather, until I really see her I shan't expect her at all.

As I look out my windows, only the tops of the trees are in sight and they are covered with snow for the first time this winter. My rooms, you know, are on the top of the house, perched up like a little nest under the eaves. The walls of the room are a sort of robin's-egg blue, the curtains are of yellow glazed chintz with a tiny little red border on them. That's the bedroom. The sitting room has the same kind of walls and the same curtains with a very slight variation. These two little rooms and the bath-room between are shut off from the rest of the house like a little apartment by a hallway and an outside door. So, you see, whenever I get cross and tired, I can lock myself away from the world.

What do you hear from old Cal? I heard from him a month or six weeks ago and he said he thought of going over to Jackson. Let me know if you see him and how he is. It always worries me to think of him living alone and his own horrible cooking and half-dead of indigestion most of the time. I suppose he hibernates like an old bear in his cabin and sits there thinking the horriblest thoughts

* Ed. note: Felicia was then nineteen years old.

about women, which he punctuates by running to the window every 10 minutes in the hope of seeing some go by. Give him my love anyhow.

Cissy could never get used to Cal's penchant for wearing clothes that smelled and needed washing. Exceptionally fastidious, she was disgusted by sloppiness in others. At times she even washed his clothes, and the task always repelled her. It was one reason they never became lovers.

In her February 26 letter to Rose, Cissy also unburdened herself about Schlesinger more than she ever had before. She wrote:

Schlesinger has been down to see me and also on business. I must add, to be perfectly fair, quite often. He went on the water wagon on Jan. 1 and really had the will to stay on, which is more than I can say for myself. Anyhow, it was the greatest improvement and he seems mentally and physically a very different and very much improved man. He is so smooth and sure of himself that it is quite impossible to ever get mad at him, and with my kind of a disposition these are very unusual characteristics.

Two months later Cissy reported to Rose that, of all the men she knew, Schlesinger was "the most interesting of all right now. He fixes up my life for me—arranges everything. Decides my troubles in two seconds—after I've been changing my mind for weeks and arrived at no conclusion. He'll be out this summer, I think."

Schlesinger had not hurt his chances with Cissy by giving a ball for Felicia at Easter. Fifty persons were invited to dinner, and another hundred guests had come afterward.

Schlesinger in New York and Washington was masterful, but in the Jackson Hole wilderness he was still a tenderfoot. That summer he became ill at the Flat Creek ranch and was secretly relieved when the doctor told him to take it easy. Cissy—who always referred to him now as "my dude"—would stand for no such inactivity. She dashed off a note, which was delivered by hand to Rose at the Crabtree Inn fifteen miles away:

I'm just leaving for the hills with George and Ed and
Rex† and the cook—and leaving my dude behind! I'll be
gone for four or five days. Must go—I simply must get
out.

Come up with Doctor Huff and spend the night? *Please*
do. I want the doctor to see Mr. Schlesinger again. Bring
some nice meat with you—and five slop jars!

Schlesinger says that the doctor has forbidden him any
violent exercise for 10 days, so you'll be quite safe here.
(That's why I thought I might as well go now. For a
while.) *Please* come. *Quick.*

During that summer of 1924, Cissy told Rose she would never
marry him. Rose's own opinion of Schlesinger was that he was
one of the nicest and kindest gentlemen she had ever met.

Rose believed Cissy meant what she said about Schlesinger, a
belief which was reinforced during Cissy's long stay in Paris
the following winter. In her letters Cissy seldom mentioned
Elmer, and on her voyage home she wrote Rose: "I fell in love
too, old fool that I am, and left just in the nick of time. I didn't
suppose this world held anyone as fascinating—just for *me*—as
that man." (Rose never did find out who this fascinating person
was.)

† Ed. note: three ranch hands.

SIX

Elmer

Toward the end of the summer of 1924 there began a chain of events which influenced Cissy's decision to marry and also brought her a son-in-law with whom she was to be linked, often turbulently, for two decades.

Like many rich, restless women, Cissy spent far less time with her daughter than did most mothers. Consequently, when they were together, their relations were likely to be either distantly formal or wildly tempestuous. She deeply loved her daughter, but was baffled by her. She remarked to Rose Crabtree, "I've got to remember every minute that Felicia is half Polish," attributing Felicia's sometimes strange moodiness to the fact that her father was a temperamental Slavic count. Felicia was as rebellious as her mother had been at the same age, but apparently less vulnerable. From an early age, she had greater inner resources and an unshakable poise.

One day at the Flat Creek ranch, after mother and daughter had collided like a couple of wildcats, Felicia decided she had had enough. She made plans to run away immediately and asked Aasta, her mother's young Swedish maid, to accompany her. She and Aasta were good friends; they had gone to Jackson together and danced with the cowboys. Aasta refused to run away, but Felicia was not to be discouraged. She made a halter out of her cotton stockings and put it on her favorite colt, scorning bridle and saddle because they belonged to her mother. Then she put all her worldly goods in a duffel bag and, while her mother napped in the cabin, rode down the canyon bareback. Halfway down, half her possessions fell off and she ended up leading the horse into Jackson. There she put up her colt in a livery stable and drew $300 in savings from her bank account. She added this to the $50 she had won from Schlesinger on a bet that she could walk a horse faster than he could. Then she looked up Rose and asked her help.

"I've got to go East," she told her. "My mama is ill."

"Mama" was Felicia's grandmother, but Rose didn't believe the girl could have received word of the illness, since there was no telephone at the ranch.

"How did you find out, Felicia, by ouija board?" Rose asked with a smile. But she still agreed to put Felicia on the stagecoach which made the 75-mile journey up over Teton Pass and down into the railroad station at Victor, Idaho, where she bought a ticket on the first train for Salt Lake City. Just as it was pulling out of the station, a slim young man leaped aboard the rear platform, strolled through three cars and sat down next to her. Felicia was startled, and then angry. The young man was Drew Pearson, a guest at the ranch. Pearson was in love with her—he wanted to marry her—and it was getting to be a bore. She had been almost as anxious to get away from him as from her mother.

Pearson explained that as soon as he had heard of her escape he had saddled up a cow pony and set out in pursuit. Now he wanted to help her out, if he couldn't persuade her to return home. Felicia made it clear that he was as unwelcome on the train as he had been on the ranch. Pearson took the hint and got off at Salt Lake City. Felica got off there too and wired her grandmother—visiting relatives in New Philadelphia, Ohio—that she was en route. This was to cover her tracks, for actually she caught the next train west.

Though he had no idea where Felicia was heading, Pearson was not yet ready to abandon the uphill courtship which had been going on for a year. It had started at a dinner party. Pearson had been taken to the dinner by Anne Hard when her husband, writer William Hard, had become too ill to attend. Mrs. Hard said the dinner was being given at a mansion on Du Pont Circle by Countess Eleanor Gizycka, "the most glamorous lady in Washington."

Pearson, then an economics instructor at Columbia University, was not unsophisticated. His father, Paul Martin Pearson of Swarthmore, Pennsylvania, was a well-known man of letters, and he himself had been educated at Swarthmore College. Nonetheless, he was dazzled by his hostess, her town house and the distinguished guests. There were monogrammed plates, and uniformed butlers waiting on him. Pearson was careful to pick up the right fork at the right time, and he pretended to be completely at ease, but he wasn't, paricularly since he was trying to catch the eye of his hostess's lovely daughter, the "young Countess." It was obvious that she was popular; her beaux, he heard, included wealthy Averell Harriman.

Pearson found plenty of excuses to return to Washington. He set out to woo Felicia, but he made no progress. Thus, it was a surprise and a pleasure, in the summer of 1925, to receive a telegram from her mother inviting him to spend a few weeks at her ranch at Jackson Hole. The wire reached him at Columbus, Ohio, when he was peddling features for a newspaper syndicate. He borrowed the train fare and set out for Wyoming the next day.

When Pearson seated himself at the table at the ranch, Rose Crabtree was reminded of John Gilbert, then the great lover of the silent screen. It was true that Pearson, like Gilbert, cultivated a small black mustache, but there the resemblance ended, in Felicia's opinion. Her suitor was earnest, but balding and diffident. Unaccountably, her mother also had taken a fancy to this proper young Quaker.

As far as her mother and Pearson knew, Felicia vanished from Salt Lake City into nowhere. For four months she kept her whereabouts a secret. Years later, her Uncle Joe said to her: "During this period your mother kept saying, 'Oh, I don't care where she is.' But I knew her heart was breaking." Pearson, too, was frantic. Finally, at Christmas, he received a card from Felicia telling him she was in San Diego. Her mother located her about the same time.

Felicia had ended up in San Diego because it was the end of the line for her westbound train back in September. Her first problem was supporting herself. She had never held a job, but she summoned up hope from the fact that she had managed to take her turn as a waitress at the Foxcroft School without dropping any dishes. She moved from the YWCA, which she decided was too expensive, to a $12.50-a-month rooming house inhabited by girls who made the doubtful claim of being married to sailors at the San Diego naval base. Through the girls, Felicia was directed to a sailors' waterfront hangout where she could apply for a job as a waitress. A hard-eyed woman in charge listened to Felicia's finishing-school accent, studied her regal poise, and said: "You're runnin' away from something. If it's a man, I don't want you." When Felicia reassured her on this point, she got a job serving the bar.

Felicia used the pseudonym "Marion Martin." (Curiously, when her mother adopted a pen name some years later in order to do an undercover series on working girls for the Washington Herald, she chose "Maude Martin.") Felicia was seeking a new life, a career if possible, which would make her independent of her mother's emotions and money. By December, though, she was getting fed up and lonely in the tough sailors' town, and so she had let her mother and Pearson find her.

When Pearson showed up, Felicia was glad to see him. His courtship was promptly renewed—and rewarded. On March 14, 1925, headlines in Chicago and Washington newspapers disclosed that the young Countess Gizycka and Drew Pearson had been married at Long Beach, California. (The Chicago Herald-American described the bride as "an international figure" ever since she had been "the most kidnaped child in the world" in 1908–09; the Washington Star noted that she was a much-traveled and "accomplished young woman" who had refused to make a formal debut in society but had "consented" to have her mother give her a ball the previous winter.)

Cissy gave the story to the newspapers after telegraphing the couple her felicitations. She was genuinely happy about the match. To help out, she offered to supply them with what Pearson later said was a fabulous income. The offer was refused.

Pearson and his bride set up housekeeping in New York City, where he was now a $125-a-week writer for the United Publishers Corp. One month after the wedding, Pearson answered the telephone after breakfast and heard his mother-in-law's husky voice saying casually: "We're getting married this morning. Come on over." Felicia made a bet that her mother would not go through with it; she was so sure of it she did not bother to get dressed and accompany her husband. She could not believe that she would marry Elmer Schlesinger.

Cissy and Elmer were married in the chapel of the License Bureau in the New York City Municipal Building. The wedding, performed by the City Clerk, was starkly simple, especially in comparison with the Gizycki-Patterson ceremony twenty-one years before. Pearson was pressed into service as a witness. A brief announcement was made to the press after the couple had boarded the steamship *Conte Verde* for a honeymoon in Italy; it was front-page news in most of the New York newspapers the next morning.

Why did Cissy marry Elmer Schlesinger? The decision was made the night before, over drinks, but it was not that impulsive. They had been seeing one another for years, and Elmer had proposed repeatedly. She had given a great deal of thought to the question.

To her friend, Senator Burton K. Wheeler, she once confided that she was "afraid" that some night, in a gay mood, she would marry Schlesinger. To Pearson she explained, afterward, that she had made the decision because she no longer had to worry about Felicia, now that Felicia was married to him. Pearson's own conclusion was that Cissy decided to get married because she had been footloose for fifteen years and was bored. And apparently her daughter's marriage had put her in a romantic mood.

In conversation with close friends in later years, Cissy rarely used the word love in connection with Schlesinger. Sometimes her explanation of how she happened to marry him was harsh—or utterly negative. To a contemporary, Prentice Coonley, who asked the question many years later, she replied: "I've thought —and thought—and thought, and, you know, I haven't a clue!"

Whatever the true motivation, the marriage at first seemed to have a good chance of success. Cissy's loneliness was gone. From the Trianon Palace Hotel at Versailles, a honeymoon stop, she wrote Rose: "Elmer sends you and Henry his love. He is the kindest, most intelligent and most patient man in all the world. And he has made me happier than I ever was before."

"Felicia is really happy too," she added. "If she isn't, it's her fault, for she has a lovely boy." (The "lovely boy" was Pearson.)

Cissy and Elmer spent the summer at the 57-acre estate at Port Washington, Long Island, purchased by Schlesinger from Vincent Astor, and spent the rest of the year at their apartment at 1010 Fifth Avenue and at the Patterson mansion on Du Pont Circle in Washington. In between, there were frequent trips to Europe, for the Schlesinger law firm had an office in Paris.

Elmer was now a member of the Wall Street firm of Chadbourne, Stanchfield and Levy, whose clients numbered not only many industrial "blue chips" but also Bernard Berenson and Lord Duveen of the art world. Louis Levy had been a brilliant young founder of the *Columbia Law Review* (he was destined to be disbarred in 1939 for improper conduct), and John B. Stanchfield was among the most prominent trial lawyers of his day. Schlesinger, a corporation counsel, proceeded on the principle that it is the job of a lawyer to keep his client out of court, and he was so successful he was almost never seen there.

The Schlesingers moved among the most brilliant and successful New Yorkers in the twenties. They were regulars at the salons in the home of Herbert Bayard Swope, and Elmer could hold his own among such compulsive talkers as Bernard Baruch and Arthur Brisbane. Indeed, his daughter, Halle, felt that, colorful as Cissy was, she failed to outscintillate her father.

"He was one of the most charming, brilliant, forceful personalities I have ever met," Halle (now Mrs. Julian S. Bach, Jr.) recalls. "He had been one of the youngest graduates Harvard ever had, and was a marvelous raconteur. He spoke French, German and Latin."

Forceful or not, Schlesinger's will was no match for Cissy's. She barred Halle's young brother, Elmer, Jr., from visiting either the Fifth Avenue apartment or their Victorian house on Long Island—simply because he resembled his mother!

In the mid-twenties, when middle-class Americans were riding the bull market, the very rich Schlesingers were living the kind of life that F. Scott Fitzgerald was capturing on paper. They had everything other rich people had, and sometimes twice as much. As a wedding present, W. C. Durant, an automobile manufacturer and a client of the Schlesinger firm, gave them a pair of matching Locomobiles, each worth $6000. (Twenty years later, they doubtless would have been monogrammed with "his" and "hers.") It was the most elegant limousine model, enclosed save for the front seat, which was unprotected from the weather and known to chauffeurs as the "pneumonia special."

Cissy needed a chauffeur for her Locomobile, and the first to apply for the job was Charles Frazier. Frazier was familiar with the Fifth Avenue trade and was not surprised when he arrived in the morning to find Cissy emerging from the apartment in a long, white mink coat and with her favorite French poodle on a leash.

Cissy had just one question for Frazier: Could he drive around Du Pont Circle without going in the wrong direction? In those days there were streetcars on Du Pont Circle, but both the northbound and the southbound tracks ran along the west side of the Circle. Thus, the northbound cars were traveling against the southbound flow of automobile traffic. Motorists unfamiliar with this ridiculous arrangement sometimes followed the northbound streetcar route, courting trouble. Periodically, there were proposals to place the northbound car tracks where they belonged, but these moves were blocked by some of the Du Pont Circle residents, including Cissy. She didn't want the streetcars rumbling in front of her house, which was on the east side of the Circle.

Frazier assured her that he could navigate the Circle.

It turned out to be one of the most unusual jobs Frazier ever had. Sometimes he was dispatched to the Port Washington home to manage the nineteen poodles there; once, he was sent all the way to the Wyoming ranch to help out; and Cissy often went out in the car after 11 P.M. Nonetheless, Frazier enjoyed working for the Schlesingers. They paid good wages and were kind and considerate.

Schlesinger looked the part of a prosperous corporation lawyer—dignified, serious, conservative and a tiny bit austere. His favorite attire was a dark-gray-and-white herringbone suit, black knit tie and stiff white collar. But he did not live austerely, and it was a great triumph for him when, as it was said, the Schlesingers "stole" the gifted French cook, Clementine, from the Vanderbilts. During dinner parties, while the other men were enjoying their brandy and cigars, Elmer had slipped into the kitchen and used the argument of a skilled advocate to convince her she should forsake the Vanderbilts for the Schlesingers.

At Port Washington, Schlesinger literally bypassed the normal problems of the New York commuter. He simply boarded his sixty-five-foot power yacht, docked in Long Island Sound, and floated toward the city, while he breakfasted, read the newspaper and had himself shaved. His chauffeur met him at the New York Athletic Club dock and drove him to the office.

Cissy and Elmer traveled in what was then known as the "fast set." On January 18, 1926, she sent Rose Crabtree a detailed account of a way of life that must have been beyond her western friend's imagination. She wrote:

Dear Rose, we got back from Paris last Tuesday. Maybe you didn't know we had sailed? I was at the dressmakers', having some clothes tried on, when Elmer telephoned and said that some frightfully important business had come up and we had to sail *next day*. We were half moved in from the country, everything just at the worst disorder, and I had no maid, having just got rid of that elegant lady who was too dainty to empty slops out in Jackson. Well— My God, it was awful. We *had* to go to dinner and dance that night at Elmer's partner's house, and then up early and out to the country and tried to pack myself and give five million orders about shutting up the house for the winter. (All nice, good, *reasonable* orders—and all carried out just about as sweet and as well as the orders I left behind up in dear Wyoming.) That was in November—the first week—about two months ago. The postcard I sent you was from Florence—beautiful Florence—Italy. We had a good time in Paris the first three or four weeks and tore around to restaurants and theaters seeing our friends —up all night and shopping all day. But got sick afterward.

At this point Cissy gave her western friend a glimpse of European night life—as enjoyed by rich Americans—in the twenties:

One night we went off on a bat with some old friends —about four in the morning Elmer wanted to go home, but I had had a lot of champagne by then and felt pretty gay and wouldn't go with him. We went to one place where the men, all painted up, were dancing together, some in women's costumes. I gave one 20 francs to go over and kiss Elmer, which he did right on the mouth. Elmer turned green and came over absolutely foaming—said he had probably got a disease and I must be drunk and had better go home where I wouldn't disgrace myself. That's when *he* left.

Then we went to a place where the women were all making love to each other, some in men's clothes. Half very masculine and half very fluffy ruffles. The head girl had a lovely face, like a young boy, and a deep, deep voice, and a tiny mustache. She was *very* well dressed in a tuxedo (excepting for a little, black straight skirt), high stiff collar and a white gardenia in her buttonhole. I thought she was grand and would have loved to talk to her, but they dragged me on to a Russian place where some of the oldtime Russian gypsies (the kind the grand dukes and nobles used to ruin themselves for, before the war). I never will forget the voice of one oldish, fat woman. It was the wildest, most passionate, heartbroken thing you ever heard. Then we went on to a nigger joint, all American coons—singing their heads off too. We ate waffles there and drank coffee. It was about 6:30 A.M. Then we thought we'd go to the great central market, which supplies (just think of it) the whole of Paris, and buy some flowers. All those big noble horses, three in line, were standing about with their carts, having walked in—miles and miles from the country—and hundreds of peasants muffled up in warm woolen stuffs, wearing wooden shoes—huddled over braziers of charcoal, lots of them, for it was bitter cold and across from food stalls; enough to feed three armies. And there we were, among those simple, poor, hard-working people—me in a white ermine coat and rose-satin slippers walking through the slush and mud.

We came back to the Ritz—it was 7:30 by then or later—arms full of the loveliest flowers and straight up to Elmer's room (not any *too* straight). He was asleep in bed. We showered him with roses and violets and mimosa and tulips—all *over* the bed and floor. But do you think he was grateful for this lovely sentiment of ours? Not a bit of it! He didn't hardly speak to me for a week.

A New York friend, the Princess Raspiglioci, recalls that during this period Cissy "seemed crazy about Elmer. No doubt about it—she was in love with him."

Cissy wrote Rose from Du Pont Circle on November 9, 1926:

Elmer is reading the financial section of the paper in bed next to me. He's got an old striped wrapper on and specs, and he looks too homely and cute and contented for anything.

Which proves that the Schlesingers spent at least one night at home. In the next breath Cissy says in her letter:

Sunday night we had a big party here and brought down from New York three quadroon girls and two men and a big band to do the "black bottom" dance after dinner. One girl wore an enormous wig and had nothing on but a few bananas around her waist. When she came on, I thought I'd die of shame. But everyone got used to it mighty quick. The girls dressed upstairs in one of the bedrooms before the show.

I knocked at the door before the show—they said come in—I opened the door—they hadn't a stitch on any of them—excepting one girl had a napkin. About every two minutes, without any knock, the door would open quick and one of our *gentlemen* guests would stick his head in, and, seeing me, pull it out again. Don't know how all those men knew where the girls were. Guess they just smelled them.

Each of Cissy's letters to Rose made some reference to the ranch, its horses and its caretakers. In this one, she reports to Rose on Cal Carrington, whom she had been parading around Long Island and Washington in all his frontier flavor, even though she had said she would never trust him again. Cal had been yearning to hunt big game in Africa, and now the Schlesingers were willing to send him there. Wrote Cissy:

C-C sailed right after the Dempsey-Tunney fight for Africa! Elmer got him a cabin on a freight boat for nothing. (I guess he would have *bought* him a ticket to get rid of him!) He is the only passenger. They sailed for Mozambique, British East Africa, by way of the Suez Canal and Arabia! I went down to see the ship—and it certainly was a Romance ship if ever I read of one. The whole crew are black East Indians. Cal wrote us from Canada (the ship went up first to St. John's, New Brunswick, to get a load). He said he had an Indian boy just to wait on him, and every morning the boy turned his socks and fixed them for him. But he had to wait till the boy left to turn them back again to get them on. Also, so he could throw the hot water out the portholes.

Early in 1927 the Patterson town house at 15 Du Pont Circle in Washington earned a place in American presidential history. The White House was forced to undergo extensive remodeling, requiring President and Mrs. Coolidge to find another home temporarily. Cissy offered them her home, and the Coolidges accepted. The Coolidges knew the Schlesingers well. Elmer as well as Cissy had impeccable Republican credentials. He had been chief adviser to Senator Hiram Johnson back in 1912 during the Roosevelt-Johnson "Bull Moose" campaign, and he had known the late President Harding.

Schlesinger felt that Coolidge was excessively parsimonious. Once, after he and Cissy had dined at the White House, he told his daughter, Halle, that the meal had been so skimpy he was hungering for a sandwich all evening. "I felt like a peanut rattling around in its shell," he remarked.

When Cissy's parents built their Washington residence, Mrs. Patterson went to fabulous expense to furnish it; virtually everything came from Tiffany's or was imported from France and Italy. It is a white-marble, four-story building in the ornamental Florentine style favored by Stanford White. The mansion (now the home of the Washington Club, a women's social and philanthropic organization) faces Du Pont Circle from the northeast. As long as the Pattersons occupied it, this was the heart of the fashionable section of Washington. In the twenties a mansion on the right was the home of the famous Levi Z. Leiter, partner of Marshall Field, and the house on the left belonged to Miss Mabel Boardman, famous for her work with the Red Cross.

When it was announced that the Coolidges would use the Patterson mansion as the temporary White House, the New York *Times* wrote:

> The Patterson mansion is impressive on the exterior and beautiful on the interior. Every room is bright and distinctive and preserves the Italian style.
>
> The first floor contains a library and smoking room at the left of the entrance. At the right is a reception room and kitchen. An immense foyer has a marble stairway. On its left wall hangs a costly Gobelin tapestry 25 by 10 feet, depicting a hunting scene, while the stairway is lined with trophies of the hunt, heads of caribou, deer, elk, mountain goats and mountain lions killed by Mrs. Schlesinger on her Jackson Hole ranch in Wyoming.

On the second floor an immense foyer leads to a library, dining room, drawing room and ballroom. The dining room, running the entire length of P Street, on which the house borders, has five windows and was then decorated in rose tapestry paper. The room seats sixty persons easily—big enough for White House state dinners in the twenties. The massive ballroom is distinguished by a balcony and was furnished then in the Louis XIV period. A smaller room connects the ballroom with the library, where Cissy was married to Count Gizycki.

On the third floor was a series of bedrooms. The President and First Lady had separate bedrooms—each with an elaborate bathroom with many mirrors—and the President's bedroom also had a fireplace and an adjoining study.

The Coolidge move was well publicized, for Coolidge was only the third President in history who had to find private quarters. In 1814 President Monroe had been forced out when the British burned the White House, and in 1902 President

Theodore Roosevelt moved across Lafayette Square to a red brick house while the White House was undergoing repairs. First, Cissy showed Mrs. Coolidge through the house, pointing out how well adapted it was for formal entertaining. Next, a special White House telephone system was installed, and a sentry box was placed in front of the mansion for security purposes.

Then a van loaded with the Coolidges' personal effects appeared at the mansion. Cissy's daughter, Felicia, who happened to be visiting her that day, discovered that the President's living habits were not as Spartan as she had been led to believe. Spread out in the bedroom she and her husband, Drew, had formerly occupied she counted no less than thirty pairs of shoes, half a dozen pairs of hip boots, an assortment of flannel nightgowns, and a hundred or so woolen socks. Fascinated with the wardrobe of this supposedly frugal Puritan, Felicia couldn't resist picking up one pair of socks and carrying them home to Drew as a souvenir. When he tried them on, they proved to be too small for his long feet. Even presidential socks are not the sort of souvenir one can keep on the mantel, so Felicia put them away, and when the moths got at them she threw them out.

On March 3, 1927, the Coolidges turned up with more baggage, several days before they were expected and just in time for dinner. They moved in—fortunately, Cissy was in the process of moving out—and stayed until midsummer.

On June 10, 1927, the Patterson "White House" became the scene of the most thrilling event in its history and one of the most wildly spontaneous demonstrations ever witnessed in Washington. A young man had just made the first nonstop flight from New York to Paris, and the nation's capital was welcoming him back. The usually unemotional *Evening Star* pulled out all the stops:

> A tired young soldier tumbled into bed last night under the roof of the President of the United States after a welcome home such as has been accorded few other individuals in the history of the world.

Col. Charles Augustus Lindbergh—25 years old, slender, blond and curly-haired—had been clasped to the bosom of an exulting nation whose heart overflowed with pride in her blue-eyed Viking boy.

After a parade and a ceremony at the Washington Monument, Coolidge had escorted Lindbergh back to the temporary White House for a state dinner graced by cabinet members and other top-ranking guests. Outside many thousands massed in Du Pont Circle, cheering the new hero and hoping to catch a glimpse of him.

Cries of "We want Lindy!" "Three cheers for Lindy!" and "Come on out, Lindy!" floated into the dining room. A dozen times before and during the dinner the shy young flyer, wearing unaccustomed white tie and tails, stepped out on the little iron balcony on the second floor of the mansion and waved his right arm. Twice he was led there by Coolidge himself.

Lindbergh spent two nights in a third-floor suite, and the bedroom still bears a Lindbergh-slept-here plaque marking the spot. Lindbergh himself could hardly have forgotten his stay at the Patterson mansion, for it was there he met his future father-in-law, Dwight Morrow, ambassador to Mexico.

Two years before, Cissy had had a haunting experience in her bedroom on the third floor. She was taking a siesta and was dreaming. Suddenly a figure loomed before her: A man was standing at the foot of the bed and his features were unmistakably those of Count Gizycki.

"This was no drab, gray dream, it was bright technicolor," Cissy told friends later, "and I was awake. He was wearing his cavalry uniform with dozens of bright campaign ribbons on his chest. As suddenly as he appeared, he vanished."

The next day a cable arrived. It informed her of the death of her former husband in Poland—at exactly the time she had seen the vision. True to the landed-gentry society which had spawned him, the Count's dying request was that he be buried in his red hunting jacket.

Although she had just married Schlesinger and was then extremely fond of him, Cissy brooded about the eerie coincidence. She was haunted by the feeling that the Count, whom she once passionately loved, was trying to speak to her.

Gradually there were signs that her match with Elmer was not a perfect one. In the spring of 1927 she wrote a long letter to Rose Crabtree in which she never even mentioned her husband. The news was that Felicia had given birth to "the cutest, darlingest little girl you ever saw—only weighed six pounds, two ounces. But that is what Felicia weighed exactly, and she grew to be a big girl."

"She did not have a hard time at all," Cissy continued enviously. "They put her out of her misery just as soon as her first bad pains came. Certainly times have changed since I was a girl! Poor Drew looked much worse than Felicia did. I guess he suffered more."

Cissy tells Rose in this letter that she is definitely coming to the ranch for two weeks and probably will have Senator Henrik Shipstead and Mrs. Shipstead with her. Tall, tow-headed, able Shipstead, the Farmer-Laborite from Minnesota, was one of Cissy's favorite senators. In an indirect swipe at tenderfoot Elmer, Cissy added:

> They are both *swell* in the woods. And she's as good a cook as you and just as good-looking, but not quite as amusing. Maybe more. She says she will do all the cooking. But that would be asking too much.
>
> Expect to leave end of August. My guns are here. I have them in the corner of my room where I can see them all the time.
>
> Next year Felicia and Drew and baby Ellen and Elinor and I are all coming. This year, though, Grandma is coming alone!! Whoop-ee!

A year later, on June 7, 1928, she wrote Rose from Port Washington her doubts about Rose's decision to run a small hotel.

"Two other careers are still open to you," Cissy went on. "One to run for Congress, and the other to run a dude place *in the summer* only. Something like that darling place where I had lunch last year, between Kelly and the Yellowstone. I'll help start you anytime you're ready to go. How about one of those cute ranches along one of the canyons between Jackson and Kelly? It should be somewhere near the road, so you can see the boys as they go by."

The letter concludes: "Elmer sends love. He is still sweet and reasonable—but one *couldn't* say that the seasons are as damp as once they were."

Cissy and Elmer had began to drift apart. In 1928 Drew and Felicia were being divorced, much to Cissy's great distress, for she had lavished attentions on them both in hopes the marriage would succeed. Now she began thinking of divorce for herself. But she was not at all prepared when on a pleasant afternoon in February 1929, she was called to the telephone. The call was from Aiken, South Carolina, and she was informed that Elmer had died after suffering a heart attack on the golf course.

Schlesinger had had heart trouble and had not improved his condition by burning the candle at both ends. He had worked hard and played hard for more than a decade. Some of his close friends believed his death in the prime of middle age—he was only fifty-three—was hastened by the news that Cissy wanted a divorce. Cissy was deeply shocked by Elmer's death. She telephoned Pearson and asked him to accompany her to South Carolina on her private car to bring back his body. En route, somewhat remorsefully, she confided that she had told Elmer she wanted a divorce.

The funeral service was held in the Du Pont Circle mansion before an impressive gathering of senators, congressmen, Supreme Court justices and cabinet members. A eulogy was delivered by John L. Elliott, of the Society of Ethical Culture in New York. That was all. And Cissy wept.

Cissy openly sorrowed over Elmer a good deal longer than was expected by those who knew how far the couple had drifted apart. When she wrote to Rose a month after the funeral she was still wearing the mourning clothes which she had had specially run up for her by Charles James, a leading New York dress designer, and she wore them for another month after that. In this letter she put into words what she finally decided Elmer's attraction for her actually was. Friends in whom she had confided in the past might have thought he represented a father figure—which made the intimate revelation in the letter all the more surprising and baffling. Cissy wrote:

> Dearest Rose: What can I say to you? I have lost above everything else *my child*. A woman can get over the loss of a man she loves but not over the loss of her baby. Outside business—at home—Elmer was my baby. You know that. All day and every waking moment of the night I want to put my arms around him and tell him not to be frightened—that I'll take care of him.
>
> I know you love me, and, believe me, that means a *whole* lot. Do write soon—love to Henry and Sonny.

The following summer she wrote Rose: "Let's meet somewhere pretty soon. I haven't had a real laugh since I saw you last. Maybe we'll never laugh like that again. Maybe we will never feel like it."

This mood did not last much longer. Soon she legally changed her name back to "Eleanor Patterson." She had been angling toward a really challenging career for some time, and in exactly one year it would be underway.

SEVEN

Author

Cissy Patterson's love affair with journalism began as a flirtation after the First World War. She got her first break, ironically, because of attempted revenge against her brother Joe, though she did not realize it at the time.

Joe was then editor of the family newspaper, the Chicago *Tribune*, whose fierce competition came from the morning Hearst paper. The city editor of the *Tribune* was Walter Howey, immortalized on the stage a decade later as the cynical managing editor of *The Front Page*.

A contemporary *Tribune* writer, Burton Rascoe, wrote in his memoirs, *Before I Forget:* "Joseph Medill Patterson was zealous in maintaining [the] incorruptibility of the news columns fostered by his father." (His father had established a tradition that the *Tribune* never took favors from anybody; reporters had been fired merely for accepting small presents from grateful persons who had been legitimately mentioned in news stories.)

Howey was earning $8000 a year and had turned down an offer of $35,000 a year from Hearst, because he was satisfied at the *Tribune*.

"The *Tribune* was a better paper, a better engine, a more respectable medium to work with," explained Rascoe. "It had solidity, permanence, power and prestige. Howey loved the *Tribune*."

One day in 1919 Howey wrote a three-paragraph story about the production plans of David Wark Griffith, the motion-picture

genius who created *The Birth of a Nation*. He had visited with
Griffith, who was a friend, as the producer was passing through
Chicago. Patterson regarded the item as "press-agent stuff." He
apologized on the editorial page for this slip-up in the news
columns, and he called Howey on the carpet. Howey insisted
the item was a legitimate news story, but Patterson would not
budge. The upshot was that Howey exploded and quit on the
spot, serving notice to Patterson that he would accept the invitation to take over the morning Hearst paper and that he would
stop at nothing to beat the *Tribune's* brains out.

In a version of the showdown scene later described by Hearst
editors (who must have heard it from Howey), Howey added
one final fillip to needle Patterson: "And what's more, I'm going
to seduce your sister!"

Within a year, partly to get Patterson's goat and partly to add
prestige to his paper, the *Herald and Examiner*, Howey hired
Cissy to do two special assignments. The first was to cover the
Republican National Convention in Chicago in June, and the
second was to do a series on her big-game hunting exploits. To
make sure that no reader missed the point, Howey inserted under
the byline "Eleanor Gizycka" this chuckling identification: "Sister
of the Editor of the Chicago *Tribune*."

Cissy's convention coverage consisted of eyewitness comments
on the action plus some interviews with prominent Republicans,
most of whom she knew. Each story carried a half-column,
rather wistful picture of her; the headline over it often carried
the word "Countess."

The convention was one of the most exciting and intricate in
G.O.P. history. Three formidable candidates were in the lists:
Major General Leonard Wood, former Chief of Staff of the
Army and former Governor General of the Philippines; Frank
O. Lowden, the able Governor of Illinois; and Senator Hiram
Johnson of California. Cissy's hero was Johnson, and it annoyed
her that everyone didn't share her view. In one story she wrote:
"'Government of the people, by the people and for the people,'

yet some delegates from the East told me today they weren't for Hiram Johnson, because he is too close to the people. Isn't that a funny thing for Americans to say?"

She defended Johnson—who had been a running mate of Theodore Roosevelt in 1912 on the progressive "Bull Moose" ticket —against the charge that he was a radical.

"Radical! Radical!—what is a radical?" she exploded. "I am sick and tired of having people denounce Hiram Johnson as a radical. When pinned down, they fail to prove that one single law advocated or passed by him as Governor of California, or as a member of the United States Senate, is unreasonable, impractical or not humane."

Hearst also was backing Johnson, but neither the Senator nor his two chief opponents was in command of a majority of delegate votes. In the now famous "smoke-filled room" at the Blackstone Hotel, the party bosses agreed on dark-horse Senator Warren G. Harding because he was "safe" and could be controlled.

No ill-feeling developed between Joe and Cissy because she wrote for the chief rival of the *Tribune*, from whose profits Cissy received a sizable income. She enjoyed expressing herself in print; and for his part, Joe would have considered it unseemly to hire his sister when the *Tribune* boasted plenty of its own established talent. Besides, unlike Hearst, the *Tribune* did not indulge itself in the practice of hiring big names to dress up the coverage of big events.

Joe Patterson was two years and ten months older than his sister and, up to this point, the more flamboyant rebel of the two. A year before his graduation from Yale he went off to China to report for the *Tribune* on the Boxer Rebellion. Starting out as a city reporter on the *Tribune*, Joe developed a zeal for municipal reform, and in 1903, at twenty-four, he was elected on the reform party ticket to the Illinois House of Representatives. Two years later he helped elect a municipal-ownership mayor of Chicago— a candidate who was opposed by the *Tribune*—and was rewarded with the post of Commissioner of Public Works. There he fought the "interests" on behalf of the city, but he soon became dissatisfied with the new administration and quit in 1906, announcing he had become converted to socialism.

Joe admitted that in a family like his becoming a Socialist was tantamount to being an Abolitionist in the Old South. "I shall go to work and try to produce hereafter at least a portion of the wealth which I consume," he said. The Socialist party placed him on its national executive committee with such men as Clarence Darrow and Big Bill Haywood. During this period Joe retired to an Illinois farm to write books and plays. Two of the novels which resulted—*Rebellion* and *A Little Brother of the Rich*—were subsequently dramatized. He wrote numerous other plays, the most successful of which was *The Fourth Estate*, written in collaboration with Harriet Ford and the then managing editor of the *Tribune*, James Keeley. In a sense, this play was a forerunner of *The Front Page*—with the significant difference that its managing editor was an idealist. The heroic editor in *The Fourth Estate* defies "the interests" and publishes the Big Story. One critic called playwright Patterson "an unpolished Galsworthy."

After the death of his father, in 1910, Joe and his cousin, Robert R. (Bertie) McCormick, divided up the job of running the *Tribune*, with Joe handling the editorial end and Bertie the business side. Joe had become disillusioned with socialism; based on his own four years as a struggling writer, he was convinced that the profit motive was what made people work.

In 1914, Patterson went off to cover the Mexican border war and then the war in Europe. In 1916 he enlisted in the Illinois National Guard as a private, and when the United States got into the war he went overseas as a lieutenant in the soon-to-be-famous Rainbow Division. He saw combat in five major battles, was wounded, and promoted to captain. After the war, his division commander, Douglas MacArthur, called him "the most brilliant natural-born soldier who ever served under me."

Although he was gassed in addition to suffering minor wounds, Patterson never received a decoration of any kind. In 1923, Cissy, ever devoted to her brother, determined to rectify this omission by working through Joe's former commanding officer, Brigadier General Henry J. Reilly.

When she told him what she was up to, Joe immediately wrote back to Cissy in great embarrassment: "You were kind enough to think of mentioning that possibly I could get a decoration through Reilly. Now darling, for gosh sakes, don't dream of mentioning this subject to him or hinting of it to anyone, because I here and now state that under no circumstances would I accept any decoration for what happened in the late unpleasantness, and no one would think of offering me one because I didn't earn it. Now remember, this is extremely important to me and to my peace of mind, and you must do as I say in this respect."

In 1919 Patterson struck out on his own and (with *Tribune* financial support) launched the *Illustrated Daily News* in New York. He had met Lord Northcliffe in London during the war and had been impressed with his *Daily Mirror*, a lively picture newspaper with an 800,000 circulation. Patterson's paper, soon to be called simply the *Daily News*, was the first successful tabloid in the United States. After an initial setback, it moved ahead swiftly, and by 1925 it hit a circulation of 1,000,000, largest in the nation. Bright, breezy, colloquial and irreverent, the *Daily News* became the perfect historian for the flapper-speakeasy-whoopee twenties. None of its main imitators over the years ever approached its success; they lacked Joe Patterson's instinct for sharp editing and his genius for knowing what interested the mass of ordinary Americans.

Joe and Cissy were as close as a brother and sister could be. Joe admired Cissy—he once told his wife, Mary King, that Cissy was the most charming woman he had ever met—and was proud of her accomplishments. In the early twenties, Cissy was just beginning to write creatively, and Joe was still making a stab at it occasionally. In 1923 he wrote her:

Dearest Cis,

. . . you didn't tell me about your play. Are you doing
anything on it? I have done two acts and have only one
to go of mine, and it looks good. I expect I will have
to back it myself to get it on, because my record as a
playwright was made long ago and was not brilliant financially, and managers would hesitate and probably stall me
along a year or two before I could persuade them. I would
rather put up the money. I could only lose half of it
anyway, because of the income tax.

Affectionately your brother
Joe

Cissy never finished her play. Instead, she began thinking in
terms of a novel set in the two locations she knew best—Washington and Jackson Hole. The novel was written in Paris in the
winter of 1924–25; on the return voyage Cissy wrote jubilantly
to Rose Crabtree:

I forgot to tell you my little novel is accepted in *French*
in Paris. It is coming out in one of the first literary
magazines in the world and later as a book. I will translate
it back into English as soon as I have the courage to look
at it again. So I put Jackson Hole on the map in France
. . . you should be proud of your old friend, although
I'm so conceited already over the whole thing there will
be no living with me.

Titled *Glass Houses,* the novel was published by Minton, Balch
and Company in March 1926. It was the first novel of its kind—a
semisatirical picture of Washington personalities and mores—and,
as such, it caused a sensation. In the town houses and embassies
along Massachusetts Avenue the book was Topic A, and in the
Senate cloakrooms it took precedence over talk about two controversial issues, the Tariff Commission and the Volstead Act.

In the relatively small, tight circle that then comprised the
ruling castes in the capital, everyone was sure that Cissy's characters were based on actual people. Judith Malcolm, the acidly

witty, lion-hunting hostess, was interpreted as a take-off on Alice Roosevelt Longworth, wife of the Speaker of the House; Bob Millar, mussy-haired, golden-tongued ex-senator from the West *had* to be Senator Borah; the suave and romantic Count de Sevaise of the French Embassy obviously was a composite of two titled diplomats; and Mary Moore, the uncertain heroine, was Cissy herself.

Judith and Mary compete for the attentions of Millar, just as their real-life counterparts did. More on the fictional side, Millar and the French Count, both wooing Mary, follow her to big-game-hunting country in Wyoming that resembles Jackson Hole (and where their dependable but ornery guide is "Ben," a name Cissy always used to disguise Cal Carrington in her writings).

The ending is not altogether a happy one. Mary married the Count, but found he still had a wandering eye for other women. Trying to make the best of it, Mary tells her rambunctious husband in the curtain line: ". . . Don't let's ask too much. But we can be happy most of the time, I suppose . . . when we have learned to compromise."

Mary Moore is a lovely young woman who lives alone in a Georgetown town house and shoots goats in Idaho. She has a "capricious shyness" and a "grave, trailing voice"; at night she can be a "romantic, silvery creature," but by day she might be found at home comfortably dressed in Turkish trousers or brown riding breeches, field boots and a discolored buckskin waistcoat.

Here is Mary Moore firing her rifle at an elusive wolf: "Her face was white, his nostrils sharp and her eyes glittered strange and black." And when the Count expresses anguish upon learning that Bob Millar and Mary have had a tryst in a mountain forest, Mary's heart is "filled with perhaps the only pity of which she was poignantly capable—pity for the weak."

In each of these vignettes, to her close friends, this was Cissy.

As for Judith Malcolm, she comes through as a completely unsympathetic poseur, and with considerably less depth than Alice Longworth, whom Washingtonians assumed Cissy was lampooning. Judith had a "bold, handsome head," "brilliant, greedy eyes," and an "uncanny scent for news" (meaning gossip). If Cissy did indeed model Judith on Alice, here is a passage intended to devastate her as an intellectual snob and phrase-dropper:

> Attired in a red brocaded man's dressing gown, Judith sat cross-legged on the floor before a cheerfully burning fire in her sitting room. She had just dipped into Gibbon's *Decline and Fall* to refresh her memory on a certain passage concerning the Seven Vestal Virgins, for she liked to be letter-perfect. She had a volume of Pope under one arm, and Fraser's *Golden Bough*, and the new *Prancing Nigger* lay on her knees. One foot rested on Fabre-Luce's *Victoire*. Although she had achieved a really fine literary taste, she occasionally struck the average; and for the moment her attention was wholly, if somewhat contemptuously, engrossed by Arlen's *Green Hat*.

On balance, *Glass Houses* drew good reviews. The New York *Times* said the novel "goes beyond a mere satirical comedy of Washington manners. Shot through and through with mischievous wit, the first portion of the book merely sets the stage for what, in any event, is a wise and human comedy."

In the view of the New York *Herald Tribune* critic, "the author has given us much more than a series of trenchant pictures as she sees it. She has given us a dispassionate—perhaps a disillusioned—story of the lives of two people whose characters were rightly placed in the environment of the capital, because in America only in that environment could they have been produced. In that respect, it was the first story of Washington life of recent years which was more than an episode."

Some reviews were less complimentary. The *Saturday Review of Literature* found the novel "more sophisticated than penetrating." The *New Republic* said of the new author: "She has a keen, ironic eye, and an accurate ear, but a facility in translating what they report to her which dilutes the natural acid that might etch a sharper plate . . . one wonders why such a brisk talent is not being better employed . . ."

Washingtonians agreed that Cissy's word painting of the Senate in action was vivid and convincing. It sets the stage in the very first paragraphs of the book:

The Senate chamber was packed that particular afternoon. On the floor itself, Senator Lodge, shadowy but erect, moved across with small, drifting steps to drop a word to Senator Curtis. Senator Curtis nodded a stolid, swarthy head. Reed of Pennsylvania, square-shouldered, thin and flexible, leaned over his colleague, Senator Pepper of Pennsylvania, and while he spoke, his brilliant glance struck in twenty different directions. Senator Pepper was fatigued. He listened absently. Perhaps he was contrasting the stale air and stale futility of the moment with a vision of promise and early springtime on the countryside at home. Across the aisle, Senator Heflin, in his grand white waistcoat, was again on his feet. He was cribbing from one of his own speeches made five years previously, at the time of the Armistice. But nobody noticed it. Behind him, in the back row, sat Senator Wheeler of Montana, in the attitude of Michelangelo's *Il Penseroso*, his fine head sunk slightly forward, the forefinger of one pale, slim gambler's hand resting against his cheek.

A page boy presented Senator Walsh of Montana with a visitor's card, and he moved away toward one of the swinging doors leading to the reception room. A handsome grayhaired man, with a curved nose and relentlessly honest blue eye. As Senator Walsh went out at one side of the chamber, the door of the Republican cloakroom flew open, and Borah of Idaho cautiously entered the arena. However, perceiving Heflin still on his feet, he changed his mind and turned to go, but paused first for a second, with one foot across the threshold, and from over his shoulder raked the ladies' gallery fore and aft with a bold, magnetic eye.

This was indeed a penetrating view from the gallery. Senators seeing their colleagues thus pinioned in print were convulsed. In the Capitol, Wheeler was asked to exhibit his "pale, slim gambler's hand," Borah was urged to demonstrate how he "raked the ladies' gallery" fore and aft, and Heflin was kidded about "cribbing" from a five-year-old speech.

Cissy was using an old novelist's trick when she mentioned Borah, so that she could pretend she was not modeling Millar on him. But there wasn't any doubt about the real-life identity of the veteran western politician with the string tie and the Shakespearean manner.

At one point in the book, Cissy has Mary Moore saying candidly: "We, all of us—girls and women, I mean—we all have our favorite hick senator. You know, it's the fashion." She then defines "hick" to the French Count:

> They are more amusing than the old-guard type, who are all snagged up in their own technique and, perhaps very wisely, are afraid to tell you anything. But the hicks are unafraid. Most of them don't take themselves too seriously. Sooner or later, if you work hard enough, they will tell you what they really think.

Cissy used "hick" affectionately. Her favorites—Borah, Wheeler, Shipstead, Hiram Johnson—all came from the West. They picturesquely reinforced her concept of westerners as being rugged individualists.

Consider Wheeler. He arrived in the Senate from Montana in 1923, a hero of the Progressives, for he had fought for justice and honesty as a lawyer, legislator and federal district attorney. He wasted no time living up to his reputation. Wheeler flouted Senate tradition for freshmen by calling for an investigation of Attorney General Harry M. Daugherty, charter member of the corrupt "Ohio Gang" which had made the late Warren G. Harding President. Wheeler charged Daugherty with protecting federal officials who were under a cloud everyone else seemed too timid to puncture.

The Wheeler speech was a bombshell. President Coolidge forced the Attorney General to resign, and a select Senate committee was created to investigate the charges, with Wheeler as its counsel. In retaliation, the Justice Department brought two indictments against the Montana senator on conflict-of-interest charges—which Wheeler denounced as a frame-up.

Cissy took quickly to this new breeze off the Rockies. After Wheeler was indicted, Cissy sent flowers to Mrs. Wheeler and invited them to a large dinner party. She seated Wheeler on her right, thus letting Washington know where she stood. Then she smiled challengingly around the table at a number of powerful personages who still had their doubts about the brash man from Montana.

She was anxious to help Wheeler fight his indictments and, typically, her suggested tactics were personal and melodramatic. For example, William J. (Wild Bill) Donovan was then Assistant Attorney General, and Wheeler believed he was one official who was pressing the indictments. Cissy passed on to Wheeler the rumor that Donovan had a secret "girl friend" and urged him to check into it, but Wheeler declined.

Wheeler was eventually acquitted of both indictments.

"Men liked Cissy and enjoyed her company," Wheeler recalls. "She had charm and she also had guts and courage."

Whenever a new and interesting man made his mark in Washington, he was likely to be invited to one of Cissy's spectacular parties. After the dining, the dancing and the champagne, the party frequently turned into early-morning poker sessions.

A pot running as high as $10,000 was common at these parties. Cissy enjoyed the drama, but she never played. She felt the same about politics: She appreciated the drama of the interplay of personality and character, but not the science.

Cissy never summed up her feelings about politics and politicians any better than she did in *Glass Houses*. Mary Moore explains to the French Count:

> . . . politics are so personal and gossipy. The very stuff we women are made of. Of course, we like to pretend we're interested in principles . . . but, as a matter of honest fact,

we're interested in personalities mostly, and when we go
down to the Senate it's not to hear the expressions for or
against a particular policy, but to hear the Particular expression of a Particular man. Matinee-idol stuff.

At another point, Mary Moore says:

I despise politics. Fawning on your enemies. Double-cross-
ing your friends. Never a spontaneous act. Never a disinter-
ested judgment. Playing your life out like a silly game of
checkers . . . ego rampant! Most professional politicians are
just actors gone wrong . . . exhibitionists . . .

Her father, Mary Moore recalled:

. . . always said the big men of this country were the
captains of industry; bankers, packers, editors, railway presidents, big manufacturers, public utility men, even corporation lawyers—men who act and not men who just talk for a
living. These men tell the politicians where to get off. They
are the real bosses.

This comment was largely true at the time; the year was 1926,
a little while before the era of big government.

Living with Schlesinger in the world of big business in New
York had opened Cissy's eyes. She has Mary Moore saying to the
Count:

Did you ever meet any of the New York crowd of really
big businessmen? They are pirates, of course, and gamblers.
They are a terribly tough lot. By tough I mean disillusioned
and merciless, but they are vital and human and courageous.
After all, that is what I despise most in politicians—they
haven't true courage.

"Vital and human and courageous"—a kind of arrogant fearlessness—were the qualities Cissy admired. She gravitated to the
Progressives from the West, of both parties, because she believed
they had this. She was a regular in the front row of the "family
gallery" at night sessions of the Senate. In that day of forensic

giants in the Senate, it was usually a good show, alive with flashing debate.

Several times she brought Wheeler back to her town house with her for champagne at midnight. On one such occasion, the Shipsteads were present and she began to kid the two senators on the subject of impatient senatorial Casanovas. "You westerners are all alike," she said with a reproving smile, shocking Mrs. Shipstead when she added: "You want a girl to be a 'pushover.' I like to be wooed and fussed over first."

Wheeler and Cissy enjoyed a close friendship for the rest of her life, and, despite rumors to the contrary, their relationship was never anything but Platonic.

In 1928, Cissy wrote and published her second novel, *Fall Flight*. She was not coy about what it represented; anytime the book was mentioned in later years, she remarked, "that's *my* story." Except for a slight alteration of characters, places and relationships, the story bears a striking resemblance to her own childhood and to her life with Count Gizycki: An American girl (Daisy Shawn), reared on Chicago's fashionable near north side by a domineering mother, is transplanted to Russia after her mother marries a rich man who becomes United States ambassador there. In St. Petersburg the romantic-minded girl meets and marries a charming Russian (Prince Serge Slavinsky). They move into his shabby castle in the Ukraine and she is quickly disillusioned. Serge turns out to be dissolute, treats her with contempt and consorts with his mistresses.

Fall Flight shows some development of Cissy as a novelist. The philosophy is less shallow, the characters more deeply drawn. Also, perhaps because the book is more autobiographical than *Glass Houses*, the love-making scenes are more convincing. In *Fall Flight* there is an amusing premarital seduction attempt in a hotel room. Abruptly the Prince abandons his maneuvers, deciding that the American girl, tipsy from champagne, is too inexperienced. Daisy nevertheless comes to with a startled, "What happened to me?" The Russian gallantly assures her she has nothing to worry about, but admonishes: "My little snowfield, you should not wear thin, black dresses like that."

If *Fall Flight* is to be taken literally, it throws light on Cissy's attraction to Count Gizycki despite their stormy married life. At one point Daisy Shawn muses:

. . . Serge seemed to like her hair (it streamed backward across the pillow nearly to the floor). He had said so, often. He liked to plunge his hand through the length of it and admired the effect of the soft, bright strands slipping along the hard, fine contour of her arm . . . since her marriage Daisy had penetrated no further beneath the surface, into the Oriental soul of the man, nor along the convolutions of his Slavic mind. In truth, she understood the real Slavinsky no better now than the night of the old Princess Catherine's ball, when he had taken a little gold key from his waistcoat pocket and laid it down beside her plate . . . they had become neither true lovers, nor true friends, for with Oriental caution he kept from his young wife the secrets of his passions; selfish in love as in all things, he had skilled his body only for his own delight.

Yet it was only their physical union which gave her any— however brief—sense of reality. When he lay relaxed in her arms sometimes, she believed that at last she possessed him. He belonged to her then, she felt, and to her alone, those few short minutes before he turned from her to fall asleep . . .

The reviews of *Fall Flight* were slightly more favorable than the reviews of *Glass Houses*. However, the most important commentary written about *Fall Flight* was a preface used only in a limited edition of 500 copies which Cissy gave her friends. The preface was written at her request by Dr. Alvan T. Barach, a New York physician and friend of hers. Dr. Barach's interpretation of Daisy's character formation was a revelation to Cissy about herself and especially her childhood. On the flyleaf of the special edition, she wrote: "I am deeply indebted to Dr. Barach for his brilliant analysis of the core of my story—hidden until now even from me."

In his preface, Dr. Barach writes: "Made continually conscious of her physical unattractiveness by a mother whom she originally loved, she developed first of all a feeling of inferiority, which tended to remove her from the world of reality, leaving her with an exaggerated respect for power, no matter how acquired. Riches, pomp and rank were influential with her, far more than she could understand or prevail against."

Daisy's love instinct, deeply hurt, failed to develop beyond the infantile stage, Dr. Barach theorized, and so she selects a man for whom she has feeling only on the level of sensation. The man (the Prince) is even more of a sensationalist than herself, "representative of a primitive, archaic, infantile capacity for love." Such a marriage could only have ended in failure.

With *Fall Flight*, Cissy was through with writing novels. She had unburdened herself of her childhood, her unhappy marriage, and the two worlds which interested her most—life in Washington, and life in the West. Otherwise, she felt she was marking time until she could find a role in the family profession. She was always on the lookout for an opportunity to play a journalistic part in recording the gaudy American sideshow that typified the twenties.

In April 1927, the public became spellbound by a pair of drab lovers on trial in a Long Island City courtroom. Ruth Snyder, a housewife, and Judd Gray, a corset salesman, were charged with the clumsy murder of Ruth's husband in his bed. Some of the most famous writers of the generation, including novelists and playwrights, were on hand to cover the trial, while crowds outside rioted trying to get into the building.

No newspaper gave its readers juicier or more complete details of the drama than the New York *Daily News*. Cissy wanted to do a feature article on Ruth Snyder's first day on the witness stand, and brother Joe gave her the chance. Her story was played relatively far back in the *Daily News*—on page 10—under the by-line "Eleanor Gizycka," but no story on the trial that day had a more arresting headline: "WHAT DO YOU KNOW OF THE SOUL OF AN INDIAN?"

Cissy wrote that out West, Indian youths who wanted to become braves were forced to hang by their armpits on long poles from sunrise to sunset. They stuck it out without a whimper, she explained, because they had no imagination and were "a different kind of an animal" from the rest of us. Then she tried to analyze why Ruth Snyder was able to maintain tight-lipped, iron self-control during a day of withering cross-examination on the stand:

> Ruth Snyder is another kind of an animal. There she sat today. Strong nose. Strong jawed. From every angle she turned her face you saw those wolfish jaws. And she has a white, seductive skin. One of those indestructible, Scandinavian white-rose skins. Neither heat nor cold affects it nor five pounds of chocolate candy nor a quart of whisky . . .

> Ruth Snyder must have smiled, turned her head, shown her teeth, flashed her eyes, only a few weeks ago. Probably she rouged her fair cheeks, curled her hair, set her hat to one side, smoked cigarettes, drank highballs, danced, kissed, loved. But it's hard to believe now, looking at this strong-jawed, implacable woman, sitting there, hour after hour, almost motionless, her hands nicely clasped like a lady's, one upon the other . . .

> How does she feel, Ruth Snyder, sitting up there hour after hour answering questions in the same inflexible, defiant voice? Sometimes louder. Never softer. How do Indians feel when they are hung on long poles from sunrise to sunset?

> We can imagine something of what is going on inside Judd Gray. It's a question of degree. But we can't—can't —get Ruth Snyder's psychology.

> What do we know about the soul of an Indian?

Ruth blamed the murder on Gray, but Gray, nervous on the stand, confessed that they both did it. The jury's verdict was "guilty," and the penalty was death in the electric chair. Ruth broke down in sobbing hysteria, while Gray went to his cell and ate three plates of Hungarian goulash. At that point, presumably, he became the Indian.

Cissy yearned to own or at least operate a newspaper or a magazine. With her second marriage turning sour, and the gay, brittle social life in New York starting to pall on her, she needed something which would engage all her considerable talents and energy. In 1928 she fixed her acquisitive eye on Washington and began to shop around.

In the late twenties, Cissy had an annual income ranging between $600,000 and $700,000, only part of which derived from stock in the *Tribune* and *Daily News*. She consulted constantly with brother Joe and cousin Bertie, and both warned her of the numerous pitfalls of publishing. Even with their undoubted talents and knowledge, their touch was not always sure. Patterson and McCormick had started the weekly *Liberty* magazine in 1925; it was foundering, and before they could get rid of it they would have sunk $15,000,000 into it.

Cissy became interested in buying the Washington *Herald*, a chronic loser in the empire of her friend, William Randolph Hearst. She sounded out Arthur Brisbane, the top Hearst lieutenant, and on July 9, 1928, Brisbane strongly advised her against buying a newspaper in Washington.

On the same day, Cissy wrote cousin Bertie a letter which revealed the dickering she was doing—and the fact that she was afraid she was getting in over her unbusinesslike head:

Although realizing "puffickly" that my judgment is based on next to nothing of knowledge and experience, I still think the small "class" paper my best bet. However, since I saw you there has been some tentative dickering with my original idea of the Washington *Herald*. Funnily enough, I had a note from Brisbane only this morning (written in answer to one from me about his wife, who is reported to be dying). Brisbane said, to quote verbatim, "Take the advice of an old man who has some wisdom . . . if you bought the *Herald*, which I would never encourage, you would literally lose millions. What's the use?" But maybe the old scallywag has some idea of his own up his sleeve.

Then Cissy discusses her attempt to buy the Washington *Post*, owned by Edward B. (Ned) McLean. She had discovered that there were several others trying quietly to do the same thing—Hearst; "a toad called Paul Block (closer than anyone to Ned McLean)"; and, of all people, Samuel E. Thomason, formerly business manager of the Chicago *Tribune*. She wrote McCormick that at first she was not concerned about Thomason, thinking he was on his own, but that now it appeared he was secretly acting for the *Tribune:*

> . . . now at last Joe opens up and tells me that you and he have an agreement to this effect. If (or, rather, let us say when) *Liberty* turns up with a safe margin, Joe wants to start a tabloid in Los Angeles. Bertie wants to "go into" Washington.
>
> I told Joe how friendly you had been, and that you had offered to "make up the books," or rather have them made up for me; given me several valuable tips and suggestions—names of managers—and most important of all promised me the inside track with the "contracts." Gee, Bertie! What does it all mean?

Competition from within her own family discouraged Cissy, and McLean wasn't ready to sell the *Post* anyway.

Cissy next began to think seriously of an idea she had flirted with ever since writing *Glass Houses*—starting a magazine of political satire in Washington, perhaps a counterpart to *The New Yorker*. She sounded so serious about it, indeed, that McCormick wrote his mother that summer:

> . . . Cissy has decided to publish a magazine in Washington. I don't know what the name of it will be, but we will know in a short time, as she is all ready to launch it. It will be a weekly publication.

Joe Patterson was proud of his sister's accomplishments as a novelist and newspaper and magazine writer. But he thought it was foolish for her to risk her money as an editor-publisher. He sent his advertising department experts to her to explain why a magazine of political satire in Washington would not succeed. So Cissy turned again to newspapers. If she couldn't buy one, she would try to do the next best thing—run one. If she couldn't buy Hearst's *Herald*, perhaps he would let her edit it. During one of her frequent visits to Hearst's San Simeon estate, she leaned over the dinner table and said she would make him a good publisher. Hearst refused to take her seriously. But Cissy would not be put off. In June 1930, she forced the issue. She prevailed on Brisbane to formally ask Hearst to give her a try. Brisbane cabled Hearst, who was abroad. Hearst replied affirmatively, suggesting she take the *Herald*. He offered to pay her $10,000 a year—a small salary by Hearst executive standards—plus a slice of whatever advertising she could attract. Cissy accepted.

The news that Washington's most unpredictable society woman had been selected to rescue the humpty-dumpty *Herald* seemed hilarious to Washington and those who knew Cissy in New York. But she was to have the last laugh.

EIGHT

The Semi-Pro

It was achingly cold at 2 o'clock on that winter morning in the mail room of the Boston *Record*. Harry Arthur (Happy) Robinson, circulation manager, was looking forward to a warm bed and a long sleep while he watched the last edition being bundled up and stacked in trucks. His anticipation was broken by the sound of a familiar voice—that of Walter Howey, trouble shooter for the Hearst papers.

"Somebody's here to see you," Howey said.

Robinson had a sinking feeling, and before he could turn his head he heard a huskily feminine voice behind him.

"How are you, Happy? Why did you leave me?"

He faced around to Mrs. Eleanor (Cissy) Patterson, editor and publisher of the Washington *Herald*. A year before, in February 1932, he had quit his job as circulation manager of the *Herald* and returned to his old post at the *Record*. Since then he had not heard a word from Mrs. Patterson. Now he stared back at her haughty gaze. She was warmer than he was—clad from head to toe in mink. Happy swallowed hard and prepared to defend himself.

"But I only agreed to stay six months."

"*You're coming back,*" she replied firmly.

"Your circulation figures are good, Lady," Robinson hurriedly explained, using the term with which he always addressed her. "I've kept track of them, and your men are doing a good job—"

"*You're coming back!*" Cissy repeated.

Howey suggested they go to the editorial department and talk it over.

Upstairs, Cissy said she would not argue. She picked up the telephone and put in a call to William Randolph Hearst at his ranch in San Simeon, California—"The Chief" would settle the matter. Robinson was told to pick up the extension.

He knew he was right, but he was none too calm. Hearst had assigned him to go to Washington and help out the new, untried woman editor for six months. At the end of six months, Robinson had simply boarded a train for Boston. He had not informed Mrs. Patterson—or even said goodby—for fear she would wheedle or bully him into staying on.

Now, when Hearst came on the phone, Cissy asked him if it was indeed true that he had given Robinson to her for only six months.

"You knew I was only loaning him to you," Hearst replied soothingly.

But Cissy knew what she wanted and she would not be diverted.

"No man can serve two masters," she told The Chief. What two masters? Hearst wondered. She replied that there was a single circulation manager for both the *Herald* and its Hearst-owned, afternoon counterpart, the *Times*—one William Shelton. She felt she was entitled to a circulation man devoted to her interests alone.

Nettled, Hearst began to address Robinson, asking him if there was anything that could induce him to return to Washington. "Anything you want you can have," The Chief added.

"But I'll be in bad trouble with my wife," Happy answered. "She's tired of living in Washington hotels—our home is here in Boston."

"Cissy will call her and explain it," Hearst suggested. That was the last thing Robinson wanted. He asked Hearst for two weeks to think it over, but The Chief hung up.

Mrs. Patterson was staring at him.

"You're coming with me—now!" she said. When Robinson again tried to tell her how wonderful her circulation looked, she told him to call his wife.

Mrs. Robinson came on the phone, groggy from a deep sleep. Her first words, with womanly intuition, were: "What is it? Is it *that woman* again?"

"What do you mean—*that* woman?" Cissy snapped. "Your husband is going back to Washington with me. We're all going. Come along!"

"Lady, I'm *not* coming," Happy hastily interposed from the extension phone.

"Everything's going to be all right," Mrs. Patterson reassured him.

"I'm *not* going!" Mrs. Robinson yelled back at her.

Robinson began to plead with his wife to be a sport and give the national capital another try. But Mrs. Robinson kept replying ominously, "Remember, now, I'm *not* going."

Happy hung up with a sigh. He met The Lady's look, imperious and expectant, and nodded his head. It *had* been an entertaining experience working for this charmingly willful woman, and he secretly admired her. Now he told her with more confidence than he felt that Mrs. Robinson might change her mind.

Actually, he was worried that his move back to Washington might break up his marriage. But his hunch paid off; his wife did go to Washington—six months later.

Back in Washington, Robinson organized the circulation departments of the *Times* and *Herald* into separate entities, then went out of his way to please Mrs. Patterson and the *Herald*. Like everyone else, she called him "Happy" and found him irresistible.

First of all, he knew everything there was to know about the roughneck business of distributing and selling newspapers. Cissy valued this skill, for her brother Joe had always emphasized the importance of a good circulation manager. She was fascinated, too, with his links to the underworld—something every good newspaper circulation man used to have.

But beyond this, Robinson functioned as a confidant and a court jester. Cissy was aware of her shoot-from-the-hip firing weakness, and in the mid-1930s she promised Happy she would not sack an employee without talking it over in advance with her circulation boss. Happy's freedom of language diverted Cissy—he was the only staff member who had the temerity to swear in her presence—and his Damon Runyon malapropisms delighted her. Toward The Lady he was respectful—but not deferential.

Robinson's shortage of syntax and vocabulary was understandable. Born in Russia on September 22, 1888, he came to America when six months old and was educated on the streets of Boston. At eight he was a newsboy, and at thirteen he had a regular job among the circulation "sluggers" of the Boston *Record*. Following World War I, Robinson had what amounted to a postgraduate course in his specialty—he was a participant in the bloody asphalt-jungle warfare in Chicago between the *Tribune* and the Hearst papers. Happy worked for both sides, at different times, and when Joe Patterson went to New York to start the tabloid New York *Daily News* in 1919 he took Happy with him to help launch the new baby. Afterward, Robinson became a trouble shooter for Hearst, diagnosing the circulatory ailments of some twenty papers during the twenties.

When Cissy took over the editorship of the *Herald* in 1930, her brother advised her to get Happy from Hearst.

Happy inspired more anecdotes than anyone else on the *Herald*. When the *Herald* was bannered with a hot headline, Robinson would get so excited he would rush into the streets and peddle the edition himself. One of the biggest street sales occurred when King Edward VIII announced he was abdicating the throne to marry Wallis Warfield Simpson. Happy dashed out of the building with a stack of fresh *Heralds*, shouting "The King is vindicated! The King is vindicated!"

When Cissy and Happy agreed on a policy, he would counsel her, on departing: "Now, remember, 'foll'y t'rue.'" Mrs. Patterson took to calling him "Foll'y T'rue Hap" and presented him with a gold watch with "Foll'y T'rue" inscribed on it.

Once, she chanced on Robinson and some of his circulation crew shooting craps. Instead of bawling them out, Cissy got down on the floor and tried out the dice herself. She quit after losing $5.60—she never did care for gambling. But a week later she presented Happy with a pair of solid-gold dice made into a bracelet by Tiffany's.

Robinson overflowed with pride over such presents, and would play the buffoon to go along with a gag. With a little coaxing, she persuaded him to come to one of her swankier parties in white tie and tails. It was Happy's first experience with formal attire, and his suffering during the evening—volubly expressed—amused Mrs. Patterson and her guests.

Robinson became one of Mrs. Patterson's most trusted sources of information on what was afoot in the *Herald* building. He was well aware of her baleful contempt for Hearst's afternoon *Times*, with which the *Herald* was obliged to share the building. She encouraged her staff to work even harder at beating the sister paper than it did other Washington rivals, and the *Times* reciprocated.

The internecine warfare was intensified when Hearst's son, George, made his friend, George P. Marshall, publisher of the *Times*. Cissy took a poor view of this appointment—Marshall was a Washington laundry owner and, what was worse, almost as strong-minded as she was. It was obvious that one partitioned building was not big enough for both of them.

One day, as Robinson entered the building, he saw workmen on the third floor painting the *Times* side of the corridor in gay buff and white—with arrows directing visitors to the *Times'* advertising and circulation offices. Presumably, few visitors would be likely to find their way to the anonymous *Herald* offices hidden behind the standard Hearstian dun color.

Robinson went to the phone and called Mrs. Patterson, who was staying at San Simeon, and passed on the news about Marshall's interior-decorating spree.

"Hap," she replied angrily, "get some painters busy and paint my side of the building a two-toned blue and gray, with signs pointing to our offices. Make the signs fluorescent and twice as big as his."

Since the *Herald* had about twice the corridor wall space of the *Times*, Marshall's paint job no longer appeared lustrous. But he was determined to give his *Times* more identity than the *Herald*—and to needle Cissy at the same time. His next promotional gimmick was daringly original in the Hearst empire. Under the eagle symbol used on all Hearst newspaper mastheads, Marshall added this incredible phrase: "The paper with a soul." Again Happy telephoned Cissy. This time her first words were, "What's he done now?" Happy teased his boss by refusing to say. He said he was mailing her six copies of the *Times*, so she could see with her own eyes this latest Marshall audacity.

As soon as she scanned the copies, Cissy called Robinson back, her languid voice unusually gay. "This is it," she told him. They both knew that, however stupid or innocuous Marshall's masthead innovation might seem, Hearst tolerated no such tinkering by mere publishers. Cissy called Hearst's attention to the aberration, and Marshall was fired. He had lasted only six months. (Marshall later became more successful as the owner of the Washington Redskins—who were played up big in Cissy's newspaper.)

The transformation of Cissy Patterson from a flighty, sometimes bitchy dilettante into a competent professional newspaper executive seemed a long way off to some of her subordinates in the early years.

To begin with, she had no knowledge of the lingo of the newspaper shop. The fact that she went off on trips frequently, and then bombarded her staff with messages after scanning the latest edition, did nothing to lessen the confusion. Once, she wired complaints from California about the "captions." The staff struggled to improve the prose beneath the photographs, but the denunciations continued to pour in. Only when Mrs. Patterson returned and laid a finger on the paper did the editors realize that when she referred to "captions" she actually meant the headlines over the articles.

Also, in her first year, she refused to publish the results of the Kentucky Derby on page one. "Horse races," she decreed, "are vulgar." (Years later she would recall this cheerfully and confess: "How stupid I was!")

But she was a willing learner, and quick to give credit to the men who educated her in the mysteries of creating a fresh, up-to-the-minute newspaper every twenty-four hours. She seemed to enjoy describing her role to friends as that of a naïve amateur who couldn't find her way to the composing room. "I'm only a kind of fake editor," she once said. But except during the first year or so, this was an act, and it fooled no one who knew her.

Week in and week out, Cissy was having more fun with the *Herald* than anything else she had ever done. She discussed her new vocation with typical frankness in an interview published in the *American Press* in November 1934. She told her interviewer: "One can't be a good reporter and a lady at the same time. I'd rather be a reporter. I think newspapermen are the most interesting people in the world, don't you? They're more interesting than society people. I like to work with them."

Cissy also said the *Herald* was the biggest thing in her life.

"Outside of newspaper work my hobbies are horses, dogs, living in the country and flowers," she said. "I don't like playing cards, or racing or polo or games of almost any sort. I seem to have no gaming instinct. I am never able to get the hang of the rules of most games.

"I like to chew gum. I don't care about anything else."

Mrs. Patterson's staff respected her. They welcomed her determination to make the *Herald* go, and they liked her admission that she had a lot to learn. One day Cissy pulled a chair up to the desk of her assistant managing editor, Frederic E. Shapiro, sat down and said, "Mr. Shapiro, tell me what I can do to help you make this a better paper."

"Mrs. Patterson," Shapiro replied, "let me spend $120 a week more to hire two good rewrite men."

"Hire them," she said, and walked away. Shapiro did. The next day he related this story to a colleague and added: "I would love Satan himself if he did that for me."

When Shapiro disagreed with Cissy, he said so. This might bring on an outburst, but later Cissy would regret it and send her city editor a box of Corona-Coronas.

In time, however, Shapiro became the victim of one of Cissy's mercurial moods. Returning from a vacation with his wife and infant son, he found a dismissal notice waiting for him. There was no explanation, and Shapiro was stunned. At the Press Club, he talked it over with Mike Flynn, the managing editor and a Cissy favorite. Flynn explained that Mrs. Patterson had walked into the city room one day and, without any preamble, told him to fire the city editor. When Flynn began to argue, he was informed bluntly that he wasn't indispensable either. Flynn then had gone through with the dismissal notice but enclosed in it two weeks' severance pay. This was contrary to the orders of Mrs. Patterson, who had insisted that Shapiro's two weeks' vacation pay was enough. When she discovered that Flynn had ignored her wishes, she fired *him*.

Flynn was rehired in two days. Shapiro shrugged philosophically and found a job on the Philadelphia *Record*, later shifting to a successful career as an editor on the Philadelphia *Inquirer*. Shapiro harbored no bitterness toward Cissy. His hat was off to an editor who would let him add two good rewrite men in the depths of the Depression.

On taking over the *Herald*, Cissy felt it was her first duty to learn to take charge of the paper competently rather than to change its face or its policies. A week after she become editor, this front-page box appeared:

ANSWERS

All kinds of people ask me if I intend to change the policies of the Washington *Herald*.

I would not if I could. I could not if I would.

Everyone should understand from the beginning that Mr. Hearst is first, last and all the time his own editor.

Aside from this rock-bottom fact, the other newspapers with which my family has for so long associated stand today with the Hearst papers on nearly all of the major issues. AGAINST prohibition. AGAINST the League of Nations. AGAINST the World Court. AGAINST the recent naval treaty. FOR an adequate defense and FOR the general debunking of our foreign relations.

Dozens of other inquiries have come in as to how a woman proposes to boss an office full of men. But why should it be a worse job to boss men in the office than to boss them in the home? Men have always been bossed by women anyway, although most of them don't know it.

Still others want to know what ideals, if any, are peculiar to the female editor. The ideal of all true newspaper folk, regardless of sex, is to keep a paper interesting, inspiring, honest, and successful.

But the question raised most frequently has to do with the practical plans for the future.

I've only to remember the first two long words I ever learned to say. And I learned them most likely sitting on my grandpa's knee—CIRCULATION, ADVERTISING.

(*signed*) ELEANOR PATTERSON

The box told quite a few things about its author:

That she recognized Hearst as the absolute boss—a fact which was to frustrate her increasingly until she acquired financial control of the paper.

That she was a natural "ag'iner."

That she was concerned about a man's feelings in having to take orders from a woman.

That she saw nothing wrong in the American tendency toward a matriarchy.

That she would go after circulation and advertising for the *Herald* aggressively.

It would be uphill all the way, for the *Herald* stood fourth in circulation among the five Washington dailies when she took over. The venerable *Evening Star* led with 109,507 daily subscribers. The *Times* had 100,365, the morning *Post* had 73,935, and the *Herald* had 62,647. Only the tabloid *News* trailed the *Herald*—with a circulation of 57,711.

Five newspapers were too many in a city whose size could ordinarily be expected to support three. Washington is probably the most difficult city in the United States for successful newspaper publishing, chiefly because major political parties and major politicians and—in the twenties and early thirties—rich playboys aspired to influence public opinion in the power-filled national capital, and were willing to spend large sums of money to do so.

Thus, when Cissy Patterson moved onto the scene, Hearst and the Scripps-Howard chain (which owned the *News*) were willing to operate newspapers at a loss in Washington in order to have their editorial views digested in the cloakrooms of Congress and on the breakfast tables of cabinet members.

The *Herald* had trouble attracting "class advertising," because it had the reputation, only partly deserved, of being a "backstairs paper." While it was not one of Hearst's most sensational products, it suffered in comparison with the *Star*, a staid Washington institution, and even with the limping, but slightly more dignified, *Post*.

Cissy's ambition was to make the *Herald* not only talked-about but admired for professional excellence. She was anxious for circulation but determined not to sacrifice quality to achieve it. Secretly, she wanted the paper to reflect her own talent and taste. If the "best people" in Washington circles noticed the *Herald*, and perhaps came to respect it, the department stores would flock to her with their advertising. Meanwhile, Cissy carried on a campaign of wooing the department-store owners and executives by inviting them to her parties.

Cissy knew that one of the first steps in improving the *Herald* was to develop the best staff in Washington. She set out to lure the brashest, most imaginative, most dedicated newspapermen she could find. Next, she gave her staff *carte blanche* to do anything necessary to get the story, or the picture that made the story.

The talented people who came to the *Herald* did not come for money but because its editor had a flair and an impudence that were setting an exciting pace in the capital. The *Herald* offered a challenging daily outlet for reporters with originality; as a result, many a reporter and rewrite man on the paper went on to national fame.

Cissy Patterson's own big-eyed innocence was no handicap; it led her to demand and expect more than ordinary editors would. After she hired Edward T. Folliard away from the *Post*, she stared at him for a moment and then drawled slowly and seriously: "Eddie, I want you to get me a scoop a day." Folliard gulped, but held his tongue. He did get a scoop the very first day, but then he fell short of Cissy's impossible objective. A few decades later Folliard, back on the *Post*, won the Pulitzer Prize.

Cissy encouraged initiative, loved exclusive stories, and backed up her reporters when their nosiness got them into trouble. In 1936, reporter Frank C. Waldrop, a large, bland Tennessean who had learned his trade on the New York *Journal* and the old New York *World*, was snooping into the activities of Representative John J. McSwain, chairman of the House Military Affairs Committee, in connection with the disposal of surplus war material.

After the *Herald* published several of Waldrop's articles exposing McSwain, the chairman visited the *Herald* office and arrogantly issued a demand—in writing—that the stories be halted immediately. If they continued, McSwain threatened, he would have his committee subpoena the reporters and compel them to disclose their sources of information and the names of the persons who inspired the series.

The abrasive *Herald* was not the type of newspaper to knuckle under to a high-handed ultimatum from a congressman. The reply was an even tougher story by Waldrop—linking the chairman with the operations of two men who were under indictment for conspiracy to defraud the government in the sale of surplus goods.

McSwain promptly carried out his threat. He issued a subpoena commanding Waldrop to appear before his committee for questioning. Elisha Hansen, the *Herald* counsel, told Waldrop that the committee would be carrying out no legislative purpose in investigating a reporter. He advised Waldrop to honor the subpoena by making an appearance—but refuse to answer questions. This decision had the strong endorsement of Mrs. Patterson, who was furious that an arm of Congress should attempt to abridge the rights and duties of a free press, especially hers.

On April 6, 1936, Waldrop appeared before the committee accompanied by Hansen. The counsel immediately stepped forward and announced that his client would answer no questions, because the committee was proceeding improperly, "pursuant to a threat by its chairman and without legislative purpose." McSwain, enraged, ordered Waldrop to take the stand, and the questioning started.

"Your name is Frank Waldrop, is it not?" he asked.

With a smile, the reporter replied: "Upon advice of counsel, I decline to answer . . ."

When it was apparent that Waldrop was declining firmly, but politely, to cooperate, several committee members jumped into the act with questions designed solely to embarrass the witness: "Are you a man of ordinary intelligence?" "How many times have you served in the penitentiary?" "Were you honorably discharged from the Army?"

The committee finally had no course except to excuse Waldrop. (He further infuriated the group by insisting on collecting his $3 witness fee.) Subsequently, at a closed session, it reluctantly agreed that the *Herald* had a right to its position under the First Amendment. The frustrated committee members thereupon voted to end the inquiry immediately and also to ignore the customary procedure of printing the proceedings and reporting its findings to the House. In other words, the sooner the whole mess was buried the better.

The episode, however, was not forgotten by the American Newspaper Publishers Association and others concerned about a free press. At its 1936 convention, the ANPA formally commended the *Herald* for standing firm, and the ANPA's committee on freedom of the press called the McSwain hearings "one of the most disgraceful exhibitions in the history of Congressional institutions."

The stand taken by the *Herald* in challenging a Congressional committee's attempt to violate guarantees under the First Amendment became a landmark in the history of Congressional investigations and the limits of their jurisdictions.

Mrs. Patterson was of course delighted with the outcome of the Waldrop-McSwain showdown. She often reminded herself that a newspaper's reason for existence is the dissemination of news. She was determined to be faithful to the heredity which traced printer's ink to grandfather Joseph Medill and Medill's own father-in-law, James Patrick, of New Philadelphia, Ohio. Analyzing the ingredients of a good newspaper, she once said: "First comes the news, because public thinking and public opinion are based on news events, and what the public thinks is the thing most important . . . what goes on now, in 120,000,000 brains in the United States represents what will happen in the United States as time goes by. The future of the country is born in the minds of today."

But she knew that to attract attention a newspaper must cater to the public appetite by serving up entertainment and useful information as well. She had little interest in sports, but she came

to realize that the sports pages were of prime importance because they "interest all men and consequently all women, interested always in things that men discuss." Second most important
in her judgment was "humor," by which she meant the comic
strips. Third came fiction. Medill had once told her that when
his friend, Horace Greeley, was running Eugene Sue's *Mysteries of Paris* in the New York *Tribune*, the upstate farmers
stood in line at the post office waiting for the latest edition of
the paper. Fourth in importance she placed "information specially for women—fashions, so-called beauty secrets, household
information and advice, care of the children, etc."

This recipe for a newspaper's success was not, of course,
unique with Cissy Patterson. In the 1930s it had become standard
for any big metropolitan daily. But Washington is a unique town,
and Cissy was adding her own unique flavor in the *Herald*. She
created news. Since she moved in the highest political and social
circles, she was in a position to learn what was going on back-
stage. What she picked up might be a news story in itself, or
perhaps a hint of something which could be run down by her
astute reporters.

The results often turned up not in the *Herald* news stories but
in its many sprightly columns carrying society doings, or sheer
gossip. For the first time, the society pages of a Washington
paper reported news that was significant to the national political
life. Washington is one of the greatest home-delivery newspaper
towns in the United States, and its newspaper readers have perhaps a higher I.Q. than any other city. When they picked up
their copy of the *Herald*, as they did in steadily increasing numbers in the mid-thirties, it became a habit to turn to the gossip
columns first for news. There cabinet members, senators, and
other leaders were reported as personalities.

Washington lawyers who earned their retainers by keeping
clients posted on every significant little-known fact had a vested
interest in scanning the *Herald*, for in Washington the Social
Lobby is of prime importance. One lawyer, for example, learned

from a society column that a certain member of the Federal
Communications Commission had accepted an invitation to a
swank party given by an "economic royalist" in Philadelphia. To
the lawyer this meant that the commissioner, who had once voted
in the poor man's interest, was now anxious to curry favor with
big business. He so reported this conclusion to his boss—who
had matters pending before the FCC—and the tip proved to be
useful to the client in analyzing his chances before the commission, and in planning his argument before it.

In creating news by reporting such gossipy items, Cissy was
herself playing a key role in the life of the capital. The New
Deal was flooding Washington with reformers, professors, intellectuals and theorists of all kinds. These planners and leaders,
whose names were becoming household words, were invited to
elaborate parties staged by Cissy and by her close friend Evalyn
Walsh McLean. What they said or did there could foreshadow
a new trend—or a new fight—in the experiment-minded administration of Franklin D. Roosevelt.

While her reluctance to sound pompous kept her from talking
about it, there lurked in Cissy a well-concealed but strong interest in civic reform. The *Herald* began to reflect it. Although
suffrage in the voteless District of Columbia was not to come in
any form until three decades later, she pioneered toward the
goal of "home rule." The *Herald* alone organized and directed a
citywide plebiscite in 1938 which gave an overwhelming "yes"
answer to the question of suffrage.

In 1933, after an investigation of conditions in District of
Columbia schools led by Cissy in person, the *Herald* distributed
free hot lunches to underprivileged school children, eventually
shaming the school system into providing the lunches itself.

She also set out to improve the Potomac River. Through feature articles, news stories and editorials she plugged for modern
wharfs, piers, and sewage disposal on the Potomac watershed.
This resulted in a $2,000,000 harbor and yacht basin. Meanwhile,
working with the Izaak Walton League in an effort to protect

fish and animal life in the upper river, the *Herald* organized a campaign which resulted in a PWA loan and giant project to improve sewage conditions.

At one time or another Cissy directed her withering editorial fire against the laxity of the police department; inadequate facilities for tuberculosis prevention; unhealthy slum and alley conditions; and inadequate schooling for crippled children. Every crusade resulted in some type of reform.

By 1936, the *Herald*—hard-hitting, newsier, brighter and breezier—had more than doubled its 1930 circulation of 62,000.

This only made Cissy chafe even more impatiently for independence. She was still, after all, only a vassal of the mighty Hearst. Much of the space in her paper had to be filled up with his syndicated national columns and features. Even worse were the "canned" editorials imposed on all Hearst papers. Cissy had strong personal opinions on everything, and inevitably she found the situation almost unbearable during the presidential campaign of 1936.

It was not that Mrs. Patterson was opposed to Alfred M. Landon. Indeed, she had accompanied Hearst on a visit to Landon's home in Topeka, Kansas, a full year ahead of the election to look him over as a possible G.O.P. nominee. Like Hearst, she had been impressed. Nor did she consider herself a New Dealer, although she sympathized with many of the Roosevelt administration's objectives, liked FDR personally, and was influenced by the pro-New Deal stand of her brother Joe in his New York *Daily News.*

During the 1936 campaign she was obliged to print in the *Herald* columns many Hearst-organization editorials and news stories which attacked the New Deal bitterly and sometimes unfairly, she felt. The savagery of the Hearst campaign coverage hurt *Herald* circulation and advertising and made her agonizingly conscious of her lack of control over the paper she supposedly headed.

For years Cissy had been importuning Hearst to sell her either

the *Herald* or both the *Times* and the *Herald*, but he was reluctant to give up his Washington outlets. But Hearst's losses in
Washington continued to mount. In 1935 they exceeded $1,400,-
000 for the two papers. Despite attempted money-saving cut-
backs, the losses went on increasing at the rate of $100,000 a
year. In addition, Hearst, the last of the big spenders in journalism, was in deep trouble financially in other areas.

In January 1937, Cissy was alarmed when she heard that
Eugene Meyer, publisher of the morning *Post*, had offered
Hearst $1,000,000 for the *Herald*. The *Herald* was the big thorn
in the side of the *Post*, which Meyer had purchased in 1933.
The *Herald*, under Cissy's satin-sheen leadership, was now being
read in the big homes and embassies on Massachusetts Avenue.
It was expected that, if he bought the *Herald*, Meyer would
add its best features to his own paper and then close it down,
giving him a morning monopoly in the capital.

Cissy telephoned Hearst, and he suggested that she take over
both his Washington papers. She asked for time to think it over,
but meanwhile, in April, she arranged to lease the *Herald*. In
June, she learned that Meyer had increased his bid. Frantically,
she put in a call to Hearst at his San Simeon estate late one
night. Friendship with the hard-pressed magnate now won out.

"Well, Cissy," said Hearst, "you tell me what you want to do
and I'll have my folks do it."

The result was a series of meetings at her Long Island home.
Cissy was represented by William C. Shelton, her shrewd business manager, and her attorney, Mabel Walker Willebrandt.
Hearst was represented by Thomas J. White, his general manager, and two attorneys. Finally, the Hearst group agreed to lease
the two papers to Mrs. Patterson for five years, with an option
to buy. In return, she gave Hearst a "loan" of $1,000,000 to bind
the agreement. Under the terms, she was to assume the losses,
but with the understanding that, if the losses exceeded a certain
amount, Hearst would benefit.

For her part, Cissy was gaining the opportunity to take over and operate a losing property as she saw fit, with the privilege of purchasing it at a later date if she wished. For his part, Hearst was getting $1,000,000 in cash when he needed it badly, while retaining title to his papers and ridding himself of the losses.

The next day Cissy wrote Hearst a characteristically frank letter. "Sometimes at the end of a long-drawn-out and difficult struggle, when you suddenly win your point," she wrote him, "you feel sort of flat and let down. Maybe I should, but I don't, feel that way now. You have contended for a long time that the responsibility of the management of your two papers . . . would prove too heavy a burden for me. But I have stubbornly believed that I could prove to you that I was right and you were wrong in this particular argument.

"Well, these past seven years have passed like a dream—the grandest and most brilliant adventure of my life. But these last seven years I hope will pale before the next five . . ."

Free at last, Cissy was off and running.

NINE

The Professional

For the first time in years, Cissy Patterson was dictating an open letter to her readers. It was January 30, 1939, and, journalistically, she was about to perform a marriage. She hoped the nuptials would carry her the last long distance toward her goal of becoming a true newspaper professional.

Pacing the floor, Cissy first reviewed in her mind the last year and a half, when she had for the first time functioned as an absolute boss. Confidently, she had started out to ride two horses—the *Times* and the *Herald*—at once, exulting in the new freedom to try out any idea that occurred to her or one of her editors. Circulation had risen, but nonetheless, both papers had remained deep in the red. It offended her pride as well as her pocketbook to operate *two* losing properties. In 1938 the total loss had come close to $1,000,000.

Washington obviously was overcrowded with five newspapers, and Cissy was advised by expert opinion in the publishing field to close the morning *Herald*, which was a bigger loser than the afternoon *Times*. She resisted this idea with all her force; the *Herald* was her first love, and she was tied to it with a passionate devotion. She had never liked or understood the *Times*. Some drastic new remedy had to be devised.

Now she was about to disclose what it was. Slowly she dictated the message which, signed and in boxed type, appeared on the front page of the next morning's *Herald* under the simple heading: "AN ANNOUNCEMENT." It read:

I would like to make a statement to end all statements concerning the lease and sale of the Washington *Herald* (morning) and the Washington *Times* (evening).

On August 7, 1937, I leased both properties from Mr. William Randolph Hearst with an option to buy. On January 28, 1939, I exercised my option and *purchased* both properties and all their physical assets, with the intention of merging the two unnaturally divided papers into one.

I use the word "unnaturally" after considerable reflection and years of intensive experience of waste of time and talent, worry and ceaseless effort to keep those twin papers separate entities and apart.

Anyone who understands anything about the operation of newspapers knows the handicaps involved in such a divided setup. The duplication of expense alone, added to the enormous increase in cost of production since 1937, became finally a problem without any reasonable solution.

There has been, contrary to general opinion, a limited duplication of circulation between the *Times* and the *Herald*—only 17.3 percent of the whole. That is, 183,309 people are reading today either the *Herald* or the *Times*, and the reason for that is simple. Some of our readers want their paper with their morning coffee, while others prefer theirs around noon or when they get home at night.

So for sound editorial as well as business reasons, we have finally decided to pull up the sluice-gates which artificially divided these properties and let the two papers merge into one.

I will close without the usual quota of pompous promise and merely say we hope you will like the new *Times-Herald* —Washington's only around-the-clock newspaper—and that you, the people of Washington, will share with us in our success.

Only a very few round-the-clock newspapers have been tried in the United States, and their success has not been conspicuous. One of the main reasons Mrs. Patterson took the risky plunge was not mentioned in the open letter. For over a year she and her key staff members had held long conferences on the problem of attracting department-store advertising. To do this, the Patterson papers would somehow have to breach the bastion of the *Star*, which virtually dictated the advertising policies of the biggest advertisers in the capital. The *Star* was a fat old dowager whom nobody, seemingly, dared offend. But Cissy and her strategists felt that if they could offer the advertisers a package which would guarantee them more readers for the same rates they could not, as hardheaded businessmen, afford to pass up the extra business.

The shotgun wedding of the *Times* and the *Herald* united two of the city's oldest and most durable newspapers. The *Times*, started in 1893, had been bought in 1901 by the famous Frank Munsey, who in turn sold it to Arthur Brisbane, then chief editorial writer for the Hearst chain. Brisbane deeded it to Hearst in 1919.

The *Herald*, founded by a group of Washington businessmen in 1906, passed first to Clinton Brainerd of the McClure syndicate. In 1919, Brainerd sold it to a syndicate in which Herbert Hoover was a principal. Surprising as it may now seem, Hoover was interested in becoming the Democratic presidential nominee in 1920. After an unprofitable two years running the *Herald*, the syndicate sold it to Hearst.

Neither paper ever prospered under Hearst, but he was determined to maintain two windows in Washington at almost any cost. In 1924 he constructed a $1,500,000, four-story building at 1317 H Street NW, and installed both the *Herald* and *Times* in it. The papers had separate offices but shared the same presses. It was this building that Mrs. Patterson acquired when she purchased the publications.

The new *Times-Herald* published ten editions over a 24-hour period—five editions from dusk to dawn, and five others through the day. The savings Cissy would achieve immediately were easy to see—the round-the-clock paper would carry the best features and comics of the *Times* and *Herald*, and the daytime editions also would offer full race results and jazzier headlines to lure street sales. Many costs would be cut in half.

But there was an immediate and significant casualty of the merger: jobs. Thirty-seven fewer staff members would be needed to put out the streamlined paper. Each of the thirty-seven was to be given the required Newspaper Guild severance pay for time served, plus a week's notice pay, plus two weeks' 1939 vacation pay—which was added over the protest of some of Cissy's financial advisers.

The vacation pay was more than was required under the Guild contract Mrs. Patterson had signed the previous summer with the *Times* and the *Herald* employees. Thus, she was surprised when she learned through the grapevine that the Guild was calling a strike meeting. But first there was to be a mass meeting to which all department heads and those who would remain on the staff were invited. Cissy herself was invited, and she went, feeling a little depressed and very tired.

When she walked into the room and faced the assembled employees, they were prepared to hear a plea or a pep talk. They got something much more dramatic, and much more in her own individual style. Cissy leaned against the table and told her story, simply, slowly, in a voice that broke only once. She said, first, that she could not understand the reason for the protest and the threatened strike; if she had taken professional advice and closed the *Herald*, hundreds of its people would have been left without jobs. She gave details of cost and duplication of running two papers, and said she could not afford to continue losing money at that rate. She thought she had found a way out: merger. She wanted to publish a good newspaper, and she knew they wanted one too. She had counted on their cooperation and loyalty. Then her voice dropped and she chose her words even more carefully.

"I want to save this paper," she said, "for you and for myself, because I think you love it as I do. If there is a strike, I will lock the doors and they will never be opened."

Then she turned and walked from the room.

Her audience, as hushed as a church congregation, included all sorts of people—newcomers, oldtimers, leaders of the strike movement, all of them imbued with the tradition that a newspaperman wears cynicism like armor. As Mrs. Patterson left, many of them were unashamedly blinking back tears.

The strike meeting was to go forward on schedule. The night before it, Cissy dined at Harvey's restaurant and seemed serene. The threatened strike had Washington buzzing, but she preferred to talk to her friends about a new type of mountain goat discovered in Idaho. When someone mentioned the Guild, she remarked quietly: "There will be no strike. If they picket, they'll picket against an empty building. There will never be a strike. I'll close the shop and lock the doors."

Later in the evening she went to a tiny office adjoining the roaring press room, where the first edition of the newly born *Times-Herald* was being spewed forth. It was a moment to be savored. She sat down at a desk and began to autograph the first editions for employees. She had, as usual, mislaid her spectacles and could scarcely see her own signature, but the name, Eleanor Patterson, in bold, feminine letters was unmistakable. Then, with a characteristic gesture, she swept off her large picture hat, pushed the heavy auburn hair from her forehead, and smiled contentedly around the room.

The next day no strike was called. Probably not a single staff member doubted for one moment that Mrs. Patterson had meant what she said.

The *Times-Herald* would continue to be a Guild paper, but the threatened strike left Mrs. Patterson wary of the Guild for a long time, and she showed definite contempt for its members in an incident that occurred the following October. The Guild shop paper carried a cartoon which showed a shepherdess labeled "Mrs. P" running after a fleeing lamb. The caption read: "Now, those mysterious people who won't join the Guild . . . I tell you sincerely, I wish you could persuade *everyone* outside the Guild to come in . . . ('stated by Mrs. Patterson to a Guild committee Tuesday, Oct. 10')." The cartoon was tacked up on the bulletin board in the city room. The next day the staff found tacked on the same board two sheets of white paper bearing the boss's handwriting in red ink. It was one of Cissy's most devastating exercises in ridicule, for the note impugned the shop-paper staff's ability to report, spell and use grammar. The note, in all its deliberate illiteracy, follows:

> dere friends of the Guild. No, wat you wrote ain't true. i argufied 2 hours & half i sed everybudy has a rite to there opinion & i wud not try to change everybudy's opinionion about guild because i dont care wat opinionion about guild everybudy's got & never did care & for you to do your own work for yourselves & wat was the matter with you & guild you ast me to do it for you
> Next time we meat i will have a couple cort stenografers along. i think you is bum reporters & should all fierre eche other offen your own paper & no severance pay neither
> Eleanor Patterson

On the morning of February 1, 1939, the first full day of the *Times-Herald's* existence, Cissy was so elated she sent a telegram to George De Witt, the night managing editor, and "Happy" Robinson, the circulation manager, reading: "I want to send my special love and particular thanks to you for your marvelous work and unfailing devotion."

The other two executives selected to run the paper were Arthur G. Newmyer, associate publisher and general manager, and Michael W. Flynn, day managing editor. Mike Flynn had been managing editor of the *Herald* when Cissy took it over in 1930. Tall, genial and gentle, he was endowed with the kind of Irish charm and humor that appealed to her.

Flynn was outstanding in his ability to smell out a political angle. He was the first to notice and "get on" a charge that Senator Hugo Black, FDR's 1937 appointee to the Supreme Court, had once been a member of the Ku Klux Klan. As in other instances, Flynn's superawareness gave the *Herald* a headstart on the press associations and other Washington papers on a big story.

Strangely, while Flynn was the only editorial executive who lasted all through Mrs. Patterson's eighteen years as an editor, he never felt secure in his job. This caused him to go along dutifully with her on all her decisions. Not so with De Witt, a short, stocky, Hearst veteran known for his explosive temper and bellowing voice.

De Witt had learned the editor's trade in the tough newspaper world of Chicago, under the tutelage of Walter Howey. In 1935 he quit as managing editor of the Chicago *Herald and Examiner* when he was faced with having to share his authority with Victor Watson, a Hearst editor who boasted the distinction of having introduced "The Chief" to Marion Davies.

De Witt went to Hearst and told him he wanted another job, and Hearst gave him a choice of applying for openings on his papers in Boston or Washington. De Witt elected to try the Washington *Herald* because of Mrs. Patterson's reputation. When he arrived in the *Herald* office, Mrs. Patterson was striding around in riding clothes, with her French poodles at her heels. He liked her flair, and she saw in him the kind of hard-boiled managing editor she felt she needed to jack up the *Herald*. Thus began a tempestuous relationship that lasted seven years.

De Witt saw no reason not to stand up to his female boss when he thought she was wrong. While she always retained her poise and quiet—dangerously quiet—composure during arguments, De Witt would get excited and raise his voice—not a wise tactic for anyone conversing with Mrs. Patterson. She respected De Witt because he was a competent, hard-working executive who tried to run a taut ship, but her temperament could stand only so much. De Witt, consequently, was fired three times.

Two nights after war broke out in August 1939, De Witt, who had gone without sleep for two days in order to stay on top of the constantly breaking news, got a call from the boss.

"I think it's disgraceful the way you've messed up this edition," she told him. The managing editor knew that Mrs. Pat-

terson had been to a champagne party and he surmised that she
actually was looking at the early edition, which was hastily
thrown together for street-sale purposes, when she *thought* she
was looking at the home edition, with which great care was
taken. When De Witt tactfully tried to explain that she might
be mixed up, she informed him *he* had been drinking and told
him he was fired.

The next morning De Witt stayed home, having taken his
dismissal at face value. Late in the day Mrs. Patterson telephoned
and upbraided him for taking the day off. When he reminded
her that she had fired him, Cissy retorted irritably: "Why, I did
not!"

To make up for the misunderstanding, she invited him to
Du Pont Circle for dinner. De Witt asked if he could bring
along William C. Shelton, her business manager, who also had
had his services terminated the night before. During dinner
Shelton was rehired, as De Witt had hoped he would be.
Carried away by her generosity, Cissy concluded the dinner by
tossing her black pearls across the table and telling De Witt
to give them to Mrs. De Witt. De Witt left the pearls on the
table. He knew she didn't mean that either.

De Witt was paid $300 a week—a decent salary for a managing
editor during the Depression—but he felt Mrs. Patterson expected a lot in return for it. She made him responsible for
her round-the-clock paper literally around the clock. He sometimes slept in his office—to be ready for her phone calls punctually at 9 A.M. and 2 P.M.

While Mrs. Patterson seemed pleased in general with the job
De Witt was doing, he found it increasingly difficult to keep
up with her moods. A climax came in 1942 when he was enjoying the office Christmas party. Suddenly there was a summons from the boss, and he found her simmering in her private
office.

"Do you think I pay you to go to parties," she demanded,
"or to do your job?"

To De Witt, who had been drinking champagne, it seemed

that Mrs. Patterson was looking for an excuse to get rid of him. She had been nagging him lately.

"Look, Mrs. Patterson," he told her with some heat, "I'm not a butler or servant in your home. If you have no confidence in me, there's no point in my continuing here. You've talked about loyalty from employees. To me, loyalty is a two-way street. With you, it's a one-way street!"

Cissy's round eyes grew wider with indignation.

"You're fired!" was all she could say. He walked out.

The next day Mrs. Patterson came to De Witt's office and saw him cleaning out his desk.

"What are we going to do with you?" she asked good-humoredly.

"Well, I'm through—you said so," De Witt reminded her. And so he was. He did not even receive severance pay.

De Witt was convinced that Mrs. Patterson was annoyed with him because of an exclusive story he had printed the week before. It exposed the activities of a lobbyist who was the husband of a close friend of hers. The repercussions were instantaneous. The friend let De Witt know he had made an enemy, and to watch out! Then Cissy herself called him about the story. De Witt explained that he had run it because it was important news.

"Well," Mrs. Patterson answered, "you know I never suppress news, but I think we ought to be a little kinder to our friends."

In all De Witt's years with Mrs. Patterson, this was the closest she had ever come to hinting that he should not always print the news.

After his third firing, he went to Chicago and got a good job on the Chicago *Sun*. There Mrs. Patterson once again tried to lure him back to the *Times-Herald*, at a bigger salary, but he had had enough.

As late as July 25, 1944, she wired De Witt in Chicago:

I do hope you'll come back as managing editor at 350 a week (or 375 if you really feel that way about it and I guess you do) but the main points are that you do come as soon as you possibly can that you and Mrs. De Witt settle down with us for good that once more we will all be together again and once more we will all be happy.

He never worked for her again.

However badly his relationship with Mrs. Patterson ended, De Witt always recalled his years with her as the most interesting period of his lively career. He gave Mrs. Patterson high marks for integrity and generosity in treatment of employees in general.

Cissy had lavished favors on De Witt, between battles. And she was not necessarily afraid to admit it when she was wrong. Once, De Witt found on his desk a gift wrapped with a bright blue ribbon. Inside was a photograph of Cissy Patterson as an infant. Scrawled under the picture in pencil was this message to De Witt: "Still only 18 months old!" De Witt chuckled and asked himself: "How can you get sore at a boss like that?"

In November 1938, while De Witt still edited the *Herald*, Cissy wired him: "I think we should get up a special Thanksgiving paper. I can think of a couple of things myself to be thankful for right off the bat, Happy and you."

Once, when Mrs. Patterson felt De Witt had presided over a too cluttered edition of the *Times-Herald*, she bawled him out in verse. The note, handwritten in pencil, started out, "Dear friend."

> I'd be so delight-y
> If the T-H weren't so type-y
> War news now is sure 'nuff right-y
> But must the paper look a fright-y
> You are stubborn, Dutch, and fight-y
> Sometimes, yes, it's true I'm flight-y
> But ain't I never proved I'm right-y?
>
> —
>
> Love to all—and night-y
>   night-y . . .
>   E. P.

Mrs. Patterson once insisted that the De Witts spend a week at her ranch in Jackson Hole, Wyoming. Before the De Witts departed in their automobile, a case of Scotch was delivered, with this note from Cissy:

A friend in need is a friend indeed. This might help out over some of those long, dry stretches *before* you get over the mountains and into Jackson Hole. Have a grand, long vacation and forget all about the office and its pesky little poison ivies.

> Your sincere friend,
> Eleanor Patterson.

The Scotch helped, but the De Witts were not fond of roughing it, and the perilous mountainside journey to the Patterson cabins—plus the relatively primitive existence there—was not their idea of relaxation. Much more to their taste was the vacation Mrs. Patterson extended to them at a house she leased on a beach at Nassau.

When the De Witts arrived in Nassau, they discovered that Cissy had sent her housekeeper, Mrs. Sibilla Campbell, on ahead to staff the house, with a maid, cook and butler. There was also a chauffeur to drive them to the docks, where a chartered yacht and crew were waiting every morning to take them fishing.

A lover of luxury, Mrs. Patterson nonetheless prided herself on her ability to cope with conditions—whether on mountain or water—which discomfited her friends. From Nassau she once wrote Mrs. De Witt this note: "We arrived during the first act of a hurricane yesterday. Luvvie Pearson was very ill coming over. My maid Hazel—a gentle and delicate soul—absented herself during most of our trip. Drew turned a faint chartreuse . . . a lovely color *off*."

Cissy's alternate use of the carrot and the stick with De Witt illustrated her ambivalent attitude toward her employees. Much as she might admire a subordinate, she never completely trusted

him. Oddly, this had something to do with changing her into a
sharp administrator as well as a good editor.

Within a year, the new *Times-Herald* was accepted in Washington. The paper flaunted a distinct personality—reflecting, as
all successful newspapers do, the personality of its boss—and
its circulation and advertising totals were encouraging. Cissy,
however, was beginning to realize that this was not enough.
There was another aspect to running a newspaper which had
never interested her but which eventually would make or break
her. This was the financial side, the esoteric world of book-
keepers, accountants, and auditors, where dollars-and-cents decisions were made that meant either a profit or loss for the
whole operation. Until she could master the management end,
she realized, she could not call herself a true publisher—nor
could she be sure that she was receiving 100 percent loyalty
from her staff.

Concern about loyalty obsessed her. Her chronic suspicion
and distrust of her executives led to her determination to know
exactly how their departments operated, down to the minutest
detail. She felt that, if she knew all there was to know about
an executive's bailiwick, she could keep an eye on his performance and—what was really interesting—perhaps trap him
in a lie.

She called in each department head and asked him, "What do
you do? . . . how does this work? . . . exactly why do you do
that? . . . how can we improve your shop? . . ." etc., etc. For
the first time, she found out what happens on a newspaper from
the moment trucks back into the building with giant rolls of
virgin newsprint until other trucks roll out of the building with
bundles of freshly minted newspapers.

Cissy's determination to keep her hand on all throttles of her
new machine brought her into violent collision with her associate publisher, Arthur Newmyer. Both of them should have
foreseen this, for it is hard to imagine two more incompatible
people working together.

Ironically, Cissy had told Hearst she would purchase the two papers only on condition that she could have Newmyer to run them. She did not know him well, but she was well aware of his distinguished record. Newmyer was a native Washingtonian who got a job on the Washington *Times* at $3.50 a week when he was seventeen years old. At twenty-one he was its advertising manager, and at twenty-four he was national advertising manager for the entire Munsey newspaper chain. For a time he was part-owner of the New Orleans *Item*, then returned to Washington in 1935 to succeed laundry-owner George Marshall as publisher of the *Times*. Under Newmyer, the *Times*, in 1935 and again in 1936, showed the largest advertising gains of any newspaper in the United States.

In 1937 Hearst promoted Newmyer to New York, where he was first publisher of the New York *Journal*, and then assistant general manager of Hearst enterprises on a five-year contract at $57,000 a year. It was this contract which Cissy assumed when she made Newmyer associate publisher of the *Times-Herald*.

Newmyer was as strong-willed as Cissy and had always insisted on running his own shop without interference. In eight months he and Cissy were not on speaking terms, communicating only through memos. Newmyer repeatedly asked to be relieved of his contract, but in vain. Eventually, Cissy stripped him of all real authority and relegated him to a smaller office. When the contract expired on July 27, 1942, he resigned to found a Washington public relations firm. He died in 1955.

One of the three or four men who were most responsible for making Cissy's creation a success was John Irving Belt, her mechanical superintendent. Belt's title hardly began to suggest the scope of his genius, or the contribution he made to the *Times-Herald*. Belt's first job had been as a reporter on the Washington *Times* back in 1900, but soon he had become fascinated with type and had learned the printing trade. Belt became an authority on the history of type dating from Guten-berg. He also became a virtuoso in his print shop.

He presided over the composing room like an aesthetic despot, although he looked less like a printer than anyone on the paper. Amid the dirty type plate and the grimier printers, he moved majestically, like a minister searching for error. He could detect the tiniest typo while reading a column of type, almost casu-ally, upside down—and simultaneously talking to an editor. Belt never removed his coat or tie, yet he never showed a speck of dirt on his meticulous person. When he actually made up a page, his long sensitive fingers throwing type together with be-wildering speed and dexterity, he was an artist at work. It was like watching Rachmaninoff at the keyboard.

But Belt was far more than composing-room royalty. He stood out in the whole rakish *Times-Herald* staff as an undoubted gentleman and scholar. He measured up to Mrs. Patterson's ideal of an executive: a "Renaissance man" who possessed knowledge, in depth, on almost every subject. Although he had no formal education beyond business high school, he had taught him-self Latin and Greek and he maintained a classical library in his office. Belt's encyclopedic fund of information was such that he would often catch some obscure historical inaccuracy in copy sent down to the composing room. He would telephone the editor in charge and call the mistake to his attention with the asperity of a schoolmaster rapping a careless pupil's knuckles.

At Mrs. Patterson's insistence, Belt sat in on all high-level con-ferences affecting the *Times-Herald,* and she consulted him on all manner of nontechnical decisions, including personnel changes or altering the style of a gossip column. She trusted him more than she trusted her other top executives.

He was mainly responsible for the technical readability of the *Times-Herald.* What Mrs. Patterson wanted was "a clean paper, easy to read," with the emphasis on the kind of artful simplicity that she admired in all things. The typeface she and Belt chose for the news columns was large, legible, and streamlined by ordinary newstype standards. In Cissy's words, it "didn't look too pretty and was perfectly clear." On the other hand, Belt picked a typeface for the women's pages which *was* pretty, that is, slightly fancy and feminine-looking.

The headlines on the news stories were kept largely to one-column width, again to keep the makeup from looking cluttered, or what Mrs. Patterson called "mixed-up."

Cissy sometimes joked about her insistence on a "clean" news-paper, typographically speaking. She said it was caused by her own myopia.

The more she learned about a newspaper's innards, the more of a perfectionist she became. "I've always wanted everything to be perfect," she once told an interviewer. "I'm the sort of bore who calls up the composing room and tells them, 'Oh, change that comma!' and then calls them back in a few minutes to say, 'Oh, put it in again!'"

Her perfectionism sometimes was carried to a matter of amaz-ingly minor detail, but staff members could not argue against its soundness.

She insisted, for example, that every page of her paper be "dummied," that is, every bit of space allotted to newsprint had to be marked out in advance for specific stories, no matter how minor they might be. The ordinary procedure on a newspaper is for the news editor to dummy only the first three pages and allow the rest of the space to be filled up, usually haphazardly, by the makeup editor in the composing room. Cissy disliked the idea of having editorial matter shoveled into her newspaper just to fill up space.

As for the stories themselves, Cissy demanded that the writer diligently search out the right word instead of falling back on the handy journalese which is characteristic of the average, hur-riedly written news story. Writing which reflected a careful and deceptively clever style delighted her.

Mason Peters, who spanned Mrs. Patterson's career in almost every editorial capacity, found that on the *Times-Herald* "you were more like a magazine editor than a newspaper editor. You had to find time to think in depth and to have the artistic sense that goes into a good magazine."

Such perfectionism may have been lost on most of Mrs. Patterson's readers, but it inspired respect and a feeling of professional challenge among her staff members. They were fascinated by the high standards set by the lady herself. She was totally different from any other editor they had ever seen or heard of. A talk with Mrs. Patterson was an event to be remembered. Even apparently casual orders and ideas came from her lips as if encased in an elegant sheen. She pronounced each word carefully, enunciating the syntax precisely. One could almost see the commas and semicolons falling into place. Her choice of words was intriguing to anyone who loved the English language. She herself obviously loved the language and sought always to suit the word to the thought exactly. Now and then her use of a rare word hinted at her cultivated tastes in reading. Most of the time she used short words and idiomatic phrases which hit straight at the target.

Cissy was equally fastidious about pictures. It was not uncommon for her to telephone the picture editor at one o'clock in the morning to tell him she had spotted a "wrinkle" in a picture and wanted it corrected. This meant the picture editor had to locate the engravers in whatever saloon they had repaired to, get them back on the job, and then run off the replated edition —finally making sure it was delivered to Mrs. Patterson at her home.

For a time she personally selected every picture that went into the *Times-Herald*. The picture editor would submit a pile of photographs connected with the day's news, and together they would pore over them, with Cissy asking the editor his opinion of each. These were tense moments for the picture editor. He would try to figure out, before answering, what might appeal to her about that particular shot.

For several years during the bellicose De Witt's reign at the

Times-Herald, no picture was used on the front page. Cissy once explained to an interviewer with a smile: "That's because Mr. De Witt and I can never agree on a picture. Poor man!"

She had no objection to "cheesecake"—the girlie pictures favored by most newspapers—as such, but she sometimes reminded her staff that a picture of a particularly handsome man should be used occasionally if one was available. "Women like to look at handsome men," she said.

Cissy seemed to favor handsome men—if they also had talent —and she would have surrounded herself with them had they been in better supply. She just as strongly preferred not to have to look upon the ugly, the deformed, the unwashed and the uncouth.

Staff members who offended Mrs. Patterson in appearance or manners did not last long as a rule. An exception to the rule was Bill Edwards, a talented but unkempt cartoonist. Edwards was in the habit of showing up at his drawing board without having bothered to shave or even clean the mud off his boots. He soon caught Cissy's eye. For four consecutive mornings she paused at the door of the art department, peered in disapprovingly at the slovenly artist, and walked on without a word. On the fifth day she veered toward an editor and told him: "I never want to see that man in here again!"

Since everybody liked Edwards, various daring stratagems were contrived to keep him on his job but out of Cissy's sight. They were, in turn, dependent on a general-warning system which had been set up long before to protect all staff members from the possibility of being caught in an idle moment when Mrs. Patterson arrived—which might be at any time of the day or night. An elevator man was the lookout. From the building entrance, he could spot the boss's Cadillac limousine nearly two blocks away. His responsibility was to ascend quickly to the editorial floors, tip off the nearest employee and then drop down again in time to meet Mrs. Patterson when she walked through the lobby to the elevator.

When "The Coming" was signaled, the *Herald* city room resembled a stage setting on which the curtain is about to go up. Even if it was long before a deadline and not much had been happening, the place exploded into action. Copyboys scurried about willy-nilly, copyreaders put pencil to paper, rewrite men pounded their typewriters furiously, editors bent over their desks with furrowed brows.

In Bill Edwards' case, of course, the trick was not to make him look busy but to make him disappear. Sometimes he was shoved into the photo darkroom, and sometimes he was simply hidden under the work table in the art department. Once, Edwards had been stashed under the table only a moment before the staff heard the familiar "yipe!" of French poodles, which meant that their mistress was emerging from the elevator. No one was worried, until it became clear that Mrs. Patterson was heading straight for the art room. There she sat down at the table and called a conference on picture trends. Lee Wade, a staff member who was sitting in on the conference, nervously placed his foot under the table on Edwards' chest. Edwards, annoyed, bit Wade in the leg. Wade managed to suppress a cry of pain, and the vanishing artist was not discovered.

Once Cissy had leased the *Herald* and *Times*, and become boss in fact as well as in name, her operation became more of a serious office and less of a salon. With full command over her consolidated empire, she knew she must streamline the administrative work of the papers and budget her own time more effectively. She no longer wanted to be consulted by staff members on every trivial thing that came up, or even a policy matter which she felt should be more properly handled by the department head. While she enjoyed "consulting" and insisted on knowing the latest intramural gossip, she tended to downgrade the subject matter, and subordinates had to learn which matters would be likely to deserve her interest.

She could look back with a touch of nostalgia on her period of apprenticeship. In an interview published in the New York

Herald Tribune on November 13, 1939, she said: "I must admit I have learned the difference between the gay and delightful editorial side and the grim business side."

"It was all delightful then [in the early thirties]," she explained. "All I had to do was build up circulation, and anything I wanted was at Mr. Hearst's expense (I must say he was always very generous). But now things are paid for out of my own dollars and cents. It is an eternal struggle to make income balance expenditures."

Finally, she had arrived as a responsible, and successful, newspaper owner and operator. Even more than the public respect this brought her was the satisfaction in knowing that she was proving herself—and in the rough Washington proving ground—in the eyes of brother Joe and cousin Bertie McCormick. Nothing less than her profit ledger could wipe out their image of her as "little Cissy," the kid sister.

TEN

"Everybody Moved at a Half-Run"

In 1928, two Chicago newspapermen, Ben Hecht and Charles MacArthur, wrote *The Front Page*, a wild and witty version of life on Chicago newspapers. It was chosen as one of the ten best plays of the season and later was made into a successful movie. *The Front Page* has remained the classic dramatization of exciting journalism.

The common reaction of veteran newspapermen has been that, while the atmosphere of the play is authentic, they never encountered so rough and tough a crew in any city room. Clearly, they never worked on the Washington *Herald* during the thirties. From 1930, when Cissy Patterson took it over, until war clouds rolled up in 1938, the *Herald* attempted to turn Hecht-Mac-Arthur fiction into fact. As an example of life imitating art, it succeeded.

The plot of *The Front Page* revolves around a managing editor who ruthlessly outsmarts his star reporters, outfoxes rival papers, outfinagles politicians, and outrages everybody. The managing editor, Walter Burns, was modeled directly on Walter Howey, the Chicago editor whose falling out with Joe Patterson led to Cissy's first journalistic writing.

After Cissy assumed command of the Washington *Herald*, Howey, then a Hearst-organization trouble shooter, dropped in frequently to contribute his unmistakable touch. Howey was nothing if not tough—he had one glass eye, and it was a *Herald*-staff wisecrack that the kindly one was the glass one. Still, in

those early days when she was trying to revitalize the *Herald*,
Cissy and her hell-for-leather staff welcomed the Howey influence.

George (Ash) De Witt, a Howey disciple, calls Howey "a
great news*maker*, who loved to go out on a story himself."

"I worked under fifteen Hearst editors, and Howey stood
taller than any of them," De Witt recalls. "He wore $50 ready-
made suits, despised pompousness and pretense, hated stupidity,
avoided society and cocktail parties, and declined all invitations
to talk before Rotarian-style affairs. 'Remember,' he once told
me, 'an editor may be a genius on his ass, but he's an ass on his
feet.'"

Howey was as unpredictable as Cissy, and pursued a similar
"work hard, play hard" philosophy. She delighted in his pranks.
One night she invited him to a party at her town house with
Fred Smith, an ex-Chicago *Tribune* foreign correspondent whom
Howey had sent to the *Herald*.

Champagne exploded through the night. As dawn stole across
Du Pont Circle plaza, Howey and Smith, the lone survivors
among the guests, peered out uncertainly from the balcony of the
mansion. Their blurred eyeballs focused on two milk wagons
parked on the Circle while the drivers made their delivery
rounds. The temptation was too much. They hurried out the
door, boarded the wagons joyously, and jerked the reins on the
horses. A chariot race, of sorts, was on.

As Howey and Smith whipped their horses on around the
Circle, they traded insults in the Ben-Hur style established in
Hollywood. Bottles rolled from the wagons and crashed, spilling
milk in the street. The milkmen rushed from the doorways, shaking their fists and yelling at the two presumably berserk newspapermen. Standing on the balcony was Cissy Patterson, laughing
and cheering on the racers. As the wagons careened across a
finish line directly in front of her, she declared Howey the
winner. Loser Smith had to settle with the milkmen.

One of the most important Howey-trained men on the *Herald*

was Ray Helgesen. Helgesen had spent his early life in Washington as the son of a Republican congressman from North Dakota, and was a nephew of the poet Eugene Field. He was sent to Cissy after solid seasoning on the Hearst papers in New York.

Helgesen was six feet four, and emaciatingly thin, with blond hair, worn long. He strongly appealed to women, and made the most of it. When he became the *Herald's* night city editor, he strove to bring a certain brand of executive glamor to its raffish setting. When he strode into the city room, a copyboy was trained to catch his wide-shouldered, belted polo coat as it fell from his shoulders; another boy had a steaming hot cup of coffee waiting at precisely the spot where his right hand would hit the desk when he slumped into the slot.

Sitting in the slot, Helgesen was almost a caricature of the *Front Page* city editor. For the edification of the staff, he might make a production out of handling two or three telephone calls simultaneously; or he might bark orders at an underling to summon no less than the Washington chief of police. ("Get that son-of-a-bitch over here in five minutes!")

It was a hammy act, but behind his flamboyance Helgesen was talented. He was exactly the kind of fast-thinking, free-wheeling city editor the *Herald* needed and Cissy wanted. He would literally stop at nothing to beat another paper to a story. Indeed, the *Herald* beat the rival morning *Post* so often it was wise-cracked that, if a man were found dead on the steps of the *Post* building, it would probably be reported first in the *Herald*.

Herald reporters outdid themselves under the garish banner raised by Helgesen. A few of the more zealous would have jumped off the Calvert Street bridge if he had said it was necessary to get the story. Some of the more sophisticated young reporters admitted Ray's ability but considered it excessively picturesque of him to carry a revolver and holster and maintain a round-the-clock bodyguard. Helgesen explained that he had been threatened by a gangster syndicate because the *Herald* was warring on the underworld. His more cynical colleagues sniggered that the only persons Ray had to fear were the local gamblers to whom he was perpetually in debt.

Quite a few *Herald* reporters also packed guns. (Probably no newspaper city room outside the Old West ever boasted such a mobile arsenal.) Most of them had more justification than Helgesen, since they were continually barging into strange places and strange characters. And the *Herald* was in fact seriously determined to expose important hoodlums. If this crusade needed any impetus, it was provided by the fatal shooting of a *Herald* newsboy, the innocent victim of a gang feud.

Cissy herself thought the gunslingers on her staff were marvelous. What could remind her more vividly that her paper was in cold fact "battling the criminals"?

Because it was crime-conscious, and the most competent paper in town in reporting crime, the *Herald* developed a close working alliance with the Washington police. The arrangement was mutually beneficial—the *Herald* usually got a story first, and the capital cops were properly rewarded. Policemen who cooperated with the *Herald* were described in the paper's pages as the bravest of men. Of course, if they didn't cooperate, they couldn't have shot their way into *Herald* print.

No Washington newspaper ever offered so much exhilaration for its staff. Working on the *Herald* after Cissy took over was fun. Many desk men and reporters found it a much more stimulating home than the one they shared with their families. Some of them left the office late and reluctantly, preferring to stick around the city room, after their shift, for the inevitable poker game and liquor refreshments which kept the office alive all night.

Herald alumni—many of whom have gone on to loftier and more dignified jobs—invariably recall their days on the *Herald* with joyful nostalgia. Mason Peters, who performed brilliantly for Mrs. Patterson in climbing the ladder all the way from teenage cub reporter to managing editor, remembers it this way:

"The clocks seemed to run faster there. There was always a

great deal of unnecessary action going on. There was more shouting and more bustle than you could possibly justify. Everybody moved at a half-run. It was normal for us to look as if we were getting out an extra on a presidential assassination. It was ridiculous . . . and wonderful."

One island of calm stood out among these extroverts. When he wasn't running a Du Pont Circle chariot race with Howey, Fred Smith was a model of deportment. He was the only man in the city room who always kept his necktie cinched up and his sleeves rolled down. While the staff went into semihysteria over a breaking news story, Smith simply puffed away on his pipe and went on competently editing copy. Smith was not only serene; he was a deep thinker. This was enough in itself, at this time, to put him under suspicion with Cissy. In the early thirties, she loved the razzle-dazzle of the unabashed imitation of *The Front Page*. Because he was able, well read, and well grounded in world affairs, Smith floated to the high post of news editor, but his tendency to be himself portended trouble. Cissy had a habit of bringing wealthy friends into the office, sometimes direct from a black-tie party, to show them how a newspaper is put together. Some staff members, notably Smith, felt there was an air of slumming about the whole thing. When Cissy's friends asked him questions, Smith felt he was being used as an errand boy in a zoo. Finally, this is exactly what he told Cissy—and was promptly fired.

On a big news story, Helgesen would throw a whole battalion of his troops into the field, in order to cover all possible angles. This is not unusual on a metropolitan newspaper, except that Helgesen did it more sweepingly; once, he even demanded a real battalion of the United States Army to go to the rescue of his "troops." That was in 1933, when the eastern shore of Maryland was the scene of an extraordinarily ugly series of lynchings.

One night, in the little town of Princess Anne, a mob of 3000 tore a Negro from his cell (where he was being held on a rape charge), dragged him through the streets, hanged him on the

courthouse lawn, then cut him down and burned him with gasoline. Twenty-five state troopers who rushed to Princess Anne
were driven back by the frenzied lynchers.

Helgesen had his contingent of reporters there while the horrible episode was still in progress. They arrived in three automobiles along with Baltimore *Sun* reporters, were instantly spotted
as outsiders and set upon. H. L. Mencken had been lashing out
in the *Sun* at the eastern shore people, and his acidulous reflection on their mob actions did not make the reporters any more
welcome.

First, the Princess Anne citizens set fire to the Ford driven by
Charley Dockarty of the *Herald* and pitched it into the river. It
was the third time a Dockarty-operated car had been burned out
from under him, an indication of the occupational hazards faced
by *Herald* reporters. The newsmen fled from the flaming car and
tried to escape the mob by taking refuge in a local hotel. When
the hotel too was set on fire, they jumped to the roof of an
adjacent hotel, slipped out the back door, and raced from the
town in the remaining two cars.

Pursued by the citizens in automobiles, the *Herald* men drove
all the way to the Delaware state line before they felt safe enough
to telephone Helgesen. The city editor, of course, was having the
time of his life. With Mrs. Patterson's backing, he had already
requested the War Department to rush combat troops to Princess
Anne to rescue his reporters and restore order. Meanwhile, the
Herald staff was able to come up with a graphic description of
the lynching in gruesome detail for the next edition.

A good murder case was an inspiration to the *Herald* staff.
The guiding rule was, "Never mind the victim, find the mur-
derer," and no one followed it more enthusiastically than gun-
toting Pat Frank, the *Herald's* most resourceful reporter. Frank,
a Jacksonville, Florida, native, came to the *Herald* in 1933 via the
New York *Journal*, where he had impressed Helgesen. On the
Herald he earned the nickname "One-Fact Frank." It was said
that Pat could spin a longer and more fascinating yarn out of a

single fact than most writers could get out of a whole file of facts. Frank eventually devoted himself to pure fiction and became one of the most productive and successful free-lance authors in the United States until his death, at 57, in 1964. He wrote a batch of best-sellers—including *Mr. Adam, Hold Back the Dawn,* and *Alas, Babylon,* plus countless short stories, magazine articles, television and movie scripts, and speeches for Democratic presidential candidates.

In the mid-thirties, Pat Frank was in a class by himself as a Washington reporter and rewrite man who could turn out smooth prose with great speed and skill, as well as imagination. He met his severest test one night in 1935. Years later he recalled it:

"So many queer things happened during my days on the *Herald* that sometimes they all whirl together in memory like an inchoate dream of a long motion picture spliced from melodramas, comedies, horror stories, and censored footage. It never seemed possible that we cover a story in the ordinary manner, that is, get it, write it, and publish it. Something incredible always intervened. Take the execution of Mais and Legenza. I think that story marked my real debut as a fiction writer."

Robert Mais and Walter Legenza were charter members of an all-purpose criminal group called the "Tri-State Gang," which preyed on Virginia, Maryland, and the District of Columbia. They had been sentenced to die in the electric chair in Richmond, Virginia. Frank was assigned to cover the execution. He arrived in Richmond the night before and found a distressing problem: News reporters would be barred from witnessing the electrocution.

Hoping the decision would be reversed, Frank late that afternoon wrote a routine story for the first edition and filed it with Western Union. Then he joined the other reporters in the office of the Richmond *Times-Dispatch* for a time-killing game of poker. At eight o'clock, holding aces back to back, he was called to the telephone. It was Helgesen.

"Pat," the city editor said, "your first-edition story stank. No action. No drama."

"Well, nothing dramatic has happened," Frank explained.

"Then we must *make* something happen," Helgesen said.

"How can I make something happen when they won't even let me in the jail?" Frank protested.

"It can happen in your head," Helgesen said. "We're in a bad spot, Pat. Our whole home edition, and the final street-sale edition, will be off the presses by 6 A.M.—when these two monkeys squat in the chair."

"What do you want me to do—kill 'em?" Frank asked, half-jokingly.

"You've seen executions before," Helgesen said. "Write it that way—now—just as it's going to happen, and we'll hold it until you give us a telephone flash at six that they're burning. Then we'll start the presses—and we'll lick hell out of the *Post*."

Frank procured a fifth of sour-mash bourbon and sat down to write. Deciding he needed more than one fact to inspire him for this occasion, he repaired briefly to the penitentiary and asked a few innocuous questions. He learned in a general way the physical layout of the execution chair and the one really necessary fact—that Mais was scheduled to die first.

Frank returned to the *Times-Dispatch* and resumed writing. He began to get involved in his story. He remembered that Legenza had a steel splint in his leg. What would happen when the voltage hit that steel? Why, it would get red hot, of course! The leg would cook, literally. Frank became inspired. He described a thin wisp of smoke rising from Legenza's leg. He told how it smelled. The description was so gruesome he began to feel sick himself.

Three thousand words, as smooth as cellophane, rolled out of Frank's typewriter. He filed it with Western Union after writing across the top of the first page, "HOLD FOR RELEASE!!"

At 3 o'clock in the morning the reporters learned they had no chance of being present for the execution.

At 5 o'clock Frank opened up a telephone line to the *Herald* office to make sure he could send the flash to release the story without a second's delay.

At 6 o'clock, however, word came that the Governor had not yet ruled on a final appeal for a stay of execution. Frank relayed this to the *Herald* city room.

At 7 o'clock the execution took place. Frank flashed his office, returned to his hotel room, and collapsed.

Meanwhile, back at the *Herald*, something had happened, and it would have horrified Frank. "Happy" Robinson, the circulation manager, had read the story in proof. His enthusiasm soared. This was much too good a story to hold for a few last-minute street sales. So at 4 o'clock the next-to-the-last edition of the *Herald* was replated to insert Frank's story under a banner headline. The trucks were loaded and carried it to the newsstands. More than two hours before Mais and Legenza died, the report of how they met their end was presented, in morbid detail, to *Herald* readers!

On his way to his morning radio stint at that hour was a budding disc jockey named Arthur Godfrey. He bought a *Herald* at a newsstand and sat down in his studio office to read all about the execution. Just then, the Associated Press ticker chattered a flash: The execution set for 6 o'clock had been postponed pending a decision by the Governor! Godfrey found the situation irresistible. On the air between six and seven o'clock he intermittently read portions of Frank's grisly description of the death-room scene. He punctuated his readings with the chortled comment: "And the poor guys ain't even dead yet!"

The Washington *Post* jeered at the *Herald's* "eyewitness description" of an execution before it happened, and Mrs. Patterson was not amused. A tigress who invariably defended her cubs, she did not take it out on Helgesen, Frank or Robinson, but on Godfrey. Forever after, his name was anathema in the *Herald*.

For the embarrassed Frank there was one consoling bit of professional satisfaction. A year later the prosecutor who had actually witnessed the execution said to him:

"One thing I'll never understand. How did you sneak into the execution? Don't tell me you didn't, because I read your story. Unless you had actually seen and smelled it, you couldn't have known about Legenza's leg."

Pat Frank in the throes of composition was one of the memorable sights in the *Herald* city room. When he got really carried away with his subject, he would pause frequently to laugh uproariously as he pounded his typewriter. Cissy liked Frank's effervescence and his resourcefulness. Whenever he had finished writing an exciting story, she would invite him into her sanctum. There she would pop some of the champagne kept in her office refrigerator, sit back and say, "All right, now, Pat, tell me what *really* happened."

The *Herald* tempo was set by Cissy herself.

"The drive and vitality of any organization comes from the top, and Cissy had it," Frank once remarked. "If you didn't have a spark, she didn't like you. If you had it, there wasn't anything you couldn't do."

What sparked the *Herald* was a spirit of devil-may-care coupled with a passionate love of newspapering. Zany incidents were almost routine. On the night of April 11, 1935, many of them came together in a sequence which probably would have seemed too preposterous to be used even by the authors of *The Front Page*.

The pressing aim of the staff early that evening was to locate a 31-year-old blonde, Mrs. Anne Lyddane, a prominent resident of nearby Rockville, Maryland. Mrs. Lyddane had been indicted for plotting with hoodlums to murder her husband and her lover's wife (neither murder took place). The case titillated the newspapers. The lovers had selected a fitting setting for their trysts—a Rockville cemetery. (During the subsequent trial, a detective's blunt eyewitness description of the lovers nestled between the graves caused two women to leave the courtroom audience in blushing haste.)

On April 11, Mrs. Lyddane, out on bail and visiting Washington, was being sought by all Washington newspapers. Lazlow Sommer, Helgesen's bodyguard, reported to the city desk at nine o'clock by telephone that he had discovered she was en route to the National Press Building in the care of Ted Huntley, a reporter on the afternoon *Times*. The fact that the *Times* was also Hearst-owned and therefore a *Herald* sibling made it no less a rival in Cissy's eyes; indeed, she took a special delight in beating the *Times* on a story.

Helgesen told Sommer he would be joined at the Press Building by three *Herald* reporters—Pat Frank, Frank Waldrop, and Adela Rogers St. Johns, star of Hearst's International News Service. The three arrived at the entrance just in time to see Sommer and Huntley fighting over the custody of Mrs. Lyddane. Sommer, a husky former football player and ex-night-club bouncer, slugged Huntley so hard that Huntley's hat flew straight up off his head in comic-strip fashion. The *Times* man took to his heels, following Mrs. Lyddane as she fled into an elevator. The *Herald* trio commandeered the next elevator. As it opened out on the lobby of the Press Club entrance on the 13th floor, they saw Mrs. Lyddane disappear through the Club's swinging doors. She was heading directly for the hideout Huntley had planned for her—the powder room of the ladies lounge!

But Adela stayed on Mrs. Lyddane's trail. Inside the powder room, she grabbed the defendant by the shoulders, but the big blonde sank her fingernails into Adela's wrists. They wrestled. Finally, Adela ended the matter by bullying the woman into agreeing that, as long as "the press" was waiting outside, she might as well submit to an interview and get it over with. "The press," of course, meant the two other *Herald* reporters. Huntley, outnumbered and disabled as well, had left the field of action.

After the interview, Adela, Sommer, Waldrop and Frank returned to the *Herald* city room preening themselves on having "hung one" (literally) on the *Times* in particular and the other Washington newspapers in general. But in the city room there was trouble brewing. Helgesen was sitting with a stranger, and he looked worried. With good reason—the stranger was talking about suing the *Herald* for $10,000,000.

The threatened suit was inspired by an organizational boo-boo. Hearst originally had ordered a series exposing the Communist propaganda being imported into the United States through foreign "art films." Hearst's lawyers read the series, scented possible libel action, and advised him to kill it. But a *Herald* editor had not seen the kill order in time to pull the first installment out of the *Herald*. The art-film company named in the story had sent one of its representatives—Matt Radin—to the *Herald* from New York to serve notice of the intended suit.

Helgesen felt that if anyone could talk Radin out of the repulsive notion of collecting millions from the *Herald*, it would be the redoubtable Adela. He asked her to go to work on Radin. He also reserved a room at the Carlton Hotel. Adela soon had charmed Radin into repairing to the Carlton for a game of bridge, with Helgesen and Waldrop. Sommer also was on hand. He ordered liquid nourishment from room service and then sat on a chair which he placed in front of the door, just in case Radin should feel an overpowering urge to leave. Radin didn't know it, but the plan was to keep him in the room until he became a friend of the *Herald*.

Helgesen had ordered the telephone cut off, but as the first hand was being dealt, his uncanny instinct caused him to ask Sommer to call the *Herald*. When Helgesen picked up the phone and talked to the city desk, he turned white. Then he slammed down the receiver.

"A B&O express just smashed into a school bus near Rockville," he told his colleagues. "Let's get going!"

They began to dash from the Carlton, with Helgesen in effect telling Radin to get lost. But Adela, whose sixth sense was also operating, insisted that Radin be allowed to accompany her and

Sommer to Rockville. Helgesen, Waldrop and Frank meanwhile hurried back to the *Herald* to handle the stories that would be coming in over the telephone from Adela and the other *Herald* reporters at the accident scene.

A large part of the *Herald* staff was already en route to Rockville; fifteen children had been killed and fourteen injured when the train struck the bus at a grade crossing in the fog.

Working with customary speed, the *Herald* reporters and photographers had funneled back, in an hour, enough eyewitness stories and pictures to fill several pages. By two o'clock, the final edition had been "locked up" and the city staff began to relax. Presently, Adela returned, accompanied by Radin, who was now bug-eyed. Adela had allowed him to help her out in interviewing survivors and their parents. He was almost speechless with excitement. The little man from New York now asked Helgesen if he could lend a hand in the office. Amused, the city editor sent Radin on some errands to the composing room and photographic darkroom. He even had a picture made of Radin playing city editor—a telephone in each hand, a big cigar in his mouth, and a derby cocked over one eye.

Radin told Helgesen he wanted to become a newspaper reporter and would even be willing to pay for the privilege of having a job on the *Herald*.

Helgesen, loath to spurn ready cash, dealt a hand for poker and said to Radin, "Give us some money." Radin produced a roll of bills, whisky was poured, and the celebration was on in earnest. The *Herald* staff felt it could afford to celebrate. The next edition was full of Mrs. Lyddane and a train wreck. Besides, Radin had been taken into camp—there was the gag picture of him playing city editor being printed in the *Herald* to prove it. He was hardly in a position to file a libel suit.

The party waxed so boisterous that the sounds of revelry floated out the *Herald* windows. Soon the policeman on the local beat strolled into the city room and looked around disdainfully. He was called "Moon Mullins" because he looked like the

comic-strip character of that name. Mullins informed the revelers
that residents of neighboring apartment buildings were complaining about the noise. He said the party was over. Unlike
most Washington cops, Mullins was held in low esteem by the
Herald staff—particularly by Helgesen.

Helgesen called out a vulgar insult by way of reply. Mullins
stepped over to the willowy city editor and struck him on the
side of the head so hard he fell from his chair, unconscious.
Then Mullins pulled out his blackjack and leaned over the
prostrate form as if to beat him.

At this point, Waldrop, who weighed 215 pounds and had
played football at West Point, intervened. He hit Mullins in the
face with a right, a left and another right, dropping the cop like
a sack of potatoes. Then Waldrop sat on the blue uniform and
methodically removed Mullins' revolver and handcuffs. A paddy
wagon was summoned. Within a few minutes Mullins was carried ingloriously from the city room by his colleagues—who
apologized to the staff for his impertinence. It was a fitting
curtain scene for the *Herald's* night of comic opera.

Late that morning Mrs. Patterson enjoyed every detail of the
evening as it was related to her by Adela. She said she was
pleased with the handling of the Lyddane case particularly. Indeed, Adela's Press Club interview with Mrs. Lyddane had been
reported in the highest-quality "sob sister" style in vogue at the
time.

"Mrs. Lyddane looked at me a moment, and I looked back at
her and I felt a sudden strange chill, as though a cold desert wind
had blown upon us," Adela wrote.

"She is tall, is Mrs. Anne Lyddane. A few years ago she must
have been pretty, after a night-club blonde sort of fashion. Now
her features are sharpened, they are too close to the bone, if you
know what I mean. Her hair is that blonde which reminds you
of too brightly polished brass . . . she looked, as she stood staring at me, rather like any other sharp-faced blonde.

"Except for the eyes. They were blue and cold, and very, very clever. They were direct. They saw things, but you couldn't see into them. The mascaraed lashes gave no warmth . . ." etc.

Adela doubted that Mrs. Lyddane had hired thugs to do the double murder, as the state charged. She wrote: "I am convinced that if she really wanted to murder her husband, she'd jolly well do it herself." Adela based this conclusion on her ferocious tangling with the defendant at the Press Club.

The jury agreed with Adela. They acquitted Mrs. Lyddane. Meanwhile, her codefendant, John Martin Boland, had elected to throw himself on the mercy of a three-judge court. On June 11, 1935, the court announced they would begin deliberating on the Boland case. The Lyddane jury was then being impaneled, and it was expected that the judges would withhold immediate disclosure of their verdict on Boland for fear of influencing the Lyddane jurors.

Helgesen, naturally, wanted the judges' verdict before they chose to announce it. He put it up to Pat Frank. Frank learned the hour the judges planned to begin their deliberations and casually strolled into the Rockville courthouse an hour beforehand. He slithered into the bathroom just off the judges' chambers and concealed himself behind the shower curtain.

When the judges met, Frank leaned against the bathroom door and eavesdropped. He heard the judges discuss the case and arrive at a verdict of guilty. Frank scribbled a single sheet of notes and, standing on the toilet seat, dropped it through the bathroom window. Waiting below to catch it was David Lee, a *Herald* reporter. Lee sped to Washington. The next morning the *Herald* published not only the Boland verdict but included some of the judges' comments during the deliberations, in direct quotes, as taken down by Frank at the keyhole. For almost any paper but the *Herald*, Frank's story would have been too hot to print.

The judges, who had decided to withhold announcement of their verdict for a week, were outraged. They angrily issued a citation for contempt of court against Frank, Lee, Helgesen, *Herald* managing editor Mike Flynn, and the *Herald* itself for "embarrassing and obstructing the administration of justice." Frank and Lee, who were still in Rockville, were arrested but released to a *Herald* attorney.

Helgesen and Flynn avoided arrest by staying out of Maryland for nearly a year. Although they failed to appreciate this, the citation doubtless saved them money, for they were unable to visit their favorite recreational haunt—the race track at Bowie.

The *Herald* was fined $5000, but neither Frank nor Lee spent a day in jail. Cissy considered the $5000 well spent.

Helgesen married Kitty Barrett, a young Alabama beauty who had become a reporter on the *Herald*, whose father owned the Birmingham, Alabama, *News*. Cissy was so fond of Kitty that she ordered up her private railroad car and took some of the staff members with her to Birmingham for the wedding.

Helgesen eventually was divorced from Kitty and in increasingly hot water with Cissy. He drank and gambled excessively, and his overblown flair began to seem tiresome. Once, when things were going badly, he walked into Mrs. Patterson's office and pointed his gun at her, threatening to shoot.

"Put down the gun, Ray," she said calmly. "You haven't got the guts to kill me."

Helgesen's hand faltered. Managing Editor George De Witt, who had been sitting talking with Cissy, rose and glared at Helgesen. Helgesen turned and left.

Helgesen was exiled to Chicago and never regained the flaming—and invaluable—role he had once enjoyed as the *Herald's* scoop-crazy city editor. He served another hitch at the *Herald* in the 1940s, then he wandered from paper to paper until he wound up as a copyreader on a weekly in Iowa. There he committed suicide in 1961.

Cissy's spontaneity kept her staff in a state of suspense. One afternoon in 1936 a grand piano was moved into the city room. Soon Duke Ellington, newly risen to fame, was at the keyboard running through some of his current favorites. Nearby stood Cissy, beaming and tapping her foot. She had heard Ellington

9

Cissy had one child, Felicia, and Felicia had one child, Ellen (below). All three loved horses, which Cissy kept at her Dower House estate in Maryland.

10

Jackie Martin

11

Cissy envied her daughter her beauty. Here is Felicia as a girl and as a young socialite in Washington in her twenties.

12

13

14

Cissy divorced the count in 1917. Four other men played key roles in her turbulent life. The most influential was her brother Joe (upper left, picture 13). Columnist Drew Pearson (upper right, picture 14) became her son-in-law for a time by marrying Felicia, and he and Cissy later carried on a famous feud. Cal Carrington (lower left, picture 15) was a Wyoming cowboy and guide who taught her to shoot big game in the Rockies. He is shown here with Cissy's granddaughter, Ellen. Elmer Schlesinger (picture 16) was Cissy's second husband.

15

16

Cissy's far-flung residences ranged from her ranch in Wyoming to what she called the "movie palace" at 15 Du Pont Circle in Washington. It served as the White House for three months in 1927. Her most intimate female friend for more than thirty years was a Wyoming woman, Rose Crabtree, shown here with her husband, Henry.

Jackie Martin

play the night before and thought the whole staff deserved to hear him. The most startled person in the room was De Witt, who had only recently taken over as managing editor. True, he had been weaned on the antics of Hearst papers in Chicago, but he had never expected to see a newspaper going to press to the jazz beat of "Drop Me Off at Harlem."

Working for both Hearst *and* Cissy Patterson accustomed staff members to offbeat assignments. Some of them put a strain on even the most versatile talents. Take the case of Sanford Jarrell, a Howey-trained Hearstman who was a *Herald* city editor for a year. One midnight Jarrell lifted the phone and heard a curious request: Someone was asking him in a high-pitched voice to write a three-act play and have it copyrighted first thing in the morning. Jarrell knew this was the witching hour for crackpots, and he was sleepy besides, so he made no effort to be tactful.

"What the hell do you think this is—a newspaper office or a playwriting bureau?" he snapped. "Write your own damned play, and copyright it yourself."

"Young man," replied the high-pitched voice, now perturbed, "do you know who you're talking to? This is W. R. Hearst speaking."

Jarrell steadied himself and said the long-distance connection at his end was poor. He apologized and asked for the instructions to be repeated. Hearst explained that he wanted a play composed, titled *Three Blondes*, and copyrighted. And he wanted it all done immediately. Hearst said that if Jarrell was editor in charge that night to have it copyrighted under his own name. Then he hung up.

Many pranksters tried to imitate Hearst, as a gag, so Jarrell first checked with the *Herald* switchboard and learned that the call had indeed originated at San Simeon, California, where Hearst had his estate. A lesser man at that point might have appealed for professional help, or been taken suddenly ill. But Jarrell had a reputation for resourcefulness to uphold.

Back in 1924, when he was on the New York *Herald Tribune*,

the city desk had a tip that a cabaret ship was operating off New York, and Jarrell was asked to check it. Stuffing a wad of expense money in his wallet, Jarrell left the office. He returned four days later and wrote a fascinating story: A yacht was indeed lying just outside the twelve-mile limit, loaded with gamblers, beautiful women, whisky and mad music. The floating orgy, as related in detail by Jarrell, filled up four columns of lurid type. No other New York paper had the story. After some thorough investigating, the reason why became obvious: Jarrell had perpetrated a hoax. The ship was pure fancy. Jarrell had gotten no further than the nearest pub. His expense allotment had been drained, but not his imagination. Such creativity went unappreciated at the *Herald Tribune*. Jarrell was fired on the spot.

Obviously, Jarrell—tough on the outside and soft on the inside—fitted in perfectly with the Washington *Herald* spirit. That night, after taking the call from Hearst, he sighed and got busy. He gave the lone copyboy in the office two orders: "Get me a pot of hot coffee and go to my home and pick up my manuscript, *Murder in the Vieux Carré.*" The manuscript was a serial which had been rejected years before by a pulp magazine. But it was full of dialogue and there were three brunettes in it who wouldn't mind having their hair dyed. During the next six and a half hours Jarrell used this plot to help him turn out a 12,000-word, three-act play. At 9 A.M. he finished writing and typed on the title page: *Three Blondes*. When the first reporter showed up for work, Jarrell handed him the manuscript with instructions to take it to the copyright office. Then he went home and flopped into bed. Later in the day Hearst asked Jarrell for a copy of the play, and ten days later sent him a check for $200.

Not until three months later did Jarrell find out what lay behind the weird playwriting assignment. Hearst's friend, Marion Davies, had her heart set on starring in a movie version of John Erskine's new novel, *The Greeks Had a Word for It*. At a party one night Hearst learned that a rival studio was planning to use the book as a vehicle for actress Ina Claire. But it considered the original title too highbrow and intended to retitle the story *Three Blondes*. It was then that Hearst had put in a call to the *Herald* with his scheme to have *Three Blondes* copyrighted and thus beat the other studio to the punch.

Later, Jarrell had a falling out with Mrs. Patterson and shifted to the Philadelphia *Evening Ledger*. One day he received a letter from a major movie studio asking if he would consider selling his rights to *Three Blondes*. His mouth watering at the prospect of big money, Jarrell was tempted to say yes. But then it occurred to him that Hearst had placed his trust in him when he told him to put the copyright in his own name. The fact that he no longer worked for a Hearst organization did not, he felt, release him from his moral obligation to report the tentative offer. He sent Hearst a night letter. The next day Hearst wired back: "I suggest that you hold onto the copyright a little longer." Wincing, Jarrell notified the studio that he was not interested in selling the rights to his play.

Meanwhile, Hearst had wired Mrs. Patterson he had just learned Jarrell was no longer with the *Herald*. "He is a good man and did me a great favor once," the telegram said. Mrs. Patterson sent word to Jarrell that she'd like to have him back. Thoroughly disgusted now, Jarrell ignored the overture—while wishing he were unchivalrous enough to tell her what she could do with her job.

Jarrell never got another offer for *Three Blondes* and he never wrote another play. For many years before his death, in 1962, he supported himself writing short stories. Not surprisingly, he became a master of the ironic twist of plot.

ELEVEN

Cissy's Henhouse

Time magazine called it "Cissy's Henhouse." In the early thirties, before it was common on other newspapers, the Washington *Herald* harbored a large percentage of females, of varying ages, shapes, temperaments and talents. To the *Herald* building they brought noise, confusion, tears, beauty, romance, and, sometimes, an air of impending panic.

The women who flocked to the wide-open chance to develop careers of their own on the *Herald* extended from the kind who could competently report and/or write a murder story to those with a knack for turning out tips to government girls on how to become sophisticated. As a result, the paper was full of women-angled news stories and also reams of practical information through features, columns, and service departments. Cissy thus attracted—and held—a faithful female readership.

The woman's touch in newspapering was not original with Cissy; she had found the precedent right in her own family. Columns by and for women began to sprout in the Chicago *Tribune* during World War I. For the first sixty years of its life, the *Tribune* had been emphatically a man's newspaper. But under the guiding hand of the pretty and brilliant young Miss Mary King, the *Tribune* began to advise women readers on such vital matters as how to cope with assaults on their virtue, how to make themselves lovelier, how to cook and sew, what to wear, what to say, and how to be helpful to the needy. *Tribune* circulation jumped from 400,000 to 700,000 during this period. Miss

King later married Joe Patterson, Cissy's brother, and became women's editor of Patterson's New York *Daily News.*

The society and gossip columns in the *Herald* which titillated Washingtonians emerged, like Minerva, full-blown from Cissy's brain. She not only told the columnist how to write to avoid being dull; she often contributed some of the spicier items herself.

Cissy's stable of spirited fillies included some crack reporters and writers, the foremost of them Adela Rogers St. Johns, the ranking female star of the Hearst syndicate who was sent to cover Washington in the early 1930s. The two most startling members of the *Herald* stable were the Poe sisters, Elizabeth Poe and Vylla Poe Wilson, direct descendants of Edgar Allen Poe. At first glance, they seemed to belong at a poetry reading club rather than to the *Herald* city room. They were genteel ladies, reminiscent of lavender and old lace. But Elizabeth and Vylla knew everyone who counted in the capital, and they proved to be useful in some murder stories.

The sisters nonetheless measured up to the *Herald* standards of toughness. As young girls their father had taught them to shoot straight, and there came a time when this knowledge was put to potential use by the eccentric Washington hostess Evalyn Walsh McLean. After the Lindbergh baby was kidnaped, Mrs. McLean offered the notorious confidence man Gaston Means $50,000 to try to get in touch with the kidnapers. However, Mrs. McLean did not completely trust Means. Just in case he should try any skulduggery when he came to her mansion to collect the money, she stationed the Poe sisters behind the draperies with drawn pistols. There was no necessity to call on gunplay, as it turned out, but Mrs. McLean's suspicions were well founded; eventually Means was sentenced to prison for offering fake clues in the Lindbergh case.

The *Herald* columns told women how to do just about everything but have a baby. Many of them carried the by-lines of Cissy's own household staff. For example, her housekeeper, Mrs. Sibilla Campbell, had a column on household hints, and the Negro chef on Cissy's private railroad car, Alonzo, furnished recipes on cooking and cocktail-shaking. Both these columns were ghosted by a versatile young reporter, Betty Nowell (although the first household column was written by Cissy herself while—as she enjoyed telling her friends—she reclined in the bathtub).

When experts in a field were not handy, Cissy told her staff members to become experts. Once, she asked a girl reporter, Virgila Stephens, what she knew about beauty culture.

"Well," the girl quipped, "all I know is that I'm lucky if I can get my lipstick on straight."

"Tomorrow," Mrs. Patterson smiled back, "you start doing a column on beauty hints."

The column became one of the best on the paper. Under the by-line "Araminta," Virgila wrote as angelically as she looked.

A writer as versatile as Betty Nowell learned to be surprised at nothing. Once, Mrs. Patterson swooped down on her in the city room and cried, "Betty! Now we shall see you with a bird of paradise in your hair!" This was how Betty learned she was to do a night-club column to be called "The Nite Owl."

"The Nite Owl," the way Betty did it, did not please the night clubs. Instead of rewriting the press releases furnished by the night clubs, Betty dropped them in the wastebasket and went to watch the floor shows with a critical eye—sometimes accompanied by a third of the *Herald* staff. She thought most of the new acts were terrible, and said so in her column.

Mrs. Patterson suffered periodic guilt feelings because she was overworking Betty. Once, when Betty was depressed after the death of her mother, Cissy brought her to her country estate, Dower House, and told her to do her writing at poolside, with champagne within easy reach. When this failed to turn Betty into Little Miss Sunshine, Cissy offered to send her abroad to consult the eminent psychiatrist Carl Jung in Vienna. Betty declined.

Soon thereafter Betty went to the hospital to have her tonsils out, but she found no refuge there. Managing Editor Mike

Flynn telephoned her as soon as she was in bed and said Mrs.
Patterson wanted her to do a new series to be called, "The
Eternal Triangle." Each installment, to be told in the first person
purportedly by an anonymous, disillusioned woman, would be
an object lesson in why one should not take a married lover.

When Betty protested that her tonsils had to have priority,
Flynn said the orders were to start the series at once, and that,
further, Mrs. Patterson didn't believe in having one's tonsils out.
The upshot was that Betty yielded up not only her tonsils but a
daily soap-opera version of pitfalls of illicit love, created in
longhand in her hospital bed and rushed to the *Herald* city room
by a copyboy. Although she managed to meet the deadline for
the final poignant installment, she did so as the doctor was packing her throat; her activity had caused a hemorrhage.

Betty's success in imagining disastrous triangles led directly
to an even more offbeat assignment. Cissy wanted a series under
Betty's name revealing the private afterhours adventures of
Washington newsmen and newswomen. The idea embarrassed
Betty. She protested that she had never experienced anything
more devilish than a late-night session at the Herald Square Bar,
the staff hangout.

"Nonsense," replied Cissy. She handed Betty a copy of *Fall
Flight*, her novelized version of her own romantic early life as
an innocent bride in Europe. "You can turn out something like
this. Put all the drunken parties in," she urged.

Betty's life in Washington had been remarkably dissimilar
from Cissy's life at court balls in Vienna and St. Petersburg, but
since one didn't say "no" to Mrs. Patterson, she dutifully wrote
two chapters covering the first eight years of her life and turned
them in. That was the last she heard of the project.

Cissy had her own spy system, which kept her informed of
who was doing what to whom on the *Herald*, and it had led her
to believe that her staff was enjoying nocturnal adventures
which would divert *Herald* readers. The truth was that the
private life of Cissy's young staff was unconventional. When

Betty took an apartment on N Street, at the end of St. Matthew's Court, she was soon joined by quite a few of her colleagues, male as well as female, though the place consisted of nothing more than a cupboard kitchen, one bedroom, a dressing room and a bath. One impecunious reporter moved in with his bride, simply because he had nowhere else to take her, and stayed several nights. Another tried to *leave* his bride until he could get a job in New York and send for her, but Betty decided that was going too far.

Betty recalled later on that she was protected by sheer numbers, if nothing else, but that her colleagues eventually decided she needed a watchman. They gave her one named Horace.

"I was embarrassed to tears about it," Betty recalls, "and am thoroughly ashamed of my part in it. Horace was a dummy who wore a watchman's uniform and sat in the window of a spark-plug factory on the road between Washington and Alexandria. The legend was that he was a real man who had fallen into a vat of spark-plug fluid and been petrified—anyway, that's what the sightseeing-bus driver said. Some of the *Herald* people stole him one night and he was instantly news—rewards were offered. The people who stole him had a problem of what to do with him. So they propped him up against my door, and he fell in one night—just like Jimmy Cagney in *The Public Enemy*. He was to be my bodyguard, sitting in the window on the fire escape that led down to the then mixed St. Matthew's Court. He made me more and more nervous, though, and finally I put him on the dressing-room floor, where he scared poor Betty Owen half to death one night. I forgot to tell her he was there."

Betty told her friends they would have to ditch Horace. One night they put him in an auto and drove around Washington looking for an appropriate place to dump him. In the car were Betty and four of the *Herald's* more free-wheeling reporters— Mason Peters, George Waters, Charley Dockarty, and Bill Flythe. On Connecticut Avenue they came upon City Editor Ray Helgesen and he flagged them down. Helgesen approached the car, opened the door and noticed the body on the floor. He asked who it was, and Waters gave him the name of a police reporter on a rival Washington paper who was known chiefly as an alcoholic. Helgesen—at that moment no model of sobriety himself —peered at the body by the light of a match and said, "So it is."

The reporters drove off and decided that Horace deserved an attention-getting finale. They hanged him from the Calvert Street bridge above Rock Creek Drive. At dawn a driver spotted him from the road below and gave the alarm. The fire department was summoned to cut the dummy down. The *Evening Star* carried a front-page story about the incident, speculating that it was the work of some cub reporters. Betty and her friends were aghast at the idea that they had behaved like cub reporters. Even more sobering was the announcement by Helgesen that he would fire anyone who he discovered had been a participant. There was not much danger of that happening, for Helgesen would have had to admit that he had mistaken a dummy for a well-known police reporter.

Betty Nowell was the first beneficiary of Cissy's penchant for giving away her clothes. One day in November 1930, Mrs. Patterson called her in and said, almost in embarrassment, "Betty, I have all these clothes. Will you take some of them off my hands?" She telephoned her chauffeur, and later in the day he appeared in front of the *Herald* building in a Packard filled to the roof with feminine apparel of every kind. Betty was approximately her boss's size and she went home that night with several expensive evening gowns—something she hadn't worn since she had gone to high school proms in 1927.

After that, Mrs. Patterson periodically invited some of the girls on her staff to "tea" at the Du Pont Circle mansion. There was no tea served, but Cissy would take them to a large room adjoining her bedroom on the third floor. It was crowded with rack after rack of suits and dresses. "Let's have a fire sale!" she would say to her secretary, and invite the girls to help themselves.

In the course of the wardrobe dispersals over the years, some of the staff blossomed out in astonishing getups. For instance, one day Cissy decided to throw out all the extensive wardrobe she had acquired after the death of her second husband, Elmer Schlesinger, in 1929. The next day the *Herald* city room looked like a funeral parlor. All the girls were wearing deep mourning.

Cissy's "hens" were thrilled to be able to sport clothes which were the best-made and the most expensive they had ever touched. Cissy's sense of style was wisely acknowledged—when Paris couturiers, in 1934, divided the title of "Best Dressed Woman in the World" between twenty famous ladies, Cissy was one of them. Her sizes were in the normal range, except for her feet. They were so small that only one girl on her staff could wear her shoes, and she became the best-shod newswoman in town.

The least popular of her hand-me-downs were her hats. Cissy had a weakness for wide, wild, floppy "creations," and affected them long after she should have sent them to the attic. She was fond of tailored suits too and also fell in love with *them*. One day, in the *Herald* corridor, she passed a girl who was striding along in a smart, tailored suit. She stopped her and admired it. The girl explained that it was Cissy's own and jokingly—she thought— remarked that if she liked it that much she'd give it back. Cissy —who was occasionally an Indian giver—promptly accepted.

The girl saw Cissy wear the suit once, and then pass it on to another staff member.

Cissy did well by her female favorites. She gave a Persian-lamb jacket with mink collar and cuffs to Betty Nowell (who shortly thereafter, in 1939, quit the *Herald* and went to Chicago with her husband, Ray Brennan, who became a top reporter on the Chicago *Sun-Times*).

Cissy's perfumes—heavy and exotic—were also available at her "fire sales," and the *Herald* was able to boast the best-scented as well as the best-dressed white-collar girls in town.

Cissy gave more and more job opportunities to women in the late thirties. In 1939, her *Times-Herald* hired what may well have been the first copygirl on any newspaper, though a few years later, when copyboys were being drafted into service, copygirls became a commonplace. The girl was Lina Hoffman, whose face, shape and personality were much appreciated in the city room. Because her ambition was to become a reporter, Lina went out of her way to catch Cissy's eye, and Cissy in turn paid more attention to her than she did to most of the older women. In fact, she continually gave Lina advice on grooming. Once, she suggested to Lina that she cut her hair shorter.

"Don't you like it?" asked Lina.

"Honey, it looks untidy around the office," her boss told her. Lina got her hair cut.

Cissy maintained many charities for her girls who fell down on their luck, but few were ever known, because she insisted on keeping them secret. When she took over as editor of the *Herald*, a reporter on Hearst's afternoon paper, the Washington *Times*, told her that a onetime top labor reporter, Millie Morris, was in sore straits. Millie, a niece of Samuel Gompers, was having trouble concentrating, and consequently could not hold a job for long. Cissy, who didn't even know her, anonymously provided an income large enough for her to eat but small enough so that she would still be inclined to seek work. She never found out who was helping her.

One of Cissy's most talked-of acts of charity happened on Christmas Eve, 1932. That night, as Cissy emerged from the third-floor elevator of the *Herald* building, she almost tripped over Matt Tighe, a *Herald* rewrite man who was witty, erratic and lovable. Matt was on his knees, crawling from the reference library toward the city room. He had barely survived an office party that was wild even by *Herald* standards. Cissy, as tolerant as only one who loves champagne can be tolerant, reacted as if it were normal to find Tighe on all fours. She smiled and wished him a Merry Christmas.

"Merry Christmas be goddamned to you!" the rewrite man said.

"Why do you say that?"

"Do you realize," Tighe asked her bitterly, "that you've got a girl in there in the library who's the sole support of her mother and you're paying her fourteen dollars a week?"

Cissy turned on her heel and strode toward her office. Arthur Reilly, an assistant city editor, had witnessed the horrifying exchange from the door of the city room. He slipped back to his desk and waited for the roll of thunder. The very least he expected was a buzz from The Lady and an order to fire Tighe on the spot. But nothing happened.

On Christmas afternoon, Reilly was again on duty at the city desk. He received a call from the *Herald* receptionist. She asked him to get the librarian—Helen Parker—on the telephone. Reilly explained that it was Helen's day off. He gathered from the receptionist's tone that the request came from Mrs. Patterson.

At that moment, Helen Parker was sitting in her two-room apartment. She had been unable to afford a turkey and was feeling sorry for herself and her mother. At four o'clock there was a knock on the door. Curious as to who might be making a Christmas call, she glanced out the window. A Cadillac limousine was at the curb, its motor running. Helen opened the door and saw a liveried chauffeur. He handed her an envelope bearing the engraved address of Mrs. Patterson. Then he bowed and left.

Helen opened the envelope and read this note:

"Dear Miss Parker, I'm so sorry. I didn't realize the circumstances. Enclosed is a check which may help. Sincerely, Eleanor Patterson."

The check in the envelope was for $1000.

The next day Helen asked Reilly what to do with it.

"Get down to the bank and cash it before she changes her mind," he advised.

Later, Mrs. Patterson heard that the girl had spent $600 of the $1000 to buy a piano. She kept an eye on Helen, liked her and eventually made her a personal secretary—temporarily. Once, when Mrs. Patterson dictated a letter to Arthur Brisbane, she ended it, "With all best wishes," but Helen transcribed it as, "With love and kisses." Mrs. Patterson took a poor view of such carelessness, and Helen wound up as women's editor.

The Tighe-Parker incident proved, to the satisfaction of the staff, that their society boss had her humanitarian moments. And all agreed that Matt Tighe on all fours was worth ten union leaders making stand-up demands.

Characteristically, while pioneering in women's wide-ranging roles on newspapers, Cissy often, inexplicably, disparaged the idea. Once, in an interview in the *American Press* in 1934, she was quoted as saying:

"I don't approve of women working on newspapers. I wouldn't hire a woman. Only one female reporter works for me. She covers fashions and begged for the job. They are more difficult to manage. Sometimes I have to take advantage of the fact that I am a woman to get things done around here."

All this proves is that Cissy Patterson was capable of saying anything at any time if it suited her mood; when she got off this remark she had a couple of dozen women working for her. It was obvious, however, that she did consider women "more difficult to manage" than men. She was certainly much harder on them. If she was in a foul mood, she took it out on the girls. On those mornings when she came steaming through the city room, the editors and subeditors hid out. They knew where she was heading—the women's department. There, in her quiet but withering voice, she would reduce one or more of the women to white-faced trembling, perhaps for some egregious blunder she had spotted in the paper that day. Then she would have lunch and settle back, more relaxed, to deal with the male editors and their problems.

Cissy's hand showed up in every phase of the women's departments. Once, her drama critic, Mabelle Jennings, wrote a review of a Mae West film which ridiculed it as being vulgar and unfunny. Mrs. Patterson read a carbon of Mabelle's review and laughed—then ordered Mabelle to write another, more favorable review. Cissy did not encourage sophisticated movie reviews in the *Herald;* she maintained that movie fans wanted to read nothing more adult than the intellectual level of movie magazines—and the movies themselves. The fact that Mae West was one of her friends just might also have influenced her.

In any case, the girls on the staff told one another that she would never have asked Mason Peters to redo a movie review during his term as critic. Cissy did not humiliate the men on her staff.

One woman on the staff whom Cissy always treated with velvet gloves was Ruth Jones, who wrote under the name of Jean Eliot and was regarded as the best society editor in town. Ruth had a sensitivity and a ladylike dignity which not even Cissy could have dented. Her first assistant was Marie McNair, later to become society editor of the Washington *Post.*

Another star in Cissy's female galaxy during the thirties was Helen Ray Hagner, who did a column on proper manners and dress. Helen was a sister of Isabella Hagner, who had been White House social secretary under Theodore Roosevelt and for many years had run the Washington Social Bureau. The cooking editor was Frances Northcross. When she lectured on cooking, as a *Herald* promotion stunt, the sessions had to be staged in one of Washington's largest movie houses in the morning to accommodate the huge audience.

Cissy's genius for creating a popular column—and her quixotic handling of the distaff side—is best illustrated by the story of Alva Brewer. In 1932, Mrs. Brewer's husband went bankrupt and she had three children to support. Kentucky-bred, she had been in Washington since 1915, was jolly, gregarious and sharp-witted, and had a wide circle of prominent persons as friends. On the advice of newspaper friends, she wrote a dozen sample gossip columns and submitted them to Mrs. Patterson's secretary. The result was a summons to Mrs. Patterson's office.

Cissy told her she would have to be trained to newspaper writing, but she added encouragingly:

"These columns are very, very personal without being vicious about the people you write about. It's a new angle. I doubt that people will like it. People are not used to having themselves, their conversations, their parties written about so intimately for public consumption."

Cissy laughed, delighted at the thought, and commented: "You might lose all your friends." She told Alva to submit items every day for use in the column then being done thrice weekly by Mabelle Jennings under the title, "Along the Rialto."

Alva worked hard at digging up items, and a month later she got another summons to see Mrs. Patterson. This time the lady was in excellent humor.

"Your own column will appear on the third of June," she told Alva. "The title will be 'Peter Carter Says.' I want you to write under a man's name. It'll be confusing—deliberately. I don't want anyone to know who's writing the column. If the public dislikes it, they won't know who to blame. If they like it, we'll let them know who's doing it."

Unnecessarily, she added: "No one on this paper will give out information until I say so."

"Peter Carter Says" was a rousing success. Its author did not remain anonymous for long, and her identity became so entwined with the column that even her own friends took to calling Alva "Peter." Then she made a mistake. At the suggestion of her husband, she had the title copyrighted under her own name. He had pointed out—wisely, she thought, at the time—that Mrs. Patterson was unpredictable and that if Alva should get fired she would have a legal claim to continue writing under "Peter Carter," the name she had built up.

Mrs. Patterson inevitably learned of the private copyrighting (how, Alva never knew) and was furious. She summoned her to her office, where she had already seated the managing editor, the circulation manager, and two lawyers. As Alva recalled the scene later:

"The silence was positively deafening. 'You wished to see me, Mrs. Patterson?' I asked. I did not get another word in for some time. Her usually rich and mellow voice was pitched to a strident key. I have heard many times the phrase, 'livid with anger,' but had never seen it before. In what seemed like a torrent of words I discovered that Mrs. Patterson had found out that the title 'Peter Carter Says' had been copyrighted and *not* by her.

" 'Did you do this?' she fairly screamed at me. I walked over to the chair facing her. 'Don't sit down—stand up!' she ordered. I had not intended sitting down. I simply wanted something to lean on. I was nauseated.

" 'Did you?' she repeated. 'Yes,' I told her and endeavored to explain why. It was useless. The session did not last long, but to me it seemed endless. Mrs. Patterson was filled with directives. The column was to be taken away from me. Who was to do it, she didn't say. I was to be demoted to third-assistant society editress. The copyright was to be turned over to Mrs. Patterson in the quickest possible time."

Alva Brewer was instructed to report to the society department every day. Each morning Mrs. Patterson looked in as she passed the society department. Alva said "good morning," but the greeting was not returned. However, the cruelest punishment was this: The column was continued but the writer was anonymous. Alva felt that the column was not being done badly but that it lacked continuity—a tipoff that it was undoubtedly being put together by several different persons.

It wasn't until after the copyright had been duly assigned to Mrs. Patterson, several weeks later, that Alva was told she could have her column back. Then she was offered a renewal of her contract—but without an expected raise. Managing Editor Flynn explained that Mrs. Patterson felt she had been disloyal. She would never give Alva a raise as long as she lived! She was true to her word. Though "Peter Carter Says" became a Washington institution for over two decades, its author never got a raise.

Alva Brewer's idea for a column coincided exactly with Cissy Patterson's concept of how to make a paper interesting: personalities were news, particularly if their goings-on were reported in a very personal way. "Peter Carter" broadened the personality category to include what she called the "burghers," that is, the Washington businessmen and their wives. Heretofore Washington newspapers had limited themselves to mentioning only the names of those in the society and diplomatic sets—and in a relentlessly stodgy manner.

Not long after she created Peter Carter, Cissy launched another column. One night during the Democratic National Convention of 1932, she was drinking with friends at Chicago's plush Tavern Club and became amused by a pretty society girl named Martha Blair.

"You talk so funny, you ought to write a Washington column for me," Mrs. Patterson told her. Mrs. Blair was thrilled. She needed a job to support her two sons; her husband, William Mitchell Blair, like Alva Brewer's, had just gone through bankruptcy. After the convention, she packed off to Washington with her children, hoping that Cissy would recall the job offer made at a time of bibulous conviviality.

In Washington, Martha put in a call to the Patterson mansion. Cissy sounded vague but asked her to come over. They chatted over mint juleps, and Martha asked if Cissy remembered the invitation to become a columnist on the *Herald*.

Although she had forgotten about the incident, Cissy replied with a throaty laugh, "Oh, darling, I'd *love* to have you do it." After more conversation, Cissy said, "You'll write a column about your friends in society and we'll call it 'These Charming People.'"

This was the title of a best-selling novel by Michael Arlen. So Martha asked, "Will Michael Arlen mind?"

"Oh, that's a book, darling," Cissy reassured her. "This is a column."

Martha approached the project with trepidation. She knew nothing about Washington, and intuition told her that pleasing Cissy would not be easy. At first, Martha Blair was more than a columnist, once she had re-established social connections in the capital. At any time she might pick up the phone and hear Cissy's voice drawling, "I want to give a *love*-ly party, darling. Now you just go and ask all these nice friends of yours—all those people you know."

This meant Martha should consult with Cissy's social secretary about the guest list, discussing how many and who should come.

In 1939 Martha, who had been divorced, married Arthur Krock, chief Washington correspondent of the New York *Times* and a good friend of Mrs. Patterson. Early in 1940, Cissy telephoned Krock late one night and said of his bride, "I'm sick of that spoiled creature. I won't have her around. Her column bores me."

When Krock asked what she didn't like about the column, Cissy said: "The column's not catty. Martha writes only nice things about nice people. It bores me."

"Why don't you fire her, then?" Krock suggested. He thought Martha had been writing "These Charming People" long enough, so he was pleased when Cissy replied that she planned to do just that. Krock said nothing to his wife. A few days later, as he expected, she told him that Mrs. Patterson had fired her.

Martha Krock was not too surprised herself and was greatly relieved. While she liked Cissy, she realized that she had always enjoyed cracking the whip. When she married Arthur, Cissy had lost her power over her.

TWELVE

Almost a Nelly Bly

Cissy Patterson stood on the edge of the Mojave Desert and squinted into the hot sun baking the mountain in the distance. Somewhere along the steep and winding trail through the rocks was the most elusive subject in the world, Albert Einstein. A few minutes ago, at a house in Palm Springs where the world-famous scientist was staying, the butler had told her he had gone for a walk up the mountain trail.

Cissy began climbing the dry, hot trail, uncertainly picking her way between rocks and crevices and mentally rehearsing the few questions she thought would be worthy of the Einstein brain. They had to do with "ether drift," relativity, space and time, subjects which had only the vaguest meaning to her utterly unscientific mind. She made her way around a huge rock and there, bangsmack in front of her, was the great man himself.

"He was gazing out across the wide and lovely and silent desert," she wrote later. "A white handkerchief, knotted at each of the four corners, rested upon the famous shock of curly gray hair.

"Evidently, the professor was taking a sun bath, whilst contemplating, for he was relativity in the nude.

"I couldn't go up, so I had to come down, crestfallen and wondering what a regular determined go-getter she-reporter would do under the circumstances."

Three nights later, Cissy had a more revealing look at Einstein, even though this time he was fully dressed. He sat directly in front of her at the preview of the Charlie Chaplin movie *City Lights* in Los Angeles. Others in the row with him were Mrs. Einstein, Gloria Swanson, Marion Davies, and Chaplin himself.

During the overture, the professor was "at peace, abstracted," Cissy reported to her readers, but when the newsreel flashed on, displaying a zigzag of pretty girls dancing across the stage, "the professor's eyebrows shot up in semicircles of astonishment." Then, as *City Lights* began to unfold, "a look of astonishment settled on the professor's face, like a child at a Christmas pantomime," even when the whole audience, including Chaplin himself, roared at Chaplin's antics.

Cissy's reportorial account continued:

When the little blind girl came on the screen, Frau Einstein began gently to shake her head. "Ach weh," she sighed. "Nu-ach weh, ach weh."

Suddenly, just at the end of *City Lights*, your heart is caught up, squeezed out, twisted. I began to cry then, and pretty hard too, but I choked, blinked and managed to take one last look at Einstein.

An enormous white handkerchief, maybe the same which covered his head while he was taking a sun bath on the Mojave Desert, almost concealed his face, but you could see his big, sorrowful eyes still wide with wonderment, brimming with tears.

There didn't seem to be much use after that in trying to get a regular interview with Professor Einstein. Why ask him if the universe, space and time are finite or infinite? It's all the same to you and me. Either way it makes your head ache just to think about it.

Isn't it more interesting to know that Einstein, who understands better than anyone else the sublime arrangement of the universe, can also understand and weep at the heartbreak of a little clown?

When the Hearst papers published Cissy's report on Einstein, including her retreat after she spied him in the nude, she got her answer as to what a "go-getter she-reporter" would have done in those circumstances. Hearst's No. 1 pundit, and Cissy's good friend, Arthur Brisbane, wrote in his column, "Today":

> Under such circumstances, Nelly Bly, best American woman reporter with the possible exception of Dorothy Dix, would have got a blanket, put it over Dr. Einstein, and got the interview, if necessary sitting on the blanket and Einstein to keep him from getting away. Mrs. Patterson is a first-class reporter. Her account of Charlie Chaplin's first night, with Dr. Einstein shedding big scientific tears, and Mrs. Einstein saying, "Ach weh," should be read by all young reporters. Unfortunately, Mrs. Patterson has more than a million dollars income, thanks to her grandfather, Joseph Medill, who founded the Chicago *Tribune,* so she won't do the things she might do. Few succeed, in spite of wealth, the worst of all handicaps.

Cissy's retreat from the naked Einstein was her only failure as a reporter. Indeed, it was the only time in her life she was ever intimidated by anything, man or beast. During the first years in which she edited the Washington *Herald,* she traveled and reported extensively. Many *Herald* reporters privately remarked that she was "the best damn reporter on the paper," and Hearst thought so highly of her work that he syndicated her writings in all his dailies. In typical Hearst fashion, he sought to capitalize on Mrs. Patterson's name value, billing her as the rich-woman-turned-editor-reporter. But he also genuinely admired Cissy's style.

The Einstein story was published as part of a series she wrote while traveling across the country in the winter of 1930–31. A month earlier, she had interviewed a man who was perhaps as well known as Einstein, though for less praiseworthy reasons.

While motoring around Miami Beach, Cissy told her chauffeur she wanted to see the residence of Alphonse "Scarface" Capone, then already a legendary gangster. As they drove slowly past the ostentatious bungalow, Cissy saw the hoodlum himself standing on the sidewalk. She recognized him, she informed her readers, from "the scar on his cheek, like the welt from the lash of a whip."

Mrs. Patterson asked her chauffeur to pull over to the curb. She alighted and approached Capone, who was wearing a sport shirt and appeared to be relaxed. She introduced herself as the sister of Joe Patterson, publisher of the New York *Daily News*. This seemed to make no great impression on the gangster, but his suspicions were overcome by his pride as a home owner. He began to talk about his house, and abruptly said to Cissy, "Come in and let me show you around."

She reported:

And in I went. The big iron gate clanked to and was bolted behind me.

He showed me through the garden to the water font. A double-storied loggia or bath house stood beside a deep, long swimming pool.

It didn't seem polite somehow, to turn around and take a look at Capone's attendants. But whenever I glanced aside, one of those neatly dressed, quiet young men, just happened along, standing there as if absent-minded, lounging in the shadow between the palm trees.

I got one good look at Capone himself right out in the sunshine. He has the neck and shoulders of a wrestler, one of those prodigious Italians, thick-chested, close to six feet tall. The muscles of his arms stretched the sleeves of his light-brown suit, so that it seemed to be cut too small for him.

Once I looked at his eyes. Ice-gray, ice-cold eyes. You can't any more look into the eyes of Capone than you can look into the eyes of a tiger . . . Capone sat impassive as a Buddha, yet you began to sense the painful, nervous tensity under the stolid exterior. His enormous hands rested half-clenched upon the table. Without raising his voice or looking around, he called for a servant. A man in a white apron simply tore into the room. "My goodness," I whispered, "I wish I could get service like that at home."

Though she did not tell her readers, Cissy accepted a straight shot of whisky—and downed it neat—to gain the gangster's confidence.

Capone—he said it was pronounced without sounding the final "e"—told Cissy he was thirty-one years old, but he looked to her to be closer to forty-five, doubtless because his way of life exacted its toll. He reminded her of Mussolini. Cissy confided to her readers she got a little scared after she brought up the subject of his recent arrest in Philadelphia. "His heavy head thrust forward, he said, 'Oh, you think I am afraid? I'll show you how afraid I was,'" Cissy reported.

The article continued:

And he went on to tell the story of his arrest in Philadelphia for carrying a revolver. Capone's eyes are dime-novel gangster's eyes . . . I could feel their menace. The stirring of the tiger. For just a second I went a little sick. I had to fight the impulse to jump up and run blindly away.

What happened was probably this . . . I had struck full on the sensitive spot. I had aroused Capone for the moment to a flash of real hate and rage. The one thing every gangster fears most is fear. One sign of weakness, one second of faltering, and his own wolf pack is upon him, tearing at his throat.

Capone bragged to his interviewer that he was still "king," but complained that "they" (government agents) were forever after him. "All the time trying to frame me," he added. "Why, they've got me framed in Chicago now. If I don't answer that tax charge, they're trying to get me on a trumped-up vagrancy act. It ain't fair."

(It was the income-tax charge that was to imprison Capone until he became ill and died behind bars.)

Bitterly, Capone told Cissy that he had paid several hundred thousand dollars for his Florida home and had as much right to live there with his wife and kids as any man. He had been arrested eleven times in three days in Florida. But, he declared, this smacked too much of persecution even for "the crackers down here." He felt the wholesale arrests had backfired on the police and won him some public sympathy.

Capone as a human being somehow had "gotten to" Cissy, and as she left she wished him good luck.

"I meant it sincerely," she told her readers. "It has been said many times, with truth, that women have a special kind of sympathy for gangsters. If you don't understand why, consult Dr. Freud."

Cissy's treatment of Capone was in tune with the times. She did not treat him as a glamorous person, as the movies in the thirties came close to doing, but her description of him—one of the most vivid eyewitness accounts of Capone on record— showed her sneaking admiration for one who defied convention and the law. The truth is that Cissy liked the company of rascals, "if they have a bit of charm about them," as she once put it. Capone had no charm, but the raw animal force of the outlaw fascinated her. Characteristically, her story pronounced no moral judgment on Capone. She was frequently critical of people, but almost never from a lofty moral viewpoint.

The reportorial assignment which brought Mrs. Patterson the most lavish buildup in the Hearst press was the kind of stunt which always has been—and doubtless always will be—a staple of journalism. Just before Christmas 1931, she disguised herself in order to find out at firsthand whether destitute women were walking the streets because they could not find honest work. She would spend several days as plain "Maude Martin," a penniless woman looking for a job.

To sharpen the metamorphosis—and to add a dash of glamor to the first installment—Cissy set out for the world of "lost women" directly from a swank embassy party. She referred to the embassy anonymously as "the most elegant and the most deliberately luxurious in Washington." She chose not to divulge the name of her luxury-loving diplomat-host, she explained, because, "after all, nothing is closer to the intimate life of a man than his dinner table, unless it is his bed."

Immediately after the elegant dinner, Cissy excused herself and was driven home. Describing the preparations for her leave-taking, she wrote as if she were taking a journey to some wild, far-off country instead of merely slipping into the capital's seamy neighborhoods only a few miles from Du Pont Circle. In her bedroom, she told her readers, a bright fire was burning in the little grate and the gold-brocaded bed was turned down, revealing peach-colored crepe-de-Chine sheets.

After tearing herself away from her inviting bed and grate, Cissy shed her shiny sequin and crepe dress and donned the "shabby-genteel" outfit which her maid had scrounged from her fabulous wardrobe. The getup may not have made her look like the poorest woman in Washington, but it must have made her seem an eccentric. It consisted of a year-old felt hat ("Any last year's hat looks strange enough"), an old corduroy brown coat and skirt, faded woolen stockings, and a pair of "historical brown golf shoes." Incredibly, only as an afterthought did the maid un-clasp Cissy's necklace and bracelets and drop them on the dress-ing table. Then, slipping into a ten-year-old tweed overcoat, Cissy told her chauffeur to drop her at Fifth and H Streets NW. There, at the end of the installment, she vanished into the night.

Unfortunately, Cissy's adventures in disguise did not live up to the exciting standard set by her departure. She finds a haven at the Salvation Army and rooms with some down-at-heel women whose miserable case histories take up a good share of the other installments. One installment is concerned with the disguised millionairess' problems in sharing cold cream, borrowing tooth-paste and makeup, and taking cold baths. It was Cissy's first—and last—taste of urban, plebeian living, and it was brief enough to divert her.

Cissy never did find a job as Maude Martin; but one experi-ence brought her face to face with an existence which made her own seem pointless, she told her readers. She had applied as a maid at a home where the mother of three young children was obviously overworked, but could afford to pay only four dollars a week, and Cissy was asking for six.

> She looked so little and so very tired, yet loving and infinitely patient. She held the big, little boy in her arms, comforted him, and went right on talking to me over his head. I looked back at her and thought, "You spend all your life giving, and I spend nearly all my life taking," and felt ashamed of myself.

This was one of the very few occasions where Cissy publicly hinted at the lack of womanly fulfillment in her outwardly brilliant life.

In her concluding installment, Cissy decides it is possible for destitute women to find a job in Washington if they are willing to work with their hands, but the white-collar woman who wants a job as stenographer, saleswoman or hairdresser had indeed fallen on "bitter, pinching times." Her only word of consolation was that she herself never heard an unkind word from anyone during her job-seeking. Indeed, this is what made the series dull reading. No one tried to rape her, or suggested she adopt the easy way to make money.

Cissy's reportorial assignments were virtually her only brush with the ill-fed, the ill-housed and the ill-clothed during the Depression. She was always moved by misery, and wanted something done about it—instantly. When many disgruntled World War I veterans converged on Washington as a vast "bonus army," in 1932, Cissy mingled with them as a reporter to find out whether they were shiftless malcontents or men who should be taken seriously. They convinced her of their sincerity.

"Don't let us try to forget it," she wrote. "It's fixed. It's fanatical. The bonus. They have just one idea, and just one emotion. Rightly or wrongly. No matter what they have been taught to tell you. Every man Jack of them believe they've been gypped—gypped by our government."

"Right now they are being fed. But supposing these men get hungry?" she asked ominously.

In 1936, Cissy undertook her most ambitious series almost by accident. Traveling north from Birmingham after Ray Helgesen's wedding to Kitty Barrett, Cissy found it hot even in her air-conditioned car. Through the train window, she saw mile after mile of shimmering fields and cabins and wondered what life was like there. The thought weighed on her as the train sped on, and she mentioned it repeatedly to her companion, Jackie Martin, who was Mrs. Patterson's special assistant in charge of art as well as the *Herald's* star photographer. By the time they pulled into the station at Chattanooga, they decided to go and see for themselves.

At Harriman, Tennessee, at the edge of the Cumberland plateau, Cissy and Jackie rented a Model-A Ford and began their tour of the economically exhausted areas of eastern Tennessee.

Cissy was deeply moved with what she saw and turned it into six long installments for *Herald* readers. The opening paragraphs of the first installment showed the impact of the experience on her:

Now I know a little more about *Pilgrim's Progress*.

For I have seen a hundred Hills Difficult, and as many Sloughs of Despond, each with its quota of good Americans whose Constitutional rights have somehow failed to put shoes on their feet and hope in their hearts . . .

Most earnestly, then, as I tell what I can of what I've seen and what I think ought to be done about it, I hope you will bear in mind that these hills and sloughs are part of the United States, and therefore your responsibility and mine.

I'll tell you my conclusion now; either Willie and his kind must be lifted up and set on the road to economic security and human decency, or we may as well "give 'em poison gas," as a friend of mine has suggested.

And I hope too that I don't get a lot of letters from indignant chambers of commerce pointing out to me the industry

and progressiveness of the towns down in the cotton and
hill country. I know about those chipper little cities and I
think they're fine. But I know, too, about pellagra, typhoid,
illiteracy and anemia in the background, and I won't be
frightened off my subject.

After all, I'm a red-haired woman editor, and I have something to say.

In her final installment Cissy quotes approvingly from a special
interview with Harry Hopkins, then WPA administrator. The
only solution Hopkins had was resettlement. He said his agencies
had already done some of that—for example, placing 600 share-
croppers on 16,000 acres in Georgia, and others in Arkansas—
but he emphasized that such projects had to be supervised and
the sharecropper "hand-picked." Cissy felt the same way—that
the federal government had to take a direct hand in solving the
economic problems in what she called the "hardscrabble South."

In 1932, Cissy again covered the G.O.P. convention for the
Hearst press, but this time she found a different situation from
her first convention in 1920. The syndicate gave her arrival on
her private car in a big buildup, complete with a photograph
published in the Chicago papers. But she soon found the fore-
ordained nomination of President Hoover a dreary affair, and
she seized the chance to vent some of her views about politics
in general.

"In the last three days," she went on to explain, "trillions of
words have been roared from the rostrum, shouted on the
streets, in the hotels, across dinner tables, whispered behind
locked doors, maybe. Plans, plots. Counterplots. Schemes. Gossip. Endless speculation. A really stupendous activity—that is,
for a flop convention—and yet everybody knew the exact text
of the end of the story beforehand."

Cissy did very few political articles as such, and perhaps her
best was an interview with John L. Lewis, then president of the
C.I.O. as well as the United Mine Workers. Lewis was a good
friend of Mrs. Patterson and a frequent guest at her parties and

those of Evalyn Walsh McLean. Yet she reported the interview as a reporter sitting at the feet of a great man, scribbling furiously in her note pad to keep up with the flow of his rumbling talk.

The Lewis interview, published on November 26, 1937, made news. In it he proposed that capital and labor join together to try to revive the sick economy of the nation—a surprising notion at that time coming from this symbol of militant labor. Lewis also revealed to Cissy that he had cooled off on the New Deal. He said he still admired Franklin D. Roosevelt's aims and ideals but was highly critical of the inefficient way FDR was trying to carry them out. This was one of the first tipoffs of Lewis' eventual complete break with Roosevelt. The interview, printed in its entirety in the Hearst papers, filled nearly three columns. Most of it consisted of blunt quotes from Lewis in answer to his interviewer's blunt questions.

Cissy was never satisfied with what she wrote. She liked to rewrite her copy many times, searching for precisely the right word to express the scene or the thought. She would like to have each paragraph polished as brightly as a jewel. She never felt that she succeeded, and she continually disparaged her writing ability. This was not false humility. She was a keen critic of writing, and bore down hardest on her own.

If Cissy was not a great journalist, she must be given her due as an interesting reporter. Almost nothing she wrote was dull, and it was never overwritten (a sin to which many mass-circulation reporters of the 1920s and 1930s—particularly those working for Hearst—were addicted). Cissy's style was distinctive without being gaudy. It was basically an ability to communicate, candidly, tersely, bitingly, often humorously.

Cissy admired good newspaper reporters more than any other professional group, and considered them the salt of the earth. Although she assumed the guise of a reporter occasionally, and with success, it was not really her trade. In February 1936, she

was interviewed about newspapering as she debarked from her
private railroad car at the depot in New Orleans.

"I'd give anything to be young and husky and a newspaper
reporter," she told her interviewer. "And would I be one hell-
roaring reporter!"

The remark was quoted in *Time* magazine, which frequently
used Cissy's peregrinations to enliven its press section.

Cissy's style and originality came through most sharply in the
unique "essays"—for want of a better word—which she played
on her front page, boxed between heavy lines. Her startling jab
at Alice Roosevelt Longworth in a front-page box shortly after
she became editor had caught Washington's fancy in 1930, and
she printed other boxes whenever she was in the mood through
the years. The boxes revealed Cissy's aggressiveness and pungent
charm.

One of her first boxes dealt with two subjects which always
fascinated her—the battle of the sexes, and part of its weaponry,
talk. Here it is:

TALK

Men have always accused women of talking too much.
Talking their heads off. Driving men wild. The truth is
that men accuse women of talking too much because men
want to talk 100 percent of the time. I know two girls who
went to a party and, on a bet, said nothing all night excepting, "Not really!" and "How wonderful!" They weren't
pretty girls but they were the belles of the ball.

Men around the office talk like women around the home.
You know what I mean. No woman can spill language
around like a man, once he gets started.

Do you know the story of young George arriving home
on vacation? He started right in to tell all about himself.
What he had done. What he was going to do. All about what
he had said and what he was going to say. His old colored
mammy, sitting on the back porch mending his sock, did
NOT look up over her glasses. But pretty soon she said,
"Fo' Gawd, Marse George, you surely am loose with lan-

gwich. Seems like maybe you were vaccinated with a victrola needle at birth."

Men will go on complaining about women's verbosity. It seems the more women babble on like the restless brook, the more men converse like the sewing machine.

Cissy got her idea for this box from the behavior of a friend whom she admired tremendously, Maude Parker Childs. Like Cissy, Maude attended many of the brilliant parties given in the late twenties and early thirties in New York City by Herbert Bayard Swope. The guests included the famous from the worlds of art and politics. Maude was beautiful, in the classic American style of the Gibson Girl, and felt she was not obligated to contribute anything beyond her look of sweet surrender. In fact, there were only three expressions she ever uttered at a party: "Yes," "No," and "How interesting!" As the party ended, many of the male guests invariably remarked to Swope that Maude was the most "brilliant" woman they had ever met. Maude actually was extremely intelligent, but she saved her ability to communicate for more commercial outlets and she became a successful magazine writer.

Maude's party behavior delighted Cissy, for she had long known the secret of how to react to men. When she was in the mood, she could charm any male simply by listening to him raptly and interjecting, at appropriate intervals, "Not really!" or "How wonderful!"

In her boxes Cissy sometimes disarmingly mixed her modesty with her pride in a very feminine manner. One box was reprinted throughout the Hearst press, accompanied by an editorial comment to the effect that Mrs. Patterson was the kind of rich woman who chose to do something worthwhile, and then did it well:

BLOW, BUGLE, BLOW

Successful women in business, political or commercial art pretty generally express a sense of their own importance. They like to tell you about their success. They like to tell you about the important people who think they are important.

They don't apologize and they don't explain. They don't poke honest fun at themselves. They are the heroines of their own stories. Sometimes they are grim, sometimes they are excessively calm, but always they are superior.

Successful women brag more than successful men, and successful men brag quite a good deal. I guess the reason is that women are fairly new at the game and are still suffering from an inferiority complex.

Now, I'm not a successful woman. I have never worked very hard and I have never worked very well. I'm always explaining. Forever explaining. It seems to me I have to. Often I think I'm silly and I say so.

But it has gradually dawned upon me that I never WILL be a SUCCESSFUL WOMAN unless I adopt a different attitude. So I have decided to blow my own trumpet, fill my lungs and blast away with the others. Of course, I don't want to overdo the thing right at the beginning. I am still willing to admit that I don't know agate type from a 228-point Gothic scarehead. I don't know news pictures or makeup. I don't know how to write and I don't know how to read. (That is, I don't know how to read newspapers.) I don't know the ABCs of circulation, advertising, editorial policy, features.

But somehow or other (I guess it's just one of those merry little coincidences), since I came on the HERALD July 31 of last year the circulation has increased 24 percent.

THIRTEEN

The Animal Lover

N'Gi was sick. N'Gi was a gorilla in the National Zoological Park in Washington, D.C., but it is doubtful if the citizens of the capital, particularly the children, would have been as concerned about the sickness of anyone else, including President Hoover himself. N'Gi's indoor and outdoor cages in the lion house had hundreds massed in front of them every day, and he never let an audience down. He played with newspapers, balloons and baseballs. He put a double boiler on his head and capered about. If that didn't get a laugh, N'Gi—a shameless ham—stood on his head. When he was presented with a medicine ball, the gorilla had all kinds of ideas for entertaining the crowd. He sat on it, he used it as a drum, he played mock battles with it, and eventually he learned to twirl it.

N'Gi had been the best show at the zoo since he made his appearance there three years before, in 1929. He had been purchased for $3000 from J. L. Buck, who had captured him in the Cameroons in West Africa. (J. L. Buck was not related to Frank "Bring 'Em Back Alive" Buck; he probably caught more wild animals but was not as famous, because he did not write a book or make a movie.) He had pursued a gorilla and her baby with the aid of twenty-three Batwa pygmies. The pygmies killed the mother with poisoned arrows and dined on roast gorilla, while Buck took off his shirt and gagged the baby with it. He was named N'Gi—Swahili for "gorilla"—and became the National Zoo's first baby gorilla.

Now, in February 1932, he had pneumonia. As N'Gi curled up inertly in the corner of his cage, the lion house was closed to visitors. Cissy's *Herald* ran a six-column picture showing his neighbors, six lions and lion cubs, looking disconsolate, presumably because of the gorilla's illness. All the Washington newspapers carried daily bulletins on N'Gi's progress. Thousands of children telephoned the zoo during the day, and zoo director William Mann in the evening, for the latest medical reports on the animal.

Even Senator Borah, the *Herald* reported, "took time off yesterday from the cares of state to visit N'Gi at the zoo, and expressed marked pleasure to hear of his improvement. The Senator rode to the zoo on horseback . . ."

But, alas, N'Gi was not improving; his pneumonia was complicated by empyema. Only oxygen could save him. Cissy, in desperation, called her friend, Dr. Alvan T. Barach, a distinguished New York internist who specialized in diseases of the chest. She offered him $2000 to rush his portable oxygen chamber to Washington. Dr. Barach refused, pointing out that the public would be outraged if a gorilla could have an oxygen chamber—then a rarity—while many human beings who needed one could not. However, he agreed to bring the smaller portable oxygen tent which he had developed and used on Floyd Bennett, the flyer, who had contracted pneumonia after a plane crash.

On February 27, N'Gi became the first animal in history to be housed in an oxygen tent. On March 4 he underwent a major operation in which more than a quart of fluid was drained from his lungs. The operation was not entrusted to veterinarians. As the *Herald* proudly reported: "Seven white-clad doctors in the bizarre setting of the lion house at the zoo last night wrote a new page in medical history by performing the first major operation ever done for a gorilla." Cissy's paper called N'Gi "the most famous ape in the world," which was true, for the oxygen tent had made him international news. The *Herald* further noted that it was bearing all the expenses of the operation as well as the cost of flying the tent and Dr. Barach from New York.

N'Gi was removed from the oxygen tent and seemed on the road to recovery. Then, suddenly, he died. Washington mourned. Dr. Mann summed up the feeling later: "I have often thought that N'Gi did more in his three years here than many people do. He gave happy entertainment to thousands of people and, through him, oxygen therapy received great publicity with resultant saving of human life." One result was that a special oxygen-therapy chamber was installed in Children's Hospital in Washington.

Cissy's concern for the gorilla was an example of the tenderness she had for animals in general, more tenderness, indeed, than she sometimes showed toward people.

In 1936, Cissy helped two directors of the Washington Animal Rescue League to organize a District of Columbia chapter of the English Tail-Waggers Club, and became its first president. The club rescues lost pets, trains dogs to be "better citizens," and supports humane legislation. As president, Cissy started a free animal clinic, donated the equipment and underwrote the deficit. Now more than 10,000 dogs, cats, birds, rabbits and wild animals are treated at the clinic.

One of Cissy's favorite people was Dr. Mann, the delightful zoo director, and she was a familiar sight at the zoo. She was especially fond of the bears, and some of her friends swear that after weeks of daily visits she taught the brown bears to sit up and wave at her.

Naturally, she was a tremendous circus buff. No child ever was more bug-eyed than Cissy over the lions, tigers, ringmasters and equestrians. On many occasions, she took several hundred children with her to the circus. Henry Ringling North, however, recalls that she preferred to go alone and that she favored matinees. She was easy to spot, for she liked to dress for the occasion—in floppy western hat and high-laced hiking boots. When the Big

Top came to Washington, it could always count on a publicity
spread in Cissy's newspaper.

Cissy doted most on horses and dogs. A couple of times, in
her kindness toward horses, she got more than she had bargained
for. There was the case of Cypress de Beau. Mrs. John Hay
Whitney had sold this big gray gelding hunter to a Detroit
woman, who directed that it be sent to her Toronto estate. En
route the horse caught cold, and the woman's head groom refused to accept the sniffling animal when he arrived. While the
two ladies brawled over who should accept responsibility for the
ailing horse, he was somehow shunted to Washington, where
he spent his time munching hay, running up a $325 feed bill.
The express company got a court order to sell the horse at auction to pay the bill. Hearing this, Cissy wanted to make sure the
once splendid hunter would not end up pulling a peddler's cart.
She sent her accountant to the auction to bid, expecting to be
able to pick up the horse for several hundred dollars.

But Cissy had not set a ceiling on the price she was willing to
pay. The bidding became spirited, due to the presence of an
agent of the Detroit woman. Cissy's man telephoned for further
instructions but was informed that Madame was taking a nap
and was not to be disturbed. The accountant went back and
continued to bid. Finally, the horse his boss didn't need was
knocked down to him for $2225. It was unquestionably the most
expensive nap she had ever taken. She gave the horse to her
daughter Felicia.

Another proud horse snatched from dark fates was Chief, the
famous palomino who had thrilled audiences in Colonel Tim
McCoy's Wild West Show. The show became stranded in Washington, and the animals were sold to meet expenses. McCoy gave
Chief to his rider, Dave Nimmo, as a partial reward for faithful
friendship. Nimmo, however, was as badly off financially as Mc-
Coy and considered selling the horse. Cissy, hearing about this
from the *Times-Herald* staff, got interested. Clambering around
railroad yards on a dank, rainy night, she found the big stallion,

covered with a torn piece of canvas and suffering from a bad cold. She bought him, installed him in her stables at the Dower House and renamed him "War Chief." The lordly stallion was out of place in the quiet Maryland countryside and drooped about until Cissy wired Nimmo to come back from Arizona, where he had settled, and keep War Chief company. Soon both Nimmo and his wife were living in a cottage on her estate. For a time he and War Chief put on exhibitions of trick riding at society horse shows, and Cissy herself learned to do some trick riding.

The horse Cissy loved best was a big hunter, "Ranger," after whom she named her private railroad car. She bought him in Wyoming. As Cissy liked to tell it, Ranger was a sportsman, born and bred. He was gifted with a perfect nose for game and could point and flush in the field as well as the best hunting dog. It was said that Ranger was born with "nineteen legs," for he was as surefooted as a mountain goat. Treacherous shale rock held no terrors for him.

One wintry day when she was out hunting with Ranger, game had been elusive and Cissy was about to turn his head for home, when the horse's ears pricked up and he pointed dead ahead toward a thick clump of brush on the side of the mountain. Not a leaf stirred, but trusting Ranger's nose rather than her own eyesight, Cissy fired her rifle. A grunt in the brush indicated she had scored. Riding into the brush she came upon a bull elk her shot had killed, breathing its last. But it was late, and Cissy thought it best to get back to camp. The next day, returning with a guide and a packhorse for the elk, she did not recognize her trail in the bright daylight, and lost her way. She gave Ranger his head and he trotted straight to the dead elk.

In 1926, Cissy brought Ranger to Washington and installed him in a riding academy. The taste of real grain was too good for the pasture-fed pony and he got fat. Cissy wrote Rose about the problems this raised:

Ranger is here in Washington. He has been fed oats and bran until his sides stick out like hoops. Went in to see him yesterday for the first time (we only arrived in Washington two days ago). He didn't know me *atall*. And when I led him out of the barn he started a rarin' and a tearin' and bucking and jumping and he pulled the rope clean out of my hand—and about sawed my hand off doing it. They say down at the stable he bucks so they're afraid to take him out. Well, *can* you beat it? I guess I was a jackass to bring him on. But I was so lonesome for him. Told them to cut down on his food and start exercising him. Otherwise, believe me, this baby will do her exercising on her own two feet.

After Cissy acquired Dower House she gave Ranger a stall there and Cissy rode him on her bridle trails often. When he died at twenty-five years old, she mourned as if she had lost one of her best friends.

Cissy's love of animals evoked a great response from them. Animals obeyed her commands flawlessly. For the last two decades of her life her most constant companions were her poodles. The seven poodles most often with her were: Toto, Togo, and Chico, brown males; Butch, a platinum-silver male; Babe and Sara, black females; and Lily Langtry, a white female. The dogs were clipped once a month in the most fashionable poodle cut, and had their teeth cleaned regularly.

Most of Cissy's domestic staff liked the poodles (unlike her newspaper staff), which was fortunate, for the poodles had to be treated with tender, loving care. When Sara had her puppies, Joe Miller, the steward, stayed up all night and acted as midwife.

When Toto ate a stone, the doctors who examined him were reluctant to operate. Cissy asked Evie Robert to get Dr. John Lyons, the famous New York surgeon, whom she knew through their mutual interest in horses. Evie telephoned the doctor, explaining that the dog was bloated and that Cissy was dying a thousand deaths over the crisis. Lyons agreed to operate on the dog if Evie would set up an operating table and get the best veterinarian in Washington to administer the anesthetic.

Late that day the doctor flew to Washington, and that night at the Du Pont Circle mansion, under a giant hospital light, a great surgeon extracted a stone from a poodle, as a handful of the household staff hovered nervously about. Toto made a full recovery. Many years later Dr. Lyons made another hasty trip to Washington, but for a somewhat higher purpose: He operated on President Eisenhower for ileitis.

Cissy's most fastidious poodle was Lily Langtry, given to her by Felicia. Lily was too shy to relieve herself while anyone was watching, and she would eat nothing but chicken. Cissy's chef refused to lower himself to the indignity of cooking a chicken and picking the meat off the bones for the dog, so the job fell to the amiable Miller. When Babe died, it was Miller who went shopping for a coffin, dug a hole in the backyard at Du Pont Circle, and buried her.

Butch was more Cissy's concern than Lily or Babe, because he was mean and dangerous. Henry Lefort, the chauffeur, once struck him, and Miller warned him that Butch would never forget. Sure enough, a few weeks later, the poodle waited until Mrs. Patterson had gotten out of her limousine, then proceeded to bite deeply into Lefort's shoulder.

Once, Charles C. Lattin, a *Times-Herald* staff member, waiting for his boss on a marble bench in the foyer of her Washington home, rubbed Butch's ears. The dog seemed to enjoy it, but when Cissy entered she said, "Has that dog bitten you yet?"

"No, is he supposed to?" Lattin inquired.

"Well, you can't trust the damn thing," Mrs. Patterson replied. "He bites me every once in a while."

She was still fond of Butch. She would take a trip to New York thinking she could get along without him, but would telephone long distance the next day instructing a staff member to bring the dog to her immediately. The staff man would take a whole Pullman for Butch and see to it that en route he was served the kind of delicacies he insisted on: chicken liver, chicken short ribs, or beef boiled soft. For breakfast Butch preferred cereal. In the opinion of Emile Bouchard, another Patterson chauffeur, "he lived better than most humans."

Every Patterson chauffeur learned that his first duty was to go to the dogs. In 1932, when Cissy had a couple of cocker spaniels on her Long Island place, Lefort took them along on a trip to buy eggs. He struck a bump on the Mariton Pike in New Jersey and the brakes jammed, the limousine skidding into a telephone pole. The $5000 car was smashed up, along with the eggs. Lefort and the dogs were thrown clear, and the dogs, yelping in fright, fled into the woods. Lefort, his head cut badly, dashed into the woods after them, refusing to have his injuries dressed until he and a posse of searchers had located the spaniels. A New York *Herald Tribune* story reporting the accident marveled that the bleeding chauffeur had evidently considered himself more expendable than the spaniels. The writer did not know what it was like to work for Mrs. Patterson. Some years later, Lefort gave up his job for more conventional chauffeuring.

Cissy carried on a vigorous crusade against vivisection. *Times-Herald* editorials regularly attacked it as an inexcusable horror and demanded that the doctors of America put a stop to the practice.

The *Times-Herald* also gave generous news space to all items concerning the work of anticruelty societies. This became as much of a bore for the staff as Cissy's passion for underprivileged dogs. Occasionally, the task of reporting the tale of a rescued canine was visited upon John Maynard, one of her cleverest feature writers. Maynard recalls one of Mrs. Patterson's Samaritan deeds, and its consequent chaos:

"Well, she picked up a doleful mongrel out in front of the office one day and charged right back up to the city room, cradling this little character against her umpty-thousand-dollar mink coat. The Animal Lover battalion was summoned, headed by George Waters, who was city-editor-of-the-day, so to speak.

Naturally George had to put his coat and tie on before addressing the dog. The dog didn't have much to say but it was in a bad temper and, if house-broken, still not city room-broken. Just the same, an Animal Lover buck sergeant (me) whipped up a Whose-Little-Doggie-Is-'Oo? deal with picture—and sure enough, some kid out in Northeast figured it was his little doggie.

"Well, Cissy had the dog up in Upper Marlboro [the Dower House], and a photographer and I went out to get the kid and his mother, and it was the sort of upstanding American boy from whom any sensible dog would run away, but this was a Cissy must, so I had to get him and his parent back to the office for pix, because Cissy was coming all the way with dog, for Krise sake. God, what a repulsive kid. But I gave it the 'Won't you be glad to get your little dog back?' bit and the kid says, 'Naaah,' he didn't care. WHAT! And Cissy on her way in right then! The mother left the room and the photog says through his teeth, listen, you little son of a bitch, you want your dog back, see, and don't forget it, and the kid starts to cry and mama gallops back in and the photog says the kid bumped his head on a table, etc.

"Anyway, we finally got them back there and the great reconciliation was duly photographed, the dog earnestly trying to bite the kid and anyone else who came near him, scared hysterical, but a happy ending for everyone except maybe the dog."

Cissy's sympathy for animals had earlier inspired an even more misbegotten mission. A sudden freeze had left wild geese on the Potomac without food, and the afternoon *Times*, then being leased by Cissy, received a telephoned tip that some of them were isolated and starving on an island in the river. Reporter Paul Conlon and a photographer were immediately alerted for a wild-geese chase.

Conlon purchased sacks of cracked corn at a local feed store and loaded them onto a Goodyear dirigible which he chartered at the Washington airport. Conlon informed the pilot that the *Times* pair was on "an errand of mercy," that is, in search of some wild ducks, or something, but didn't know where they were. The pilot assured them that on that very day he had sighted a flock of birds apparently starving on the frozen Potomac. Off sailed the blimp; inside it was unbearably cold because Conlon had tied the door open so that the grain bags could be dropped and the operation photographed.

Over Roach's Run, an inlet about five miles south, the pilot maneuvered the dirigible to an altitude of some 200 feet, giving a clear view of a flock of ducks. While the cameraman leaned out and adjusted his lens, Conlon made an opening in the sacks with his jackknife and then threw them overboard. In four passes, the bags were gone and the birds were bombed. An hour later, Conlon was back at his typewriter relating dramatically for readers how the poor ducks had been fed, courtesy of the *Times*. The story, complete with a picture layout, ran in the first edition of the *Times* at 10 A.M. the next day.

Conlon was happily feeling like the poor man's Admiral Byrd —until a disquieting development occurred at noon. The second edition of the rival *News* headlined a deadpan statement from the Interior Department reporting that person or persons unknown had been dropping unidentified pellets on a bunch of defenseless ducks with such force that the duck population at Roach's Run had been decimated! What's more, the Interior Department had been feeding these ducks, who were now dead.

The rescue mission vanished from the next edition of the embarrassed *Times*. It turned out that the dirigible pilot had led the *Times* team to the wrong ducks. The tipster had in mind some ducks who were some ten to fifteen miles further down the Potomac and not at all well fed.

Ducks appealed to Cissy. Baby ducks graced the placid surface of the picturesque little lake which could be seen from the drive leading into the Dower House estate. Presently, they began to disappear, with no hint of how they were meeting their fate. Cissy called upon George Waters to solve the case of the vanishing ducks; Waters was then a crack police reporter. He was assigned to spend the night lying on the shore of the lake, and to stay there as many nights as it took him to find out where the ducks were going. The butler was instructed to furnish Waters with sufficient champagne and other victuals from the gourmet pantry to nourish him during his lonely vigil.

Waters kept the butler busy running back and forth to the lake and managed to have a satisfactory one-man beach party. He also found out that the ducks were being eaten by turtles. The next day the versatile Lattin was again told to drop everything and make haste to Dower House. There Mrs. Patterson informed him that turtles were eating her ducks, and asked for a solution. Lattin sought out a contractor who had done reliable work for him and they drove out to inspect the lake. It was too deep to wade into and too large to reach the center from the shore with an instrument. They finally hit upon a solution. Two tractors were run along opposite sides of the lake, dragging back and forth a stout steel cable suspended loosely between them. The lake was thus cleared of seaweed and there were no further complaints about turtles.

The only animals Cissy hated and feared were snakes. She had seen more snakes than she cared to out West, and had learned something about them. When she moved into Dower House, they seemed to be popping up everywhere. She telephoned the ever-ready Lattin and, without even saying hello, told him: "I want you to snake-proof Dower House." Lattin was told to proceed there forthwith.

When he was shown in, Mrs. Patterson was seated broodingly before the gigantic fireplace. She told Lattin she was sick and tired of living with snakes. Sometimes she would find one in her bed or curled on a book on the shelves. Once a snake poked its head through the drawing-room door when it was left ajar. Horrified, the auditor asked: "What did you do?" Matter-of-factly, Cissy related that she simply rang for the butler and he slammed the door, cutting off the snake's head.

Lattin did not fancy taking on St. Patrick's role all by himself. He went back to the contractor who had turtle-proofed the lake, and for $300 they were able to have the Dower House snake-proofed.

The snake-proofing was not completely successful. One day Cissy and Evie Robert were visited by a black snake in the dining room. Evie rushed to the kitchen looking for a paper bag, telling Cissy she would catch the snake by the tail, drop it in the bag and throw the bag out. By the time she returned, Cissy had smashed the snake to death with a poker. Another time they caught a snake and got into a disagreement over whether it was a coral species. Mrs. Robert said she would take it back to the Washington Zoo and have Dr. Mann identify it. When Evie reached her Mayflower Hotel apartment it was late, so she put the snake in a jar in her refrigerator. The next morning when the maid opened the refrigerator and saw the snake, she awakened the neighbors with her screams and ran out the door. She never came back.

FOURTEEN

Feuds

Eleanor Patterson's secretary, Mrs. Carolyn Hagner Shaw, picked up the ringing telephone in the Du Pont Circle town house and heard a long-distance operator announce that "Mr. Brisbane is calling." Mrs. Shaw was surprised, for she was sure that Brisbane knew Mrs. Patterson was in her private railroad car, rolling back across the country from a visit at William Randolph Hearst's estate in California.

Brisbane's tone was urgent. He told Mrs. Shaw to drop everything and intercept her boss before her car reached Washington.

"Get to her, and sit on her, if necessary, until I can get there later this afternoon," he said. He explained that he had been reading a book, *More Merry-Go-Round*, just off the presses.

"When she reads the first chapter," Brisbane continued, "she'll explode, and I can see a box coming. Keep her from getting her hands on a copy until I get a chance to talk with her first. I'm going to stop that box. It won't do her any good, and she'll regret it."

It was 1932, one of the years in which Cissy was most addicted to using her front page to skewer those who had incurred her scorn. Brisbane and other close friends could recognize these symptoms of displeasure in their early stages and accurately predict several paragraphs of jagged personal comment, bordered in black lines and boldly signed "ELEANOR PATTERSON." For Cissy, publishing the box accomplished two good ends: her blood pressure went down, and her circulation went up. In Wash-

ington, a personality fight is delicious entertainment, and this
kind could be purchased for two cents.

Mrs. Shaw knew that no one had ever talked Cissy out of a
box, once she had set her mind on one, but the great Brisbane
was supposed to be Cissy's journalistic mentor and the only person, aside from brother Joe, who could handle her. Until Brisbane could get there she faced the task of catching the boss and
bridling her. A railroad timetable told her that the train to which
Mrs. Patterson's car was attached was scheduled to pass through
Baltimore in an hour and a half. Mrs. Shaw was on the next train
to Baltimore.

When she alighted there, she gazed around quickly and spotted
the Patterson car, "The Ranger," halted at an adjoining platform.
Mrs. Shaw made a dash for the car and, as she hopped aboard,
ran smack into Cissy herself. Cissy drew back, looked at her
secretary in surprise, then broke into a triumphant chuckle.
Clutched in her hands was a copy of the orange-colored *More
Merry-Go-Round*, and she had already guessed that this was the
reason she was being intercepted.

"Was this Mr. Brisbane's idea?" she drawled. "I'll bet he
wanted you to keep me from getting a copy! Well, I beat him
to it. But I'm glad you're here. Get out your pad and pencil.
We've got work to do."

As they seated themselves in the chintz-covered chairs of The
Ranger, Cissy's gloating amusement turned to anger. All the way
to Washington she dictated sentences that sizzled. In Mrs. Shaw's
experience with Cissy, she had never heard her scorch a victim
with such fury. The target was Drew Pearson.

For the record, *More Merry-Go-Round* was anonymous; the
title page stated that it was "by the authors of *Washington
Merry-Go-Round*"—which was likewise officially anonymous.
Washington Merry-Go-Round, published a year before, was
written by Pearson in collaboration with Robert S. Allen, as all
Washington knew. Their aim was to give a racy and irreverent

19

In the Du Pont Circle town house Cissy's favorite attire for her fabulous
parties was exotic hostess pajamas.

When Cissy became editor of the Washington *Herald* in 1930, she occasionally gave herself assignments as a reporter. Here she is disguised as a destitute woman, "Maude Martin,"
seeking work. A series of articles resulted.

Harris & Ewing

Cissy, a born actress, loved self-dramatization and played many roles. Here she is in a harlequin costume at a "Bal Bohème" in the twenties.

22

Though she preferred lounging pajamas or riding clothes, Cissy had hundreds of gowns and could dress as elaborately as anyone in the ornate twenties.

peek at the capital. In one way or another, virtually every personage was derided—President Hoover, his cabinet, Congress, the press, diplomats, hostesses, generals—in the heady mixture of juicy gossip and little-known fact whipped up by Pearson and Allen.

Nothing quite like *Washington Merry-Go-Round* had ever been published before. It was an immediate best-seller and went through nineteen printings in five months. The authors did not remain anonymous very long; and as soon as they were unmasked, Pearson lost his job as a reporter on the Baltimore *Sun*, and Allen was fired from the *Christian Science Monitor*.

Washington Merry-Go-Round relates, presumably tongue-in-cheek, that Pearson "married Countess Felicia and came to Washington to get a veneer of respectability." This is the only reference to his ex-wife. As for his ex-mother-in-law, she gets off comparatively easy. The book introduces Cissy as one of the capital's four "whip-cracking hostesses" and describes her as "one of the most gifted women in Washington but who has dissipated her gifts, for the most part on trivialities."

Taking note of the "Patterson-Longworth war," *Washington Merry-Go-Round* also brings in the perennial anecdote about the feminine articles Cissy left in Alice's chandelier, except that the word "panties" is changed to "shoes," doubtless by one of the publisher's prissier editors.

But in *More Merry-Go-Round*, as Brisbane had anticipated, Cissy felt Pearson had gone too far. Tailored to follow its predecessor to the best-seller lists, the sequel makes sport of her luxurious boudoir.

In *More Merry-Go-Round* Cissy is graduated from a "whip-cracker" to one of the "chief fox-trotters in Washington's Dance of the Depression." "While editing the capital's most interesting newspaper," the book reports, Cissy has "made her parties the most fascinating, albeit the most bizarre in Washington."

It continues:

. . . For the first time in her life she found herself doing something more useful than ordering servants around, hunting big game in the Rockies or taking the Herbert Swopes down to Florida in her private car, "Ranger." With no journalistic experience and only the blind belief that the granddaughter of the founder of the Chicago *Tribune* could edit any newspaper, Cissy had cajoled, stormed and goaded the staff of the Washington *Herald* into putting out a first-class sheet . . . it showed flashes of the genius of a woman who has spent all her life groping for an opportunity to do just exactly what she is doing now.

Fair enough. So far, so good. But Cissy's lips tightened when the book detailed the strange quest of Ralph Palmer, the managing editor of the Washington *News*. When Cissy had showed up in his office determined to thrash a *News* columnist, Palmer had been impressed by a vocabulary which had bullied teams of horses across the Teton Pass. He was further enchanted when he read Cissy's first-person "Maude Martin" series in the *Herald* and learned that the same woman slept on peach crepe-de-Chine sheets. *More Merry-Go-Round* relates the editor's reaction:

Mr. Palmer was one who did not suffer from suppressed desires. He called Mrs. Patterson up and told her of his great admiration for any woman who had her command of profanity and of his overwhelming curiosity to come into closer contact with those embroidered crepe-de-Chine sheets. Mrs. Patterson in turn invited him to come to a Christmas party.

When he arrived he pulled his hostess to one side.

"I have come," he said, "both prepared and determined to enjoy the exquisite luxury of those sheets."

Whereupon he pulled up his trousers, exhibiting underneath a silken cerise pajama leg.

Cissy was convulsed. She took her latest arrival over to Senator Capper of Kansas.

"Mr. Palmer has come to sleep with me," she announced, assisting in the ceremony of pulling up the trouser leg.

Senator Capper, just the moment before, had had one

shock and was not at all prepared for another. Having been handed a large flat package from which other gentlemen extracted handkerchiefs, the aged widower pulled from the box a pair of ladies' underpants. They were made of black transparent lace, and on a card inside was written, "To Rose Nano."

The lady in question, wife of the Roumanian chargé d'affaires, and most bewitching beauty in the diplomatic corps, is famous for her scantiness of attire.

Although a widower, the Senator, after all, comes from Kansas. Also, he is a very mild man. So with the climax of Cissy's latest confidence, he quietly got his hat and went home.

Palmer himself went home that night feeling badly let down, *More Merry-Go-Round* relates, for, despite the naughty joke she had made about his wearing pajamas, Cissy had not invited him to her bedroom for a peek at the heavenly sheets. And so the next time he was invited to Cissy's town house at Du Pont Circle he vowed to make a second try at satisfying his curiosity. When he arrived, Palmer wondered if he had come on the wrong night; not only was there no large party in full swing but Cissy herself was not at home. The butler asked the editor to wait in the library and sought to make his waiting more palatable by serving a series of highballs. The hours dragged on, but still no Cissy. Finally, emboldened by the distilled spirits, Palmer set out to explore the house in hopes of locating the exquisite bedroom.

Upstairs, Palmer found a bedroom with a double bed on which were laid out green silk pajamas, a green negligee and green crepe-de-Chine sheets. He renewed his vigil, but presently grew so tired that he took off his clothes, slipped into the green negligee, and lay on the coverlet, resisting only the impulse to crawl between the famous sheets.

Palmer was awakened hours later by a high-pitched woman's voice crying out that "this is Countess Gizycka's room," followed by the voices of two housemen promising to get him out of the mansion forthwith.

Out went Palmer, befuddled and befogged, but painfully
aware that he had blundered into the wrong bedroom. "Countess
Gizycka" was of course Cissy's daughter and Pearson's former
wife, a blonde, lovely and sophisticated adornment of the town's
younger set.

This episode closes with a giggling sentence:

The embroidered crepe-de-Chine sheets, both peach and
green, retained their pristine purity.

Cissy boiled. Now, as her private car rushed toward the capital,
she dictated to Mrs. Shaw as fast as she could think of original
ways of barbecuing Pearson. She was sure that he, not Allen,
had contributed this chapter, because, even after his divorce
from Felicia, she had given Pearson the run of the mansion. He
had entertained his friends there, and thus had an insider's
knowledge of the family—which he was turning to profit in
More Merry-Go-Round.

Arriving in Washington, Cissy took her secretary home with
her so that the shorthand notes could be transcribed without
delay. It was past four o'clock and Cissy wanted to make sure
the box got into the first edition of the *Herald*. For poor Mrs.
Shaw, time was indeed running out, and there was no sign of
Brisbane's arrival. So she stalled. She dropped her notebook repeatedly. She made one stupid typing error after the other. She
smeared the typewritten page and laboriously erased. Finally,
running out of butterfingered delays, she began putting the copy
paper into the typewriter upside down. This was too much for
Cissy, who had been pacing the floor and railing at the secretary
for her awkwardness. She told Mrs. Shaw that if she could no
longer do her job well she would lose it. This made the secretary so nervous she started making mistakes without even trying.

At long last, after an hour, the box was neatly typed and
ready for the presses. Cissy read it on the telephone to the
Herald managing editor, Mike Flynn, told him to be sure to get
it into the first edition, and hung up.

Mrs. Shaw left for home feeling she had failed Brisbane. She had had no word from him; but a half hour later he hurried through the door of the *Herald* building just as Mrs. Patterson herself was entering. They went into her private office and shut the door. An argument erupted, and Brisbane won. Somehow he was able to convince Cissy that the blast at Pearson would only make her look petty and undignified—also, that it would be reprinted all across the country and give Pearson's book $1,000,-000 worth of free advertising. Cissy picked up the phone and ordered the box snatched back from the composing room just as the first edition was going to press.

Cissy was still boiling. She put in a call to the publishers of *More Merry-Go-Round*—Liveright, Inc., in New York City—and demanded that they delete the crepe-de-Chine sheets episode from all future editions. That accomplished, she simmered down quickly. She and Pearson became friends again, and in 1934 she capitalized on the notoriety of the now famous Pearson-Allen exposé team by signing a contract to run its new syndicated column, "Washington Merry-Go-Round," in the *Herald*.

While Cissy's fury at Pearson died down for the time being, her feud with Alice Longworth continued apace. Cissy had used Alice as the basis of a scheming Washington hostess in *Glass Houses*, and she had needled her on the front page after she took over the *Herald*. But why? They had been friends since almost the turn of the century. Yet Cissy and Alice were also competitors. It was an open secret that they had competed for the attentions of Senator Borah in the twenties, and they were still competing, whether they liked it or not, for the unofficial title of "Sharpest Observer on the Washington Scene."

The fact is that Cissy, who enjoyed bringing down big game, simply could not resist shooting at Alice. She thought that Alice's reputation as a longtime resident wit of the capital's top echelons was tiresome, and also that in trying to live up to her once radiant image as the "princess" of the House of Roosevelt, Oyster Bay branch, she was an anachronism.

Alice, wisely, did not choose to counterattack publicly. Whatever barbs she might fashion for Cissy by candlelight, she did not utter them for publication (perhaps because it would only have goaded Cissy to new heights).

On October 16, 1932, Cissy was at it again, with this box:

FIFTY-FIFTY

Alice Longworth in the fascinating first installment of *Some Reminiscences*, published this month, tells the world that Franklin Roosevelt is only her fourth cousin once removed. Yet "some people have actually congratulated me on the nomination of 'my brother,'" writes Mrs. Longworth.

It is evident that Mrs. Longworth and her family are irritated by the possibility of a confusion between Governor Roosevelt and Junior T.R. But what is the Governor's reaction to this case of mistaken identity, as reported by Mrs. Longworth? Maybe he feels flattered and complimented to be mistaken for Mrs. Longworth's brother. Maybe, though, he isn't crazy about it at all.

That reminds me somewhat of a story about the magnificent old Norseman, Andy Furuseth—head of the Seaman's Union. Some years ago when he was lying very sick indeed, in a little sailor's hospital in San Francisco, a "society" lady came to visit him, her arms full of roses, her heart full of romance. "Oh, Mr. Furuseth," she said, "come to my house and let me take care of you. You will have a flowered chintz room, fine linen, servants to wait on you." Andy looked up from his narrow, iron cot. "Madame," he said, "that would be turrible for both of us."

ELEANOR PATTERSON

With a Hyde Park Roosevelt running for President, Cissy liked to hint that the old Roosevelts, preserved by Alice, were going out of style. After FDR was inaugurated, Cissy appeared in a skit at a Woman's Press Club stunt show in honor of the new Roosevelts. With both Alice and Eleanor Roosevelt sitting in the audience, she sang a parody built around the theme:

"Alice? Alice? Where could she be? I wonder what ever happened to *her?*"

Cissy next struck at Alice in an article in *Cosmopolitan* magazine. It probably revealed what really irritated Cissy about Alice; in any case, it was regarded as a particularly penetrating thrust by longtime observers of Mrs. Longworth.

In the article Cissy said that "women brag too much, far more than men." She noted that Alice Longworth never bragged. This sounded magnanimous, but she was only setting up Alice for a haymaker:

> On the contrary, Alice seems to take an odd, malicious satisfaction in poking fun at herself. She believes herself to be a failure because she was not born a man. She cannot hope to be a second Teddy Roosevelt. No substitute for this particular choice of success has ever satisfied her purely dynamic type of ambition.

The feud inspired George S. Kaufman and Katherine Drayton to write a comedy, *First Lady*, which opened on Broadway in December 1935. The play picks up the style of Washington satire pioneered by Cissy in *Glass Houses* nearly a decade earlier, and adds brittle gags. In the first act the hard-bitten wife of an oldtime senator remarks: "What I like about Washington is that everybody is somebody. This puts gossip on such a high plane."

Time magazine called *First Lady* the "lowdown on highups in the nation's capital of the sort that is whispered over a cocktail at the Carlton by someone who got it straight from a secretary at the British Embassy who got it straight from his girl in the Post Office Department who got it straight from a reporter on the White House run who eavesdropped on a sub-cabinet member in the Mayflower washroom."

Time saw the plot and its real-life counterparts this way:

> Without libeling either Eleanor Medill ("Cissy") Patterson or Alice Roosevelt Longworth, Playwrights Dayton and Kaufman call them strongly to mind when they pose

Irene Hibbard (Lily Cahill) and Lucy Chase Wayne (Jane Cowl) in opposite corners for a three-act social grudge fight. Mrs. Wayne, now the wife of the Secretary of State, was a White House bride when her grandfather was President. She has been "patted on the head by every member of the Party," is a gracious hostess, an incorrigible meddler in affairs of state and, she happily admits, a "dirty politician." Irene Hibbard was married to a Balkan prince before a Supreme Court justice became her husband. For years she and Lucy have fought over freshmen senators from the West. Now the spoils are nothing less than a presidential nomination, which Lucy almost hands to Irene's second husband only to snatch it for her own spouse because of Irene's first.

In real life, the Patterson-Longworth feud was conducted entirely in public. There were no eyeball-to-eyeball showdowns, nor even any sly ripostes, when they encountered one another at parties. Both women were too well bred to resort to drawing-room stilettos.

But as the thirties ended and Cissy became a more serious newspaper publisher, she tired of baiting Alice. Besides, she really liked her. Once, when they ran into one another on a Massachusetts Avenue sidewalk—their houses were only a few blocks apart—Cissy halted and said abruptly, "I think it's time we made up."

"Oh, I don't think so," Alice replied with a laugh. "It's too soon."

She said it half-teasingly, but Cissy was annoyed at being rebuffed, and Alice could feel her "towering scorn" as she walked on down the street.

The reconciliation did not come until 1942, and then almost by accident. Adela Rogers St. Johns, the author and Hearst-syndicate writer, had lunched with Alice at the Mayflower Hotel. As she stepped into her car, Alice said goodby and asked Adela where she was going. Adela said she was returning to Dower House, Cissy's country estate in Maryland, where she was staying.

"Oh, how *is* Cissy?" Alice asked, with concern.

"Why don't you come with me and find out?" Adela suggested.

"Oh, I don't think she'd want to see me," Alice demurred.

Adela convinced her that she was mistaken. Alice got into the car and rode with Adela to Dower House. When they arrived at the front door, Adela asked Alice to remain in the car while she talked with Cissy first. She found her in an upstairs bedroom and told her Mrs. Longworth was waiting outside. Tears sprang into Cissy's eyes. While Adela hung back at the window, she left the room and went downstairs. A few minutes later, through the window, Adela watched the two old friends greet one another affectionately at the car. Then Adela went for a walk on the estate, leaving them alone for a long talk.

Discussing the feud years later, Alice Longworth said, "It was a love-hate thing. I don't think she was really provoked at me when she ran that first front-page box. I knew it was coming —after what she had done in *Glass Houses*—once she got a newspaper. It was good for circulation."

She then went on to reveal that, despite the feud, she couldn't help liking and admiring Cissy.

"Her charm was that she was so unpredictable and eccentric. Cissy was one of the most engaging people I've ever met— *great* fun to be with, *so* personable! She was interested in *everything*. And she had so much talent she could have been anything she wanted to be."

Cissy broke with Pearson the same year she made up with Alice. She had always been personally fond of Drew, and the column "Washington Merry-Go-Round" had proved a top drawing card for the *Herald*. When Pearson remarried, Cissy made his wife, Luvvie, a columnist.

In 1937, Pearson wrote a complimentary profile of his former mother-in-law for *Redbook* magazine entitled "Our Leading Lady Publisher," but after 1937 Cissy and Drew found themselves on opposite sides in the national debate that waxed hotter and hotter over the gathering war storm in Europe. Cissy sided with those senators in Congress who believed the United States should pursue a hands-off policy; Pearson and Allen were violently interventionist and used their column to attack Burton K. Wheeler and Henrik Shipstead, who were personal as well as ideological friends of hers. Cissy was irked, but she published the column more or less intact.

Despite these differences, in 1941 Cissy came to the Pearsons' house for dinner on her birthday, November 7, and the atmosphere was as serene as in the old days. But a month later Pearl Harbor was attacked, and from then on tension built up steadily between the *Times-Herald* publisher and her pair of controversial columnists. They continued to hammer personally at former isolationist senators who were fully supporting the war but criticized the Roosevelt administration's policy of giving priority to the war in Europe. Pearson and Allen also raked up snide items about General Douglas MacArthur; Cissy passionately admired MacArthur and argued that FDR should send more help to the beleaguered MacArthur forces in the Pacific.

Finally, she ordered Frank Waldrop, editor of the editorial page, to blue-pencil the more offensive items in "Washington Merry-Go-Round." Pearson and Allen began to complain that they were being "censored." Cissy scoffed. She felt no obligation to give valuable space in her newspaper to what she regarded as the personal vendettas of columnists.

Early in 1942, "Washington Merry-Go-Round" was banished from its choice center spot on the *Herald* editorial page and tucked away under a single-column headline well back in the news pages. Readers as often as not had to look below the center fold to find the column sharing nonpremium space with an advertisement for linseed oil. From there, after several paragraphs, it was jumped to the rear of the paper, where it was flanked by ads for curing "excessive drinking" and "jittery headaches." This gave Cissy an idea, for she took to calling Pearson and Allen "the Headache Boys."

It is hard to conceive of any other newspaper ridiculing its own columnists. In the April 2, 1942, issue, Cissy gleefully published a page-one box headlined: "PEARSON AND ALLEN, THE HEADACHE BOYS." It printed a letter from Secretary of Commerce Jesse Jones denying that there was any truth in a Pearson-Allen item about him on the day before and accused them of having "maliciously distorted" facts about him for years through "innuendo." The *Times-Herald* added its "sincere apologies" to Jones.

Suddenly it became a kind of game for readers to try to find the Pearson-Allen column. It did not disappear altogether; one simply had to look for bits and pieces, for it was dismembered and scattered through the various sections of the paper in chunks. A faithful Pearson-Allen fan attempting to track the column through the *Times-Herald* was in danger of losing his mind.

On April 28, Cissy omitted "Washington Merry-Go-Round" entirely and carried a long box in the center of page one head-lined:

THE HEADACHE BOYS AND GENERAL MACARTHUR
Our readers may inquire WHY Pearson and Allen over a period of years have, by false and sneering innuendo, at-tempted to smear the reputation of a great man, General MacArthur.
Well . . . WHY a Winchell?
WHY . . . a cockroach?

E.P.

(The *Times-Herald* also published the column of Walter Winchell and, as is apparent, Mrs. Patterson liked him even less than Pearson and Allen.)

The April 28 box recalled that in *More Merry-Go-Round* Pearson and Allen had castigated MacArthur for using troops to disperse the bonus army in 1931. According to the book, MacArthur had received a letter after the bonus army incident suggesting that he be given another ribbon "down the middle of his back which will be a long streak of yellow, with a piece of bologna at the end."

After Pearl Harbor, Pearson and Allen continually jabbed away at MacArthur for his "swaggering vanity" and other traits, while the *Times-Herald* otherwise seldom let a day go by without some favorable mention of the general. A day of reckoning was inevitable.

In May 1942, "Washington Merry-Go-Round" suddenly showed up regularly in the *Times-Herald's* rival, the Washington *Post*.

Mrs. Patterson did not often let personal feelings interfere with running a newspaper. "Washington Merry-Go-Round" had star quality for a Washington audience. Before deciding to get rid of it she had consulted her shrewd circulation manager, "Happy" Robinson, and asked him whether loss of Pearson and Allen would hurt *Times-Herald* circulation badly. Robinson advised her that it would—at first—but not if she put her reasons on page one in characteristic style. Whenever Cissy uttered a front-page blast, Robinson had his newsboys hawk their papers with: "Have you heard what Mrs. Patterson says today?"

Cissy was so incensed at Pearson that she fired his wife, Luvvie, who had been doing movie reviews for the *Times-Herald*, and hired Luvvie's ex-husband, George Abell, to do a column, "Diplomat's Diary," in a choice spot on the editorial page. Cissy had changed her mind about Abell since that day back in 1931 when she had gone looking for him with a horsewhip.

Pearson and Allen claimed Cissy could not have fired them, because they had quit. Irritated with her editing, they had gone to Eugene Meyer, publisher of the Washington *Post*, and negotiated a contract to replace their *Times-Herald* one when it ran out in August.

Cissy nonetheless insisted she was not the one who had been jilted. She told a *Newsweek* interviewer: "I'm fond of him [Pearson]—he's been a wonderful father to my grandchild—but he and Bob both were spoiled by the promotion I gave them in this columnists' show town. . . . I got tired also of lawyers coming and going in the office here on possible libel suits."

In his memoirs, "Confessions of an S.O.B.," in *The Saturday Evening Post*, Pearson related:

> Bob and I tried to buy a full page in the Washington *Post* to print correspondence showing we, not she, had canceled the column. Eugene Meyer, the man who had helped maneuver us into all this, spurned our $2000 and turned down our ad. I don't blame him. He knew the lady's wrath.
>
> We approached Fleming Newbold, then the vice president of the Washington *Evening Star*. He read our ad with interest and amusement, but said no. He was not going to get into a row with the redheaded publisher of the *Times-Herald*. Publishers, he said, must stick together.
>
> Next the Washington *News*, a Scripps-Howard paper, declined our money but said the ad was news, and ran it as news—free.

But Pearson hadn't seen anything yet. Once the contract for the column had run out, Cissy decided to give her ex-son-in-law her full treatment, running to a page and a half in a Sunday edition. It was part of a series entitled "Having a Wonderful Time," designed to expose prominent figures who had wanted the war and were enjoying it—at their desks in Washington.

Cissy savored the idea of doing justice to Drew in print, but she had a hard time getting it done right. She wrote it first herself, but the *Times-Herald* lawyers advised her the article was libelous. She assigned the task to Frank Waldrop, her pontifical chief editorial writer. Dissatisfied with Waldrop's version, she turned the chore over to Vincent X. Flaherty, a sports columnist who could turn a phrase, and finally to John Maynard, a flippant feature writer. None of these drafts suited Cissy; they simply were not nasty enough. So she obtained permission from her brother Joe to recruit the services of a member of his Washington bureau—jaunty, wise-cracking

George Dixon (later to become a humor columnist for the King
Features syndicate).

Dixon's version made no concessions to subtlety, and Cissy
was delighted with it. To add a dash of mystery to the whole
thing, she gave Dixon a female *non de plume*—Georgiana X.
Preston. Typically, she forbade anyone on the staff to identify
Dixon as the author—and then went around giving out the
secret herself at every party.

The clobbering of Pearson, which caused a stir in the capital,
ran under this headline and subhead:

QUAKER OAT TURNED
INTO SOUR MASH

Tale Strictly for Adults, but Full
of Model Instruction for
Evildoers

Dixon adopted the jargon of a chautauqua lecturer (Pearson
and his father had both been associated with chautauquas) and
asked his readers to inspect "the weirdest specimen of humanity
since Nemo, the Turtle Boy." Nemo, he explains, is able to face
both ways at the same time because he is two-faced.

Pearson is then jeeringly taken apart, physically and mentally.
Dixon reviewed Pearson's controversies dating back to the publication of *Washington Merry-Go-Round*. He said the book
"took half of Washington apart, with particular emphasis on
those who had consistently ignored the authors. Tidbits picked
up at small, intimate dinner parties where one or the other was
a guest were thrown in, embarrassing no end of hostesses."

One of the milder phrases Dixon used on Pearson was "America's outstanding journalistic heel." He said that "possibly no
man in Washington ever had so many doors slammed in his
face . . . former friends relate that, green around the gills, he
used to roll on the floor in hysterical rages."

When Bill Flythe, then a *Times-Herald* desk man, read the
Dixon version, he said it sounded libelous. "Good," Cissy re-

plied, "I can afford it. I'd gladly pay $1,000,000 to get that S.O.B. into court."

Pearson did consider suing Cissy and discussed it with his daughter, Ellen, then aged fifteen.

"That's just exactly what grandmother wants," Ellen pointed out. "Don't give her the satisfaction."

Over the next several years Cissy continued to publicize Pearson as "the Headache Boy" whenever he was into another controversy, which was often. Pearson's keyhole level of journalism has built-in hazards, since the squiggles of backstairs information that slither to him so often prove to be misleading, malicious or just plain wrong. As he himself puts it, he has been sued for libel more times than he can remember; and he has boasted that a letter addressed simply to "The S.O.B.," with no city or state indicated, was unerringly delivered to his door by the Post Office.

Pearson was one object of Cissy's derision who did not excite sympathy. For one thing, he could strike back in his widely syndicated column—and did. And after all, Cissy was far from being alone in her swipes at Pearson. Altogether, two Presidents (Truman and F. D. Roosevelt) have called him a liar, fifty-four senators and congressmen have questioned his integrity, and eight Congressional committees have interrogated him.

Cissy once asked her friend, Senator Burton K. Wheeler, whom she often consulted for legal advice, whether he could dig up evidence showing Pearson to be a pro-Communist. Wheeler told her he could not. To George Abell she remarked half-seriously that it was a pity they weren't in Chicago, because "then I could have Drew 'rubbed out.'"

Of the dozen or so persons Cissy feuded with, Pearson was the one she came closest to hating, perhaps because she had been fond of him for many years and looked upon him as an ex-member of her family who had unaccountably betrayed her.

Her determination to cut her former son-in-law into small

bits in public never ceased. On October 28, 1945, she published under her own by-line, in the Sunday *Times-Herald*, a full-page article entitled, "Crazy—Crazy Like Foxes." She wrote that Pearson bore a strange physical resemblance to Robespierre in the French Revolution, and she ran portrait pictures of them, facing one another, to prove it. Also pictured were Cissy's other villains among the liberals of the era—Henry Wallace ("Crystal-Gazing Crackpot"), Marshall Field II ("Poor Puppet King"), and Walter Winchell ("Middle-Aged Chorus Boy").

Having just visited Washington's St. Elizabeth's hospital for the insane, she wrote, she could better understand "what could be going on inside the screwy heads of the poor jerks" who called themselves liberals. Rambling in her wrath, she said at one point:

> Incidentally, you G.I. Joes, when you happen to listen to the Phony Quaker Pearson on a Sunday night—Bleeding-Heart Drew—never forget that, although he was 20 and in perfect health in 1917, he managed to "thee and thou" himself out of service in World War I. Then, as now, Drew was a yellow-bellied slacker (for further information, please write in).*

In his radio broadcast that night, Pearson shrewdly laughed off the outburst: "The British have organized a society for protection against mothers-in-law, but what we really need in this country is an organization for protection against ex-mothers-in-law. I would like to be a charter member."

Meanwhile, he was in a running legal battle with Cissy. Back in 1936, she had presented her granddaughter, Ellen, with her 280-acre farm on the Potomac River in Maryland. Since Ellen was then only ten, Cissy had named Pearson as trustee to run the property for his daughter. In January 1945, she filed suit

---

* Ed. note: Pearson was inducted into the Students Army Training Corps, United States Army, at Swarthmore College, on October 29, 1918, and was granted an honorable discharge one month later.

against him, charging that he was operating the farm for his own commercial use. She asked the court to sell the farm, invest the proceeds, and turn the income over to Ellen.

Ellen remained loyal to her father. She accepted his offer to buy the farm from her for $100,000, though she understood her grandmother would be willing to pay her three times that much to keep it out of Pearson's hands. The suit was dropped.

Meanwhile, Cissy had been further enraged at Pearson for failing to invite her to Ellen's wedding in March 1947. Ellen's marriage to George Arnold, son of Thurman Arnold, Washington lawyer and New Dealer, was a posh affair and Cissy took pains to play it up in the *Times-Herald*.

Winchell's reaction on the radio to Cissy's "Crazy—Crazy Like Foxes" article was to call her "the craziest woman in Washington, D.C."

More than three years before, Winchell, too, had begun to vanish from the pages of the *Times-Herald*, and for much the same reason. Though at one time he had served as a judge of the paper's "Golden Mirror" beauty contests, he had fallen far from grace. When war came, Cissy did not suffer gladly Winchell's shrill superpatriotism, which included running around New York night spots in the uniform of a lieutenant commander in the naval reserve (he had been a yeoman in World War I).

"There isn't a night goes by that I don't get down on my knees and pray that they take the —— off shore duty and put him on a destroyer that will sink," she remarked privately.

The Navy used Winchell for recruiting stunts to raise money for Navy Relief. But when he began doing his radio broadcasts in uniform, it was too much for Representative Carl Vinson, powerful chairman of the House Naval Affairs Committee. He advised the Navy Department to either call Winchell into active service or to "disenroll him." The Navy returned Winchell to the inactive reserve.

Exasperated at the gossip columnist for sniping at everyone

who disagreed with him as an "appeaser," Cissy sometimes had
such attacks deleted and sometimes killed the column altogether.
In the month of February 1942, the *Times-Herald* printed only
nine of Winchell's twenty-eight columns.

Virtual suppression in a city which has the most influential
breakfast reading audience in the country is of course cata-
strophic for a columnist. In his first radio broadcast in March
1942, Winchell threatened a lawsuit to cancel his contract with
Cissy. He charged that the *Times-Herald* was meeting telephoned complaints about his missing column with the statement
that they were available only three times a week.

Over the next Winchell column Cissy printed this precede:

Editor's Note: Walter Winchell's column is a part of a
general purchase of features the *Times-Herald* makes from
King Features Syndicate. We are under no compulsion to
print any of it any time. Winchell writes six times a week.

If anyone has told you that Winchell "writes three times
a week," he was not speaking for the Washington *Times-
Herald*.

To an interviewer, Cissy further explained: "My contract is
with King Features Syndicate, not Winchell, and it has two and
a half years to run. Winchell, unless he breaks his contract with
King Features, will run in the *Times-Herald* when and as we
decide. Who runs a paper anyhow—the editor or its columnists?"

Later in March, Cissy sued Winchell for $100,000 as punitive
damages for defamatory remarks about her on his radio program,
and sued his sponsor, the Andrew Jergens Company, and the
National Broadcasting Co. for another $100,000.

In this program Winchell had dug out a *Times-Herald* editorial
which had been reprinted in the *Congressional Record* two
years before. He noted that the column was inserted in the
Record with praise by the late Senator Ernest Lundeen of
Minnesota, who was shown in court to have worked with the
convicted Nazi agent Viereck. "It fascinates me to see how the
pieces of the jigsaw puzzle fit together," Winchell had com-

mented. He added his customary complaint that the paper which printed the editorial "buys but suppresses and handcuffs my column."

Cissy promptly reprinted the two-year-old editorial; all it had done was to sensibly urge that the United States assume the protection of Greenland in the wake of Hitler's occupation of Denmark, of which Greenland was a colony. "The logical 'sun' for the western hemisphere nations to revolve around is the United States," the editorial concluded.

Cissy informed her readers in reprinting the editorial that she was proud of it, as she was of every one of her editorials. She entitled her reply to Winchell "SQUASH" and said: "Nobody *likes* to step on a cockroach, but occasionally it is necessary in the interest of cleanliness and hygiene."

Haled into court for a pretrial examination in the libel suit, Winchell did an about-face and said meekly under oath that the editorial he had singled out was indeed a "very patriotic piece." He disclaimed any desire to besmirch or harm the *Times-Herald*. Mrs. Patterson testified that neither Lundeen nor Viereck had anything to do with the publication of the editorial, as Winchell well knew, and Winchell did not dispute her.

Cissy dropped her suit when she learned that Winchell's contract with the Jergens Company allowed him to escape payment of any judgment that might be rendered against him, including lawyer's fees and all other expenses. If she could not stick Winchell personally for damages, she saw no point in pressing the suit.

But Cissy was not through with Winchell yet. In her "Having a Wonderful Time" series that summer she devoted one article to him as "The Popgun Patriot." It noted that a *New Yorker* profile of Winchell, written by St. Clair McKelway, discovered, by checking back on Winchell items appearing in a single month, that 41.2 percent were completely inaccurate, 18.3 percent were partially inaccurate, and 40.5 percent were accurate. Winchell's career from obscure vaudeville hoofer to what Westbrook Pegler called "The Gents' Room Journalist" was given a typical going-over by Dixon writing as Georgiana X. Preston.

Winchell never did succeed in following Pearson to the Washington *Post* and, indeed, never got another daily newspaper outlet in Washington. In this sense, he was a Patterson-feud casualty.

FIFTEEN

More Feuds

Not many American men, and probably no other American woman, had the temerity or the gusto to engage in as many public feuds as Cissy Patterson. Besides her open quarrels with Alice Longworth, Drew Pearson and Walter Winchell, she wrangled with Harold Ickes, Eugene Meyer, Franklin D. Roosevelt, Marshall Field, Henry Wallace, Harry Truman, and Henry and Claire Boothe Luce. The list would be a good deal longer if a number of prospective victims had matched her zest for a verbal tangle.

Save for Roosevelt, the two most interesting feuds Cissy had were those with Ickes and Meyer. Both were worthy antagonists.

Eugene Meyer was a California-born millionaire banker, bald, scholarly, witty, and tough, with a taste for combat. With a white goatee, he could have passed for a Spanish grandee. He came to Washington in 1917 to help President Wilson finance the war, and remained to serve in government posts under five more Presidents.

Shortly after he arrived in the capital, Meyer's wife, Agnes, was invited to a large luncheon given by Mrs. Bernard Baruch. At this point, she still did not know a soul in the city. Sitting directly across the table from her was a fascinating young woman, the Countess Gizycka. They fell to talking and became so engrossed with each other they spoke to no one else at the luncheon.

The next day Cissy invited Agnes to lunch, and saw to it that

from then on the Meyers were brought into social affairs. The
Meyers themselves began to entertain, and Cissy and Agnes became close friends. The most important party the Meyers gave
at that time was in honor of the Secretary of the Treasury, Carter Glass. Meyer was then managing director of the War Finance
Corporation, which was under the Treasury Department. Agnes
knew all about Cissy's tardiness—she came to a party when she
felt like it. So she stressed that this party was for "Eugene's boss"
and could Cissy please try to be reasonably prompt? Cissy promised, and made good on it. She was the very first guest to show
up.

"Agnes," she announced, "I'm not only on time, I've got a
corset on! I wanted to do you proud."

After Cissy married Elmer Schlesinger, they saw a good deal
of the Meyers. But the time came when Cissy's warmth toward
Eugene Meyer evaporated. It began on the morning of June 2,
1933, with a strange scene on the steps of the old Washington
Post building on E Street NW. A small crowd, which included
some of the town's most influential citizens, was gathered there
for the sale of the *Post* at public auction. The once respected old
paper had fallen on evil days. Thanks to some unwise financing
and neglectful stewardship by playboy Ned McLean, who had
inherited the paper (and was to die in a mental institution), it
was $700,000 in debt. Its circulation, gouged by three years of
stiff competition from Cissy's *Herald*, had plummeted all the
way down to 19,000. The *Post* was in receivership and was up
for the highest bid in order to satisfy its creditors.

The most dramatic figure present was Ned's estranged wife,
Evalyn, appropriately dressed in black. She was anxious to save
the paper for their two sons, but her own fortune was running
out and she had not even been able to hock or sell the Hope
Diamond (which she was wearing) to raise a substantial amount
of cash. Also in the crowd were the other two members of what
were called "The Three Furies"—Cissy Patterson and Alice
Longworth. Bascom Timmons, a Washington correspondent

from Texas, opened the bidding at $250,000 and soon dropped
out. Mrs. McLean bid up to $600,000 and then she had to quit.
The rest of the bidding was done by lawyers on behalf of un-
disclosed principals. The bidder for Cissy, who was trying to
buy the *Post* for Hearst, went as high as $800,000. The paper
was then sold for $825,000 on a bid by George E. Hamilton, Jr.
Not until four days later was it disclosed that the paper had been
bought by Meyer.

Cissy was furious at her good friend for jumping into the
newspaper business as her rival. She regarded it as nothing short
of a declaration of war, and she buckled on her sword and shield.
So did Meyer. Both had been advised by professionals that two
morning newspapers in Washington could not both make a profit.
Both were determined to win the battle at any cost.

It promised to be a fairly even scrap. Meyer had more liquid
assets to pour into his enterprise than Cissy, but he was, after all,
a banker, and he looked on a newspaper strictly as a business.
Cissy, on the other hand, had the flair for eye-catching journalism but was somewhat restricted by the Hearst-organization
straitjacket.

Meyer learned which part of a newspaper has most reader
appeal the very moment he acquired the *Post*. He was informed
that the paper had already lost its best circulation asset: its comic
strips. When the *Post* was in receivership, Cissy had snapped up
some folk characters who were better known than the President
of the United States in virtually every American household—
Andy Gump, Winnie Winkle, Dick Tracy and Skeezix.

All these strips, and some others only slightly less popular,
were distributed by the Chicago *Tribune* syndicate, owned by
the Patterson-McCormick family. Indeed, Cissy's own brother
Joe had coined the names Winnie Winkle and Andy Gump. Cissy
persuaded the syndicate to give her an exclusive contract in
Washington for its comics and sports and medical-advice features which had been carried by the *Post*. She triumphantly an-

nounced her coup in full-page advertisements—while the strips were still running in the *Post*.

Meyer got a court order to restrain the *Herald* from printing the features, but another court dissolved it. In New York, Meyer lawyers sought to enjoin the *Tribune* from selling to the *Herald*, but in vain. Meyer next filed a suit against the *Herald*, insisting that the old contracts with the *Post* were still in effect and now belonged to him alone. Cissy fought back, and for twenty months the legal battle raged, as injunctions were issued and dismissed and the case climbed from court to court. All the while, Washingtonians were saturated with the misadventures of Andy Gump and his fellow comics. They were available in both the *Post* and *Herald* simultaneously.

At last, in April 1935, the United States Supreme Court declared Meyer the winner. The *Post* celebrated its victory with a six-column cartoon showing an imposingly robed justice sternly pointing to a facsimile of the *Post's* front page, toward which Dick Tracy, Skeezix, et al, obediently trudged. The caption said: "To your Post!"

The *Herald* obeyed the Court and dropped its forbidden strips the next day. But its Sunday color pages were already made up, with the now *verboten* comics included. Cissy asked Meyer for permission to publish them for one last time, sparing her the expense of a last-minute change. Meyer agreed, after some hesitation, on condition that the *Herald* print a front-page box acknowledging the *Post's* courtesy. Cissy asked time to consider. The deadline came and went, with no further word from the *Herald* publisher. Whereupon the *Post* published its own announcement that the *Herald* would appear next day with Sunday comics by special courtesy of the *Post*. After one edition, the *Post* blushingly killed its own announcement, for Cissy had quietly removed the disputed features and substituted Brick Bradford, Mandrake the Magician, Rose O'Neill's Kewpies and an animal feature by Frank Buck, rushed to her from New York by air express.

Cissy simmered over losing the strips. Then she sent to the meat market for one pound of hamburger—no more and no less. She wrapped it up in a gorgeously decorated box fit to encase an orchid and told her chauffeur to deliver it to Meyer's door. When the banker opened the box, he found the raw meat beneath a spray of freesia, sweet peas and forget-me-nots. Attached to it was a note: "So as not to disappoint you—take your pound of flesh."

Meyer delightedly told the story on himself, and it was all over Washington the next day. He could not help but like Cissy. He had always aided and abetted suffragettes; back in 1910, when he was one of the chief financiers of Maxwell Motors, he had pioneered in employing female auto salesmen (on the theory that it was the wife who made the family decision on the choice of car). He respected a woman who was a good, tough manager, and Cissy had charm besides.

Just the same, their war was real, and out in the open. Most metropolitan publishers—for mutual protection—keep their private squabbles discreetly hidden from the public, but not these two former friends. As the circulation war between the *Post* and *Herald* waxed bitter, they played up one another's blunders in front-page jibes. For example, when in February 1935 the jury ended its deliberations over Bruno Richard Hauptmann in the Lindbergh baby's kidnap-slaying, the Associated Press sent out a premature flash, "Hauptmann gets life." The *Post* rushed the flash into print, but luckily the corrected flash came through ("Hauptmann gets chair") in time to call back the edition before it hit the newsstands. A *Herald* staff member bought a copy of the embarrassing edition from a *Post* printer for $50, and the *Herald* gleefully ran a photograph of it on page one, paying back the *Post* for having enjoyed a journalistic Bronx cheer when the *Herald* had prematurely announced the "eyewitness description" of the execution of a couple of gangsters.

On its masthead the *Post* carried the picture of a crowing rooster. One day the *Herald* carried the drawing of a sick chicken, with its feet in the air, together with a picture showing a shed piled with copies of the *Post* and another showing newsboys dumping batches of the paper in the woods just outside the city limits. Under a headline, "YOU ASKED FOR IT, EUGENE," Cissy alleged that the *Post* was counting these unread papers in claiming circulation gains.

Meanwhile, both papers raided one another's staff and continued to try to buy up one another's best features.

Cissy's feud with Meyer in no way affected her friendship with Agnes Meyer.

"I always liked her because she was one of the most fascinating women I have ever known—a great woman," Mrs. Meyer explained years later. "You never knew what Cissy was going to do or say next—but it was always interesting. Her appeal was indefinable, and irresistible, to women as well as men."

Once, Cissy and Agnes turned up at the same party wearing exactly the same new dress. Neither woman was happy about it, but such was Cissy's reputation for making mischief that many people jumped to the conclusion that she had done it deliberately to discomfit her friend, though it was not so.

Cissy and Eugene made up several times. Once, there was a chance confrontation at a meeting of the Soroptimist Club, an organization of women chosen from every profession, at the Willard Hotel. Meyer was guest of honor, and was seated at the table right beside his rival. An indispensable part of every club luncheon was a ritual in which each member puts his arm around his neighbor and sings the club song. As the time for the ritual approached, Mrs. Patterson and Mr. Meyer eyed each other coldly. Finally, Cissy, unable to suppress a smile, threw an arm around her competitor's shoulder and together they sang the corny lyrics ending: ". . . so now we get together, as happy as can be."

In the last years of her life there was no bitterness between them. They were still keen competitors for circulation and they were direct ideological opposites: Meyer's paper was liberal and internationalist; Cissy's paper was conservative in domestic affairs and for "America First" in foreign affairs. But Cissy's paper, now the merged, round-the-clock *Times-Herald*, was showing a good profit by 1943, and the *Post* was doing better too.

Cissy's feud with Ickes was livelier, from an etymological standpoint, because he was her equal in turning a destructive phrase. Ickes shared her joy in pugnacity for pugnacity's sake, a Scotch Presbyterian heritage and a Chicago background. The Cissy-Ickes feud, too, followed after a close friendship and was occasionally interrupted by further spurts of amiability.

In Chicago, Harold Ickes had been a highly successful lawyer and a reform politician. He came to Washington with the New Deal. Although he was to serve as a cabinet member longer than anyone in history—thirteen years—he got into FDR's cabinet almost by accident. A progressive Republican since Teddy Roosevelt's Bull Moose campaign in 1912, Ickes had backed Roosevelt in 1932. After the election, he had ambitions to become Indian Commissioner; he had made a hobby of studying Indians, though no one but Ickes himself could have considered him the best-qualified man for the post.

FDR, however, was shopping around for a Secretary of the Interior, having been turned down by two liberal Republicans, Senators Hiram Johnson and Bronson Cutting. Then Ickes was recommended, Roosevelt had a chat with him and said, "I like the cut of his jib." FDR liked Ickes' obvious aggressiveness and the fact that he had fought the private utilities, including the notorious Samuel Insull. But it was a hasty decision when he picked Ickes for Interior Secretary and it flabbergasted the men around him. To their amusement, Roosevelt knew Ickes so little that at first he kept pronouncing the name as "Icks" instead of "Ickees."

Ickes did not become close to Cissy Patterson until after his wife, the former Anna Wilmarth, was killed in an auto accident.

He was hardly the handsome or rugged type that usually attracted Cissy. Ickes was below medium height, a bespectacled, dumpy man with a heavy chin and a petulant eye. But people, including Cissy, admired Ickes' fearlessness and enjoyed his Puckish sense of humor. Typically, when someone called him a "curmudgeon," Ickes adopted the word and played the role with perfection. A worried aide reminded his boss that the dictionary defines "curmudgeon" as "an irascible, churlish fellow." Fine, replied Ickes, this is exactly what he was. Aside from the fact that he was a shrewd administrator, Ickes was useful to FDR as a hatchet man and hairshirt.

Ickes' published diaries are replete with references to Cissy. He admired her as a woman and as a journalist; he believed that if she had been a man she would have been a better editor than either her brother or her cousin in Chicago. Here is a typical entry, dated September 18, 1935:

> Last night I had dinner with Cissy Patterson at Dower House. She is very friendly and understanding. I have liked her since I came to know her in Washington, and my liking for her has not grown less as I have known her better.

Later in the year he met Joe Patterson at a party at Cissy's and had this to say about her brother: "I have never really known him but I have always felt that I wanted to know him. He is not afraid to do some independent thinking, despite his wealth and social position, and he is a forthright, hard-hitting individual, with a social outlook . . . I would rank him now as a real progressive."

On another occasion in 1935, Cissy telephoned Ickes to tell him that the first edition of the *Herald* had carried a bitter attack on him as a "Communist." She explained that, when she saw it, she ordered this Hearst-syndicate editorial pulled out. "She said that the editorial was not only mean, it was stupid," Ickes noted with satisfaction in his diary. "I told her that I appreciated her doing what she had but that she should not have done it. She said, in a facetious vein, that both of us might lose our jobs."

In 1936, Hearst broke with Roosevelt, and Cissy had to run Hearst's anti-New Deal editorials in the *Herald*, although she did not always agree with them. During a visit in July, according to Ickes:

> She asked me if I was going to attack her boss again, meaning Hearst, and I told her that I was. She asked me what I had against him, and I replied that I thought he was unscrupulous. Then I asked her what her brother Joe thought about him. She said that he too thought he was unscrupulous.

A month later, according to the diary, Cissy was helping the Interior Secretary feel sorry for himself, and he loved it:

> Mrs. Patterson asked me out to Dower House for dinner last night. I was dreadfully tired but I thought it might be a good thing for me to go. There were only four other guests, one of them being White, the general manager of the Hearst newspapers. Cissy noticed that I was pretty tired and, after dinner, she took me down to the swimming pool where we sat and talked for quite some time. She told me how foolish she thought I was to work so hard and allow things to worry me, and of course I had to admit the force of everything she said. I know that I looked tired and acted tired, because I couldn't do otherwise, considering the way I felt.
>
> I was impressed again with Cissy's gentleness and friendly understanding. I have come to be very fond indeed of her. I have found in her the best friend I have made in Washington. She seems to me to be a very genuine person with broad sympathies. She doesn't see why I stay on in the cabinet, considering the difficulties under which I have had to work during the last year or more. I have wondered myself why I do it, but she agreed with me that at least until after the election I have no alternative but to stick, because otherwise I would be regarded as a quitter.

Hearst was all-out in backing Governor Alfred M. Landon of Kansas against Roosevelt in the 1936 election, and Cissy was in the middle, between her boss and her friend. Ickes was making more campaign speeches for FDR than all the other cabinet members combined—a prime target for Hearst. Ickes spent the following weekend at Cissy's Long Island estate and, together, they listened to Landon's speeches on the radio.

In his diary Ickes reveals that on this weekend he was preparing another speech, "Hearst Over Topeka," to be given over a radio network, and "chuckled to myself that I should be polishing up an attack on her boss" while staying at her place.

After Roosevelt's election landslide, Ickes continued to be a regular at Cissy's parties, but Cissy and Harold were on a collision course. When Ickes assailed monopolies, as he often did, he usually took out after certain newspapers. In the mimeographed text of a speech to be delivered in December 1937, he used the phrase "certain kept newspapers and kept commentators," but he dropped the phrases in his actual delivery.

The next day he telephoned Cissy to invite her to his house for dinner and got a surprise.

As soon as I was connected with her, she almost jumped down my throat about the speech. She thought it was terrible and would hurt both me and the Administration. She especially resented the expression, "kept newspapers," and I asked her why she had put on a slipper that was not intended for her. The *Herald* yesterday had an editorial taking violent exception to my speech, and she told me that she had written it herself. I told her that this had been my guess. She spoke of the cartoon also, saying that she had called to her cartoonist asking him if he could get a cartoon out on Ickes right away. I told her that it was a good cartoon and that she ought to raise the young man's salary. She sputtered and sputtered. She said that she still loved me but that she didn't like the speech, although she thought that it might be nice to come out to dinner next week. She warned me, however, that the *Herald* was not through with me, and I told her that was all right.

Cissy did not hesitate to print any story which would get under Ickes' skin. One day, when Pat Frank was vacationing at Cape Hatteras, North Carolina, he was standing on the beach when he saw an incongruous sight. Further down the beach was a Packard touring car loaded to the running boards with men, all of them carrying stop watches. They had their eyes on a flock of sanderlings. Each time these shore birds ran down the beach, the car would roar along with them; when the frightened birds ran back, the car would follow them back.

The third time the men in the Packard followed the sanderlings up the beach toward Frank, his curiosity overcame him and he asked what they were doing. One of the men said they were from the Fish and Wildlife Service and were undertaking a bit of research: timing the speed of the sanderling.

"You know what we discovered?" the spokesman asked. "The sanderling can travel three miles an hour faster downwind than he can upwind!"

Frank went directly to the nearest telegraph office and filed a story to the *Herald* about this evidence of imbecility. It was Frank at his funniest, and the *Herald* played it on the front page. The story caused cries of antibureaucratic indignation in Congress, and this, in turn, brought a protest phone call from Ickes to Cissy. The Fish and Wildlife Service is a division of the Interior Department, and Ickes was put on the spot by what Frank had described as a "prize example of boondoggling."

In April 1938, Cissy telephoned Ickes from New York to urge him as Interior Secretary to develop springs that possess therapeutic and medicinal qualities, "in connection with the possible expatriation of Jewish doctors who have been running the spas in Austria." Ickes promised to pass on the idea to the President. The next day she called him again to arrange a dinner meeting and, according to the diary, was "her old friendly self."

"She told me that she didn't like my speeches but that she loved me as much as ever," the diary continues. "I countered that I didn't believe it and that her editorials had not shown any such attitude."

At dinner, Ickes reported, "we had a very pleasant evening, though when it came to discussing newspapers we had to watch our step. She thinks that I am even more critical of the newspapers than the Administration."

That spring the sixty-four-year-old widower was paying court to twenty-five-year-old Jane Cudahy Dahlman. Jane was a redheaded, athletic, outspoken beauty who worked for the Interior Department; her sister was married to Ickes' stepson. Cissy, sensing that they were serious, informed Ickes that she expected him to give her a scoop when the wedding plans were made.

Meanwhile, George De Witt, the *Herald* managing editor, was informed by a nurse—one of his tipsters—that when Jane was in the hospital for a few days she had hinted that she would be married soon. When De Witt called Jane to get the story, she begged him not to print it. She and Harold would be embarrassed by premature publicity. De Witt went to Cissy and explained the situation. Cissy wanted to print the scoop, but she fully expected her friend Harold to tip her off anyway. She told De Witt to sit on the story for the time being.

In June, Jane Dahlman announced she was taking off for Ireland to visit her uncle, John Cudahy, who was U.S. minister in Dublin. Shortly afterward, Ickes quietly boarded a ship, incognito, for France. His trip was a tightly kept secret for several days; Michael Straus, Interior Department press secretary, issued mimeographed announcements of actions and statements by the Secretary to leave the impression that Ickes was in the United States and on the job.

When Ickes left Washington, he told Straus that he would meet Jane in Dublin and they would be married there. Only one other person was in on the secret—the President. Straus was told to await a cablegram from Ickes and then "break the story." Edward Folliard of the Washington *Post* had a tip about the wedding, but when he tried to check it with Straus the bland reply was: "I'm the Department information officer. How would I know?"

At 8 o'clock one morning Straus got the expected cable ("Done this day . . ." was the way Ickes put it) and issued an announcement that the Secretary had been married in Dublin. At 10 o'clock, Straus answered the telephone and found himself being upbraided by Mrs. Patterson, for whom he had formerly worked as a reporter.

"How could you let them do it?" she demanded.

Straus pointed out that he had had no control over his boss's private life.

"After all, Mrs. Patterson," he said, "I'm not their chatelaine."

Cissy made it clear that she did not approve of Ickes marrying a girl thirty-nine years his junior.

Nonetheless, Cissy got Ickes on the overseas telephone when the happy couple were two days out on the voyage home and extended her congratulations and love. She also offered the use of her apartment at the Carlton House while they were in New York.

Cissy not only forgave Ickes for marrying without telling her; she telephoned him late in July with what she called "a crazy thought." She asked him to write a column for her afternoon paper, the *Times*. She said she was having trouble with the *Times* and that his punditry would give it a boost.

Ickes replied that he was flattered and attracted by the offer but was uncertain whether he would be allowed to do a column. He had good reason for his doubts; the idea of a cabinet member commenting on political affairs regularly in a newspaper was unheard of, and obviously fraught with pitfalls. The next afternoon Cissy called again and suggested that, if Ickes himself could not do the column, perhaps Jane could. Ickes realized this meant that he would really be writing it under his wife's name. Nonetheless, he promised to think it over on a trip he was about to make to Alaska and would let Cissy know when he returned.

When he got back from Alaska, Ickes mentioned the offer over
lunch with Roosevelt. The President made the sensible point
that Ickes would be unable to write about anything except his
own department and would run out of material. Ickes nodded,
realizing that as a member of the Administration he could not
very well criticize other departments, nor could he frankly discuss political affairs at home or abroad.

According to Ickes' diary, FDR added a personal comment:
"The President said that he had known Cissy since she was a
girl and that he liked her but thought she was somewhat
'cracked.' "

Cissy was right in believing that Ickes could write a lively
column, for he did so after he stormed out of Truman's cabinet,
but that was not until 1946.

Ickes continued to annoy Cissy by his public statements in
which, as the Administration's public prosecutor, he excoriated
the newspapers which were hammering at the New Deal. Finally, in late April, she decided to answer his latest speech and let
"Honest Harold" have it broadside over a national radio hookup.
Her speech was entitled, "The Jawbone of an Acidulous Man."
It began:

> Harold is a friend of mine but I am not pretending now
> that I am speaking more in sorrow than in anger. Oh, no! I
> am mad clear through, and this is why:
>
> The purpose of his speech was as evident to me as is the
> purpose of those many lectures on "Journalism" which the
> President has seen fit to deliver at his press conferences. I
> can see the same purpose in other acts and allegations of the
> Administration now in office. The purpose is to discredit the
> press of the United States as the purveyor of the truth of
> what goes on in Washington. To most of us the incentive
> behind the attack is plain.
>
> For some time the New Deal has been slipping. Its con-
> fusions have been multiplied; its failures have been increased.
> These facts are well known. How do they become known?
> Because that section of the press which is on duty in Wash-

ington and those editors away from Washington who comment on the news they send, have revealed the facts. It is this which is the animus of the Administration's steady attacks on the press.

The New Dealers fear only the press as the revealer of their errors and accidents. The radio is licensed by the government. The newsreels impart government good-will. Only the press, under the Constitution, is wholly free from the restricting hand of politicians in power. What, then, more natural than that men who love power and want to keep it should attack the press for discovering and publishing the truths which foreshadow the loss of that power?

Cissy charged that Ickes' most recent speeches were timed to "besmirch the American press" and offset newspaper criticism that was certain to come in the wake of bellicose statements by Administration leaders on the growing war clouds in Europe.

She declared that Ickes "suppresses views and prejudices which are a deterrent to his ambition, and only reveals those he thinks will aid him."

Cissy then disclosed into the microphone that she had made an offer to Ickes to write a column and that he had been "forbidden to write, presumably by his boss." She added:

From his standpoint, this was indeed a pity. For if Mr. Ickes has ever conducted a column, I am sure that it would have been a column that ended all columns, including those he now attacks. And instead of speaking to you here tonight —a free woman—I—because of his venoms, irresponsibilities and inaccuracies, would probably be in jail serving out a sentence for criminal libel.

Attacking columnists, Mr. Ickes shows himself a purveyor of more baseless gossip than any he so describes. Attacking reporters, Mr. Ickes shows himself too incompetent to hold a job on any paper with which I am familiar.

Cissy's blast at Ickes was widely reported in newspapers, and there were many in Washington who felt that the crusty Secretary had been "Cissified"—a term which Ickes himself had coined.

In his diary Ickes complained that in her speech Cissy had been catty and personal about him, to the point of having blatted on the radio things he had told her privately. He grumbled that her version of how she offered him a chance to become a columnist was twisted and unfair. And he said he had learned that the speech had been written for Cissy by Arthur Krock, chief Washington correspondent for the New York *Times*.

Krock, a good friend of Cissy, had indeed helped her compose her blast, as had Frank Waldrop, *Times-Herald* editorial writer.

When Cissy and Ickes met within a week after the speech was delivered, their friends were expecting a clawing match. However, it developed otherwise, as Ickes notes happily in his diary:

> Drew Pearson had invited Jane and me to a cocktail party Friday given in honor of the newspaper editors who had been in session in Washington . . . Cissy Patterson came in to the cocktail party as we were standing in groups about the lawn. Of course she saw me but she kept on the outskirts until it became clear to me that it was her purpose to get away without speaking to me. So I disengaged myself from the group I was with and went up to her. She turned in affected surprise and said, "Why, Harold." I said, "Cissy, dear," and we threw our arms around one another and demonstrably kissed. Everyone was watching us and everyone was much amused. Then we stood with our arms around each other while we discussed her speech over the air. One guest came up and remarked that we were afraid not to have our arms around each other, which I thought was a good *bon mot.*
>
> Cissy could not believe that I had not listened to her radio speech, but I assured her that I hadn't. I consoled her, however, by saying that I had read it the day following. I kidded her about it and declined at any point to show that I had minded anything she had said . . .
>
> Jane did not want to speak to Cissy at the cocktail party,

but she could not avoid doing this without it being obvious. Jane used to like Cissy, but she resents her attack on me and insists it is all jealousy on Cissy's part. I had never felt that Cissy had any matrimonial aspirations, so far as I was concerned, but we were very good friends and I sincerely liked her. It is a fact that, from the time Jane and I became attached to each other, Cissy has gone out of her way to hammer at me in her editorials, and now, on this last occasion, over the air.

To Cissy's friends it was laughable even to suggest that Cissy might have had "matrimonial aspirations" toward the arrogant old curmudgeon. But Ickes naturally did not look at it that way.

The publisher and the cabinet officer continued to bombard one another at long range as war came and Ickes was given a number of additional home-front posts which got him into hot water.

One of his new jobs was that of Petroleum Coordinator, in which he laid down gasoline- and tire-rationing restrictions. The *Times-Herald* kept an investigative eye on Ickes' activities, and occasionally it was rewarded. During the summer of 1941, the paper reported that at the very time the "gas czar" had imposed a 7 P.M.-to-7 A.M. curfew on wayside filling stations in the East he kept a private filling station and underground tank hidden away on his 250-acre estate in Olney, Maryland (the estate was known as "Bellyacres" because of its owner's role as the Administration scold).

In May 1942, shoppers on Connecticut Avenue in Washington noticed a Department of Interior truck delivering eggs to a grocery store. It was known that the Secretary did a wholesale business in eggs laid on his farm. Some of the shoppers phoned the Interior Department and said they too were in the egg business and could they too have the use of a Department truck to distribute their produce? The *Times-Herald* assigned a reporter to tail Ickes' official limousine from his farm; the reporter learned that farmer Ickes was putting all his eggs in one basket and carrying them to town in the car.

Ickes explained it all: it was actually a plan to save gasoline and rubber. Ordinarily, he told newsmen, Jane would carry the eggs to market in her car, using up valuable fuel and tires. By acting as the egg-bearer himself, he could transport them to the Department in his government car and there transfer them to a government truck for the actual delivery to stores.

The *Times-Herald* quoted Washington taxpayers as conceding that the plan certainly saved Mrs. Ickes some mileage, but they failed to see any saving for the government. After that, the government truck was no longer seen delivering Ickes' eggs.

The *Times-Herald's* stable of irreverent columnists similarly enjoyed needling Ickes. The witty Evie Robert, in her column, "Eve's Rib," speculated on what to name her new German dog. She ran through a list of prominent New Dealers, rejecting each. Finally, she wrote, she would "call him 'Harold Ickes' until he's housebroken." Cissy was tickled—and so was the President. At the next cabinet meeting, FDR mentioned the column and teased the Secretary.

"Well, now you've finally made good, Harold," he quipped. "You've had a dog named after you!"

The fact that Eve's husband, Lawrence (Chip) Robert, was a prominent party member—treasurer of the Democratic National Committee—added to Roosevelt's enjoyment of Ickes' discomfort.

Ickes of course was quite capable of defending himself, even against Cissy Patterson. Once, Igor Cassini gave him the opportunity to write his column, "These Charming People." Ickes, as expected, hit Cassini as hard as he could. He wrote that "the two of you make a pretty pair, 'as the Devil said when he looked at his feet,'" but he warned Cassini not to anticipate a lifetime job on the paper.

At the end of the column Cissy appended an editor's note: "Come again, Harold. We welcome you anytime as a space writer, and forward herewith your accustomed check for ten dollars ($10.00)."

Cissy increasingly lost her patience as the home-front World War II controversies continued, however, and one of her last anti-Ickes editorials was headed simply: "Oh, Shut Up!"

SIXTEEN

War Declared—on FDR

A few of Cissy Patterson's closest friends had a theory that her animosity toward Franklin D. Roosevelt had its origins in an incident that supposedly happened on the golf course of the Chevy Chase Club, just outside Washington, back in 1916. According to this story, Assistant Secretary of the Navy Roosevelt was searching for his ball in the rough when he spied Cissy holding hands with a brand-new beau under a tree. He called out a joshing remark which embarrassed Cissy—and then proceeded to kid her about the scene for years after.

It is easy to believe that Roosevelt, famous for his teasing, would have made the most of the situation, but the story is very probably apocryphal. It may have been confused with another incident which *did* happen on the Chevy Chase golf course in 1916. The ebullient Assistant Secretary of the Navy hit a long drive which struck Cissy's beau in the leg as they were strolling near the green.

In any event, the theory that Cissy nursed a grudge toward Roosevelt for two decades and more is nonsense. They had known one another since they were young, and until the late 1930s she had no reason to dislike this Hyde Park Roosevelt either personally or as a politician. Although her family background was stoutly Republican (save for her brother's temporary lapse into Socialism in the early part of the century), Cissy's best friends among senators were the progressives of both parties. She enthusiastically covered the 1932 Democratic convention for the Hearst press and came out of it convinced that Roosevelt was just what the Depression-struck country needed. In fact, Cissy was regarded as being sufficiently non-Republican to be offered the post of associate chairman of the Democratic Central Committee of the District of Columbia in September of 1932. She declined.

By September, Cissy was busy interviewing Roosevelts for the Hearst syndicate. Her first article was a long one based on a visit with Mrs. James Roosevelt, the candidate's mother, after lunching with her, the Governor and the other guests at their home in Hyde Park, New York. Cissy wrote:

> The conversation scattered up and down the big, hospitable table. The Governor joining in, freely, frankly, with none of the usual man-in-the-limelight, crablike caution. Yet Roosevelt is quick and sensitive of eye and ear. Warm, responsive. For all his gaiety and freedom of manner, sitting there at home in his family circle, you feel that he is aware of each personality in the room.
>
> When I left her, finally, I felt even prouder of my country than I ever felt before, and convinced that this time we are going to have a real American of the finest type once more in the White House—Franklin Roosevelt.

Three weeks after Roosevelt was elected, Cissy journeyed to Warm Springs, Georgia, in her private railroad car to do an interview with the President-elect there. It frothed over with admiration:

> I don't want to sound as if I were getting exalted or anything, but there surely is a special radiance about this man which makes you feel better just to be around him. A "bonnie," frank manner. A high, free spirit. And natural warmth and subtle understanding.
>
> Well, unfortunately, the President-elect put me immediately at my ease by reminding me of the day, about eighteen years ago, when he cracked an old beau of mine on the shinbone at the Chevy Chase Club with one of those marvelous long balls he used to drive.

In this story, Cissy also had fulsome praise for the President's daughter, Anna Roosevelt Dall ("tall, built like a racehorse, with the kind of milk and wild-rose complexion you just don't see any more").

That night she threw a party on her private car for the President-elect's new "brain-trusters" and some newspaper correspondents. The champagne flowed freely and the only sober guests at the party were two who arrived late, after dining with Roosevelt. They were Congressman James F. Byrnes and Professor Raymond Moley, a brain-truster. At that moment, Cissy was pacing up and down, furious at Louis Ruppel, a New York *Daily News* correspondent, who was never a man to suppress his opinions and was complaining about how hard it was to please Joe Patterson. To Cissy this was *lèse majesté*.

"I think, Mr. Ruppel," she finally exploded, "you are a very cheap type of reporter to criticize the man who happens to be your employer and my brother."

Moley promptly lost *his* temper, drew himself up, and said, "I think you are the one that's cheap, Mrs. Patterson, for making a remark like that to one of your guests."

Cissy fired back that she had a good mind to ask both of them to leave. Moley snapped, "That's unnecessary, I'm going anyway." He took Byrnes and Ruppel with him. By the time they saw Ruppel back to his hotel, he was weeping. The argument had shaken him badly—perhaps, he feared, right out of his job.

Moley soon regretted his own outburst, but he had no chance to apologize; Cissy left Warm Springs later in the night. A few days later, Moley asked Fred Essary, a *Herald* reporter, to call Cissy on his behalf, but word came back that she would not talk to him.

Moley next went to Roosevelt, expressing fears that he had laid the basis for an unfriendly press in Washington for the new President. Roosevelt laughed it off with, "Why don't you send some sort of insulting telegram to her train?" Moley, however, was serious about making amends.

After the inauguration in March 1933, William E. Bullitt arranged a reconciliation over cocktails at Du Pont Circle. Cissy blithely opened the conversation by remarking that she had never hated anyone as she had been hating Moley. This cleared the atmosphere, and before the cocktail hour was over a friendship had ripened. Moley, who soon broke with FDR and became a columnist, has regarded Cissy with great admiration and affection ever since.

Cissy's feeling for the new President was reinforced by the fact that her brother was going all out for him. Joe Patterson gave Roosevelt more than political help. After the 1932 election, the New York *Daily News* enlisted the aid of other newspapers around the country and asked the public to donate their nickels and pennies to build a swimming pool in the White House so the polio-crippled President would have a place to exercise. The *News* launched the campaign with its own $1000 contribution, and, in all, some $25,000 was collected nationwide.

FDR wrote Patterson a warm note of thanks:

> It is not alone the material contributions you and the others have made but the kindliness and generosity of all contributors that I appreciate. The thought that this campaign was initiated voluntarily, without my knowledge or sanction, and subscribed to so generously means as much, if not more, than the pool itself.

When Hearst and other publishers jumped off the Roosevelt bandwagon in the 1936 campaign, the *Daily News* stuck with him, which was important, for the New York tabloid had by far the largest circulation in the United States—more than 1,500,000 daily and 3,000,000 on Sunday. After FDR was elected by a landslide, he wrote on November 9, 1936:

> Dear Joe:
> Many thanks for sending me that very nice telegram from Lord Beaverbrook. I knew him during the war when he was doing excellent work in helping to take care of Amer-

ican and British overseas soldiers and sailors on their way through England.

And—what is more important than that—I think I do not need to tell you how very splendid you have been throughout. I have a very strong feeling that the NEWS was worth more to us in the city in the way of votes than all the political meetings and speeches put together. And, incidentally, you must be proud of the NEWS poll—and I only wish you had been able to get the *Literary Digest* to back their crazy poll with a million dollars.

During the first five years of the Roosevelt administration, Joe Patterson's influence in the shaping of the New Deal was considerable. He spent weekends in the White House frequently and sailed down the Potomac with the President on the presidential yacht, and not purely for social relaxation.

Cissy saw a good deal more of Eleanor Roosevelt, and admired her tremendously. In a long interview with Mrs. Roosevelt for the Hearst papers, Cissy revealed quite a bit about herself. After vainly trying to get the First Lady to admit that her serenity of spirit and "beautiful adjustment" to a crowded life were due to utter selflessness, Cissy said she asked her:

It must be, Mrs. Roosevelt, that you don't doubt and wonder much about yourself. There can't be any drain of sick vanity or wounded ego in you, as there is in most of us. That wastage which comes from forever wondering whether we're right or whether we're wrong. Whether we're being admired. What other people are thinking about.

Mrs. Roosevelt turned with a little chuckle by answering that she was too busy to think about such things.

The interview concludes:

Mrs. Roosevelt has solved the problem of living better than any woman I have ever known. There is none of this business of self-destruction going on within her heart or soul, as with most of us. No longer any anger, envy, uncharitableness, remorse, you would say. No longer any falling down just to pick yourself up, just to fall down again. Eleanor Roosevelt is the master of her soul.

The First Lady was an occasional guest at Cissy's parties, and their friendship never cooled. As for her feelings toward the President in the election year of 1936, Harold Ickes summed them up accurately in his diary entry of April 21, 1936:

> I had dinner with Cissy Patterson at her home Thursday night . . . she seemed to think that President Roosevelt's election is inevitable. She isn't for Roosevelt, although she isn't strongly against him. She said that she was pulled both ways between Hearst and her brother Joe. Hearst is bitterly fighting Roosevelt, and she is publisher of the Washington *Herald*. Naturally, she is loyal to him, but she adores Joe. Her state of mind seems to be significant of what the Hearst organization really believes.

In the opinion of editorial writer Frank Waldrop, Cissy "was more of a New Dealer than she was not."

While Joe Patterson continued to back the President in virtually everything he did (including the unsuccessful plan to "pack" the Supreme Court), Cissy felt, as the second New Deal proceeded, that it was about time FDR policies showed more solid results. She finally concluded that it was the domineering Roosevelt personality, together with his personification of power, that was stifling the economy. When she first stated this in print, it came about, ironically enough, because Managing Editor George De Witt was trying to bring her closer together with the President. He felt that adding to the stature of the great Cissy Patterson would give her paper prestige.

In April 1938, it occurred to De Witt that if FDR would appoint Mrs. Patterson to a cabinet post it would be wonderful for her and a stroke of political genius for the President, since it would be a fine gesture toward her pro-New Deal brother and just might please her anti-New Deal cousin in Chicago.

FDR already had one woman in his cabinet (Secretary of

Labor Frances Perkins), and exactly how he could be persuaded that he needed another one—and a tigress named Patterson, at that—was not fully developed in De Witt's mind. Nonetheless, De Witt went ahead and arranged a meeting, without telling Cissy in advance.

(Afterward, De Witt remarked ruefully that, despite his best-laid plans, "Mrs. Patterson kicked over the apple-cart.")

About the only thing that went right at the meeting was that, for once, Cissy was on time. She arrived at the door of the White House exactly at noon, after picking up a speeding ticket en route from Dower House. The clash with the President—probably inevitable—occurred soon after they began talking. Cissy told him bluntly that the economic slump was due to fear on the part of businessmen, and that it was up to Roosevelt to do something dramatic to reassure them. Stung, FDR snapped that it was easy enough to sit back and criticize without proposing solutions. He taunted his redheaded visitor: "All right. You go ahead. Write out exactly what you think I should do to banish fear!"

Cissy accepted the dare. She returned to her office under a full head of steam and called her top editorial advisers together. What resulted was a front-page open letter headed: "WHAT YOU COULD SAY, PRESIDENT ROOSEVELT." (She had her chauffeur deliver the letter in a huge white envelope to the front door of the White House.)

In the letter, Cissy said to FDR:

> You once said, with eternal truth, that the only thing to fear is fear itself. Fear is depressing industry. With due respect, you should concede the obvious. This fear is fear of you.
>
> It is fear of shifting policies; of a hostile attitude toward legitimate business; of insistence on discredited tax methods and other laws which prevent the earning and retaining of fair and honest profits.
>
> It is fear that, if you work out a constructive plan, you

won't stay put. It is fear that if a plan of yours is proved bad, you will stick to it stubbornly because you are unwilling to admit that, like all the rest of us, you make mistakes.

Mr. President, you can eliminate this basic cause of the Depression very simply. You command an instant audience of the whole nation. Through a message to Congress or some other vehicle, you should address yourself at once and convincingly to remove the fear that keeps applicants for loans away from banks full of money, and prevents us from turning into profits the greatest store of natural resources and industrial ingenuity in the world.

The open letter went on to suggest that the President should promise that his whole effort would be to raise the national income and that he would do so without favoritism and without attacking any individuals or groups, and ended:

> . . . the chief thing is to eliminate fear and thus restore confidence. You alone can do that. But you must do it thoroughly, forsaking hate and vanity, and resuming that patience with which you so nobly and courageously conquered an illness that would have broken the spirit of most of us.
>
> You have been a great leader and a great man. You can be again.

ELEANOR PATTERSON

Many newspapers, including the New York *Times*, ran stories about Cissy's public lecturing of the President. The Hearst press not only carried the open letter in full but Hearst himself was moved to print an open letter to Cissy, congratulating her and urging her to throw the columns of the *Herald* open to suggestions from readers.

In November, the Democratic party suffered a smashing defeat at the polls, losing seven seats in the Senate and eighty in the House. They were the first gains by the Republicans since 1928. The *Herald* called the election a rejection of Roosevelt's "philosophy of paternalistic security—attained by the government and exemplified by the WPA."

Meanwhile, Cissy was heading for a showdown with the President over, of all things, trees. The Administration was proposing to build a marble memorial to Thomas Jefferson in the Tidal Basin. Frank Waldrop urged his boss to oppose the project; he said it would be more sensible to put up a large assembly hall—something the capital really needed—and dedicate it to free speech. Waldrop argued that an empty memorial would desecrate Jefferson's express wishes. For Cissy's edification he dug out the long-forgotten fact that Jefferson had sketched on the back of an envelope the type of simple memorial he wanted: a plain six-foot obelisk with this inscription: "Here was buried Thomas Jefferson, author of the Declaration of Independence, of the statute of Virginia for religious freedom, and father of the University of Virginia."

Cissy cited the quotation in the *Herald*, adding that the proposed $3,000,000 memorial would be "a meaningless, useless, hideous scramble of cold marble and bronze." But what really fired her up was the admission that three hundred Japanese cherry trees, which had made the Tidal Basin famous, would have to be chopped down to make room for the grandiose project. Thousands of other Washingtonians were similarly aroused about decimating those almost sacred trees, and they made their views clear when the memorial bill came up in Congress.

The reaction indeed was so violent that the project was revised and a promise made that few trees would be chopped down. On Sunday, November 13, she urged in an editorial that "not one cherry tree shall fall to make room for this blasphemous proposition to 'honor' Jefferson with a mess of marble . . ."

The Washington Hotel Men's Association, worried that hundreds of thousands of tourists might lose interest in coming to the capital if there were no cherry trees, called an emergency meeting. Civic officials, clergymen and congressmen joined in a plea to have the start on the project delayed.

On Tuesday, the President reluctantly summoned the executive committee of the Memorial Commission to the White House to discuss the trees, but no action encouraging to the tree-savers resulted.

On Wednesday afternoon, Cissy herself led a march of three-dozen angry women on the White House. They halted at the door of the west executive wing while she went inside. She was met by Marvin McIntyre, the President's appointments secretary. McIntyre said the President was too busy to receive the ladies. Cissy handed him a petition from organizations representing 60,000 women. It urged Roosevelt to "save the trees." Cissy went back to her women and reported the rebuff. They sang Joyce Kilmer's "Trees" and dispersed.

Back in her office, Cissy confessed to her editors that she felt foolish leading the march. Yet she had an even wilder ploy up her sleeve. The *Herald* announced the next day that "militant District citizens—fighting mad over the threat to hack down the cherry trees—will take their stand this morning at the south Tidal Basin . . . and defy workmen to so much as break a twig.

"Leaders of today's demonstration," it continued, "are the women who executed yesterday's march on the White House—the most dramatic demonstration since suffragettes moved on the mansion years ago."

It amounted to a "tie-in," a forerunner of the "sit-ins" to come twenty-five years later. The clubwomen were to bring locks and chains, fasten themselves to the trees, and remain chained until the President promised to stay his "death sentence."

The result was the oddest exhibition of distaff determination in the history of demonstrations in the capital. Some 150 women marched with chains to the Tidal Basin. The CCC (Civilian Conservation Corps) workmen, who were quickly surrounded, feebly protested, "We're just digging, we're just digging." But the ladies snatched the shovels and spades from their hands.

Several buxom ones filled up a hole around a spruce tree, and others wrested a holly tree from a laborer who was trying to place it on a truck. But most of the women were busily engaged in chaining themselves to the trees and clamping locks on the chains. One group chained a park policeman to a tree, just to show that they would stand for no nonsense from *him*.

In the White House at that moment Roosevelt was holding a press conference. And far from retreating on trees, he was taking the offensive. He told the newsmen that the campaign to save the trees was "one of the most interesting cases of newspaper flimflam" he had ever seen. In effect, he was blaming Cissy's two newspapers for trumping up a phony issue.

At the Interior Department (which has jurisdiction over the Tidal Basin), the question of dealing with the female chain gang was being debated. Mike Straus, the Department's imaginative press secretary, proposed that the workmen be dismissed for the day and that the women be treated with exquisite hospitality. If gallons of coffee were served to the ladies, Straus reasoned, they would have to leave to go to the bathroom. Sure enough, the ladies drank the coffee, and as the day wore on they unshackled themselves, one by one, and hurried away. They never came back.

All that day, Cissy was sure that what the President was saying privately would be the tipoff to whether he was going through with his project. She asked her friend, Evie Robert, who was well connected at the White House, to go over there and find out.

Evie telephoned McIntyre at 5 o'clock, and McIntyre said to come right over, that Roosevelt would love to see her. As she walked into the President's office a few minutes later, he greeted her in his most buoyant manner.

"Evie! How are you?" FDR called out. "People have been bothering me all day about those damn trees. I'm so glad you've come for a *social* call."

The President mixed some old-fashioneds, leaning heavily on

the bourbon, and they had a convivial cocktail hour—chatting about everything but trees. FDR avoided the subject and skillfully steered Evie away every time she got near it.

Evie arrived back at Du Pont Circle and reported her lack of success. Cissy just nodded in disappointment and then muttered, with undisguised admiration: "He always *was* smart!"

The President, as Cissy suspected, *had* said something on the subject privately earlier in the day, and she subsequently found out what it was. He had shown his merry contempt for the demonstrators by suggesting that a hoisting device be employed to lift each tree and chained clubwoman out of the earth. Larger holes would then be dug and the trees and ladies planted in them—"all to be done in a strictly humane manner."

Boiling mad at FDR's "flimflam" crack at her papers, Cissy wrote him an open letter on the day after the demonstration. She said, "we accept the slap on the wrist proudly—though as workers in words we shudder at the word 'flimflam.'" And she thanked him for the "complimentary publicity" in making her papers responsible for the cherry-tree crusade.

On Sunday night a group of spokesmen for the tree-saving women went on the Mutual radio network to broadcast their frustration. They urged listeners all over the country to wire or write their protest to the President. Cissy played this up in the *Herald* and also used the issue to argue again for one of her pet campaigns. She said that such a thing would never have come to pass if the citizens of the District of Columbia had the right to vote.

Nonetheless, the trees were cut down, the Memorial was started, and soon the cherry-tree hullabaloo would seem trivial. The same edition of the *Herald* which called the memorial plan perfidious carried another editorial which quoted an internationally known psychiatrist as saying that Hitler was a "paranoiac seething with hatred and malice and a crazy determination to 'get even' with a world which does not recognize his godlike genius." "Why isn't he locked away, anyhow?" the editorial asked, adding that there were hopeful signs that the Germans might be sickening of his brutal ways.

The top headline in the same edition read: "JEWS FINED $400,-000,000 BY NAZIS, BARRED FROM ALL BUSINESS IN GERMANY." Another article on the front page told of Jews in Vienna going hungry as a result of anti-Jewish decrees promulgated by Germany. A third article, written by David Lloyd George, World War I Prime Minister of Great Britain, was headlined: "MUNICH ACCORD HASTENS WAR."

James Henry Whigham, a friend of Cissy's, was then writing editorials for the *Herald*. Whigham was a brother of a director of the Bank of England and was prone to write the Chamberlain government's official line—that the Munich pact would prevent the outbreak of war. Frank Waldrop complained that the *Herald* should not take a pro-Munich stand, and Cissy agreed, giving Waldrop specific authority to kill Whigham editorials.

About this time, Joe Patterson's *Daily News* was beginning to worry about the fact that the Roosevelt administration was studying ways and means to take economic reprisals against Germany and Japan. The *News* pointed out that economic reprisals "often lead to war." Actually, Patterson for some time had believed that war with the imperialistic Japanese was probably inevitable, and that we should prepare for it. As early as September 1934, he warned that the United States should build two ships for every ship the Japanese built. For the next seven years, hundreds of editorials headlined "TWO SHIPS FOR ONE" appeared in the *Daily News*. When FDR signed the "Big Navy bill" in July 1940, he gave Patterson a great deal of credit for making it possible and sent him the pen with which he signed the bill. After Cissy got the *Herald* away from Hearst in 1937, she began running many such editorials written for the *Daily News*.

Patterson was more worried about the Japanese aggressors than about the Germans; he felt that, if the Japanese conquered Asia, nothing but a huge U.S. navy and air corps would prevent them from making things hot for Uncle Sam. Cissy, on the other hand, was more interested in the war in Europe. While her brother had no emotional ties with Europe, she had quite a few. She had become thoroughly familiar with Paris, Vienna, and St. Petersburg as a young woman, and her marriage to Gizycki had resulted in an affection for Warsaw and the Polish people. She had nurtured her friendships in her frequent trips to Europe since the war, and now she was fearful of what would become of those old countries at the hands of the barbarian Nazis and Communists.

Nonetheless, Joe and Cissy were in complete agreement that the United States should keep hands off while Europe was going through its agony; they felt that direct intervention by America would not help. It was not up to this country to stop Hitler; it was up to the Europeans. While both condemned acts of appeasement like the one made at Munich, they were opposed to expending American blood or treasure to stop the Nazis in their tracks. Much as Cissy hated to think of Poland being sacrificed again, she was opposed to America plunging into the European maelstrom. For once, her heart was not ruling her head.

Patterson and Roosevelt continued to see a good deal of one another, however, and even after the war broke out in Europe on September 1, 1939, there was no break between them. Both Pattersons made no secret of their isolationist leanings, but, unlike many other isolationists, they believed in the utmost military preparedness. Joe Patterson pressed hard, for example, for not only a big navy and big air corps but a peacetime draft. In 1940, Patterson also—after FDR took him aside privately and explained it in advance—supported the "destroyer deal," in which Great Britain received fifty overaged destroyers in return for granting us certain of their outlying bases.

Despite these misgivings, the *Daily News* backed the President for a third term in 1940 against Republican Wendell Willkie (it even urged the Democratic National Convention to "draft" the President if necessary). Cissy was not very happy about her brother's unflagging enthusiasm for FDR, yet she ran the *Daily News* editorials in her *Times-Herald*, and it thus became the only Washington newspaper to support Roosevelt in 1940. (The Pattersons' pro-FDR stand was of course in direct conflict with the policy of their cousin in Chicago who ran the *Tribune*.)

(Joe Patterson's support of the third-term campaign is a fact which has escaped many FDR Boswells. Among others, Professor James McGregor Burns got it wrong in his *Roosevelt: The Lion and the Fox*. Interestingly, it was these third-term editorials, as well as others written in 1940 by chief *Daily News* editorial writer Reuben Maury, which won him a Pulitzer Prize in 1941. The vast majority of these editorials ran in Cissy's *Times-Herald*.)

The Pattersons' conviction that the war was not America's war remained unshaken in the fall of 1940, but they were fairly certain FDR did not feel the same way. The President was walking on eggs in his pre-election effort to please everybody. The Pattersons were reassured when he pledged in a campaign speech in Boston: "I have said this before, but I shall say it again—and again—and again—your boys are not going to be sent into any foreign wars."

Their break with Roosevelt came when he asked Congress right after the election for blank-check authority to sell, transfer, exchange or lease equipment and supplies to any country whose defense he deemed vital to that of the United States. Joe Patterson called this the "dictator bill," on the ground that it would be the greatest grant of power ever given any American President, and branded it as an act of war. After the Lend-Lease Bill passed Congress overwhelmingly in March 1941, Joe and Cissy Patterson opposed one brinkmanship measure after the other.

Cissy summed up her attitude in a letter to Rose Crabtree on April 21, 1941:

Some few of us think the President has always intended to get us into war, and that he has led this country as if it were a blindfolded little child—little step by little step along the road into the kind of hell this war will surely be.

Unlike Joe, Cissy was living in the midst of the interventionist activity sweeping Washington in 1941. It infuriated her. Among other things, she resented the government officials who, themselves too old to fight, were urging young men either to get into uniform or to demonstrate their devotion to the Allies by filling the rapidly growing pool of civilian wartime jobs.

One morning in October 1941, *Times-Herald* readers turned to the editorial page and stared at a headline reading, "A Letter to a Young Man." The open letter was addressed "Dear friend," and signed "Eleanor Patterson." Cissy's readers were accustomed to her personal vendettas in print, but in this instance the person on the receiving end of her scorn was not identified. It was apparent only that it was someone who had quit her to join the Government.

The victim was Dick Hollander, a young man whom she had hired away from the Washington *Daily News* to become her city editor early in 1941. She liked Hollander's work and promised him that he would eventually succeed to managing editor. When the *Times-Herald* became increasingly isolationist, Hollander, an interventionist, became increasingly unhappy. Besides, he was being importuned by friends in government to do his duty and join the new Office of Coordination of Information. Cissy urged him not to do so, but he notified her in September that he was leaving, and he did. A short while later, she had another talk with Hollander to get him to come back, but he said it was too late.

A few days after this conversation, Hollander was sitting at home late at night when an ex-colleague on the *Times-Herald* telephoned him and said, "I'm going to read you something you'll be interested in." As the open letter was read to him, Hollander had the eerie sensation that surely this must be one long typographical error.

The letter began by classifying him as a "rather mixed-up

young man—mentally, emotionally, spiritually," and went on to say that he was not being completely honest with himself. Cissy's main point was that her departing editor was "obsessed" with the idea of "personal sacrifice for the defeat of Hitlerism." She said he had heeded the propaganda of the elders who were now calling for the service of young minds and would later call for the service of young bodies as well. She reminded him that, as a goodby present, she had given him a copy of Fraser's *Golden Bough*, with special reference to the "scapegoat" in volume seven.

Cissy continued:

> But yours is a common case. Washington is crowded to-day, just as it was in the last war, with sacrificial young men, some in uniform, some in mufti, some smug and complacent, blithely engaged in having the time of their lives; others, like yourself, bewildered, unhappy, and thoroughly dissatisfied.

If he had really wanted to make a sacrifice, Cissy said, he should have joined the armed forces of the United States.

Washington was diverted by the letter as a new Cissy Patterson caper. The ex-editor was soon identified by word of mouth to anyone who wanted to know, and Hollander dined out for several weeks on the strength of being the man whom Cissy had taken the trouble to bawl out in 1000 words of valuable wartime newsprint. (Serious-minded professors of journalism doubtless deplore Cissy's open-letter outbursts. Her attitude was: Why own a newspaper if you can't use it the way you want to?)

After Pearl Harbor, Hollander spent four years in the Army's psychological warfare branch, seeing service in North Africa and at SHAEF. He won two decorations. Since World War II, he has been managing editor of the Washington *News*.

On the Sunday Pearl Harbor was attacked, the *Times-Herald* was on the street with an "Extra" four hours before the other Washington papers, thanks to the fact that Waldrop had happened to be in his office reading his mail when the flash came through. Once the United States was at war with Germany and

Japan, Cissy was for prosecuting the war to the limit. She was proud of the high percentage of her young staff who volunteered for the armed forces. Not once during the war did her newspaper file a request for a deferment from the draft.

The outbreak of war in Europe, and the subsequent national quarrel in the United States over what Americans should do about it, had broken many friendships and engendered an ugly atmosphere in Washington. Pearl Harbor did not clear the air; now the bitterness was over where and how the war should be fought. The interventionists were still more interested in Europe, and the isolationists had their eye on the Pacific. As America rushed into wars on two fronts, there were mistakes, bungling and outright stupidity, and the tension in the national capital was always at the breaking point. Many people found it hard to handle their feelings, and Cissy was particularly vulnerable because she was intense and volatile even under normal conditions. Where some people would react to a controversy with some discretion, she always reacted in technicolor.

Cissy did not believe that in supporting the war she was under any obligation to refrain from criticizing government policies or strategy when she thought it unwise, or from exposing phoniness and scandals on the home front when she found them. A dramatic scene which occurred in the White House a few days after Pearl Harbor had supercharged her feelings toward the President.

When Pearl Harbor was attacked, Joe Patterson was at a hunting lodge in North Carolina. Four days later he was standing in Roosevelt's study, at a meeting arranged in the hope that the two proud men could be reconciled for a common war effort. The day before, Patterson, then sixty-two years old, had formally written the War Department an application for readmission to the Army, pointing to his combat experience in five major engagements in France in 1918, as a major in the reserves.

Patterson remained standing while the President took five minutes to sign documents. He remained standing for another fifteen minutes, he recorded later in a memorandum, "while he gave me a pretty severe criticism for the way the *News* had conducted itself during the year 1941. He said he would give me a task, which was to read over the *News* editorials for 1941."

According to the memorandum, Roosevelt also told Patterson that the editorials appearing in 1941 in the *News* and *Times-Herald* had slowed up the "effort" from sixty to ninety days—without specifying what he meant by "the effort," whether it was the war or preparation for the war.

Patterson did manage to get in a reminder to the President that the editorials in question "were written in peacetime, not in wartime."

"At the end," the memo continued, "he seemed a bit mollified and told me to pass on the word to Cissy to behave herself also."

Joe Patterson, to his deep disappointment, never did get a wartime assignment from Roosevelt, and he returned to New York embittered. As for Cissy, telling her to behave herself was enough to invite the full measure of her wrath. Now she told friends she had never really trusted FDR anyway, because his eyes were set too close together.

Cissy not only took on the President; she aimed her shafts at all the men who had clamored to get into the war and were now, she contended, enjoying it. She did not confine herself to interventionists in government. Two of her favorite targets were Henry Luce, publisher of *Time*, and his lovely blonde wife, Clare Boothe, who had once been good friends and inhabited the same social plane.

Mrs. Luce threw the first punch. A few days after Pearl Harbor, Cissy received a mammoth bouquet of roses. Attached was Mrs. Luce's card. On it was penned: "Hiyi: How do you like everything now? Affectionately, Clare Luce."

Cissy always admired intelligent women who were lovely and lively. She had once remarked that Clare Boothe Luce combined the power drive of Catherine the Great with the wit of Athene (the Greek goddess of wisdom) and the physical allure of a movie star. Now she wired a reply which revealed a good deal about herself and made the Luces sound like cold fish indeed:

> Roses are beautiful. I still think you have the great Catherine, Athene, and that Tierney girl fried to a crisp. How do I like it? I hate it. How do you and Henry like it? The terrible thing about you two is that you neither hate nor like very much. You just go on having a wonderful time.

In the "Having a Wonderful Time" series, Cissy inspired the author, George Dixon, to write of Henry Luce:

> In his career of profitable malice he has a wonderful helpmeet. A friend once referred to Mrs. Luce as "that lovely asp." They make a remarkable pair.
> In all this country it would probably be difficult to find another ostensibly patriotic American woman who thought the attack on Pearl Harbor was a matter for light banter.

In the article, Luce was charged with stooping to "the lowest type of scandal" in the guise of printing the news, of appealing to the most malicious instincts in humanity for circulation purposes. *Time* magazine consistently reported the doings of Cissy, her brother, and her cousin, in a not altogether complimentary fashion, and she was paying the Luces back.

The interventionists who felt Cissy's lash in the "Having a Wonderful Time" series had this in common, she said: "They all sang, and are still singing, the same refrain: 'Joe Doakes is an isolationist! He's a traitor! He doesn't want America to win the war! He's an agent of the Axis!' "

In early August of that bitter summer of 1942, when Washington was worried because the war was going badly on both fronts, the accusations against Cissy's *Times-Herald* and her brother's New York *News* climactically reached the floor of the House of Representatives. Representative Elmer Holland, a Pennsylvania Democrat elected to an unexpired term, was making his maiden speech. He had campaigned with a promise to "deal firmly with the defeatists, the sowers of dissension," and now he was calling the Pattersons "America's No. 1 and No. 2 exponents of the Nazi propaganda line . . . doing their best to bring about a fascist victory, hoping that in the victory they were to be rewarded."

The *Daily News* editorials were usually blunt, but the editorial the next day was blunter than usual. It was signed by "Joseph M. Patterson"—the only editorial he ever signed—and headed: "YOU'RE A LIAR, CONGRESSMAN HOLLAND."

Patterson noted in the editorial that, while Holland's statement was "privileged" (members of Congress cannot be sued for remarks which go into the *Congressional Record*), his, Patterson's, were not. He recalled that his forebears had come to the United States several generations before and members of the family had served in the Revolutionary, Civil and World wars. He said there was no trace of German, Italian or Japanese blood in himself or his sister, adding that "we are of Irish extraction (both North and South), with a trace of Holland Dutch."

The editorial continued:

> This country has treated us well—superlatively well. What could we gain by having it fall?
>
> We do not know whether you were inspired to your lie by higher-ups. But we do know that servile fawning upon this or any other Administration is not a test of love of America.
>
> We again suggest to other newspapers that they watch out for encroachment on freedom of the press. Their turn will come if they don't.
>
> To repeat: Congressman Holland: You are a liar. Make what you like of that.

Cissy, printing the editorial in the *Times-Herald*, added:

> To the above statement, I heartily subscribe. You are a liar, Congressman Holland. And you know it.

Holland replied to the editorial with another privileged vitriolic attack, charging that "daily these publishers rub at the morale of the American people. Daily they sow suspicion . . ."

This time the reply came from Patterson's daughter, Alicia Guggenheim, owner, editor and publisher of the Long Island paper *Newsday*. In the editorial, reprinted in the *Times-Herald*, Alicia stated that she knew Joe Patterson perhaps better than most daughters know their fathers, having hunted, fished, and learned to fly an airplane with him. She explained:

> I have seen him under all sorts of circumstances: when he enlisted as a private and went to the Mexican border in 1916; when he joined up with the Rainbow Division in the last war, although he was 38 years old with a wife and three children; when he came back from France in 1918 looking older and grimmer; when he fought for the Roosevelt Administration because he believed that the underprivileged of the country should get a better break; when he pounded week after week in his editorials for a two-ocean navy so that we might never have to bow to an aggressor nation; when he opposed our entry into this war because he thought that we were unprepared. As long as I can remember, he was carrying the torch for the U.S.A.

Alicia recalled that she and her father disagreed over the Administration's prewar foreign policies. But, she went on:

> After the Japs bombed Hawaii—and I was with him at the time—his one thought was that we must win at all costs—that nothing must stop us. He tried to enlist but was told that he was too old.
>
> Isolationism was a dead issue so far as my father was concerned, but it apparently wasn't with a lot of pre-Pearl Harbor interventionists . . . [these] fanatics stumped the country from end to end denouncing anyone who happened to have believed before the war that America should look before she leaped.
>
> . . . it is true that my father had from time to time

criticized the Administration. Does that make him a traitor? If it does, then anyone who questions the policies laid down in Washington is likewise treasonable.

Are we no longer allowed to disagree with the elected "servants of the people"? If that is so, we have lost our democracy before we have begun to fight for it.

After that acrimonious year, when the tide slowly but irresistibly turned in favor of the Allies, the feud between the Pattersons and the Roosevelt administration continued. Cissy resorted to a World War I term—"slacker"—to castigate the young men who, she said, were sitting out the war at Washington desks when they should have been in uniform. Once, slashing at the President for refusing to allow any draft deferments for boys in premedical courses in college, she snorted: "If the Army needs all the able-bodied young men it can get, we politely suggest that the Army cast its eye on the State Department. There it will discover, like so many pearls in so many oyster shells, an assortment of rich, able-bodied and unmarried boys of no particular use to anyone.

"We do recall," Cissy continued in this story, "that quite a few of these State Department members of the 'panty-waist brigade' (and isn't that vulgar?) have declared they'd 'give up their eye teeth' to get into this war. Well, why don't they give them up and throw their molars in for good measure? Is it because they are a bit shy about risking their blood and guts and tears into the bargain?

"The President himself," she added, "has no firsthand knowledge of war either . . . he stayed away from the battlefields in the First World War. Although at the time a young man and in perfect physical condition, he 'did his bit' as Assistant Secretary of the Navy—right here in Washington."

The *Times-Herald* in the same edition ran photographs of twenty State Department men under the heading: "SOME STATE DEPARTMENT BOYS WHO DO NOT CHOOSE TO FIGHT."

In another widely discussed thrust at the Administration, Cissy ran a full page of pictures of fallen American soldiers, with a caption implying that Roosevelt was responsible for their deaths. According to legend, her managing editor, George A. De Witt, served notice that either it went or *he* would go. And he went. According to De Witt himself, this cherished anecdote is a complete fabrication.

FDR was the biggest fish Cissy ever hunted, both in terms of his personality and the resources at his command. She saw him in wartime as arrogant, vain and power-hungry, a man with dictator tendencies who would surely run for a fourth term in 1944, despite signs of failing health. And she was convinced that he would have the Justice Department crack down on her or the *Times-Herald* if some wartime legal justification could be found.

But if this antagonist was on the highest level, she viewed it as a level no higher than her own. Cissy was too sophisticated to glorify herself in her own mind as a heroine standing off the forces of evil. If she had, she might have paraphrased one of the proudest lines uttered by Queen Elizabeth I—with whom Cissy had more in common than red hair: "I know I have the body of a weak, feeble woman, but I have the heart and stomach of a king, and a king of England too . . ." Cissy was quite conscious that she had the heart and stomach of the Medills and the Pattersons—to whom it was important never to show the slightest sign of fear.

During the wartime years she often reminded herself of her heritage, and sometimes, to close associates, she told two stories illustrating that the red-whiskered founder of the newspaper dynasty considered himself the equal of any man. The first tells of the time Medill's good friend, Abraham Lincoln, dropped into his office (before he was nominated for President), put his muddy boots on Medill's desk, and talked politics—and talked politics and talked politics. Finally, Medill, exasperated at the untidy Lincoln, snapped, "Abe, please take your goddamned feet off my desk!"

The other story concerns Marshall Field, the Chicago merchant prince. In 1873, Field loaned Medill enough money to enable him to buy out the other stockholders of the Chicago *Tribune*. However, Field took advantage of the relationship to meddle in the running of the *Tribune*. This so annoyed Medill that by various means he raised the amount of his debt. Then he walked into Field's office, slapped the repayment and interest on Field's desk, and announced with satisfaction, "Now we're equals!"

One who was a close friend of Cissy Patterson believes that the only man she really hated was Roosevelt. But surprising as it may seem to anyone who watched her in full cry, Cissy thought of a feud as a game, a game with very few rules and one which she enjoyed playing seriously. Very few of her feuds caused her bitterness. Her basic emotions were engaged only if her antagonist was someone, like Drew Pearson, of whom she had previously been fond.

She did give the impression of wishing nothing but the worst for her opponents. FDR was probably half-serious in a letter to Harry Hopkins, May 18, 1944, at White Sulphur Springs (where Hopkins was recuperating) urging him not to return to his job before the middle of June.

"If you do come back before then," the President wrote, "you will be extremely unpopular in Washington, with the exception of Cissy Patterson, who wants to kill you off as soon as possible—just as she does me."

One of the many reasons for Cissy's opposition to FDR for a fourth term was her conviction that he was a sick man. When he died in March of the following year, she responded with a flash of her old flair that was to be cited in journalism circles for a long time. Informed on the telephone that her editors were planning to put a three-column portrait picture of Roosevelt on the front page, together with the start of his obituary, she snapped: "Hold everything! All we need for page one is the picture of the President, with just the dates of his birth and death underneath."

In Washington, if not elsewhere, this was the most original handling of the Story of the Year.

The next day she said, "Fill up the paper with Truman—he's the story now."

SEVENTEEN

Huntress and Hostess

Of the many magazine profiles which tried to fathom Cissy Patterson, none was more perceptive than a two-part treatment written in 1939 by Jean Stansbury in *The Senator*, a Washington magazine which had a brief life. Miss Stansbury had worked in various editorial capacities on the *Herald* and had had a close rapport with her boss. Cissy, who was always intellectually honest about herself, read the article in manuscript and then gave the authoress a handwritten testimonial which the magazine ran along with the article. The note read: "Here I is, 'tis pity is 'tis true. Cissy."

Miss Stansbury wrote:

> More than any other quality, and she is myriad-faceted, the huntress is predominant in Eleanor Patterson. The more dangerous or difficult the quarry, the more patient and deadly the stalking. She hung up her imported rifles about ten years ago, but she will never hang up her tenacity of purpose, her determination to conquer. . . .
>
> Now and then one meets a woman or man who utterly defeats the imagination. Mrs. Patterson is such a woman. Watching her move through the city room of her newspaper office, or about her drawing room, it is impossible to dismiss her as a categorical personality. It is impossible to point a finger at her and say, "This is so and that is not so about this woman." She challenges and eludes one's mental grasp always. . . .
>
> . . . her sub-editors walk in dread of a summons to one

of her nightmare interviews on their particular departments. Curled in a corner of a deep leather couch in her private office with her feet tucked under her childishly, she dissects each section of the paper, page by page, picture by picture, column by column. Her comments are pertinent and she rarely errs on the side of assumption. She knows what she wants and if it is possible. With languid tones and words dropped sparingly as vitriol drips from an eye-dropper her criticisms, like a black snake whip, start lazily and end with a crack in the listener's innermost soul.

While lacking the normal impulse to yield to men, Cissy was emotionally insecure enough to wish for—subconsciously, at least—a man who would master her. She enjoyed the game of charming men, an art which she had refined to a very high polish. And there was her nagging worry, as an editor, that men resent taking orders from a woman.

Yet the fact remains that, by and large, she treated the men around her like courtiers in a monarchy. She sought their advice, but if their behavior irritated her, she would explode, only to regret it later. A number of times she even resorted to that most feminine of outlets, the slap.

There was the case of one Bart Guild, who functioned in the early thirties as an efficiency expert for Hearst. Guild traveled from city to city, calling the top executives of each paper to his luxurious hotel suite, going over their books, and shouting, "You're costing Mr. Hearst too much money!" Then he would specifically order salaries cut or employees fired.

Guild was hated and feared by every Hearst editor. Cissy met him for the first time in Chicago, and he told her the Washington *Herald* was next on his list. She invited him to ride to Washington with her in her private railroad car. The next day, as the car was rolling through the Midwest, Guild was lounging on Cissy's chintz-covered sofa, swishing a highball in his hand and beginning to fancy himself a social as well as a fiscal critic. His auditor's eye roved over the three bedrooms with bath, the cozy kitchen, the eight-chair dining room, the easy chairs and the settees.

"How can you live like a queen," he suddenly asked her with a forced grin, "and then make a fuss over a Socialist like Shipstead?"

(Senator Henrik Shipstead was an illustrious member of the Farmer-Labor Party in Minnesota, and Cissy often entertained him and his wife.)

Cissy was also seated on the sofa. Her round eyes stared coldly at her guest for a few seconds as if she couldn't believe she was listening to such effrontery. Then she leaned across and carefully slapped the accountant on the face so hard that he fell to the floor of the swaying car.

And there was the incident involving Mike Flynn, the *Herald* managing editor of whom Cissy was so fond. One morning Mike showed up in the city room with a black eye. Cissy was not in one of her best moods that morning and she jumped to the conclusion that her managing editor had gone on a weekend spree and gotten into a fight. In calling attention to the bruise, she became so angry she slapped his face.

"You promised me you wouldn't get drunk!" she said, turned and strode toward her own office. Flynn had no chance to explain, but the next day when his wife, Dolly, was talking with Cissy (they were good friends), she told her that Mike had come by his black eye in the most innocent and wholesome possible way—being hit by a batted ball while playing with their two sons at a summer camp. He hadn't had a drop all weekend.

On her bad days, anything could happen in the editorial rooms. Once, sitting in her own office, with a reporter, the late Fraser (Tex) Edwards, she said to him suddenly: "I'm going downstairs and raise hell. I don't know what about, but I'm going to raise hell." And she did.

Cissy expected 200 percent loyalty from her staff. The fact that so few of her editors and reporters resigned is probably traceable in part to anxiety over how she would react. When

Robert Considine, a sports columnist, received a summons to meet William Randolph Hearst in the Hotel Warwick in New York, he was unnerved at the thought of how Cissy would react. Undoubtedly, the summons meant that Hearst would offer him a contract to write for all the Hearst papers and he would have to quit the *Herald* as such. Cissy would probably call him an ingrate, because she had taken a personal interest in him and given him a chance to shine. He could imagine the scene, and dreaded it.

To Considine's surprise, Cissy beamed when he broke the news. She immediately took him by the hand and led him into the city room. There, after assembling the staff, she said in her sweetest tones: "What do you think has happened to my illegitimate son by Calvin Coolidge? He's making good!"

Having concluded this ceremony, Cissy invited her sports writer to Du Pont Circle for a champagne dinner to celebrate. By the time the exhilarated Considine boarded the train for New York the next morning, he felt he was truly on top of the world. At the Hotel Warwick, Hearst, sure enough, told him he wanted to "push him along" and that a contract would be submitted in due time.

Riding back to Washington on the train, Considine wrote his regular sports column for the *Herald*. When he tossed it on the desk of Bernie Harter, the sports editor, Harter looked embarrassed. "I can't use it, I'm sorry," he said. Considine asked why not.

"Mrs. Patterson said you were off the payroll as of today," Harter explained.

Considine was amazed and no little concerned. His syndicate contract would not come through for several weeks, and he was in no position to live without income in the meantime. He picked up the phone and asked for Cissy, but her secretary confided that Mrs. Patterson would not talk to him, because she considered him "disloyal" for quitting her!

Cissy did not usually stay mad at anyone. Soon she was inviting

Considine and his wife, Millie, to her parties. In 1938, she telephoned Considine about an editorial Joe had run in his New York *Daily News*, very critical of Hearst.

"I'll show that brother of mine," she told Considine. "I'll print a whole-page tribute to Mr. Hearst in my own paper. You write it."

Considine worked on the Hearst testimonial for a month, sent it to Cissy and heard no more about it. Wondering if it had been received, he called her. Oh, yes, she had gotten it and it was great . . . only, she wasn't going to run it. Considine asked why.

There was a long pause. "I made up with Joe," she finally said. "But I want to pay for all that work. What did you make for your last article in *Cosmopolitan?*"

"Seven hundred and fifty bucks," he told her.

Two weeks later he received a check for $500. Attached to it was a note in Cissy's neat handwriting. "Dear Bob," it read. "I called *Cosmo*."

Cissy's devotion to her brother is the main thread running through the whole of her life. She considered Joe admirable as a creative publisher and perfect as a brother. Anyone who criticized Joe had his sister's wrath to reckon with. When, in the summer of 1938, the *New Yorker* magazine ran a two-part profile of Joe Patterson by Jack Alexander, it should have expected to hear from Cissy. On balance, Alexander's portrayal of Patterson was favorable, but Cissy took a different view in a letter she wrote Harold Ross, the *New Yorker* editor, on August 28, 1938:

Dear sir:
   Some months ago a man from your office told me over the telephone that he was writing a Profile of my brother Joseph Medill Patterson, and he asked me if I would help him with some stories of Joe's childhood. We got to talking back and forth, and I pulled out this story, my earliest recollection of him.
   When we were very little children, we came into a room —it was my mother's—to find the canary bird dead, lying

on the bottom of the cage. I was afraid to touch it. But Joe reached in, took it out and stood holding it in the palm of his fat little hand; tears poured down his cheeks. I can still see the stiff, tiny claws, and I can still feel my sense of guilt because there was Joe weeping for our pet and I wasn't sorry at all. Only scared and a little sick. You know, sometimes an incident like that sticks with you all your life.

I gave this story to your Mr. Alexander, and what does he do with it?

"Old friends relate that when he was a child, he once wrung the neck of a canary whose trilling he resented. Then he ran to his room and wept. As he grew older, he learned the folly of weeping over wrung necks."

Obviously, this perversion of a simple story I told Mr. Alexander, of a kid crying for his dead pet, springs from some morbid twist in Mr. Alexander's own mind. I have a hunch that Lennie of *Mice and Men* got into Mr. Alexander's blood, and that he drew his inspiration from him. One hears of odder things.

Your Mr. Alexander goes on to say that Joe went to the family opera box (we never had one) wearing wrinkled tails, mud-caked tan shoes, a flannel shirt open at the throat, and a lot of other hooey too long to quote.

All of this, of course, is just wild-eyed reporting. Aside from any other fact or reason, Joe, like any other normal man, hates to be conspicuous.

Your Mr. Alexander, still in pursuit of a portrait of a demented genius, strives for an impression of disorderliness —muddy boots, sloppy uniforms, etc. Now, as a matter of fact, Joe is exceptionally neat. A trait he inherits from his mother.

Joe's broad, short nails are always immaculate. I don't know how he manages this—certainly never by way of a manicure—possibly with the aid of a penknife. His hair is cut too short ever to be tousled. His skin is so healthy and so clean that he never looks "greasy" even when the sweat is pouring down his face. His shoes, square-toed, are polished neatly. His plain, dark-blue suits (I've never seen him in any other color) are well set, well pressed, well made. His white cheviot shirts somehow look fresh even at the end of the day.

On the other hand, I can well believe the story about the "houseman kissing your little girl," in the first issue of the series.

When I lived opposite the Metropolitan Museum in New York, Joe dropped by early one morning, wearing track shoes, a turtle-neck sweater, and a check-cloth visor cap. He was on his way to trot a couple of times around the reservoir, along with a sizable bunch of other men in training. Maybe he should have spared the feelings of the elevator boy. But I guess it didn't occur to him.

The last time I saw Joe, it was a very hot day. He left the office hatless, coatless, his white shirt open at the throat. No tie. But right here is where your Mr. Alexander would skate wide of the mark. As Joe walked off, down 42nd Street, on his way to his favorite movie, he melted into the crowd, utterly unconscious of himself, one of the whole of them.

I have talked a lot about Joe's appearance, because Mr. Alexander, in his anxiety to make a sensational cross between his Lennie of *Mice and Men* and Lord Northcliffe, has placed great emphasis upon Joe's personal appearance . . .

There are several bits of bad reporting in the second installment, and some others in the third.

A western friend once said to me—"horses hates to fall down." Now, we publishers "hates to fall down" too, isn't that true? That's one reason why I've taken all this trouble to set you right. Not paragraph by paragraph, because that would be tiresome for both of us, but just in a general way. Mr. Alexander is an excellent writer, but if you want to use him again, do check for sloppy reporting and watch out for that morbid twist of his mind.

Sincerely yours,
(*signed*) Eleanor Patterson

Patterson was embarrassed by his sister's rushing to his defense. He wrote Ross:

Dear Mr. Ross,

I have just seen a letter which apparently is a duplicate of one which my sister has sent to you. If so, may I express the hope that you will consider it to be not for publication. I would much prefer to leave things lay.

As a matter of fact, I was not troubled by the articles and realize that they contained much that was highly complimentary, and indeed too complimentary toward me.

Sincerely yours,
J. M. Patterson

Ross immediately replied:

Dear Mr. Patterson,

I have your letter and will do as you say. Your attitude is understood and appreciated. I will write your sister accordingly.

As a matter of fact, we had already made up our minds not to use the letter. For one thing, it is largely disqualified because she thinks she saw Mr. Alexander, the author, whereas he did not see her at all. Who did talk to her is a mystery, but it was not any authorized person from this office. She seemed to be concerned principally about whether or not you killed a bird as a small boy. The general theory here is that all boys go through a period of killing things.

Sincerely yours,
H. Ross

What had aroused the sisterly pride was Alexander's description of her brother as "the worst-dressed man of means in New York." A good many persons meeting Patterson for the first time might have been inclined to agree. What they did not know was that he was a modest aristocrat who went out of his way to avoid ostentation. He was indeed a little dismayed by Cissy's taste for luxury. ("Poor Cissy," he once remarked, "she makes her life so complicated.")

When Patterson commissioned Raymond Hood to design a home for him in Ossining, New York, he said, "Make it look as if I didn't have any money." Being a stylish dresser was not important to him; comfort was—and he campaigned editorially in the *Daily News* for the wearing of open-necked shirts with short sleeves and no jacket during the summer. Looking like an ordinary person also made it possible for him to melt easily into a crowd on the sidewalk, or in a bar to find out what the masses were talking about. Like the masses, he was a hero-worshiper and a movie fan. He originated the ideas for some of the *Daily News'* most popular comic strips, including "Terry and the Pirates," and he introduced the revolutionary idea that even newspaper editorials should talk the language of the people.

These were the qualities which helped make Patterson America's first and most successful tabloid publisher. What is even more interesting is the fact that his sister became one of America's two most successful female newspaper publishers. Unlike her brother, Cissy had never had any philosophical interest in the masses, or any firsthand knowledge of their dreams or anxieties. Yet her ability to spot the kind of story people would read and talk about was infallible.

One has to conclude that both of them, born to wealth, were born, too, with the common touch. It was an inheritance strong enough to be passed on to the next generation, for America's other outstanding woman newspaper publisher was Patterson's daughter, Alicia Patterson Guggenheim, who created from scratch the highly profitable tabloid *Newsday* in suburban Long Island.

In temperament, however, Cissy was spectacular compared to Joe. Her mercurial nature put a strain on the most steadfast of private secretaries, but her way of life was so intriguingly eccentric that each of her secretaries found the job exciting. It was fun, at any rate, for Mrs. Carolyn Hagner Shaw, who was hired in the fall of 1931.

Dealing with the rich and the famous was nothing new for "Callie." Her aunt, Isabella Hagner, had been White House social secretary in the Theodore Roosevelt and Woodrow Wilson years. Callie's mother, Helen Ray Hagner, ran the Washington Social Bureau for many years and also wrote a column on good manners and correct attire for Cissy's *Herald*.

But Callie Shaw—who has been the author of the *Green Book*, a social "Who's who in Washington," as well as a protocol authority, for many years—has never met anyone like Cissy. She has never forgotten her introduction to the job.

Hired by telephone, she was told to report to the Port Washington, Long Island, estate. There the butler took her to a lovely suite and left her alone. For four days she waited to be summoned to meet Mrs. Patterson, taking her meals with the servants but not leaving her room otherwise, for fear she would not be available when the summons came. She became so bored that on the fifth day she washed her hair. Just as she had herself fully lathered, the butler informed her that Mrs. Patterson wanted her immediately.

Afraid to take the time to dry her hair, Callie rushed down to the living room and walked in nervously dripping suds and apologies. Her new employer silenced her by motioning her to a chair with a languid wave of the hand and starting to dictate as if they had been working together for years.

From then on, it seemed every day was like that, one way or another.

"Nonchalance—or poise—certainly was necessary," Mrs. Shaw recalls. "You could get so mad at her for some of the things she did you'd want to choke her. But the more you knew her the more you respected her. If she blew off, you knew it wasn't *you* she was attacking. She was just getting rid of steam, and she never held a grudge."

Callie took dictation from many of Cissy's famous guests, including William Randolph Hearst, Marion Davies and Arthur Brisbane. She learned to take each celebrity in stride. At first she was frightened when Hearst's high-pitched voice rose in anger, but she managed to remain calm.

Callie faced an unusual etiquette problem one morning when Brisbane came downstairs fully clothed except for one item: his trousers. Seemingly lost in thought, he seated himself in her office and dictated for nearly an hour. Then he rose and left, bare-legged but dignified. Varied though her duties were, the secretary decided it was not her place to inform the great editor that he had forgotten his pants. She was confident that someone else in the mansion would tip him off before he ventured forth into Massachusetts Avenue for a luncheon date.

Callie was in charge of the mansion's eighteen servants. She reported at the mansion at 11 o'clock in the morning and began her day; but she was also expected to be at the *Herald* office before Mrs. Patterson arrived there. She had the butler tip her off the minute "Madame" ordered her limousine, then she hailed a taxi and beat her there.

Later in the day, Cissy might tell her secretary she wanted to have a dinner party for thirty that very evening. Usually, she would leave it entirely up to Callie to make up a guest list, plan the menu and every detail.

"At times she could be very human," Mrs. Shaw recalls. "Sometimes after one of her elegant parties, she would sit cross-legged on the kitchen table, drinking a bottle of beer with the night watchman. She could talk his language. I always thought she had a man's mind and preferred the company of men."

The friends who passed through Cissy's door fascinated Margaret Barney, her secretary for seventeen years after Callie. Once, Ethel Barrymore stayed there a month during a Washington theater engagement. One afternoon she spent several hours drinking potent martinis, and Cissy feared that the great actress might be unable to find her dressing room, much less speak her

lines distinctly. She was mightily impressed when Miss Barrymore, in true family tradition, gave a smashing performance.

"Barney," as everyone called the secretary, was more Irish and
more redheaded than Cissy. She could not always shrug off her
boss's temper without wanting to fight back.

"You know what a low boiling point I have," Cissy advised
her. "When I blow up, you shouldn't pay any attention."

Nonetheless, Barney quit after one explosion and stayed away
for six months. Mrs. Patterson called her and begged her to return, because "you know I didn't mean it." She learned that her
secretary had contracted iritis and had been laid up for six
weeks. She told her to take a rest at her expense and then "come
back where you belong."

"She was *so* colorful," Barney explains. "You were never
bored. No two days were alike. You might come in one morning
and find out you were going to California in the private railroad car. She would say casually, 'I have to go out and discuss
something with Mr. Hearst . . .'"

Barney considered Cissy the most feminine person she had
ever met. When Cissy returned from a European trip, the staff
of servants helped her unpack her Schiaparelli gowns and $30-
an-ounce perfume from Paris, and Cissy was just as excited as
they were.

Cissy never went in for curls and never had a permanent wave.
She subjected her waist-long hair to constant brushings, three
times a week, and pulled it straight back on her head. It gave off
a deep-red luster.

She could not read without spectacles, and she owned hundreds of pairs of them so that one pair could be left on every
table in each of her five houses. She wanted them always within
easy reach because she couldn't bother keeping track of them.

To Barney, Cissy insisted that she was shy. She confided that
she hated to appear before large assemblages of people and was
ill at ease when she performed in skits for the Women's National
Press Club. No shyness was ever more perfectly concealed. Cissy

gave the impression of being supremely self-confident at all times.

Guests at her parties remember her as the most skilled of hostesses. Regardless of any animosity she might harbor, when a guest arrived, he was treated as royalty. When a party was underway, Cissy seemed to have eyes in the back of her head. It was actually a kind of built-in radar which told her what every guest was thinking. During the cocktail hour, she had an uncanny instinct for knowing who had painted himself into a conversational corner, who should meet someone important who had just arrived, who should be culled from a group for excessive drinking.

At dinner—like several other Washington hostesses who had sparkled in the twenties—Cissy believed in mixing her guests daringly. On most occasions, the guests would be divided into tables of six or eight. She deliberately seated a senator with a cabinet member he hated, or, for example, a columnist with a politician he had been feuding with. At somewhat smaller dinner parties, the men, including some mortal enemies, were left alone together over coffee and brandy, while the women temporarily foregathered elsewhere. High-level decisions of government often resulted from such forced integration.

In the recollection of everyone who attended the parties, all went smoothly under the spell of Cissy's silky charm and seductive wit.

When the guests assembled in the ballroom for a large party, hundreds of candles flickered down on them from three great crystal chandeliers, reflecting the flashing jewels of the women. It took a full hour for Cissy's butler to light the candelabra, each of which held fifteen slender white tapers. The elegance in the ballroom was Old World. The Aubusson carpet, the walls of moss green so faint it was almost a cream, and the brocade curtains a rich, warm, old gold. On one wall was an enormous Beauvais tapestry. Contributing an exotic touch to the room were two carved Chinese cabinets.

After dinner, served late in the evening, an orchestra played. One night in 1936, Cissy threw a birthday party for herself. The cake held 135 candles, and Cissy made a little speech in which she said there was no point in trying to hide her age, because, after all, "didn't we remember the great scandal about me and Methuselah?" Then a larger, fake cake was brought in, with little white ribbons to pull. At the end of each ribbon were an amusing present and verses and comments, the contributions of some of the hostess's clever friends.

The fifty couples were a "Who's who" of the New Deal, including Harry Hopkins, Harold Ickes, Donald Richberg, Raymond Moley, and their wives, plus Anna Dall, daughter of the President and Mrs. Roosevelt. Since the Democrats had just enjoyed an historic landslide in the election, the speeches and toasts were on the wisecracking side and sometimes brilliant. The entertainment wound up on a rousing note with John Charles Thomas singing children's songs and old English and German songs.

Cissy that night lived up to her reputation of being always the most original and sensationally dressed woman present. She was in her favorite attire—pajamas—long before they were accepted as evening wear. The full trousers were in ruby velvet. The coat was brocaded velvet in all the warm, rich tones of an old church window—midnight blue, emerald green, bits of gold and dashes of scarlet.

Cissy had dozens of varieties of Oriental-brocade pajamas, and wore them anywhere she pleased. On Christmas Day in 1947 she received the whole of official Washington in what looked suspiciously like an old Japanese kimono. "Is it really a kimono?" several women whispered.

"My dear, that is not what matters," a veteran diplomat kept saying. "What does matter is that it *looks* like one—and that only our Cissy would dare to wear such a thing."

Cissy's parties were also anticipated eagerly because one expected to meet celebrities one didn't ordinarily meet in Washington. Perhaps Sinclair Lewis would be present, or some other reigning star, for Cissy seemed to know everybody. And she loved to upset precedent. One night in the spring of 1933 she reversed the usual process in staging a party for Alexander Woollcott; she invited sixty guests from the world of politics, literature and journalism to dine and had the diplomatic corps and the capital's professional sophisticates come in after dinner.

An unscheduled bit of entertainment was contributed during the dinner by Senator Huey Long. Long announced that he liked to mix his own salad. He shouted for bowls and lettuce heads, oil and chives, sauces and condiments. To the trembling footman—who had never before seen the notorious "kingfish" in action—he cried, "Hey, you! What kind of a dump is this—no Tabasco?—get some, quick!" All sixty guests watched as the Louisiana senator deftly whipped up a tangy salad.

The diplomatic corps came to dinner a few nights later when Cissy gave a farewell party for Frederick Nano, counselor of the Roumanian legation, and his beautiful wife, who were being returned to Bucharest after ornamenting the Washington scene for some years. "Freddy," brother of Madam Cardenas, wife of the Spanish ambassador, was tall, handsome, cynical and humorous. He wore a monocle even in his gray flannels and polo shirt, insisting he couldn't see without it. Rose Nano, whose sister was wife of the ambassador from Brazil, was one of the most striking belles on the capital circuit. Washington *Herald* society columnist Martha Blair drooled over her in print:

> She has dark-auburn hair, worn in a short, curly bob, huge velvet eyes, a retrousse nose, a full curved mouth, and a perfectly divine figure which is emphasized by the beautiful and graceful way she walks. Besides that, she has one of those deep, husky voices that makes a chill run up and down your spine.

An orchestra brought from the Surf Club in Miami Beach played after dinner, and then Cissy took the center of the floor and announced with a twinkle in her eye:

"Now we have some singers who will sing some sweet old English folk songs. They are very sensitive artists, so let's have absolute silence, so quiet that we could hear a pin drop."

When the guests began to compose themselves for these "sensitive artists," a band of young Negro musicians from the South burst into the ballroom in a profusion of gay voices, hot colors and jazz rhythms. A foot-stomping mood took hold of the party. Still later there was dancing.

When Cissy was stimulated by entertainers, she wanted everyone to share her pleasure. Once, Bernie Harrison, her movie critic, suggested that she would like Miss Deloyd Mackaye, a new singer and pianist then performing at Paul Young's restaurant. Cissy liked the girl's style so much that she invited her to perform in the mansion during the cocktail hour and assembled an influential audience of diplomats and politicos to hear her.

The singer made a big hit and went back to her hotel full of gratitude for the famous lady who had given her the unique opportunity to exhibit her talents. She hardly expected to hear from Mrs. Patterson again, but that evening a liveried chauffeur delivered an envelope. Inside was a note from Cissy thanking her for her performance and a check for $500.

Washington's most fabulous hostess between the two world wars was Cissy's good friend, Evalyn Walsh McLean. "Evie" was the daughter of Thomas F. Walsh, who had struck it rich in Colorado gold and silver mines, and the wife of Edward B. (Ned) McLean, owner of the Cincinnati *Enquirer* and, until 1933, of the Washington *Post*. When they were married, Ned was twenty-two years old, and their parents gave them $100,000 to spend on a European honeymoon. Mrs. Walsh had one parting bit of advice. "Now, children," she said, "be careful!"

The McLeans lived on an eighty-acre estate, called "Friendship," in northwest Washington. There were greenhouses, stables, lovely gardens and a private golf course where President Harding had frequently played. There were also mallards, donkeys, goats, geese, ponies and cows on the place, in addition to a monkey in Mrs. McLean's bathroom, a llama on the front lawn, and a brightly painted coach for children that had once belonged to General Tom Thumb, the midget. The corridors of Friendship were shrill with the profanity of a parrot who had been trained by a frustrated diplomat.

"A mad place, truly!" Evie gaily conceded. Her parties were the most elaborate and expensive Washington has ever seen.

Cissy and Evie had much in common—fame, too much money, and flights of boredom—and they enjoyed being on the same nonsensical wave length when they got together. Once, Evie, a Catholic, was given a huge diamond-studded crucifix by Cissy. She was entranced and wore it, hanging down to her waist, to Cissy's next party. When Cissy saw her coming up the staircase thus adorned, she cried out: "Evie! I told you, you're supposed to hang it on your bed!"

"Well, I couldn't bring the whole bed to the party," Evie protested.

Cissy's poise as a hostess was unshakable. No unseemly incident fazed her. Once, one of Washington's better-looking young wives imbibed too freely and had the misfortune to tumble all the way down the grand staircase. There she lay spread out, momentarily motionless, with her gown, miraculously, arranged decently about her legs. Cissy looked down the stairs and drawled admiringly, "My, doesn't Jane look beautiful there!"

At one end of the Du Point Circle town house is a balcony. A bizarre balcony scene was played there one night by none other than Cissy's redoubtable cousin, Colonel Robert R. (Bertie) McCormick, publisher of the Chicago *Tribune*. The "Colonel," with his grave and stately military bearing, was the guest of honor, and Cissy pretended to be in awe of his somewhat imposing personality. Often when there was a lull in the conversation during the cocktail period, she would drawl in tones that echoed around the ballroom, "Isn't Bertie marvelous!"

Dinner did not start until nearly 10 o'clock. McCormick, who liked to retire early, announced to Cissy immediately afterward that he was going to bed. She protested that he couldn't do that to her—she had invited scores of guests to come in and meet him after dinner, and the party was just getting started. But tired Bertie was adamant; he vanished into the Coolidge bedroom, which has double doors opening out onto the balcony.

An orchestra arrived in the ballroom, the guests danced, and the noise of revelry grew steadily louder. Suddenly, the music died, and most heads were turned toward the balcony. The double doors had flown open and McCormick had stepped out, an outraged, pajamaed, patriarch.

"Dammit, stop that noise," he called down. "Is there no place where a decent man can go to bed before midnight and get some sleep?"

For just a few seconds, as the words hung in the smoky ballroom air, the silence was embarrassing. Then Cissy's voice, resonant with concern, soared toward the balcony:

"Bert!" she cried out. "You've got the top of one pajama on and the bottoms of another!"

It was true. The publishing genius looked at his blue pajama trousers and white top and angrily went back to bed.

Cissy always threw a spectacular party when Hearst and Marion Davies were in town. Madcap Marion, a good friend of Cissy, invariably added sparks to the atmosphere. She had promised Hearst she would strictly limit her drinking, but in the swirl of a large affair at Du Pont Circle, Marion had other guests slip her drinks out of range of the publisher's watchful eye. One night so many extra glasses were bootlegged to her that she had to be carried out. Another time she cut down on her liquid consumption but kissed and snuggled with some of the guests, displeasing Hearst even more.

Cissy retained a childlike quality that bloomed at parties. She loved surprises and impersonations. One night she gave a party at Du Pont Circle for Hearst on his birthday, but before it was over she announced that she had to leave to catch a plane to go to her ranch.

"I'm leaving the head butler in charge," she explained. Just then Eddie Rickenbacker popped into the room wearing the butler's clothes. The World War I ace ceremoniously escorted Cissy to the front door and, as the assembled guests watched, kissed her goodby and cried, "You may be 'Cissy' to millions, but you'll always be 'Mumsie' to me!"

When Cissy visited Hearst's San Simeon estate in California, his guests, with arms full of flowers, met her at her private railroad car with a band to serenade her. In Cissy's honor, Hearst also staged impromptu entertainment in the form of charades and specially written blackout skits, in which she exuberantly joined. Cissy might find herself acting with Clark Gable, Bebe Daniels, Norma and Constance Talmadge and other guests who were box-office stars.

On one such trip to San Simeon, Cissy took along Dolly Flynn, wife of Managing Editor Mike Flynn. Mrs. Flynn recalls it as "the experience of my lifetime." There was a party every evening starting at 6 o'clock, and it was Hearst's rule that no one should take a drink before six. If you violated the rule, even if you were a movie star, you were never invited again. Mrs. Flynn discovered that the rule was nonetheless circumvented. Marion Davies kept gin in the powder room, for those poor girls who had played tennis or had a swim and were thirsty. The gin was sneaked outside to the men, away from the sight of a butler who doubled as a daytime-drinking spy.

In later years Cissy several times gave a party after the Gridiron Club's stag dinner. The white-tied newsmen and their distinguished guests would proceed from their politics-spoofing show to join their wives at the Du Pont Circle house. Writer Adela Rogers St. Johns, who regards Cissy as the most "hypnotically-enchanting woman" she ever met, thought she was at her best in this most brilliant of gatherings.

"She dominated it," Adela recalls, "by her great presence—gliding about in an elegant black net dress with great flounces, displaying her black pearls and that copper hair, and those topaz eyes . . . she was beyond compare as a conversationalist herself, but even better at bringing out her guests in conversation. She was a most inspiring and awe-struck listener."

Cissy preferred giving smaller parties where she could flip badinage back and forth with her favorites. Her little thrusts— disparagements of others and sometimes of herself—were uttered in a low, "aside voice," and you had to turn quickly to be sure you caught the needle point. She particularly enjoyed the contest of a running dialogue with George Dixon, the shameless quipster who was never impressed with anyone, or with handsome, black-haired George Holmes, the Washington Bureau chief of the International News Service. Cissy thought that Holmes' combination of looks, intellect and personality made him the ultimate among correspondents. He was married to the sister of Steve Early, press secretary to President Roosevelt. FDR shared Cissy's admiration of Holmes. The President once remarked to Adela that he would rather get an honest opinion from Holmes than anyone else, because Holmes could not be influenced by any living person.

Cissy did not take herself seriously as a leading Washington hostess, and in fact had no ambition to be considered No. 1. But she was interested in creating one. One morning in 1938 she told Luvvie Pearson, Drew's wife, that Evie McLean was tired and that the town needed a colorful new hostess. She picked up the telephone and called Mrs. Gwen Cafritz, the exotic Hungarian-born wife of Morris Cafritz, Washington's biggest builder. She asked Gwen if she could visit her and made a date for that afternoon. She explained to Luvvie that Mrs. Cafritz had the ambition, the vitality, the savoir faire and the wealth to make an excellent hostess, and she had a lovely new home on fashionable Foxhall Road to do it in. Being completely frank, she added that Morris Cafritz was a big advertiser, and she liked to keep big advertisers happy.

Cissy brought Luvvie with her, and when they arrived it was apparent that Gwen sensed she was being auditioned. She was dressed in an exquisite tea gown and was served champagne and caviar. Talking excitedly, she gave them a tour of her just completed home, which has a picturesque view of the capital, and she and Cissy "darlinged" one another to the limit.

The upshot of the visit was that Cissy decided Mrs. Cafritz would do. Soon she was glorified in the *Herald* as the "beauty of the week," and her name began turning up with increasing frequency in the *Herald's* society and gossip columns. And the top people in town came to her parties.

Gwen Cafritz was launched, and for the next several decades she made Cissy look good as a drawing-room talent scout.

EIGHTEEN

"If They Scratch, They Are Real"

Some fifteen miles south of Washington, D.C., near Upper Marlboro, Maryland, you turn off Rosaryville Road at an historic
marker, "Mt. Airy," and follow a rough gravel road past a
shimmering little lake a mile through the woods. Then, abruptly,
rounding a circular driveway, you find yourself at the door of a
hybrid residence. One end of it is a conventional red-brick struc-
ture, obviously very old. The rest of it, a kind of elongated
double wing, looks like an Italian villa. It is of stucco, painted
a bright, un-Maryland-like yellow. It turns out to have loggias
both front and rear, as well as a patio and semicourtyard in
the rear. This is the Dower House. Of all Cissy Patterson's
many residences, this was her favorite, from the day she purchased it in 1930 until she died there in 1948.

The Dower House is a Maryland landmark, haunted, some
insist, by the ghosts of colonial America. The red-brick part
was built as a hunting lodge in 1660 by Charles Calvert, the third
Lord Baltimore and first to come to the New World. In 1721,
Calvert descendants built the wing at right angles. They introduced the Italian style because they traveled often in Italy and
were fond of it.

"Mt. Airy," as the estate was known until the twentieth century, has had distinguished inhabitants. George Washington often stayed there on his way to or from Annapolis. Washington
also witnessed a wedding there on February 4, 1774, when his

stepson, John Parke Custis, married Benedict Calvert's beautiful
daughter, Nelly.

Later the house passed into the hands of other Maryland
families and was the scene of fashionable parties during the
Taft, Wilson and Harding administrations. Legend has it that
intrigue was hatched and scandal created behind its thick, protective walls.

The place was renamed the "Dower House" when it was
turned into a smart restaurant during the twenties.

When Cissy first saw it in 1930, the Dower House was run-
down, but she imagined its captivating possibilities. She envi-
sioned it as a retreat where she could relax virtually alone—or
entertain lavishly. The fifty-foot drawing room that forms the
main part of the old hunting lodge has fireplaces at both ends,
one of them huge enough for several adults to stand up in. A
long foyer leads to the dining room and kitchen forming the
wing. There were other rooms which could be converted into
bedrooms, dens or libraries.

What Cissy liked most of all was the sensation of being miles
away from anywhere, reminding her a little of her Flat Creek
ranch. From the patio one looked over a broad terrace toward
grazing sheep and, beyond, to a dense grove of tall trees.

Cissy converted the Dower House into a summer place, with
a greenhouse, a swimming pool, tennis courts, stables for five
horses, and a battery of telephones so she could keep in touch
with the office. She engaged an interior decorator, but his ideas
ran to ruffled curtains and flowered chintzes, and Cissy took one
look and ripped it all out. She herself decorated it as a comfortable country house, or elegant hunting lodge, redolent of tweeds
and old leather. The drawing room was painted a cool slate-blue,
and the dining-room walls were covered with $3500 worth of
midnight-blue silk wallpaper with enormous birds and flowers
painted in white. She put an old spinning wheel in the den and
filled the rooms with antique furniture.

From 1931 on, Cissy not only spent every summer at the

Dower House but also many weekends in the spring and autumn. A tenant farmed its six hundred acres, and she loved the fresh vegetables, berries and mushrooms brought to her table.

As a place to entertain, she much preferred it to her town house, which she sometimes contemptuously called "the movie palace."

In 1936, Cissy gave a party for Eleanor Roosevelt at Dower House and invited many members of the Women's National Press Club. Mrs. George De Witt, wife of the new managing editor of the *Herald*, was startled to see the First Lady holding her nose and jumping off the side of the pool. Mrs. Roosevelt confessed she wished she could learn to dive.

The First Lady came to Dower House on three other occasions. Once, she was Cissy's only guest, and the two highly opinionated ladies got into a vehement argument about politics.

Perhaps because she felt it was more of a reflection of her own taste, Cissy scintillated at Dower House even more than she did at Du Pont Circle. On Sundays Cissy's friends came out from Washington by the score for tennis, swimming and cocktails. Perhaps a dozen or two would remain behind for dinner at small tables on the lawn.

Four times Cissy used Dower House as the setting for the *Times-Herald's* "Golden Mirror" contest, to select the most beautiful girl in Washington. In 1947 she asked Arthur F. Reilly, a newscaster on the *Times-Herald* radio station, to act as master of ceremonies and to put Drew Pearson on the jury. Cissy at the time was feuding with Pearson, and so was Reilly. Pearson and his co-author, Robert S. Allen, were suing Reilly for $1,000,-000 for having described them on the airwaves as "editorial beachcombers" and "editorial maggots." Cissy seated Reilly and Pearson next to one another at dinner; but, doubtless to her disappointment, no blows were struck, verbal or otherwise.

When it came time for the judging, Cissy excused herself, explaining that she was about to take a nap and warning the jury to pick the right girl. When she returned an hour later and the

winner was pointed out, she privately pretended that the jury
had not kept its mind on its business.

"You didn't pick the prettiest," she kidded. "You picked the
one you'd most like to go to bed with."

It was said that Cissy was the perfect hostess because she
had a knack of making every guest feel that the party was given
just for him, and that he could do no wrong. One guest who
could testify to this was sports writer Robert Considine, a Cissy
favorite. When he was invited to Dower House for the first
time, Considine gallantly bought a $6 orchid, the best he could
afford. He presented it to his hostess at the door almost shyly,
and she feigned a swoon, exclaiming, "Oh, how perfectly ador-
able!"

Cissy pinned the flower on herself and made such a fuss about
the gift that Considine congratulated himself all through luncheon. Afterward, while Cissy was napping, Margaret Barney,
the secretary, took him on a tour which included the greenhouse.
There he found hundreds of the loveliest orchids he had ever
seen, and felt like crawling under the floor.

As a hostess, Cissy would overlook any gaucherie—almost.
There was another luncheon Considine and his wife, Millie, attended, this one at Cissy's Long Island estate. They were seated
beside the swimming pool, and Cissy, in a wet bathing suit,
was combing out her long, wet hair when Eugene Warner, another *Herald* writer who had been invited, arrived in the pool
area.

"Guess what the old bitch just did?" Cissy was asking the
Considines, referring to one of her poodles. Warner either did
not realize this, or was in a suicidally witty mood.

"I can see," he called out, "you've been in swimming."

Cissy laughed, without mirth. Warner, obviously, no longer
had a great future at the *Herald*. Cissy eventually let Warner go,
for the Puckish reason that he was "too handsome."

After Cissy acquired the Dower House, she visited her Long
Island estate less. It consisted of sixty-five acres at Sands Point,

near the town of Port Washington. The big, frame, rambling Victorian house was surrounded by trees on the top of a hill, with a vista down to the harbor, where J. Pierpont Morgan's yacht, the *Corsair*, often rode at anchor. Elmer Schlesinger had purchased the place from Vincent Astor after their marriage, and Cissy later added a cottage on the grounds where she could retreat to write alone. There were well-kept gardens and a salt-water swimming pool.

In the winter, during the thirties, Cissy either took a villa at Nassau or rented a house on the ocean at Palm Beach, Florida. In 1941 she acquired a frame house on Siesta Key, on the Gulf at Sarasota, Florida, and began spending her winter vacations there. This was one of her smaller residences, though the living room was even larger than the one at Du Pont Circle.

It was not happpenstance that Cissy bought a house in the same Florida town where Ringling Brothers had their winter quarters. Nothing fascinated her more than the circus and circus people. Many circus people lived in retirement in Sarasota, and she made a point of seeking them out. Sometimes they were worth a story. F. M. (Jack) Flynn, general manager of the New York *News*, was Cissy's guest at Sarasota in March 1948, and complimented her on a circus article which had appeared in the *Times-Herald* without a by-line.

"Well, thank you, thank you, thank you," Cissy replied. "I wrote it."

"Oh, come *on* now," Flynn laughed. "*You* wrote it?"

Cissy was annoyed at Flynn for his apparent skepticism that she could write that well, and she did not let him forget it. After Flynn returned to New York, he received a large envelope containing a tearsheet of the article. Across the top of the page-length story was scrawled in her handwriting, "By—E.P.," and to prove it she attached her original manuscript, done in her own elegant longhand. It was a tender, true love story about Ella Bradna, the most celebrated bareback rider of her time, and her husband, Fred Bradna, formerly a famous high-jump rider, ring-

master and equestrian director for the Ringling shows. They
were past seventy and living in retirement at Sarasota. Cissy told
their story in dialogue between them as they reminisced.

In Sarasota, Cissy was more isolated from her newspaper staff,
largely because the telephone connections were frequently poor.
Nonetheless, if an editor failed to get through to her for an
important decision, no excuse was sufficient; he should have
hired a plane, a boat, or Superman to bridge the gap. Whenever
direct telephonic communications failed, Mason Peters, *Times-
Herald* managing editor, called John Ringling North, who would
dispatch one of his flunkies to Cissy's house with the message.

Peters' problems from the receiving end were equally uncertain. Several times he was instructed to drop everything and proceed to Sarasota immediately. On one such occasion, he dashed
to the airport and luckily caught a plane which got him to
Florida in a relatively few hours. He checked into the Ringling
Hotel at Sarasota and was unpacking when Cissy telephoned.
Peters, a little out of breath, asked when she wanted him to
come over.

"Oh, don't bother," his boss drawled.

He caught the next plane back to Washington.

As an editor, Peters' duties were not entirely editorial. Early
one afternoon Cissy directed him via long distance to be in
Sarasota in time for a dinner party. Peters again managed a swift
trip, slipped into his tuxedo and arrived just as the soup was being
served.

A lovely girl was seated on his left, and John Ringling North
was seated directly across the table. After dinner, as he was
circulating, drink in hand, Peters was drawn aside by his hostess.

"Mason," she whispered, "do you find that girl attractive?"

"Oh, yes, Mrs. Patterson, very attractive," the editor replied.

"Help Johnny out, won't you?" Cissy murmured, giving him a
pat on the back and a gentle shove into the eddying crowd.
It was then that Peters, who was young and good-looking,
learned that he had been brought to Sarasota to protect the circus

man from a predatory female. Peters obediently cut the girl out of a pack of admirers and turned on all his considerable charm in an effort to monopolize her. This was not easy, for she kept craning her neck for "Johnny." North had slipped out of the party and was boarding a train.

Peters' assignment—hardly the most disagreeable he had ever had in the line of duty—was not completed. Cissy told him to keep the beauty occupied for a few days, until North was safely on shipboard, bound for Europe.

When Ringling Brothers played Washington a few months later, Frank Craven, the circus press agent, sought out Peters and advised him to "get out of town." He reported that North, back from Europe, had rediscovered the girl's charms, while the girl was bent on revenge against Peters for having let the circus owner get away from her in Florida.

Knowing that his boss would be tickled by this sequel to her plot, Peters telephoned Mrs. Patterson and explained how the Sarasota caper had left him with an angry woman gunning for him. He suggested that perhaps he *ought* to get out of town until the circus left.

Cissy replied with a throaty chuckle.

"Well, we can't spare you *now*, Mason, can we?" she said, and hung up.

Peters stayed in town but laid low and managed to survive.

Keeping two people apart was unusual for Cissy; it was more characteristic of her to play a matchmaker's role. When she was not throwing two people together, she was trying to find out who was pursuing whom—and liked to let them know *she* knew. Once, when she learned that a male overnight guest at Du Pont Circle was interested in a female overnight guest, she tacked a hand-lettered sign at the first landing of the staircase: "Beware! The Stairs Creak!"

Platoons of servants were necessary to maintain Cissy on her mobile plane of living. At both Dower House and Du Pont Circle she kept permanent staffs the year around. Dower House sufficed with a cook and maid, who were augmented by a butler and others when she came for a weekend or more. But the estate also required a superintendent of grounds, two grooms for the horses, and half a dozen gardeners and farm hands.

At Du Pont Circle there were two butlers, a personal secretary, a housekeeper, a parlor maid, two housemaids, a personal maid, a seamstress, two laundresses, a houseman, a chauffeur, a chef, a second cook and a kitchen boy. There were even servants for the servants—a cook solely for the employees, and a maid who waited on them in the employees' dining room.

Boarding The Ranger, her private railroad car, Cissy was accompanied by her traveling retinue: steward, assistant steward, chef, maid and secretary. This chintz-suite-on-wheels answered the needs at once of her roving spirit and her taste for luxury. She had purchased the car in 1928 for $100,000 and spent another $90,000 to refit the interior.

The fixtures in the main bathroom were gold-plated, and the lights in the main bedroom were silver-plated. A regulation-sized Pullman, with a glassed-in rear platform, the car included a drawing room, dining room, two guest bedrooms, kitchen, and servants quarters, complete with bedroom for two, a shower and their own pantry. The two stewards spelled one another in staying awake all night long; one never knew where the train might make an emergency stop, or who might come aboard. The additional staff members slept in the train's regular Pullmans.

Also aboard the car were at least four poodles, twenty-five to thirty pieces of luggage, half of which Cissy would never open, seven sets of chintz slipcovers and seven sets of silk sheets. These were changed daily because Cissy couldn't bear to look at the same colors every day. The bedcovers were usually changed more often than that; if she happened to lie down on the bed for a few minutes, the coverlet was changed. Cissy had an obsession about neatness and cleanliness and used dozens of fresh towels every day. She often bathed two or three times a day.

Cissy's indifference to the time of day caused crises on The

23

William Randolph Hearst gave Cissy her start as an editor when her own family refused to encourage her journalistic ambitions. It gave her a bond with Hearst and she became a good friend of Hearst's good friend, Marion Davies. Cissy bought out Hearst and in 1939 created her own round-the-clock newspaper, the *Times-Herald*. She was a dynamic, if mercurial, executive and developed a talented and loyal staff.

24

25

Cissy was a good friend of both the famous Roosevelt women. For years she feuded with Alice (above, picture 25), daughter of President Theodore Roosevelt. She was an outspoken admirer of Eleanor Roosevelt (below).

26

27 *Jackie Martin*

28 *Jackie Martin*

Cissy's parties drew the top names from the diplomatic, political, social and literary worlds. At this party in the Du Pont Circle house were FBI chief J. Edgar Hoover, socialite Evie Robert and GOP presidential candidate Thomas E. Dewey (top) and columnist Igor Cassini, his wife Austine (now Mrs. William Randolph Hearst, Jr.), and Senator Arthur Vandenberg (center). Cissy was a regular at even more elaborate parties staged by millionaire Evalyn Walsh McLean. In the lower picture Cissy clowns at a McLean party with Senator Warren Austin, left, and Senator Burton K. Wheeler, right.

29 *Jackie Martin*

30

Cissy willed her newspaper to seven of her top executives: (seated) Mason Peters and William Shelton; (standing; left to right) Happy Robinson, J. Irving Belt, Frank Waldrop, Edmund F. Jewell, and Michael W. Flynn. She decided too late she would rather leave the paper to Alicia Patterson Guggenheim, her niece (right, picture 31). Below is one of the last pictures taken of Cissy before she died in 1948. She is shown with her favorite poodle, Butch.

31

32

Ranger. She would have ten guests and order "dinner at eight." But she might delay having it served until 10 o'clock. Once, the chef got so rattled by the confusion that he threw the peas out the window and kept the shells.

The steward on the private car, for all but its first few years, was Joseph Miller, a light-skinned Washington Negro. At Banff, in September 1929, Miller was a pantry boy on the private railroad car of the Governor-General of Canada. The car was far outglittered one day when Cissy's car was parked alongside it. Alonzo, then her steward, invited Miller aboard to have a look around, and there he met Cissy. She was charmed when he spoke to her in French. After a few minutes conversation, she told him he was a "nice young man" and offered him a job. In early 1931, after a year in a premedical course at Howard University, Miller accepted.

Miller became Alonzo's assistant, and after Alonzo died in 1936 he became chief steward. He was the one member of the staff who accompanied Mrs. Patterson wherever she traveled. Miller was intelligent, made a good appearance, and could do anything. In a pinch, he would cheerfully double as butler, cook, chauffeur, veterinarian, laundress (he could wield a mean iron), and even maid. He also maintained a discreet anonymity, in contrast to Alonzo, who had been given a lavish buildup in Cissy's *Herald*. Reporters were assigned to write lyrically about Alonzo's sauces and his exotic cocktail recipes. Miller did become famous at Dower House for his mint juleps, served in frosted silver goblets with generous, unmeasured, dollops of bourbon, brandy *and* cognac. He also concocted a zombie cocktail which proved so devastating it had to be discontinued.

Miller quit Cissy three times, after disputes, and the third time, in 1945, he refused her pleas to return. Looking back, he recalls that this fourteen-year period was "hell, fun and an *experience*." He was well compensated; no Washington employer of that time, he believes, was as generous as Mrs. Patterson was with her help.

Miller received a salary of $125 a month, plus expenses. Food, lodgings and laundry were, of course, free, and he also had a charge account in New York at Abercrombie & Fitch. He did not stint on his wardrobe, and may well have been the best-dressed private-car steward in the United States—which was what Cissy wanted him to be. She frequently gave him checks for $500 or $1000 as a bonus, and always gave him $1000 at Christmas, though one year, when she was mad at Miller, she sent the $1000 to his wife, Helen. She also often gave the Millers tickets to fights and Broadway shows, and she urged Mrs. Miller, without avail, to travel with them—as a guest—on The Ranger.

This generosity was not out of line with her treatment of other servants. Cissy paid her kitchen boy $90 a month during the depths of the Depression, when she could have hired one for $25 a month. Mrs. Emile Bouchard, the cook who lived at Dower House in the forties, received $300 a month, more than the going wage, and felt she could have had even more if she had demanded it. When Mrs. Bouchard motored to the city on her day off, Cissy paid her auto expenses.

In the long-lost world of very private railroad cars (today they exist largely as executives' cars for business purposes), the car's position on the train was important. It was a case of "the last shall be first"—in prestige. Every car owner wanted a so-called "rear-end movement," permitting maximum use of his observation platform. But railroads were reluctant to hook the private car on last, so it usually required string-pulling. Cissy knew how to pull. In fact, during Miller's time her car failed to achieve this privilege only twice. Some kind of peak in such one-upmanship was reached when six private cars were hooked onto a special train for the Kentucky Derby. Other owners in this blue-ribbon half dozen included Mrs. Evalyn Walsh McLean, a Whitney, a Donohue, and a Woolworth; nonetheless, The Ranger proudly rode last. Mrs. McLean was second to last, making it easier for them to visit back and forth during the trip.

The railroads charged the equivalent of eighteen first-class tickets to haul a private car on a regular run. The charge for hiring a locomotive à la carte, so to speak, and not hitching on to a scheduled train, was the equivalent of 150 first-class tickets, or more, depending on the circumstances. Because she hated to wait for anything, Cissy several times paid through the nose for the convenience of having her own train.

On her 1929 visit to Banff, for example, she had an overpowering desire to head south for her ranch. Informed that there were no trains scheduled southward until the next day, she paid $6000 for a special locomotive to pull The Ranger that night.

Another time, en route to Sarasota on a rented private car (she sold The Ranger after the outbreak of World War II to the Baltimore & Ohio), she was hooked onto a slow train which missed the connection at Tampa. There were only two trains a day from Tampa to Sarasota, so Cissy paid for the privilege of being hauled the last sixty miles in solitary splendor.

Upon leaving Sarasota, she always instructed her chauffeur to follow her car in the limousine as far as Tampa—just in case she should change her mind and decide to return to Sarasota and stay a bit longer in the sun. Her leave-taking at the Sarasota station would have been hard to ignore. First there was the sound of four yapping poodles. Then came the tall woman in smoked glasses, gliding confidently amid a retinue of friends and servants. A big floppy hat was pushed back over the Titian hair. A three-quarter-length coat partly covered pink slacks, wide-cuffed in the style of the 1940s. Cissy created the same sense of exotic excitement as her Hollywood movie-star friends. Perhaps it was contagious. When she rode her railroad car to Hearst's San Simeon castle, she sometimes stopped off in Hollywood to pick up a cargo of stars and starlets who were to grace the Hearst's soirees.

In equipping her car with luxuries, Cissy may have been exceeded in ingenuity by the late Augustus Busch, the St. Louis brewer who had beer piped into every compartment of his car. Of course, she probably would have considered that vulgar, for her taste ran to champagne. But Cissy may well have gone further than others in the way she used her car. Once, she had

Miller take Rebecca, the cook, to New York on The Ranger, for the sole purpose of whipping up her famed terrapin dish for William Randolph Hearst at the Ritz Tower.

Hearst was also the reason for The Ranger's mystery trip. One day he confided to Cissy that he was anxious to slip out of New York and travel to the Far West without being detected. He was convinced that some sort of "summons" was out for him, and that the Roosevelt administration—which he had been fighting fang and claw—was behind it. Cissy asked no further questions and took charge of the escape, playing it for the last ounce of melodrama. At great expense, she leased a special train, consisting of a locomotive, a coal car, a day coach, a Pullman and The Ranger. Miller was put in charge of the bobtailed train, armed with a letter of authorization from the Pennsylvania Railroad's head passenger agent which would ensure a right-of-way all across the country.

The train started at the Port Washington, Long Island, station, where the curtains of the private car were drawn and Cissy, heavily powdered to look pale, was helped aboard from a wheel chair. At the Sunnyside, Long Island, switching yard a limousine drew right up to the siding and out stepped the great Hearst, Marion Davies, Joseph Willicombe (Hearst's top secretary) and two servants. They boarded The Ranger while Cissy, heavily veiled, took their place in the limousine.

Miller's orders were to "seal" the car, that is, to keep the curtains drawn and let no one board, on the excuse that Mrs. Patterson was ill. The little train puffed out of New York with its hidden passengers and headed for the Southwest. It passed through Texas, New Mexico and Arizona without apparently attracting any more attention than raised eyebrows. In Arizona, the Hearst entourage departed for an airplane connection, and proceeded to California.

Until the mid-thirties, Cissy traveled almost exclusively on The Ranger. After that, she used airplanes more often. (She liked the idea of getting places faster, and on the spur of the moment she chartered an airplane to take her and eleven friends to Atlanta for the movie premiere of *Gone With the Wind* that evening.) On her trips across the country in her private car, she might take along a favorite staff member or two, the wife of one of her editors, or perhaps some personal friends. Miller recalls no uneventful trips. Once, Eugene Meyer, Cissy's friendly enemy who published the rival Washington *Post*, got into an argument with Cissy and was so angry he refused to spend the night on the car. Miller engaged a drawing room for Meyer in a Pullman up forward.

Miller always wired ahead to have fresh-cut flowers brought aboard at every scheduled stop. Wherever she was, Cissy insisted on being surrounded by a profusion of flowers. Flowers were more than a luxury for her—they were a necessity. Her greenhouses were consequently among the finest in the United States.

Halfway across the country Cissy might decide to change her destination, so the steward would consult a railroad timetable and find another train to hook onto. Once, outside Oakland, California, they were snowbound for twenty-four hours. Another time the car was smothered by dust in Kansas, and the staff wondered if Cissy would stand for this act of God. However, as Alonzo put it in a wire to Cissy's secretary in Washington: "Madame has accepted the dust storms chawmingly."

Cissy's other residence was a $12,000-a-year suite she kept at the Carlton House in New York City. Located on the tenth floor, overlooking Madison Avenue, it included a dining room, library, music room, two bedrooms, kitchen and a den with a bar.

Cissy cached her main liquor supply in Manhattan Transfer storage vaults in New York City. It was drawn on, as necessity demanded, to replenish the stocks at Du Pont Circle and other residences. The Du Pont Circle wine cellar would have been adequate for a luxury hotel. Besides countless cases of vintage wines, there were sherries, Scotch, thirty-year-old cognac and five different kinds of French champagne worth about $30 a fifth

during the early thirties. (In those days, Cissy's bootlegger was
the late Sam Beard, who, after Prohibition, went on to greater
local fame and became "king of the Washington bookmakers.")

With so much temptation in the cellar, Cissy wanted to prevent her servants from acquiring too fine a palate at her expense.
The butler kept a notebook in which he recorded every bottle
withdrawn from the shelves, and for what purpose. Cissy's con-
genital suspicion of servants had been increased by a gaudy case
in point.

In the late twenties, when she was Mrs. Schlesinger, she had
returned to her Long Island estate one night unexpectedly and
discovered a Bacchanalian revel in full swing. Obviously, a party
was going on in the house, and down at the swimming pool the
rites of Dionysius seemed to be underway. The celebrators were
her servants and their friends. The butler, though somewhat
foggy-eyed, did not lose his aplomb when he saw Cissy striding
in through the darkness. He invited his mistress to join the fun.
He explained that he was throwing his own "butler's ball" for
the maids and butlers of adjoining estates. All the refreshments
were coming from the Schlesinger kitchen.

Cissy smiled and called for more of her best wine. She stayed
at the party and appeared to be having a good time. The other
butlers and maids went home thinking how lucky were the servants in the employ of Mrs. Schlesinger.

The Schlesinger servants were in a glow. But the next day
every man jack of them was fired.

Unlike rich Americans today, Cissy Patterson was not a bit
afraid to appear to be rich. Since she supported numerous private
charities, she saw no reason why she should not also use her
wealth for her own gratification. She suspected that her servants
and her newspaper staff got a vicarious thrill out of abetting her
preoccupation with comfort and glamor; they did—and they
also drew a wry satisfaction from the fact that her millions did
not keep her from being lonely and unhappy much of the time.

Cissy's extensive wardrobe and jewels were basic components

in her image of elegance. She had ten fur coats, including two minks, a sable and a silver fox, and a mink lap robe. For many years, starting in the late twenties, her clothes were made by Charles James, a New York couturier who was selected in 1947 by American fashion critics as the outstanding dress designer. Cissy liked tea gowns—sweeping, trailing things—and she liked James because he was daring and exotic. When James was starting out he would have been willing to dress her at a loss because of the prestige she gave him in wearing his creations.

"She had magic, absolute magic," James recalls. Still, trying to satisfy her could be a near hysterical experience.

"With her unquenchable frankness," James says, "she used her charm like a horsewhip. She never ordered a dress except by telephone, and usually in the middle of the night, and everything had to be made in less time than it takes to fry an egg. On top of that, she wouldn't pay for the things unless they passed the strictest muster. But just the same . . . she brought inspiration."

Cissy was easy to dress because of her height and her figure, which remained girlish and small-waisted until late in her life. She never went in for diets; her secret, if there was any, was her regular exercise. She liked to ride and swim, but her main form of regular exercise throughout her life was walking. She would walk the mile from Dower House to the highway every day.

In Washington she walked in Rock Creek Park. When she sallied forth in the Park on Sunday mornings her hiking attire was a comic contrast to her Schiaparelli dresses. (Actually, although she wore clothes beautifully, she hated to dress up; her customary attire at home was comfortable—though exquisite—pajamas.) The main elements of this costume were old patent-leather laced boots, a short woolen skirt reaching just below the knees, and a very shabby buckskin jacket worn many years before on hunting trips out West. Her hair was pulled back in a knot under a shapeless, battered riding hat, and her disguise, she naïvely hoped, was completed by pitch-black glasses. Accompanied by her poodles, she would not have been easier to identify if she had carried a placard with her name on it. Cissy nonetheless always seemed surprised when she was instantly recognized.

Cissy had a whole rack of riding clothes, including both jodhpurs and skirted habits, for she rode both sidesaddle and astride, depending on her mood. However, she preferred "western riders"—tight riding pants worn over the boots.

When she went on a clothes spree, Cissy sometimes purchased with the abandon of a buyer for a department store. She would order twenty pairs of identical shoes from Bergdorf Goodman, and once she bought one each in the entire line of Tina Leser bathing suits.

Even in buying jewels she was impulsive. One day in 1934, passing Cartier's in New York, Cissy noticed a string of twenty-two black pearls and two black-pearl earrings. She went inside and made inquiries of Jacques Cartier, head of the firm. Cartier explained that he had just acquired the rare gems from the Russian Prince Youssoupoff, father of Felix Youssoupoff, who had murdered Rasputin. Two of the pearls had belonged to Catherine the Great. But, the jeweler explained, the price had not yet been set and he would have to consult the Prince in Europe before it could be determined.

"I haven't got time to wait around for that," Cissy told Cartier impatiently. She proposed a settlement on the spot. Cartier looked surprised, but she wrote out a check, handed it to him, and said, "Here's what I'll pay you." Cartier accepted. The price she paid has remained a secret, but some of Cissy's friends believe it could have been as much as $1,000,000.

Cissy seldom wore her black pearls, fearful that a knowledgeable jewel thief would do almost anything to acquire them. Occasionally, she carried them to New York in her traveling jewel box, which was approximately the size of an attaché case and contained a selection of her diamond earrings, Russian crosses, carved emerald bracelets and diamond rings. (The comb she wore on her knot of hair sparkled with diamonds and rubies, and her hairpins were solid gold.)

Still, she thought the black pearls were worth her price. She was amused, for example, to hear that the black pearl's dark, rich color is caused by an oyster who has the equivalent of cirrhosis of the liver. The pearls were irresistible as a conversation piece.

Cissy liked to believe the story that one of her pearls had belonged to Cleopatra, and that once, when Mark Antony was about to return from Egypt to Rome, he asked her what he could get that would bring her pleasure. "Match this stone for me!" Cleopatra had told her lover, holding up a black-pearl earring. Later, when she came to Rome, Antony sent her a black pearl and then threw a big banquet in her honor.

"How do you like your present?" he asked as they toasted one another. "Fine," she is said to have replied, "but it's not real." When Antony raised his eyebrows, Cleopatra, with a wise smile, called for vinegar. An imitation pearl, she knew, would dissolve in it. When a goblet of vinegar was handed to her, she dropped in the pearl and watched it dissolve. Then, with a flourish, she drank the vinegar.

Back in the twenties, when Rose Crabtree wrote that she had come into the possession of some diamonds, Cissy had replied: "Try the diamonds on the window pane. If they scratch, they are real." She worried about being able to tell the real from the phony in all things, and she often wished it was as easy to tell her true friends from her false friends as it was to assay pearls and diamonds.

NINETEEN

"Off with Their Heads"

After Cissy created her own newspaper in 1939 and was in full command, the atmosphere was suggestive of that at the court of Queen Elizabeth I. Cissy maintained her own unofficial but discernible hierarchy, in which there were American counterparts for dukes, duchesses, ladies-in-waiting and court jesters. Columnists were made and broken, royal charmers like the Kennedys and Cassinis entered the scene, and intrigue for the new high stakes was rampant, with the Queen herself playing an enthusiastic role. One never knew from one moment to the next whether he would be feted, prepared for the chopping block, or just kept dangling.

Much of the suspense was generated by Cissy's penchant for impulsive dismissals, which could on occasion be extremely serious. With her characteristic honesty in self-dissection, Cissy admitted the satisfaction that came from lopping off a head. She even regretted that Harold Ickes never became one of her columnists, because "it would have given me such joy to have fired him."

One victim who never did figure out how he fell into disfavor was Sol Roogow. One night when Roogow was acting managing editor of the *Times-Herald* he received a call from Charley Duffy, the city editor, asking him to phone Mrs. Patterson at her New York hotel. On the phone, she took exception to a picture on page three that morning. Roogow tried to explain that it was used at the request of Duffy, but Mrs. Patterson would not listen.

The following day she called him into her office and in the presence of Duffy ordered Roogow to bring in all the pictures he could gather up.

Roogow returned with some fifty assorted photos from the United Press and International News Service. The editress glanced at each picture and discarded each with the remark, "If you can't do better than this, I'll put you back on the copy desk where you came from." Roogow, having never worked on the *Times-Herald* copy desk, was fit to be tied and ready to explode, but Duffy pushed him out of the office.

The next day Duffy notified Roogow that Mrs. Patterson wanted him out as managing editor and Duffy in. Roogow put in a call to Managing Editor George De Witt, who had placed him in charge before he left for a vacation in Nassau. De Witt said he would return immediately. Two days after De Witt came back, he informed Roogow that Mrs. Patterson had vowed never to come to the editorial floor of the building while Roogow was on it. She did indeed stay away, and her mail piled up at her door until De Witt sent Roogow to Boston for a week to cool things off. But he never did get back on the *Times-Herald* on a permanent basis. While he was a competent newspaperman, he lacked a certain spark which Cissy demanded in her editors.

Sometimes Mrs. Patterson's dismissal was more abrupt, but easier to understand. There was the case of Carroll Peake. Peake was a San Franciscan who lived up to his home town's reputation for sophistication. It was somehow appropriate that his middle names were Eugene Beauchamp, for he was a gourmet, a raconteur, a bon vivant, and a boulevardier. No Washington newsman could match him sartorially. When newsmen turned out for the annual White House Correspondents Association dinner in black tie, Peake was dazzling in white tie, top hat, tailcoat, ivory-headed cane, and black cape.

After one banquet, Peake repaired to the *Times-Herald* city room at midnight to taper off. When the nearest phone rang, he automatically reached over and, suiting the words to his mood, barked:

"Patterson's Madhouse!"

A low, husky voice demanded to know who was speaking. Peake continued to talk flippantly. Suddenly he heard a click at the other end of the wire. Only then did it come over him that he had been speaking to the lady for whom he worked.

Peake was too numbed to move, so he simply sat and waited for "The Presence." Fifteen minutes later Mrs. Patterson swept in and spotted the caped and top-hatted reporter sitting as stiffly as a misplaced mannequin in the raffish city room.

"What about that phone call?" she asked icily.

"I'm sorry, Mrs. Patterson," said Peake.

"Get out, you're fired!" she told him.

This sacking dismayed City Editor Duffy. Charles Gavin Duffy was one of many *Times-Herald* staff members who acted as if they were doing a remake of *The Front Page*. He was a black-haired, black-browed, jut-jawed, compact Bostonian, complete with accent. He walked as though he was getting up momentum to smash through a brick wall. Duffy commanded his editorial quarterdeck with hair askew, tie ajar, and trousers in imminent danger of rapid descent. When he rose up and bellowed "Boy!" it sounded as if The Story of the Year had broken—when all Duffy might want was a cup of coffee.

But Duffy's heart was sentimental, and Peake was one of his better reporters. He hated to lose him. So he began a sly campaign to have Peake restored to the payroll. He slipped this delicated topic into every news conference with Cissy. Finally, after three months, it paid off. One day Cissy sailed into the news conference in high spirits, smiled, and said, "All right, today's the day." She even agreed with the fast-talking city editor that Peake should be paid his accumulated pay for the period of his enforced absence.

Another *Times-Herald* editor whose dynamic behavior masked a soft heart was Mason Peters, whose career had been meteoric. Son of a newsman father who took him all over Europe as a child, Peters entered the newspaper business at sixteen. With an occasional year out to work his way around the world as a seaman, Peters was a reporter, movie and drama critic, and desk-man at the *Herald* and *Times-Herald*. At twenty-four he was city editor, and at thirty he was managing editor.

Peters brought not only talent but a driving, electric, nervous energy which sparked a staff that needed little sparking. Writing or editing copy near deadline, his excitement was characterized by the frenetic jitter of his right leg.

Cissy liked this young man's zest, as well as his feeling for language and literature, and Peters became the youngest duke in her domain. Yet, unlike his boss, Peters was so consecrated to the newspaper life that he found it next to impossible to fire a reporter.

It is said that once, when he had to get rid of an incompetent, Peters compromised by putting a hand on the condemned man's shoulder and telling him he had just the job for him: They needed someone with the necessary passion for anonymity to be able to put on his hat and coat, leave the city room and never come back. The trick was to vanish absolutely and forever into the night! According to the story, the reporter rose as if hypnotized and staggered from the room in a glow of exhilaration, unaware that his head had just been separated from his shoulders.

At some time Cissy must have fired an employee because she didn't like the way he parted his hair. Many dismissals were made for equally whimsical reasons. Visiting the city room one day, she pointed to the picture editor and ordered Duffy to fire him. She didn't like his flamboyant tie.

On the very first day she leased the *Herald*, Cissy noticed an editorial writer with a waxed mustache. "Fire him," she told the managing editor. Another clever rewrite man never advanced as he should have, because Mrs. Patterson complained to an editor about his body odor.

One staff member swore that he heard her approach a colleague and say: "Oh, what's your name? . . . you're fired!"

Sometimes she was mixed up as to who she *was* firing. She once told her managing editor to dismiss a subeditor. The next day she asked where he was. She was informed that the man had collected his severance pay and was already out of town looking for another job. "Oh, I didn't mean *him*," Mrs. Patterson protested. The editor was recalled.

It must be noted that many employees, discharged for nonsensical reasons, were rehired, or otherwise rewarded. There was the occasion when Virgilia Peterson, of the women's page, incurred The Lady's displeasure. Cissy fired her. But the next day she invited Virgilia to Du Pont Circle to select a fur and any piece of furniture she might need for her apartment.

When star reporter Una Franklin was abruptly fired, it was recalled that Cissy had complained about Una's eyes being set too close together. That might indeed have constituted grounds for sacking; actually, the reasons for it were almost as arbitrary. Cissy had had a dislike for Miss Franklin ever since the girl had charged seventy-five cents on her expense account for a pair of stockings, explaining that she had gotten a run while covering the *Times-Herald* art fair. She had worked her way further into the doghouse by writing a series on houses which reflected on the changing neighborhood around Du Pont Circle, where several pieces of property were Patterson-owned.

On the other hand, a pleasing physical attribute could help a career as much as close-set eyes could hurt one. When Bernie Harrison was promoted to be movie critic, he asked Jackie Martin, head of art, what the boss liked about him.

"She likes the shape of the back of your head," Jackie said. "It's so 'classic.'"

Mrs. Patterson thought the shape of Harrison's head had something to do with his Greek ancestry—which in itself entranced her.

Harrison became the movie critic after the regular critic, Harold Phillips, went to the wrong movie. Phillips assigned Harrison, then his assistant, to review a Greta Garbo film, *Ninotchka*, and went to a second-rate movie himself. Cissy liked Harrison's review but thought Phillips should have assigned himself to the more important production. She fired him.

Harrison, who later was to become radio and television editor of the Washington *Star*, had no trouble with the boss as movie critic. He even got away with a rave review of the movie *Citizen Kane*, which was an unflattering study of William Randolph Hearst. Harrison had been treated with generosity by Cissy ever since he had started as a copyboy on the *Herald*. Once, when he told her the doctor wanted him to take a rest because he was underweight, she ordered him to go home and stay there as long as he felt like it. Harrison stayed home until he got bored several weeks later; he not only remained on the payroll, but periodically Mrs. Patterson's chauffeur appeared at his door with a basket of fruit or a box of books.

Cissy did not show up at the *Times-Herald* office every day but she telephoned frequently, at any hour of the day or night. When she called the managing editor, a red light on his telephone flashed a warning. When she called on some other line, disaster sometimes resulted. Carroll Peake was not the only staff member who took her call and assumed that some kind of nut was on the wire. Cissy could not be bothered with a preliminary "hello." She started right in giving her opinions in her languid, modulated contralto, and those not accustomed to her voice might miss the first half-dozen words. If she were asked to repeat, she was furious. When the Queen spoke, she expected to be understood— it would be absurd for her not to get through.

Her message was usually terse. For example, she might say to Peters, "Mason, that cut on page three is terrible." Then the phone would click off. Or she might call and ask who wrote the cute story on page two. "John White," Peters might say. A throaty chuckle could be heard. Then—click.

One telegraph editor, Charles Henry Beneman, lived in terror of handling the red-lit private line. If Peters was in the composing room, Beneman was supposed to answer, but he preferred to go loping downstairs in search of Peters. A minute's conversation with Mrs. Patterson on the phone would leave him quivering, on the verge of tears.

Mrs. Patterson would not put up with rudeness on the telephone, however inadvertent, but she was tolerant of a great deal of bad behavior. She seldom fired anyone for drinking, and if she did he was usually rehired. She did dismiss one female alcoholic, but paid for her treatment and eventually settled on her a generous lifetime pension. Cissy treated alcoholics as "sick" people long before the word was fashionable in that context.

Cissy was devoted to those she considered competent, regardless of their drinking habits. It did not bother her if a reporter or editor had to be dug out of a saloon or speakeasy, so long as he was available when needed, and did the job well. Sometimes, indeed, sobering up an editor could be as important as writing the lead story of the day. Managing Editor Mike Flynn had just signed a new contract and was celebrating with Pete Daley, a reporter. Cissy sent her chauffeur out to find them, but they hid out in their favorite saloon. Finally, Cissy assigned Bill Flythe, a young reporter, to join Daley and Flynn, drink with them, and not to return until he had sobered them up. Flythe carried out both parts of his assignment with distinction, that is, he got himself convincingly drunk, but he also managed the rescue. (Flynn was not dismissed this time, but on another occasion Cissy got so mad at him she wrote him a sad, five-page, handwritten note telling him he was through and enclosing a goodby check for $10,000. A week later he had his job back and was $10,000 richer.)

Another time Flythe's tolerance for whisky was less spectacular. He made the abysmal mistake of weaving into Mrs. Patterson's empty office and passing out there on the couch. When she returned, Cissy forced him to down a whole tumbler of bourbon, to teach him a cruel lesson, and sent him home.

The making and unmaking of columnists was a world of its own. The breezy columns in Cissy's newspapers were a key factor in her success. They played up personalities—built them up, if necessary—and treated their doings as news. During the hectic days of the New Deal and World War II the private lives of such people very often *were* pertinent news.

Cissy believed that columnists were made, not born. She went on the theory that anybody who had something interesting to say could do a column, as long as there was a copy desk to correct the spelling and add the syntax. Even the flighty Evalyn Walsh McLean was writing a column for Cissy during one period.

Cissy "invented" some columnists simply by providing them space and letting them write as they talked. As long as they interested the public they had security; if they grew dull, they were out, even if they were her personal friends. One who became a columnist by happenstance but never bored Cissy was Evie Robert, who filled the double role of lady-in-waiting and court jester.

Evie happened to be in Dublin, as a guest of John Cudahy, the United States ambassador to Ireland, when Douglas Corrigan landed his airplane there without authorization and insisted he thought he was flying west rather than east. Evie phoned Cissy about the hilarious arrival of "Wrong-Way Corrigan" and Cissy told her to write a story for the *Herald* about Corrigan every day. This led to a permanent column titled "Eve's Rib." It became the wittiest in the *Times-Herald*.

Cissy's streak of snobbery made her proud to have good, upper-class names writing for her newspaper. Evie, a tall, slender blonde with Grecian features, was the daughter of Harold Walker, head of the legal department of Standard Oil of New Jersey, and in the thirties was considered the most glamorous glamor girl in Washington. In 1935 she married a wealthy, prominent Democrat from Atlanta, Lawrence (Chip) Robert, then Assistant Secretary of the Treasury.

One of the best-known *Times-Herald* columnists was hired originally as a reporter, and because Cissy had known his mother, Countess Marguerite Cassini, as a young woman, Igor Cassini was taken on by the *Herald* in 1937. In October of that year, Igor came up with a scoop about Italian Dictator Benito Mussolini's son, Vittorio, visiting Washington and staying at the Chevy Chase Club. A few days later Igor went to the Russian Embassy and got a story from Ambassador Troyanowsky on the basis of his being able to speak Russian.

But Igor's international background was not quite fruitful enough to guarantee a scoop a day, and so he wound up doing obituaries. One day, City Editor Duffy called him aside and advised him that he was not, after all, cut out to be a reporter. Igor assured Duffy that he felt sure he would turn out to be a great reporter, but he was canned just the same. This was bad news at home, where Igor was the sole support of his mother and his brother, Oleg.

But the Countess Cassini—as her two sons would also prove to be—was a resourceful refugee. Though their family name opened many doors, it was their talent, drive and ability to charm that made it possible to go much further. The Countess's father had been the Russian ambassador to the United States when President McKinley was in office and during part of President Theodore Roosevelt's term. She had been child-hostess to her father's embassy at sixteen and, in time, had become friends with Cissy Patterson and Alice Longworth.

When her husband, Count Alexander Loiewski died, the Countess tried running a dress shop in Florence during the thirties; there she was known as "La Lupa" (the She Wolf) because of the way she fought for Oleg and Igor. In 1937 she came back to Washington seeking jobs for her two clever but unskilled sons. In her memoirs, *Never a Dull Moment*, published before she died in 1961, the Countess describes how she reluctantly looked up Cissy to find employment for them. She wrote:

. . . There was a mocking note in her voice, and I could not wonder. We were about the same age but I looked and felt much older. Cissy, now rich and powerful, was still slender, red-haired, smartly dressed, still rode horse-back every morning though she may not have gone to bed until dawn, still gave off a kind of electric zest. While I, living in Florence, had assumed the habits of Florentine women, who do not resist age. I was tired. I had let myself go, put on weight, my hair was gray, and I dressed always in black . . . and it was clear I was neither rich or powerful.

Cissy agreed to give Igor a job, though not before she had given the opinion that journalism was an "infernal business" unless you were a publisher and warned that if the Countess's son should become a newspaperman he would end up "a drunk and married to the upstairs maid." Also, there was a condition to giving Igor a job—she wanted the Countess's life story for the *Herald*.

Countess Cassini agreed to do her story for $800. Cissy assigned Carol Frink, a highly skilled "sob sister" to do the writing. Miss Frink interviewed the Countess at length, but the Countess did not see the finished product until it began to run in daily installments in the *Herald*. What she saw appalled her. Cissy had suggested that the title would be "Washington by Candlelight" or something of the sort. But the title that screamed across the page over her by-line in the *Herald* was "I Lived for Love." The sensationalized tone employed by Miss Frink also alarmed the Countess. She complained to Cissy, but Cissy blithely explained, according to the Countess's memoirs, that it was "good for the paper, though bad for me."

For Igor the transition to the breezy *Herald* style was easier. He was assigned to write an untitled column consisting of 100 words for $25 a week. He got around socially, thanks to his excellent diplomatic connections, and turned out to be right on Cissy's journalistic wave length. In October 1938, Igor had his first occasional by-line column, "Petit Point, by Ghighi Cassini," which carried a half-column profile of him in a John Barrymore-like pose. Early in 1939, he was promoted to doing "Petit Point" regularly.

Igor entertained his readers by dropping names and reporting the latest society behavior patterns; anyone who needed to be identified did not merit space. He was attempting to develop a tongue-in-cheek style; once, he did a column in the traditional sugary society-column style of Martha Blair, with whom he was then feuding. When Martha was fired, Igor was given her column, "These Charming People."

In early 1943, Bernard Baruch gave a plush party at the Carlton Hotel for Mr. and Mrs. Harry Hopkins, complete with imported Hollywood stars. This was during the height of what was supposedly the austerity period, and Igor devoted his column to the delicious irony of the situation. His story was picked up by other papers around the country and he earned a $100 bonus. Three days later he was called by his draft board. Almost simultaneously he received a call from the Hearst organization. So he signed a contract with Hearst for three times what he had been making with Cissy and went off to war. At first Igor did not tell Cissy about the contract—he, too, feared the Patterson lightning and thunder—but she found it out after he recommended that his wife, "Bootsie," succeed him with the column. En route overseas with the Army, Cassini received a vitriolic letter. He was, after all, a vassal in her kingdom, and Cissy felt it was traitorous of him to have stolen away to a bigger monarch behind her back. Besides upbraiding him in the letter, she told him that his wife was a better columnist than he was anyway.

Not content with this parting shot, Igor now contends, Cissy did everything possible to ruin his marriage while he was overseas—by promoting a romance with William Randolph Hearst, Jr. No doubt Cissy had impishly decided that if Igor was going over to the senior Hearst, his wife should go over to the junior

Hearst. In any event, "Bootsie" and Igor were divorced right after the war and she married Hearst in 1948.

"Bootsie"—nee Austine McDonnell—was another lady-in-waiting to Cissy and a beautiful ornament at court. She was the daughter of Major Austin McDonnell, a retired army officer with a distinguished Virginia and Maryland lineage. In June 1939, while she was attending a horse-show dance at Warrenton with the young *Times-Herald* columnist, Igor was abducted by five men who objected to something he had written, and was tarred and feathered. He described the adventure in his column and it was picked up by the news services. Three of his assailants were found guilty of assault and battery and given suspended jail sentences.

When she succeeded her husband in doing "These Charming People" in 1943, "Bootsie" gave it her own touch and, if anything, it made the column more popular. She developed a sprightly feminine style which was not overly cute. Cissy thought up a gimmick—having "Bootsie" photographed in a different hat every day for the picture which appeared in her column.

Meanwhile, Igor went on to become "Cholly Knickerbocker" in the New York *Journal-American*, with a claimed syndication of some 20,000,000 readers. He also claimed in *Esquire* (April 1964) that "I reigned supreme . . . over the International Set, the Smart Set, the Jet Set, the Cafe Society Set, and the Awful Set." By this time he also had been fined $10,000 by a federal judge for failure to register as a paid publicity agent of Dictator Trujillo and was no longer "Cholly Knickerbocker."

Oleg Cassini started more slowly but went further. There was no place for the Countess Cassini's other son at the *Times-Herald*. Just before the war broke out, he did a cartoon of the Polish Embassy ball, but Cissy thought it was too cruelly satirical of her friends, the hapless aristocratic Poles. Twenty-one years later, Oleg designed Mrs. Jacqueline Kennedy's inaugural wardrobe. He was made.

The Kennedys also had columnist links with the *Times-*

Herald. In 1940, chief editorial writer Frank Waldrop hired Kathleen (Kick) Kennedy as his assistant and secretary. Her father, United States ambassador to the Court of St. James's, was a favorite of Cissy Patterson's because their views on the war coincided, though they were not close friends. Kathleen was able, willing and extremely likable, and soon she was assigned to do "Did You Happen to See—," a column about interesting personalities on the Washington scene.

In 1943, Kathleen went to England and became the bride of the Marquis of Hartington, and in 1948 she was killed in a plane crash. When the news came across the ticker, the *Times-Herald* staff wept openly. The feeling about Kathleen was summed up well by Austine Cassini in "These Charming People":

> Thursday night hard-working Eunice Kennedy (she's been working for months on the Juvenile Delinquent Benefit golf tournament program) was dining at the Sulgrave Club with her brother, Rep. Jack Kennedy . . . 'Twas the Bob Schenck's dinner at the Sulgrave dance . . . after this merry evening the Kennedys returned home to Georgetown to hear by phone of the death of their sister, Lady Hartington . . . "Kick" Kennedy Hartington, outstanding in a remarkable family, had besides good looks and wealth, an uncanny knack for making and holding friends. No young woman that I know attracted more widespread and sincere admiration. Though only 28 years old, that girl had won friendships all over the world . . . Waiters, shop girls, dukes, ambassadors, authors, paupers and prime ministers adored her . . .

Representative Jack Kennedy was an occasional visitor in the *Times-Herald* city room, partly because it boasted the prettiest distaff staff in town. Cissy liked him, and the *Times-Herald* had carried the stories on the UN charter meeting in San Francisco that he wrote for International News Service. But Kennedy made no more impression than that of any pleasant, skinny, good-looking young man. Indeed, while being interviewed in a

"Did You Happen to See—" column in February 1947, he remarked wryly to the interviewer: "For a long time I was Joseph P. Kennedy's son, then I was Kathleen's brother, then Eunice's brother. Someday I hope to stand on my own feet!"

In 1951, Waldrop hired another attractive young girl—Jacqueline Bouvier—and she became the *Times-Herald's* "Inquiring Photographer." One of her subjects was her future husband, Representative Jack Kennedy, whom she had met at a dinner party.

Photography was of consuming interest to Cissy. Hearst called the *Times-Herald* the best-illustrated paper in the nation, and Cissy regarded Jackie Martin as the best of all picture editors. She had hired Jackie away from the Washington *News* in 1931 to write one-picture features of her choosing. Three weeks later, after firing two successive picture editors, Cissy installed Jackie in the job, and she remained ten years before leaving to become a free-lance war correspondent.

Jackie was more than a lady-in-waiting. She was a special assistant to Mrs. Patterson in charge of all art. She not only knew how to make and select pictures, she had a mind with imagination and depth, and was a good organizer. She also became a close friend of "The Boss," as she called Mrs. Patterson, and traveled widely with her on The Ranger.

"She was the most brilliant woman I have ever known," Miss Martin recalls. "She was the first one to bring the women's pages to their present flowering. She had absolute knowledge of the way a story should be written or a picture layout should go. And at the same time she was a catalyst who brought the efforts of many peoples and various departments into one mosaic which would tie together.

"The result was that the morale was good. People liked to work for her because she made use of talent and knew how to make the most of it. You learned a lot."

In other words, the apprentice publisher of 1930 had now become the teacher.

Often Cissy would spend hours poring over photographic prints. As she scrutinized each picture, she would ask the picture editor's opinion. She wanted each day's layout to be as different as possible from the day before, and what she liked best of all was a layout that was so eloquent it required no caption at all.

The indestructible prime minister in Mrs. Patterson's kingdom, Frank Waldrop, also felt he benefited from her exacting standards.

"For me, Mrs. Patterson was pure gold as an editor," Waldrop explains. "She had the best judgment of what a piece ought to be of anyone I have ever met. Every time she criticized me I learned something. Unfailingly, she could take the piece of writing and show you how it could be made better. 'An editorial should never say one word more than it needs,' she used to stress."

"Mrs. Patterson had a real intellectual grasp of what she was after," Waldrop recalls. "She wanted good, clear, clean writing. Her own trouble was lack of self-discipline. She was lazy or timid or something about sitting down and writing it herself. She would talk it out with me, and what came out of the typewriter would be her thought and language. She was very good at operating the language."

Cissy so loved language that she distrusted translations. She once tried reading Tolstoy in English, but gave it up and sent Waldrop for an edition in Russian. Besides reading Russian, she spoke excellent French and understandable Polish and Spanish, and had a smattering of German.

Cissy was thoroughly familiar with the works of De Maupassant. Once, when Robert Considine was turning out daily short stories using the Washington scene, he ran out of plots. His boss had a simple solution. She tossed him a copy of De Maupassant.

"Rewrite these plots," Cissy told him, "and put some government girls in."

Considine followed orders, and had an interesting time up-

dating such a classic as "The Pearl Necklace" with typically
New Deal characters. (For a girl staff member who earlier had
done a daily short story designed for government girls, Cissy
herself had supplied the characters and plots; the girl suspected
that all of them were taken right out of Cissy's encyclopedic
knowledge of real-life Washington.)

Among modern authors, Cissy most admired Rebecca West,
a friend who visited her occasionally. She was especially enthusiastic about Miss West's *Black Lamb and Grey Falcon.*
When Thomas Wolfe's novels were published, she dismissed
them with a wave of her hand—no discussion of their claimed
merits were possible. Yet she had an intensely analytical approach and would often reread a book to find out if she might
have been wrong in her first reaction to it.

Cissy strove to inject a literary flavor into her otherwise racy
newspaper, and she continually set her editors to digging into
old volumes in order to use a quotation accurately. Once she
caught editor Mason Peters in a slightly wrong De Maupassant
quote and never let him forget it.

"When you goofed," Peters recalls with a smile, "the impression she gave was: Are you out of your mind? Making a
mistake in *my* paper!"

Beneath the surface excitement of working for Cissy throbbed
a strain and tension that scraped the nerve ends. There was no
security among the talented who were competing for the boss's
favor. Instead, there was never-ending suspense as to who next
would fall from grace, or who would be raised up. In a monarchy the elite at the king's court were looked after and taken
care of; all they had to do in return was to swear loyalty and
give up all rights to a private life of their own. They owed their
existence to their monarch. And so it was with Cissy.

When a man at the *Times-Herald* fell from favor after being
close to the Patterson throne, he had to be strong enough to
withstand the blow. Otherwise he (or she) was never the same.
Cissy had a personal grapevine running through the building

which told her the next morning whether, for example, a woman's editor had missed a deadline or an editor had been drunk and disorderly.

It was impossible to fool her for long. Cissy had extraordinary perceptiveness which seemed to tell her what another person was thinking half a block down the street. It was uncanny enough to unnerve anyone trying to deal with her to his advantage. If there was something devious afoot, her sense of melodrama compelled her to engage it directly. She "played" with people, for she could not resist beating someone at what he thought was his own game.

The following letter, written on January 30, 1941, to her business manager, William C. Shelton, is a perfect illustration of her executive personality—at once imperious, blunt, suspicious, demanding, feminine, and highly aware:

Dear Mr. Shelton:

Will you kindly tell me what has happened to the Cooking School Program? It's over a year now since I first urged that we should resurrect our cooking schools, but under a wider scope—following the Chicago program.

One after another objection followed from Mr. Newmyer and his department.

Finally, Mr. McDevitt comes across with some heavy artillery and the rest was silence for awhile.

Next we hear from Mr. Newmyer, via Mr. McDevitt, a detailed account of another type of school—Philadelphia style.

That didn't click; it wasn't applicable to our situation here . . .

More conferences, no enthusiasm, no real willingness to *get going.* I hear this-a and that-a and you all agree that the school will go ahead, but must be after the Holidays—"sometime in February."

Although these cooking schools could and would vitally affect Mr. Newmyer's department, he was yesterday about as clear as a London fog about the whole matter . . .

Out of all this dumb opposition, a few truths stick out clear and sharp.

Tom White has made a brilliant success on the *Herald-American*. He is a very able man, as we all know. So is Newmyer. But the difference between the two men, and the reason why one is successful and one is not, is because one is a generous and loyal worker. He goes "all out" for any property he works on. And Newmyer works for Newmyer alone.

Sincerely yours,
Eleanor Patterson

With her record as a mercurial queen-boss, why then did talented people want to work for her? Aside from the excitement she created and the opportunity she gave talent to shine, there was a general recognition that here was a "great lady." And there was the disarming fact that—to those who knew her well —Cissy was aware of her faults, and candidly rued them.

Once, in a moment of dismay, she confided to Waldrop: "I'm a lot like Mr. Hearst—I give things away, and then I start plotting to get them back . . ."

Waldrop wondered to himself how anyone could resist working for a boss like that.

TWENTY

Success Sweet and Bitter

The year 1943 gave Cissy something to cheer about. For the first time since she walked into the *Herald* building as a novice editor and publisher in August 1930, Cissy's newspaper was in the black. What's more, *this* newspaper was entirely her own creation, born through her marriage of the *Herald* with the *Times* only four and a half years before.

In 1943 the *Times-Herald* made a profit, before taxes, of $44,-700, and Cissy shared this with her top employees in the form of bonuses to the extent that wartime wage ceilings set by the government would allow. Once the corner of prosperity was turned, the *Times-Herald* profits spiraled. In 1944 the profit was $639,000, and in 1945 it was a cool million (of which $110,500 was funneled back to twenty-six executives and subexecutives in bonuses).

Thus, by 1945 Cissy could look back and remind herself that in just ten years since the *Herald* and *Times* had run up a combined deficit of $1,363,000, she had turned the whole thing around.

As a professional woman and as a Patterson, Cissy was proud of herself. Her critics had sneered that she considered her paper a "plaything," and even her brother and cousin had long persisted in the notion that it was a hobby of which she would grow tired when she found she could not afford it. Whenever her circulation manager, "Happy" Robinson, met Joe Patterson on trips to New York, Patterson would ask him, "When's she going to quit, Hap?"

"She's not going to quit!" Robinson always replied. One day, after the *Times-Herald* began to make gains, Robinson related to Patterson that he had said to Cissy, "Cheer up—you've got more circulation than he has."

"What!" Patterson exclaimed. Robinson chuckled and explained that he was referring to percentages: The *Times-Herald* had a larger share of potential newspaper buyers in the Washington area than the *Daily News*, with its 2,000,000-plus circulation, had in New York.

"In that case, you stick with her, then," Patterson had told Robinson.

Cissy was constantly stimulated by the thought that she had the largest circulation of any newspaper in the city that was made up of one of the most influential audiences in the world. The morning editions of her round-the-clock paper were on the breakfast tables or desks of senators, congressmen, diplomats, cabinet members, and the White House hierarchy.

The White House and cabinet officials might choke on their toast as they scanned the *Times-Herald*, but they realized they could hardly afford to ignore whatever new trouble Cissy might be brewing for them.

Cissy asked no favors and received none. The *Evening Star* had close ties with the Board of Trade, the powerful Riggs Bank, and the local merchandisers, while the *Post* under Eugene Meyer was backing the Roosevelt war policies and courting the approval of his policy-makers. In a sense, Cissy was succeeding in the face of the old saw that "you can't fight city hall." She was bucking the Administration in a one-industry town. It is interesting to speculate on how much more successful the *Times-Herald* might have been if it had become a mouthpiece for the Administration instead of its chief gadfly. On the other hand, one of the attractions in reading the *Times-Herald* was its very abrasiveness—not to mention the periodic eruptions of its publisher.

Owning the most-read newspaper in Washington should have made Cissy happy, but on the whole it did not. She had her finger into everything connected with the daily operation, and it took a lot out of her. She became involved in her job emotionally, which is an occupational hazard.

There was the problem of advertising. The disproportionate share of local advertising traditionally claimed by the *Star* was the main reason why no morning newspaper in Washington had ever been able to make money. There was simply not enough left to divide between two morning papers. Beyond this, Cissy had always had a special problem. Her papers had a hard time obtaining "class advertising," that is, ads displaying "prestige merchandise," and as a woman of wealth and taste this bothered her. The higher-quality Washington department stores looked on Cissy's breezy product—despite steady circulation gains—as a market primarily for selling cheaper goods.

This meant that her advertising solicitors had to be twice as ingenious as rival solicitors in their approach. One of them who succeeded in being creative in display advertising long before it became "smart" was Richard Borwick, whom Mrs. Patterson shrewdly converted from a reporter into a salesman overnight. Cissy felt strongly that an employee who was talented in one way might very well be just as talented in another. In October 1937, Borwick made the first real breakthrough in winning over Woodward & Lothrop, the largest high-quality department store in town. He succeeded by offering to write some eye-catching copy for an advertisement of the store's famous China collection.

This became a whole series of ads, written with a literary and historic flavor, complete with classical drawings. The first, entitled "Napoleon Dined Off Wedgewood China," showed the Conqueror in exile, being served on Wedgewood by his "faithful Corsican butler." The use of the elegant China, the ad said, proved that Napoleon was "still as proud on St. Helena as when

all Europe was awaiting his orders." The series lent prestige to
Woodward's and appealed subtly to the *Herald* reader's snobbery. It was the kind of originality that delighted Cissy, and
she passed along a congratulatory note to Borwick.

Nor would Cissy let advertising encroach on her first love,
the women's pages. Once, she gave Frank Gatewood, retail advertising manager, the privilege of selling one fourth of her
fashion page. Gatewood sold the space to Woodward & Lothrop
and was elated. But when Cissy saw the page laid out, she
ordered Gatewood to remove the ad because she felt it was
taking up too much editorial space.

"I'm sorry, Mrs. Patterson," Gatewood replied, "I can't remove it without reasonable notice to the advertiser. We have a
contract for a long period."

"It's my paper," she replied. "I can take it out if I want to."

"Don't you realize the value of an account like this?" Gatewood remonstrated, but to no avail. Gatewood was backed up
in refusing to dump the advertisement by J. Irving Belt, head of
the composing room, Business Manager William C. Shelton, and
Al Rubenstein, who scheduled the production of advertising.
The upshot was that Cissy composed a blistering two-page memo
in which she fired Gatewood, Belt, Shelton and Rubenstein.

Gatewood urged the other three to wait a few days and let
the boss cool off. They continued to observe business as usual
and were not cut off the payroll. A week afterward, Gatewood
was standing at the elevator when Mrs. Patterson approached.
She peered at him and remarked, before entering the elevator,
"I'm not through with you yet!"

Gatewood was "fired" on three other occasions for so-called
advertising "indiscretions." In recent years he has enjoyed a
more tranquil existence as advertising manager of the Washington
Post.

Cissy was strait-laced on one point: under no circumstance
was editorial space to be traded for advertising, as it is on some
newspapers. She was fanatical about the pre-eminence of the

news side over the business side. And if advertisers complained about the isolationist ideas of some columnists—such as the cocky, colorful John P. O'Donnell—she always let them know she would sooner sacrifice revenue than journalistic independence. By and large, the advertisers were Jewish and had no sympathy for the "America First" attitude of the *Times-Herald*. Cissy's stand on the war inevitably led to whisperings that she was anti-Semitic. These insinuations were answered by the fact that her second husband was a Jew; her circulation manager and confidante, Robinson, was Jewish; and she had from the start given top play in the *Herald* to Hitler's crimes against the Jews.

At a time when the Washington population was exploding in the 1940s, the three leading newspapers in the capital had three distinctive personalities. The *Star* was a fat old dowager, the *Post* was a liberal professor of political science, and the *Times-Herald* was a gum-chewing government girl. Sassy and sexy, the *Times-Herald* was too lively and too full of information to be snooted, even by those who pretended to deplore its titillating daily report on interesting rapes and divorces.

The *Times-Herald* was highly readable both in makeup and prose style. Cissy believed that a newspaper should be as open, direct and gossipy as conversation. It was the same formula that made her brother's *Daily News* a reading habit for the New York subway riders, though she would not concede that she imitated the *Daily News*, nor did she. The *Times-Herald* did, however, carry a great deal of the *Daily News'* national and international stories, because they were tightly and brightly written.

The *Times-Herald* was a boon to writers with a piquant imagination. While it was considered a "women's newspaper," on the basis of its many columns dealing with cooking, society, fashions, night clubs, movies, etc., there was also in later years an advice-to-the-lovelorn-male column, and another, "The Male Animal," which discussed men's fashions. Both were done in a tongue-in-cheek style. And on Sundays the longer features might range from a report on an archaeological expedition in nearby Virginia to the inside story of the life of a butler.

Cissy told her staff not to write down to the reader. She insisted that she herself was an average reader, and she continually proved it by her unerring instinct for knowing whether a story would interest the public.

At the same time, she recognized the responsibility of a newspaper to do more than inform and entertain. She plugged hard for long-needed improvements in the badly run District of Columbia, ruled by three commissioners who are at the mercy of Congress. Her longest crusade was unsuccessful—a drive to bring "home rule" to the voteless District. Her stand was not shared by the Washington business community or its "cave-dweller" old settlers (nor, more importantly, by the southerners who commanded the key committees in Congress), all of whom feared that the capital's large Negro population would bring about the election of a Negro mayor. (While Cissy's enemies would like to have accused her of racism, there was no evidence to support the charge. When Negro singer Marian Anderson was refused permission to sing at Constitution Hall by the Daughters of the American Revolution in 1939, Cissy's *Herald* criticized the D.A.R. and backed the Interior Department in permitting Miss Anderson to be heard instead on the steps of the Lincoln Memorial. Joe Miller, Cissy's butler-steward for fourteen years, regards her as having been generous and enlightened toward colored people.)

Cissy was more successful in editorially pressing for a $2,000,000 Potomac River face-lifting, better schooling for crippled children, and free hot lunches for underprivileged school children. She insisted on a more efficient police force and helped to combat juvenile delinquency by providing financial and editorial backing for the Boys Clubs of Washington.

It might come as a shock to those who remember her paper for other reasons that there was not a single forward-looking issue in the District of Columbia—including slum conditions and social welfare problems—in which the *Herald* or *Times-Herald* was not first in the field. Cissy lived right in the center of the capital and bore toward it the love one has for his home town.

The *Times-Herald* consumed her. Every edition was delivered to her home or sent to her by air wherever she was. First she scanned each page the way a woman looks at a rival's new hat—quickly but taking it all in. If she spotted a blemish she picked up the phone and ordered it removed. If the scanning satisfied her, she went over the paper again minutely, including an inspection of the advertisements. She would interrupt any conversation at her home to take a call from an editor.

Cissy thought of her newspaper staff as a family of unruly relatives who had to be advised, prodded, punished and rewarded. Unlike the typical standoffish publisher, she invited staff members to her parties and interfered in their private lives.

At Christmas, Cissy gave her staff a lavish party in the Du Pont Circle house. She managed this unwieldy throng with the finesse of a ringmaster who has let all the animals out of their cages; everyone was allowed to drink to excess if he wished, and everyone had a very good time.

The paper also staged an annual banquet for the 1200 carrier boys who worked so hard under the great circulation manager, "Happy" Robinson. The party customarily was dressed up with the appearance of civic leaders and sports stars. Once, all the delivery boys were taken to New York on a special train to a Redskins-Giants championship football game, and treated to dinner at Jack Dempsey's afterward.

Cissy ruled her own bustling world, peopled by hundreds she saw every day and scores she knew as friends. Men and women anxious to demonstrate their loyalty were at her elbow, as many and as often as she wanted them to be. Nonetheless, she was lonely, and sometimes she was loneliest in the midst of a crowd, a crowd of her own choosing. Increasingly during the 1940s, she would abruptly excuse herself halfway through one of her parties and say she was going to bed to read.

Her loneliness was due partly to the fact that she was unsure about her friends. The wealth which magically opened the doors to owning a newspaper and living exactly as she pleased also was a barrier. She knew that her money and her whole heritage made her different from all but a relatively few friends, no matter how close the relationship might seem. Always just below the surface of the relationship lurked the nagging suspicion that the friend or employee wanted something from her—now or when she was dead.

"This was the tragedy of someone who didn't know who her real friends were," says George De Witt, who was her managing editor for eight years.

"She had one big weakness," De Witt explains. "It was a chronic distrust and suspicion of her executives, perhaps sometimes very well founded. It was to this weakness that a few self-seeking persons pitched in their efforts to serve their own ends. In her office and in her drawing room she was constantly subjected to sinister whispers from these relentless malcontents.

"In perspective, I think one must excuse Cissy on that score. She had had no previous organization experience whatever, and she never learned the necessity for organization discipline."

A basic ingredient of Cissy's emotional insecurity was her lack of fulfillment as a woman. In her sea of troubled relationships the mooring was always her brother. Theirs was the ideal of what a sister-brother relationship should be. Otherwise, she was wary of men, if not actually afraid of them. A satisfactory relationship with a man for any length of time eluded her. She never got over the failure of both her marriages. Time after time, with women friends, she brought up Count Gizycki. She would laugh about how he could not pass a mirror without stopping to admire himself, and wanted to be buried in his pink hunting coat; yet she would add with a wry fondness that he "had the charm of the Devil himself."

She enjoyed relating to close friends how Gizycki had taken her, a virgin, so brutally on their wedding night in the Waldorf-Astoria.

"It was rape," she would say, adding, with all her power at self-dramatization: "But he was a *man!*"

To one friend, Dolly Flynn, Cissy several times confided that the only man she was ever happy with was Elmer Schlesinger. Although she would have divorced Schlesinger if he had not died, she recalled that while she was married to him she always thought of Elmer as being a very wonderful man. Undoubtedly, Cissy's second husband personified a stability of temperament which she missed so much in herself.

Arthur Reilly, the newscaster on the radio station tied in with Cissy's newspaper, got the impression from her that Schlesinger was the love of her life, while Mrs. Ann Bowie Smith remembers Cissy "laughing about her experiences" with her second husband. Yet even this memory was tainted with bitterness. Schlesinger had died without a will, incredibly enough for a Wall Street lawyer, and there had been a court dispute over his $2,000,000 estate. Ultimately it was divided into thirds, with Cissy sharing equally with his daughter, Halle, and son, Elmer, Jr.

The question remains: Who *was* the love of her life? Cissy had told Rose Crabtree that it was Frederic McLaughlin, the Chicago sportsman. At various times, she told Evie Robert and Ann Bowie Smith, that the Count was the only man she ever loved, and to the latter she recalled bitterly that her mother had made her burn all the pictures of Gizycki she had saved after the divorce.

To her sister-in-law, Mary King Patterson, Cissy once remarked of Gizycki: "He was the only man I ever loved. I should have stayed married and tried harder to make it work. I was a spoiled darling." This must have been voiced in a wave of romanticism, for it is completely unrealistic to imagine that the marriage could have worked out.

All these sentiments she expressed were doubtless true at the moment she uttered them—but not, necessarily, two minutes later.

Nonetheless, it does seem clear that Count Gizycki was the romantic love of her life. He was the prince out of her dreams, but, what may be more important, he was the only man who ever dominated her. Subconsciously, Cissy wanted to be dominated by a man; consciously, due to her lack of impulse to yield, it was always a question of time before she was trying to dominate him.

The mature love of Cissy's life appears to have been Tom White. Thomas Justin White was born in Dublin County, Ireland, and when twelve years old was brought to America, where the family settled in Chicago. The Whites were typical of many Irish-Catholic families in the United States after the turn of the century; as one observer put it, "charming, talented, and suffering." (Tom's sister, Carmel, became the famous Carmel Snow, longtime editor of *Harper's Bazaar,* and his daughter, Nancy, has succeeded her.)

White joined a paper company and became acquainted with the Hearst organization by selling it large quantities of newsprint. Soon he was employed by the Hearst magazines and rose rapidly within the organization. In three years he was general manager of all the Hearst enterprises. According to *Citizen Hearst,* the biography by W. A. Swanberg, White was one of the few high-priced Hearst executives who remained loyal to Hearst in times of financial stress.

After Cissy headed up the *Herald* in 1930, business reasons often brought her together with Tom White. His advice was invaluable—as was his companionship, for Tom White was amply endowed with personality as well as brains. He had charm, warmth, good manners and an occasional, lightninglike wit. Of stocky build, he looked somewhat like the movie actor Thomas Mitchell, though he was better-looking and stronger-looking.

Over the years, Tom White was a frequent guest at Long Island, Du Pont Circle, and Dower House. There was no other man, save of course her brother, whose friendship she valued so much. She would like to have married him, but White was married and had no desire to break up his home.

There was a third person toward whom Cissy directed her love: her only child, Felicia. But this was the most difficult emotional region of all. Just as she, as a young girl, was continually at odds with her own mother (who died in 1933), Cissy found herself in almost continual conflict with her daughter.

Born of a troubled marriage, carried off by her mother, kidnaped back by her father, the prize in an international tug of war, Felicia never saw her father after the age of four. Cissy tried to make up for this by lavishing on her the best of everything. Still, Cissy was a busy, restless woman, and Felicia was raised largely by governesses, so that her relationship with her mother became distant and formal.

There were times when Felicia had actually to ask permission to eat dinner with her mother, and there were times when she ate alone in her room from a tray. At the same time, Felicia as a girl showed an extraordinary self-assurance, as if stubbornly refusing to be overwhelmed by her mother's personality. As the years went on, they found it increasingly difficult to communicate with one another, and violent clashes became the rule rather than the exception.

The result was that Felicia was fiercely determined to assert her independence of her mother just as early as possible. She inherited her mother's powerful will, and also a kind of Slavic moodiness from her father, which her mother did not understand.

When Felicia's marriage to Drew Pearson ended in divorce after only three years, she married, some years later, an Englishman, Dudley de Lavigne.

Lavigne's sister, Doris, was married to the Viscount Castleross, who wrote a gossip column for the London Sunday *Express*. "Cholly Knickerbocker" described Lavigne as a well-known insurance broker who was "tall, slim and not very energetic." He also did not have much money. Divorce came four years later.

In 1958, Felicia married John Magruder, a Washington, D.C., landscape architect, and this too ended in divorce.

Cissy envied and admired her daughter's poise and dash. On August 2, 1929, she wrote Rose Crabtree:

> There isn't any news—except that Felicia is going abroad this month—I guess I will have to join her later and pick her out of that and any new love affair she has fallen in. She is as beautiful as the day—and so sweet and good nearly all the time. Her baby is with us now. But she's kind of skinny and long like her grandma and will never have her mother's beauty.

After her divorce from Pearson in 1928, Felicia increasingly became an international glamor girl and gay divorcee in the then popular F. Scott Fitzgerald style. During the thirties she shuttled from Washington to London, to Paris, to Biarritz, to Deauville, to New York, and to the fashionable hunt country of Virginia.

After Felicia's second divorce, the gossip columns reported that she would marry Count Alfred Potocki, brother of Joseph Potocki, then Polish ambassador to the United States. Alfred was a sallow, middle-aged bachelor who had gone to Oxford and was now a member of the international aristocracy. Alfred was the "master of Lancut," a 308-room castle on a 40,000-acre estate, but the days of high living as a feudal lord were gone forever. Alfred Potocki did indeed wish to marry Felicia, but he also needed money and, like many another titled European, he had fixed ideas about what came with the hand of an American heiress. With his old friend Cissy he discussed frankly his expectations of a suitable dowry. The Count's idea of a suitable dowry from the Patterson family, it turned out, was a well-rounded sum—no less than $1,000,000. Cissy said that the price was too high, and there was no marriage.

That was all right with Cissy. Much as she liked the Potocki family, she could not help but brood about the eerie parallel of another Polish count of thirty-five years before—who also had the dollar sign lighting up his vision of an American bride.

While Cissy envied her daughter her beauty, Felicia envied her mother her ability to write. Felicia has the Patterson compulsion to write, and she writes well. For quite a time she carefully followed her mother's literary footsteps. Like Cissy, she wrote for *Harper's Bazaar*. Like Cissy, she also published two novels. They were *House of Violence* (1931) and *Flower of Smoke* (1939). Though in later years Felicia was to disparage both her novels, they actually won better reviews, on the whole, than the two books written by her mother. Less autobiographical than Cissy's novels, they reveal a nervous, almost painfully sensitive viewpoint which reflected her unhappiness-without-hope, and the pleasure-bound world in which she moved.

Flower of Smoke did nothing to improve the relations between mother and daughter, for Cissy considered that one of the characters was an unflattering take-off on herself: a self-centered and "brilliantly conspicuous" New York sophisticate who becomes the guardian in New York of her bewildered, self-pitying niece (who, like Felicia, was born in Austria).

Felicia meanwhile reported regularly in *Harper's Bazaar* on the good life in all the right places on the Continent.

Cissy loved her daughter, and her inability to achieve a close relationship with Felicia was perhaps the major disappointment of her life and one of the keys to her loneliness.

More and more, while directing her newspaper during the tense war period in Washington, Cissy longed for the peace and isolation of Jackson Hole. It seemed as if her summers long ago in the Happy Valley she had found under Sheep Mountain were the most rewarding in her life. But somehow it was harder and harder to make the effort to travel over 2000 miles to the ranch. On July 11, 1939, she had written Rose Crabtree:

> If I could telegraph myself out to Flat Creek, and if I weren't as afraid as you are of that old grisly bear out there, and if the whole place were sweet and clean, and if the whole of Jackson Hole hadn't slept in my beds for

the past several years, and if I had a cook, and if there weren't mosquitoes and trout flies, and if I weren't too old and decrepit to sit on a horse—far less ride up and snaggle down Sheep Mountain—I'd come out to see you all. But it really is too far, and I am too old and weary.

(The "old grisly bear" referred to was Forney Cole, who was now the caretaker of her ranch. The burly Cole was not only said to look like a grizzly, but he had once won a hand-to-hand encounter with a black bear at Flat Creek. Cole was bitten badly by the bear but still managed to beat her to death with a long pole with which he had been tearing down a beaver dam. Then, bleeding profusely, he climbed into a Jeep and drove down the rocky mountainside to Jackson, where he spent one night in a hospital.)

Returning from a trip to Santa Barbara, California, in 1940, Cissy was aboard a train which stopped at Rock Springs, Wyoming, at Thanksgiving time. She wired Rose that if she was able to "get through to Jackson" she would stop off there. But she did not. Cissy felt unbearably lonely spending Thanksgiving Day in her Pullman drawing room without friends. A month later she wrote: "Look for me in the springtime."

On April 21, 1941, she again wrote Rose:

> I would truly like to come out to Jackson this summer. But it is very difficult to make arrangements. Is there anyone around to rebuild the cabins? *And* the road?

Cissy was reaching out for old friends she believed were true friends, and Rose, to whom she had unburdened herself for twenty-five years, seemed the truest of all. On January 25, 1943, she wrote Rose at West Palm Beach, Florida, where Rose and her husband, Henry, were vacationing, urging them to stop off in Washington on their way back West, adding:

> . . . I don't know why you find so many excuses not to visit me any more as you used to. Remember the good times we had in New York? You didn't hesitate then to just board the train in your pants and sombrero, perfectly

sure of the fact (and you were right, too) that you were
the best-looking woman in town.

I don't believe you realize how old I am. Really, Ma
Reed was a beauty compared to me now—and, what's
more, she hasn't got a doggone thing on me today for
unadulterated meanness . . .

You know, darling, years may come and years may go,
but you know how much I have always loved you, and
I think it is kind of mean of you not to make a little
effort. With love to you all, dearest friend . . .

The letter was typical of Cissy's self-criticism. She had always
been ruthlessly honest about her failings, continually downgrad-
ing her looks, her temperament, her writing ability. Once, incredibly, she even refused to attend an important wedding on the
grounds that she didn't have any clothes she would look good in.
The most she would say for herself was that "I've never been
pretty, but I've always had a good figure." She had a preoccupation with beauty in women and once assigned Austine Cassini to
do a series on "Beauty in the Past," deciding who were the most
beautiful women of all time, and why.

Cissy's berating of herself impressed the late Stanley Walker
when he did a profile of her for *The Saturday Evening Post* in
1939. In the course of an hour's conversation, he reported, she
made the following remarks:

Sometimes I think I haven't any sense . . . I was a fool
to do that; maybe I'll know better next time . . . Don't
read those books I wrote; they are no good . . . I was
wrong about that man; I should have known he wouldn't
do . . . I don't know much . . . What a sap I was! . . .
I guess I was taken in, that time . . . I don't know what
was the matter with me, but my judgment was certainly
off . . . It was all my fault, of course.

"It is one of the charming qualities of the unpredictable Cissy
that she can give herself a bawling out," Walker commented.

Interviewers who had been sure they would dislike Cissy were

invariably disarmed. Here was the fiery red-haired woman publisher, famous for skinning enemies alive, sitting on one foot,
curled up like a forlorn cat at the end of a divan—cutting herself down with a flow of words. The paradox was irresistible.

TWENTY-ONE

"I Don't Want to Die Alone"

During the 1940s it was generally felt that Cissy Patterson was in excellent health. She often poked fun at herself as a "tired old lady," but this seemed in keeping with her usual self-disparagement. She still rode horseback, hiked several miles a day and looked younger than she was.

Then one very hot, humid day in July 1943, she suffered a heart attack just before dinner in her town house and fainted. The doctors told her to stay in bed for several weeks and to "travel in second gear" for the rest of her life.

Writing this news to Rose, she said:

> But, you know, I don't know whether to believe them or not. Maybe if I didn't live in this outrageous house with cupids stringing marble wreaths and flowers all over the G.D. place (excepting for the back side—plain brick garbage cans and old rubbage cans out there), they wouldn't try to keep me an *invalide*.
>
> Anyhow, I feel perfectly well this morning and as if I had given birth to that baby "under the heart," which is where the little darlings were supposed to grow, according to what my mother told me. But she never got as far as to tell me how they ever got *in* there, she being very refined. And of course I was too smart to ask her, knowing all about "it" anyway.
>
> But the point of this letter *so far*, besides thanking you for your two letters, is to tell you that I don't believe the doctors will let me go into a high altitude. But I'll tell

you this much, and *sincerely*. Rather than be a sick old
woman with nurses and doctors around me for the rest
of my life, I'll *come anyway*.

Tired—must stop. Remember—I'm coming out if I can
get there.

For several weeks Cissy remained in bed in a third-floor bedroom in which an air conditioner was installed—the July heat
was awful. However, after that she did not slow down, as she
should have.

A number of times during the next five years Cissy suffered
what she called "spells." Even some of her best friends did not
know about them. A "spell" seems to have been a feeling of
faintness, accompanied by severe pain in the chest. It was not a
heart attack, but it alarmed her. Once, she and her friend, Dolly
Flynn, were alone in the drawing room at Dower House when
Cissy clutched at her heart and said, "Oh! I'm having one of my
spells." She took some medicine and moved to her bedroom on
the first floor. She refused to let Dolly call a doctor.

Lying on her bed, she confided to her, "This is a mild one
compared to some I've had." Then she murmured quietly:

"I know that one of my spells is going to take me someday.
Oh, Dolly, pray that there will be someone around. I don't want
to die alone."

Cissy continued nonetheless to drink and to smoke three or
four packs of her imported cigarettes a day. Still proud of her
figure, she worried if she gained even a few pounds, so she
bought a rowing machine, and sent another to Dolly. But she
didn't use it much.

Often when she was lonely, Cissy called up Evie Robert or
George Dixon and asked them to come over and amuse her.
She liked Dixon's flippant wisecracks, and she was always convulsed by Evie's shockingly frank offbeat wit. In the middle
and late forties, again reaching out for old friends, she sometimes
telephoned George De Witt, who was now executive editor of
the Chicago *Herald-American*, "just for a chat." She usually com-

plained of feeling very tired, and twice asked De Witt to return to the *Times-Herald* and relieve her of her editorial headaches.

Then, on May 26, 1946, Cissy's mooring was cut away from her. Joseph Patterson died. He had been under treatment for a liver ailment in a New York hospital for two weeks.

His body lay in state first at Patterson's home in Ossining, New York, and then at his sister's Du Pont Circle house. Burial was in Arlington National Cemetery, on the crest of a green Virginia hillside overlooking the Lincoln Memorial, and full military honors were accorded the captain who had served so splendidly in the Rainbow Division in the First World War.

Cissy took the blow better than many expected, but she was the personification of sorrow as she stood at the graveside in her long black dress and heavy black veil. Patterson had been converted to Catholicism late in life, and Cissy's head was bowed down as she listened to the solemn words of the Catholic committal service.

In general, the obituaries treated Patterson's death as "the passing of a giant." Even Cissy's chief rival, the Washington *Post*, pleased her by editorializing that in spite of its disagreement with Patterson's attitude on World War II, it regarded him as a "genius in the newspaper world," explaining:

> He achieved a phenomenal success. Indeed, his was the greatest circulation of any newspaper in the country. Not only that, of all morning newspapers, his newspaper held first place for retail advertising. It was his organ, stamped in every line of it with his own personality, and his guidance was felt throughout the organization. He made the *Daily News* a real community newspaper in New York devoted to the betterment of conditions of life as well as to entertainment and information. None could ever say, in spite of his position as one of the greatest tycoons of journalism, that he was ever the tool of any interest; he served nothing but the light as he saw it.

The same week her brother died, Cissy was described in *The Saturday Evening Post* by authors Hugh and Elise Morrow as "a tall, tired-eyed, cultivated, capricious woman of about 60, full of a wispy and rather wistful appeal." Increasingly, she looked tired and sadly bored by life. Her unhappiness was written in her face; indeed, many who knew her well considered her one of the unhappiest persons they had ever known. Here is a woman, that face said, who has had traumatic experiences and has known deep disappointment, rejection and tragedy. True to herself, she made no attempt to put on a merry mask, though when she felt in the mood, Cissy could still be the most gracious of hostesses or could put on an hilarious act mimicking a pompous friend.

More than ever before, Cissy was realizing the truism that the state of one's interpersonal relationships have a lot more to do with happiness than wealth, fame or power. Her compulsion to corrode her relationships intensified rather than diminished with the passage of years. After the death of her brother, for instance, she developed a running battle with her cousin, Colonel Robert R. McCormick, over operation of the family publishing properties.

When Patterson died, he left a gaping double vacancy—as publisher of the New York *News* and president of the News Syndicate Company, Inc., which owns the *News* and its related interests. There was speculation in newspaper publishing circles that a member of the family, either Cissy or Colonel McCormick, would run the *News*. However, Patterson was succeeded by Roy C. Holliss, vice president and general manager of the *News*. Then, a few months later, Holliss was killed in an automobile accident, and the question of succession had to be faced again.

Colonel McCormick immediately asked Cissy to become chairman of the News Syndicate Company board until a solution could be worked out. McCormick and Cissy were both members of the board of directors of the Tribune Company of Illinois, which owned the Chicago *Tribune*, the News Syndicate Company, Inc., newsprint mills, a shipping line and various other enterprises in the United States and Canada.

Cissy agreed to become board chairman with genuine reluctance, because she didn't think it needed one. She wrote Mc-Cormick on September 7, 1946, her strong conviction that the *News* must be allowed to continue to operate autonomously. She felt the independence of the *News* would honor the spirit of her dead brother and was also essential to the paper's continued success. (For reasons of personal pride as well as sound business, Cissy, her brother and her cousin always jealously guarded the independence of their respective newspapers; about the only editorial viewpoint the three papers happened to agree on completely was their attitude toward World War II—and, as a result, they became known as the McCormick-Patterson "axis.")

In her letter to Colonel McCormick, she wrote:

> Now, listen, Bert, you and I have all the money—and then some—that we either want or need. We have all the "power and the glory" that either of us care to be bothered with. I don't know how you feel about it, but I have more than I want. I don't like it . . . Another thing: I have been greatly disturbed by the number of letters coming in congratulating me as the new head of the New York *News*—as the new president of the New York *News*—as chairman of the board, and so on. I particularly dislike the goofy stories which appeared along these lines in the various publications.
>
> . . . Now, Bert, as you must well understand, all of these exaggerated reports of my rise to power are bad for the *News*. They are pure joy for our competitors and ill-wishers all over the country. It is bad for the *News* to have the idea get across that a tired and already overworked old woman like myself is either head of the *News*, or figurehead of the *News*, or, in fact, at the head of any job on the *News* of great authority.

Less than three months later, a *Collier's* magazine article ("No Prissy Is Cissy") billed her as "probably the most powerful woman in America" because she was now board chairman of the most-read paper in the country as well as boss of the most-read paper in Washington. Ironically, Cissy was discovering at the very same time that being a board chairman invested her with no real power.

Once she learned this, the thought of herself presiding over a board meeting struck Cissy as being funny. She appealed to her friend, F. M. (Jack) Flynn, general manager of the *News*, to coach her in what to say and how to act. The first time she sat at the head of the table she was armed with a "script" prepared by Flynn, and she read from it in a deliberately hammy voice: "The meeting of the board of directors of the News Syndicate Company will come to order. . . ." Then she leaned over to Flynn and in a stage whisper asked how she was doing and what to do next. Flynn told her to ask that the reports be read. When she did this, her duties as presiding officer were largely completed, and she sat back, bored. Sitting on her right, and watching stony-faced, was the gravely dignified Colonel McCormick.

At each board meeting the members were handed a traditional printed form on which they were to itemize expenses incurred in making the trip to New York for the meeting. How would she know, Cissy asked herself out loud, how much it cost to come to New York on a private railroad car and spend a night at her year-round suite at the Carlton House? She turned to another director and startled him by asking, "How much do you think I can get away with?" She conferred with him, then scrawled "200 bucks" across the top of the form, with no itemization, and tossed it across the table.

Cissy never made a single suggestion about the operation of the *News* and regarded it as a waste of time for her to be its board chairman. She proposed that Flynn should become board chairman and president. Her wishes were followed at the annual Tribune Company board meeting the following spring.

Meanwhile, Cissy was campaigning to persuade Colonel McCormick to give her niece, Mrs. Alicia Patterson Guggenheim, a place on the News Syndicate board of directors. Alicia had the Patterson touch in journalism. Her Long Island daily, *Newsday*, was fabulously successful. As Cissy put it, "Alicia is a smart little cookie. She has a lot to contribute." Colonel McCormick, however, boggled at the thought of having to cope with another strong-minded Patterson woman, and, what was worse, Alicia was a liberal in politics. He felt she would only cause dissension on the *News* board. Cissy could not get Alicia appointed to the *News* board without the Colonel's approval, but she kept plugging away, and at the May 1948, Tribune Company board meeting he agreed to put Alicia on the *News* board—if Cissy got off. She agreed, and the substitution was made.

That was a turbulent session, in which Cissy had startled Colonel McCormick by announcing that Alicia would be her principal heir. It was a decision which could materially affect the family fortune and all three newspapers concerned. Both Cissy and the Colonel were growing old and were increasingly worried about the ultimate disposition of their holdings. Upon her brother's death, Cissy had succeeded him as a cotrustee—with McCormick—of the McCormick-Patterson trust, which holds 51 percent of the stock of the far-flung Tribune empire.

In June 1948, Cissy spent a week writing and rewriting a letter to McCormick in order to clarify the issues—and to get a few more things off her chest. The final version was in longhand and covered eight pages of unambiguous opinion. Not trusting the United States mails with so important a document, Cissy assigned editor Frank Waldrop to hand-carry the message all the way to Colonel McCormick's door in Wheaton, Illinois, some 700 miles from Washington.

The letter began without shuffling preliminaries:

> In the name of God, Bert, why did you pull that "ham" act at the last directors' meeting in Chicago, and at the stockholders' meeting a few minutes later, go into the same kind of song and dance?

There you stood, putting on the six-foot-four business, waving your arms about, glaring like a maniac shouting your denunciations of Alicia. Why?

After bringing up past disputes at board meetings, she went on:

I bring up these past episodes because you should realize that you have never, and can never, *stampede* me off my chosen ground.

Neither could Joe. Joe could appeal to my reason, sentiment or affection easily enough, but he could not bully me into doing anything I did not care to do. This is a matter of record.

To stress that she was not dependent entirely on her Tribune Company stockholdings, Cissy told Colonel McCormick in this letter:

Within the last three weeks I refused an offer of $5,000,-000 for my *Times-Herald*. Outside of that offer, both Eugene Meyer and two well-established newspaper chains want to buy my paper and have said so. Outside of my newspaper property . . . I have quite a few dollars and cents invested in excellent stocks and bonds.

She concluded the letter on this note:

I don't want to quarrel with you, Bertie. I have a deep affection for you which nothing can alter.

In the future don't you think we had better turn such "dissensions" as may arise between us over to our lawyers to discuss and settle?

According to Maryland McCormick, the Colonel's widow, he did not even read this letter, because he anticipated its tone and did not share his readheaded cousin's enjoyment of a family quarrel. He simply turned it over to his attorneys to file.

A week after she sent this letter to Colonel McCormick, Cissy suffered another shock when she learned of the death of her dear friend, Tom White. A year earlier her close friend of many decades, Evalyn Walsh McLean, had died. The death of someone close to her always left Cissy tied up in emotional knots. Now she told friends she found it hard to carry on without Joe, Evalyn and Tom White.

The loss of three such close friends in two years made her brood about her own death. Never much interested in religion (although always interested in psychic phenomena), she began to think about the hellfire sermons preached by her grandfather, the Rev. Dr. Robert W. Patterson, in the First Presbyterian Church in Chicago. She had never forgotten his warning that one must not waste one's time on earth; now it bothered her that she had been forty-nine years old before she had found something constructive to do—running a newspaper.

The conversion of her brother, late in life, to the Catholic faith of Mary, his wife, impressed Cissy. Perhaps the Catholic Church could bring her consolation, or at least bring her to terms with herself. She never missed the eloquent radio talks of the Rt. Rev. Msgr. Fulton J. Sheen, who had converted several famous intellectuals, and she began reading "A Testimonial to Grace," the story of the conversion to Catholicism of the Rev. Avery Dulles, S.J., son of the late John Foster Dulles.

Finally, she was decisively influenced by the Rev. Edmund A. Walsh, a vice president of Georgetown University and regent of its Foreign Service School. Father Walsh started a course of instruction in Catholicism for Cissy, and early in the summer of 1948 she confided to a Catholic friend, Ann Bowie Smith, that she intended to become a Catholic.

Father Walsh was a distinguished author of numerous diplomatic and historical books, and Cissy strongly endorsed his views in *Times-Herald* editorials. He was a special consultant to the U.S. chief counsel for the War Crimes Commission at Nuremberg, but was better known for his warnings about Russian Communist imperialism. These warnings were as ahead of the times as was Cissy's concern about Communists as potential traitors, long before the Hiss-Chambers case broke.

During 1948, Cissy had developed fears of being robbed, kidnaped, or attacked. She had received letters threatening her with bodily harm, though any assailant would have been badly outgunned. At this time she always carried a revolver in her pocketbook and kept a collection of twenty-five revolvers, some of them pearl-handled, in a box at Dower House. When she went out in her limousine at night, the chauffeur, Emile Bouchard, kept a gun in the pocket of the car, and she held another in her hand in the back seat. But that was not all. The night watchman, also armed, was assigned to trail the limousine in another car.

All in all, it was shaping up as a bad summer. In June she had been driven to distraction by the shattering staccato of heavy drills coming through the windows at Du Pont Circle. The District of Columbia was digging an underpass which would take Connecticut Avenue traffic and streetcars underneath the Circle. Cissy had fought the building of the underpass, on the ground that the streetcar tracks would be obsolete within a decade and that the isolated underground areas would only be an invitation to violence and crime. Also, Cissy argued, if there had to be an underpass it should handle Massachusetts Avenue traffic instead of Connecticut Avenue's, because the former would be denser in the long run. She was to be proved right in each of these three objections, but the underpass was nonetheless built.

After the construction work began to annoy her, Cissy sought out Edward K. Wheeler, lawyer son of her old friend, former Senator Burton K. Wheeler, and asked him to get an injunction which would stop the digging. Wheeler pointed out the difficulty of obtaining an injunction and suggested she move to Dower House until the underpass was built.

At Dower House, Cissy was further distracted by the increasing number of airplanes flying over her estate toward nearby Andrews airfield.

She finally decided there was only one cure for her depressions and distractions. She would go West, where in the past she had found renewal of her spirit. She was desperate for a whiff of the bracing air off the Grand Tetons. It had been fourteen years since she had visited the ranch. She decided to make the most of the trip by going on to visit Hearst at San Simeon in California, and she asked Frank and Eleanor Waldrop to accompany her.

Arrangements were made to rent a private railroad car and to leave at the end of July for a month's trek that would take them to California, via Wyoming and permit them to return via the Canadian Pacific route.

Cissy's health seemed good during the week starting July 18, though her moods swung all the way from high to very low. At a party given Thursday night by Evie Robert at the home of Mary Holmes, widow of George Holmes, the distinguished newspaperman, Cissy entertained the guests with a take-off of Colonel McCormick doing an imitation of how Alicia Patterson Guggenheim would behave at the first meeting of the board of directors of the New York *Daily News*.

After dinner, Evie took newspaper columnist Ruth Montgomery aside and whispered that a process server was waiting at the front door to serve Cissy a summons. Cissy had refused to pay for the cleaning of an expensive rug, because she said that the cleaners had ruined it. Evie was afraid she would be upset and asked Ruth to try to delay Cissy's departure until the man got tired and went away.

However, Cissy found out what they were whispering about and exclaimed, "Good! This is the most exciting thing I've heard all evening." She announced she would leave immediately. As Ruth's husband, Bob, took Cissy by the elbow and escorted her toward her limousine at the curb, a man jumped out from behind a bush and handed her a document. She glanced at the summons disdainfully and snapped in her haughtiest manner, "How dare you!" She threw the paper on the ground, walked to her car, and was taken back to Dower House.

Early Friday morning Cissy put in a call to Rose Crabtree in

Jackson Hole, Wyoming, and told her that she was coming back to the ranch at long last. She asked Rose to get the ranch in shape and have her met at the Rock Springs, Wyoming, station. Five automobiles, she estimated, would be needed for the whole party—the Waldrops, maid, cook, baggage, and so on. She told Rose she had gone on a shopping spree at Abercrombie & Fitch and was looking forward to the trip more than anything in many years. To Rose, Cissy was in an upbeat, holiday mood, but the transcontinental conversation was a long one, and before she hung up Cissy said something which startled Rose.

"If I should die out there," she said, "I want to be buried on the side of 'The Hill.'"

Rose knew that she meant the hill that rose steeply from the south end of the town. (It has since been turned into a ski run.)

At 4 o'clock Cissy drove to the nearby home of Ann Smith. To Ann she looked wonderful and seemed in good spirits. They chatted about a lot of different things, and Cissy made a great fuss over her namesake, Ann's baby daughter, who had been named Eleanor Medill Patterson Smith and was already being called "Cissy." Cissy did not discuss her trip West but complained that she could not stay the summer at Dower House, because it would take a distressingly long time to install the new pipes to replace the ancient water system.

Back at Dower House, around 6 o'clock, Cissy suddenly remembered that she had invited Mr. and Mrs. Edwin S. Holloway, who lived across Rosaryville Road, for dinner. Bea Bouchard, the cook, reassured her that she could fix a dinner in a hurry. The Holloways arrived soon afterward and stayed until 10:30 o'clock. They saw no evidence that Cissy was not feeling well.

Earlier, however, she had dispatched Emile Bouchard into Washington to pick up some pills prescribed for her by her heart specialist, Dr. Bernard J. Walsh. She had remarked to the chauffeur that early on Friday she had felt very low, but felt better after her visit with Ann Smith. Bouchard returned with the pills two hours later and gave them to Robert Lye, the butler.

At 11 o'clock she retired to her bedroom to read, taking with her the latest edition of the *Times-Herald* and several books. The bedroom is a small one, directly behind the huge drawing room on the first floor. A small passageway leads into the bedroom from the end of a foyer adjacent to the drawing room. The night watchman was supposed to sit in this passageway, about twelve feet from the bedroom door, in case she should ring for something during the night. At about 1 A.M., Cissy told him to take Butch, her favorite poodle, for a walk.

It was hot, and the watchman spent most of the rest of the night out on the grounds. At 7 A.M. he let Butch into the house and went off duty.

It was Mrs. Patterson's daily habit to ring the bellpull around 8 o'clock in the morning. This was the signal to the servants to let Butch out and serve her her breakfast in her bedroom in exactly fifteen minutes. But on Saturday morning, July 24, no bell had been heard well after the hour of eight. At 9 o'clock Butch padded forlornly into the kitchen. He wore such a sad look that Bea Bouchard quipped, "Who spilt your milk?" The servants had fallen into Cissy's habit of treating the poodle as a person. Because he was mean, a servant had to whip him occasionally—when Cissy was not around; when this was done, he pouted for days, like a sensitive child, until the servant made up with him.

The dog continued to droop around the kitchen. Around 10 o'clock Mrs. Bouchard and Lye discussed the fact that there was still no signal from the bedroom, and she suggested he knock on the door. "Do you want to get me fired?" Lye replied. Like the other servants, Lye had no desire to risk Mrs. Patterson's wrath by awakening her from a sound sleep. Cissy suffered from insomnia and normally did not fall asleep until the early hours of the morning.

During lunch none of the servants hid their concern about the unusual stillness emanating from the bedroom. It was four and a

half hours after Mrs. Patterson almost invariably woke up. Finally
Lye and Eve Borowik, Cissy's personal maid, agreed to investigate. A few minutes later they returned to the kitchen
looking pale.

"Go and take a look at her," Lye told Mrs. Bouchard. "She's
dead."

Bea and her husband, Emile, edged into the bedroom. Mrs.
Patterson was lying crosswise on the coverlet of her white-
canopied, four-poster, rather small bed. She had apparently died
in a paroxysm, while reading. Her right hand was still rigidly
pressing a book into her face. (The book was *The Golden
Violet*. Lipstick remained on its opened pages.) Cissy was wearing lounging pajamas, and the bedroom lights were still lit.

Lye telephoned Waldrop, Dr. Walsh and the Prince Georges
County coroner's office. First to arrive was Dr. James I. Boyd,
deputy county medical examiner. Dr. Boyd estimated Cissy
had died at approximately 1:30 A.M. Some of the servants suddenly remembered that approximately at this time they had
heard Butch howling like a banshee at the front door. Since
Cissy had asked the watchman to take Butch out and he had not
returned, there was no one within hearing distance if she had
called out for help.

Cissy had died, as she told Dolly Flynn she feared she would,
alone.

Dr. Boyd issued a certificate of death due to natural causes—
acute heart failure.

At 2:15 P.M. Dr. Walsh arrived. One of the outstanding heart
specialists in Washington, he had been treating her since her
heart attack in 1943. She had not seen him for the last seven
weeks. Friends and employees alike agreed that Cissy had
seemed in good health, though to one editor she recently had
complained of a tightness in the chest and of the heart.

Some of Dr. Walsh's pills were scattered on the floor, but they
were pills for her heart condition and there was no evidence of
suicide.

Waldrop arrived just before Dr. Walsh and prepared to make the announcement to the public. The news jolted everyone who knew Cissy. Most surprised of all was the *Times-Herald* staff. Upon telephoning the paper, Waldrop learned that there was no obituary of Mrs. Patterson in the files! Waldrop telephoned the New York *Daily News* Washington bureau in the National Press Building, where this writer happened to be on duty, and said he would like to use the *Daily News'* obituary. Thus, the story of Mrs. Patterson's death which appeared in the *Times-Herald* was written by me, with the help of the previously prepared obituary in the *Daily News* files.

Relatives gathered quickly—Felicia, and Cissy's sister-in-law, Mary King Patterson, from New York, Alicia from her home at Hempstead, Long Island, granddaughter Ellen from her home in Los Angeles. On Sunday the body was removed to Gawler's funeral home in Washington. On Monday the casket was placed in the Du Pont Circle mansion—where, nearly a half century before, Cissy had married the Count—blanketed with her favorite flowers, yellow roses.

Messages of condolence poured in from all over the United States and from abroad. On Monday night the house was kept open during the early hours of the morning to accommodate the night workers of the *Times-Herald* who came to pay their respects to their departed "Lady."

Private services were held on Tuesday in the huge ballroom where Cissy had presided with such *élan*. Present were diplomats and high officials of the government, and all the friends who had basked in her glow over the years. One, the beautiful Austine (Bootsie) Hearst, wept openly.

The Rev. Dudley E. Stark, of St. Chrysostom's Episcopal Church, came on from Chicago to conduct the funeral service. Ironically, as he read the prayers, the mourners could hear the sounds of blasting for the Du Pont Circle underpass.

For once, Cissy was surrounded by enough flowers. A Washington florist estimated that the wreaths sent to the house represented a total cost of some $35,000. They covered two floors, three and four deep. Their scent was so overpowering in the summer heat that Margaret Barney, Cissy's secretary, and Callie Shaw, a former secretary, fainted as they arranged them.

Later on Tuesday, when the casket was being shipped to Chicago for burial, two freight cars were filled with the flowers, and enough flowers to fill two more freight cars were left behind.

On Wednesday morning Dr. Stark read prayers at the chapel of Graceland Cemetery in Chicago. The mourners were limited to relatives and the executives of the three family newspapers. Cissy's body was cremated and buried in the family plot.

Colonel McCormick missed the funeral. He and Mrs. Mc-Cormick had been touring Europe, and engine trouble in his converted B-17 prevented a quick return. He called the death of his cousin a "terrible blow" and the *Tribune* published a long editorial which eulogized her as "the most effective woman publisher that this country has ever known."

Cissy had specified that she wanted no eulogy in her own newspaper, but the editorial column was filled on the day of her funeral service with seven brief, poignant paragraphs in large type. The first paragraph said: "How do you say goodby? None of us here at the *Times-Herald* knows quite how to do it." The last sentence read: "And so, we say here in the only way we know how: 'Goodby. We'll see you one day.'" It was signed "The Staff."

The stories of Cissy's death paid tribute to her greatness. *Newsweek* sounded the note for all when it declared that, while opinions of this controversial woman varied widely—to her staff she was "the greatest newspaper editor in America," and to some others she was an unholy terror—Mrs. Patterson unquestionably had "left a gap in America's newspaper ranks."

The editorial in the Washington *Star* saw Cissy's newspaper success as the adventure which gave meaning to a life otherwise marked by disappointment and tragedy:

Her paper reflected the idiosyncrasies of her own personality, for she believed in that sort of paper, and she used it for the exploitation of ideas, good or bad, that appealed to her. Under her ownership it became one of the diminishing few of the highly personalized journals of the country. In making it so she was completely indifferent to criticism and intent on her own vagaries. The paper became her consuming interest, she became a skilled craftsman in her own right, and the ends she sought had nothing to do with any desire for personal aggrandizement. Outside of the newspaper, there were things she kept strictly to herself, such as her warm if unpredictable generosity, her loyalty to old friends, and the loneliness that came to her toward the end of her life . . .

The Washington *News* editorial noted that "there were few things she didn't do," and that to those who watched her, Cissy's life was "practically everything—except dull." The *News* saw Cissy as a "throwback to a somewhat more feudal era," one who resented the postwar world. Her means of expressing that resentment, the *News* felt, "were often something less than well-considered." But the editorial concluded that no "usual clichés of regret" would do in the case of this unusual woman. So it was reminded of a quatrain:

> She was gay and she was witty,
> She was wise and she was pretty.
> Now she's dead, let's not flout her
> Let's not say dull things about her.

The *News'* society editor, Evelyn Peyton Gordon, wrote a more perceptive column about Cissy, for whom she had once served as society editor. She recalled a night when she was standing outside the Soviet Embassy in freezing weather, covering a reception, while the diplomats moved in and out of the building. Cissy, leaving the party, stopped and said hello. She asked Miss Gordon why she was standing there, and chuckled when the reporter replied that she had been banned from Russian functions because of what she had written.

Then Cissy impulsively removed her mink coat and flung it around the reporter's shoulders, remarking, "Well, you can't freeze just because they're a narrow, ignorant people." The coat kept Miss Gordon snug for the rest of the evening. The next morning she dropped it off at 15 Du Pont Circle. An hour later her phone rang and she heard Mrs. Patterson's languid, musical voice saying, "Why did you bother to return the coat, my dear? I've dozens of them."

Another columnist she had launched, Robert Considine, wrote a head-shaking tribute:

> Cissy Patterson was a wonder. She could be as touchy as an adder and as sweet as a lamb, as nickel-nursing as Scrooge and more generous than the Rockefeller Foundation. She had a horse shot once for throwing her, then virtually adopted all the stray dogs, cats and horses in the District of Columbia.

Drew Pearson wrote that "a great lady died the other day—a lady who had caused me much happiness—and much pain."

Cissy's brand of journalism had made her many enemies. After talking at length with scores of her friends, associates and employees, some of whom had suffered from her whims, one found that, almost without exception, those who got to know her well not only respected her for her ability but liked her in spite of her faults.

The testimonials cannot be dismissed as mere gallantry. They are an appreciation of a gallant spirit and a very human human being. One quality even her enemies conceded, and doubtless admired, was her blazing individuality in an age of growing conformity, and the courage which made that possible. It never failed her.

FBI Chief J. Edgar Hoover, who has viewed the Washington scene from the inside since 1919 (and who, on occasion, felt Cissy's printed sting) put it this way:

During the decade that she headed the Washington *Times-Herald*, I knew and respected her as a tough executive who made no attempt to follow the conventional, and as a gracious hostess whose charm and courtesy warmed many a social evening.

Mrs. Patterson was always ready to stand up for her beliefs and, good newspaperwoman that she was, never flinched from the controversy and criticism that often lashed her editorial policies. She was unpredictable, and her moves raised many an orthodox eyebrow in Washington. But she generated an excitement in everything she did that was refreshing and unusual.

I recall with pleasure the parties I attended in Washington at which Mrs. Patterson was present. She was possessed of tremendous energy and wit which enlivened even the most staid affair. But most of all, I remember her friendship and support, which made my job a little easier in the hectic days before and during World War II.

The best one-line eulogy came from Mike Flynn, a managing editor during Cissy's entire eighteen-year newspaper career. Flynn was speaking for more than one moist-eyed staff member when he muttered, upon hearing the news of her death, "She was a hell of a sight better newspaperman than I am."

TWENTY-TWO

The Will

Cissy Patterson's death posed some intriguing questions. Who would inherit her estate, which some thought would run to as high as $25 million? What would become of Washington's most-read newspaper? Which friends and employees would that unpredictable woman reward from the grave?

What if the *Times-Herald* were left to daughter Felicia, who lived in New York and moved in the liberal circles which detested her mother? But Felicia had no newspaper experience, and she and her mother were estranged at the time of Cissy's death. There were reports in Washington that the will contained some bonanzas for employees.

On Thursday morning, the day after the funeral, the will was filed in court, and it held stunning news. The *Times-Herald* was bequeathed to seven top executives with no strings attached —they could sell it if they wanted to. Cissy's Long Island estate, North Dakota property (she had acquired a variety of real estate holdings over the years), household furnishings, wardrobe, most of her jewelry, and a lifetime tax-free allowance of $25,000 a year would go to Felicia. The Du Pont Circle house was left to the Red Cross, and there were other large bequests for a favored few.

There was apparently no precedent for the willing of a large metropolitan newspaper to a handful of employees, although at least one newspaper has been willed as a trust for all the employees.

The lucky seven were: Frank Waldrop, editor of the editorial page; William C. Shelton, general manager; Michael W. Flynn, supervising managing editor; Mason S. Peters, III, night managing editor; Edmund F. Jewell, advertising director; H. A. (Happy) Robinson, circulation manager; and J. Irving Belt, mechanical superintendent. At first labeled "overnight millionaires," they were later dubbed the "Seven Dwarfs."

On Thursday afternoon, Waldrop, who also was named an executor of the estate, held a press conference in the National Press Club auditorium. Forty newspapermen came to find out what the seven planned to do with their windfall. Waldrop promised that the *Times-Herald* would continue to be what Mrs. Patterson wanted it to be—an independent newspaper. He added with a grin: "After this meeting I invite anyone who cares to join me in the bar for a drink. For once the drinks are on the *Times-Herald.*"

Offering to stand drinks at the Press Club bar is normally risky. But they could afford to buy drinks, and to preen themselves. Up to then, all had had to work for a living. Now they could look forward to being instant capitalists. Their suspense— they thought—was over. The idea that Cissy might leave the *Times-Herald* to employees was not a surprise, for she had broached it often and had even tipped off some of her heirs. But there had remained the disturbing fact that she had a penchant for playing around with her will. No one had been absolutely certain he would wind up as a beneficiary.

But why seven—surely an unwieldy number for the smooth direction of a newspaper—and why *these* seven?

Waldrop, forty-two years old, and Shelton, fifty-five, were the two most logical heirs. Waldrop, running the editorial page, had necessarily been around the boss more than any other staff member, day in and day out, for more than a decade. An adroit, intelligent, soft-voiced southerner, he had managed skillfully to stay in Cissy's good graces while his colleagues were being shunted into and out of the doghouse.

The equally unexcitable Shelton, who looked both crafty and humble, possessed a knowledge of the financial intricacies of running a newspaper that was indispensable to Mrs. Patterson. Whenever she had a problem on the business side, she said, "Get Bill Shelton."

Cissy had known Shelton longer than any of the other six. Back in 1930, when Hearst had made her editor of the *Herald*, she had sought out Shelton immediately and told him her brother had advised her to be sure to get acquainted with the "sales manager," as she then, in her innocence, called the circulation chief. A native Washingtonian, Shelton had been a newsboy at ten, and circulation manager of the Washington *Post* at the tender age of nineteen. When Cissy sought him out, he was circulation manager of both Hearst papers, the *Herald* and the *Times*. He was to become business manager of both these papers during Cissy's regime, and ended up as general manager of the *Times-Herald*.

"I'm going to depend on you," Cissy had told him at their first meeting, and Shelton had shrewdly replied, "Then I'm going to depend on *you!*" Shelton kept after her to do those things which would help Cissy's papers make a profit. Cissy was inclined to shrug it off by pointing out, "Why should I make money?—You only have to give it to the government." Shelton told her there was only one real way to measure success: by a profit-and-loss statement. And she could always share the profits with her employees. This led to the bonuses given out after the *Times-Herald* turned the corner in 1943—and perhaps also to the decision to will it to her executives.

Like Waldrop, Shelton was named an executor of the estate, along with two attorneys—Joseph Brooks, former husband of Alicia Patterson Guggenheim; and Rudolph Yeatman, who had died since the will was made.

Flynn, fifty-nine, the veteran, unaggressive, charming Gael, had served Mrs. Patterson faithfully as an editor for eighteen years and she was fond of him. Robinson, also fifty-nine, had

been Cissy's circulation chief for nearly all of her editorial career
and was a confidant besides. Belt, sixty-four, was a surprise, but
many outsiders did not realize how Cissy appreciated his erudi-
tion, which ranged far beyond the composing room. Peters was
a surprise only because he was thirty-three years old and had
been away from the paper for four years during the war, serving
as a naval gunnery officer in the Pacific. But Peters had started
working for Cissy as an eighteen-year-old cub reporter, and
now he was the managing editor who made the staff hum.

Jewell, fifty-two, was a surprise. He had been on the *Times-
Herald* relatively few years, although he had been general manager of the Washington *Times* when Cissy had the *Herald* back
in 1931. Jewell was the able former publisher of the Man-
chester *Union-Leader* and had been a captain in the Navy
during World War II.

Events were soon to disturb the dreams of the lucky seven
and keep them in suspense; and equally on edge were the other
beneficiaries, who had a great deal at stake in seeing the court
uphold the will, which had been executed on June 21, 1946.

The two chief beneficiaries after Felicia and the seven executives were Cissy's close friends, Ann Bowie Smith and Evie
Robert. Mrs. Smith is a thirteenth-generation, direct descendant
of Lord Calvert, who built Dower House, and she then lived
with her husband, Darnell, and their eight children four miles
from it. Now she was left the entire 600-acre Dower House
estate, with all its furnishings, farm equipment and livestock,
and for five years the estate was to pay Mrs. Smith $5000 a year.

To Evie Robert, Cissy's socialite friend, went the fabulous
black-pearl earrings and necklace, a sable scarf, and three buildings on Du Pont Circle. The Du Pont Circle property alone was
believed to be worth $500,000.

The ranch in Wyoming went to a niece, Josephine Patterson
Reeve, and to a Maryland friend and *Times-Herald* columnist,
Rhoda Christmas, went all the horses and dogs, with a stipulation
that none was to be sold and that, if they were put to death, it

must be done painlessly. But no money was left to pay for the care and feeding of the animals.

If Cissy seemed extraordinarily generous to Ann Smith and Evie Robert, she was relatively stingy toward some of her most faithful employees. Miss Margaret Barney, her personal secretary for seventeen years, received $10,000, and Sibilla Campbell, her housekeeper, got a mere $1000. Elizabeth Kenney (Betty) Hines, who had in the past been Cissy's secretary and, later, society editor of the *Times-Herald*, got nothing.

Rose Crabtree was willed $3000, and Jerry Lefort, son of the former chauffeur, Henry Lefort, $5000. Joe Miller, who had quit as her butler and steward back in 1945, was to receive $1000, as was his brother, Emmet, who had worked temporarily for Mrs. Patterson. The Bouchards, who had been with her relatively few years, were not mentioned.

Provision No. 12 was this single sentence: "I am making no provision in the will for my granddaughter, Ellen Pearson Arnold, inasmuch as I have made a substantial gift to her during my lifetime."

This was a reference to the Maryland farm which Cissy had given Ellen as a child and which Ellen had sold to her father. Ellen, who grew up to be a tall, slender, good-looking blonde, was an innocent victim of the crossfire between her father and her grandmother. In 1943, Cissy had provided in her will that Ellen was to receive $10,000 a year during her mother's lifetime, but this provision was deleted a few years later.

Cissy liked Ellen, and the feeling was mutual, but Drew Pearson was a barrier between them. Ellen named her first-born Drew Pearson Arnold. His hair was as red as Joseph Medill's, redder than Cissy's. When Cissy held the baby for the first time at the home of the Thurman Arnolds, Ellen's in-laws, she remarked dryly: "I always wanted a redheaded boy—it's too bad he had to have that name."

The will also specified that the trustees use the balance of the net income from her estate to support Cissy's favorite charities

—the Cradle Society of Evanston, Illinois; the Florence Critten-
den Anchorage and the Illinois Children's Home and Aid Society
in Chicago; and the Spence Chapin Adoption Service in New
York. She also requested that some income be distributed to
"an organization aiding Polish refugee children of Catholic or-
igin."

After the 1946 will was filed, attorneys discovered a cache of
old wills in her safe-deposit box. There was a total of seven
previous wills and two codicils—the final proof of her chameleon
nature. To a relatively few persons it was known that Cissy had
been drawing up still another will during the months before her
death. Amid the confusion, this became the most provocative fact
of all.

Cissy was probably will-happy because her wealth was a mill-
stone around her conscience. Once, she was sitting on the edge of
her Dower House swimming pool with Jackie Martin, and Jackie
remarked idly that it was nice to be able to afford such a luxurious place.

"No," Cissy replied glumly, "the more you have, the more
you have to worry about."

Cissy worried about the disposition of her riches increasingly
as she grew older. It was soon after she acquired the *Herald* and
Times that the idea first came to her to leave them to some of
her trusted employees. Apparently the first hint of this occurred
when she showed Jackie a new will under which the newspaper would go to Jackie, "Happy" Robinson, and Mike Flynn.
(It bothered her that Jackie—in an effort to maintain her independence—was refusing all gifts. At one point she made a fantas-
tic offer to build a complete replica of Dower House for Jackie
right across the road from it.)

The will which Jackie saw must be counted as a ninth will; it
was either lost or previously destroyed, because it was not found
with the other old wills, after Cissy's death.

Cissy was incapable of keeping still about the changes she con-
templated in her wills. By leaking the news that certain em-

ployees would become beneficiaries, she only intensified the web of plotting, backbiting, tale-bearing and apple-polishing which pervaded her office in later years.

Some of her friends were embarrassed by her tendency to tell who was out and who was in. Once, on a Wyoming mountain trail, Cissy began talking about her current will and held up ten fingers to show Rose Crabtree how many thousands she could expect to get. Rose protested; she tried to impress on Cissy that she was not interested in her money and did not expect to receive any of it.

The eight wills charted Cissy's shifting attitudes toward relatives, friends and employees. The first will, dated January 1924, named "my beloved daughter" as sole heir. Felicia survived as the heir in minor changes made in 1933 and 1934, but in 1942 a new will took Dower House away from her and bequeathed it to Rhoda Christmas.

More vitally, under the 1942 will the *Times-Herald*, which had come into being three years previously, would not go to Felicia. Instead, it was directed that the paper be offered at a fair price for sale to, first, her brother, then her niece, Alicia Guggenheim, and then to her cousin, Colonel McCormick. If none of them wanted it, the trustees were empowered to sell the *Times-Herald* elsewhere.

A year later, Cissy changed her mind and left the paper to her brother. In 1944 she thought better of that and decided on a complicated four-way division of the paper's income, with ultimate disposition to these four heirs. This is the year Waldrop and Shelton made their first entrance. The other two executives named for the split were Advertising Director Howard R. Weaver and Circulation Director Charles R. Corcoran (who later become circulation manager of the Chicago *Tribune*).

Under the 1943 will, the Wyoming ranch was to go to Cissy's nephew, James Patterson, then at West Point. But Joseph Patterson wrote his sister that his son expected to make a career of the Army and that an Army officer should not be bothered with worrying about a ranch in the Rockies. The result was that the only male member of this generation of Pattersons was jettisoned from the next of Cissy's wills and never showed up in one again. As it turned out, he chose a career on his father's newspaper rather than the Army, but he never did get the ranch.

In 1944, Felicia lost another house; this time it was the "palace" on Du Pont Circle, which went to the Red Cross, and in this will Cissy also took Dower House away from Rhoda Christmas and bequeathed it to Ann Smith.

It was the proposed will, incomplete and unsigned at the time of her death, which was so revealing of Cissy's change of heart in the last year of her life. Why should she be thinking of a new will, having just made a completely new one after the death of her brother in 1946? The answer lies in her resolution to make sure that her newspaper lived on after her in the independent family tradition.

Early in February 1948, Cissy wrote F. M. (Jack) Flynn, whom she had successfully sponsored for the presidency of the New York *News*, to the effect that she had been "ill on and off for over a month" with "some kind of flu infection" and was about to leave for her house in Sarasota, Florida. She wondered if Flynn could arrange to visit her there to discuss some business matters, "among others, my will."

Flynn arrived in Sarasota in March and was amazed when Cissy revealed that she was embarking on another will—and considering making him a major beneficiary. She was thinking of leaving him the *Times-Herald*, or her stock in the Tribune Company, or both! Flynn had plenty to do already in running the *News*, and was amply compensated for it. Cissy made it clear she was trying to figure out a way to keep the *Times-Herald* out of the hands of Colonel McCormick or some outsider. Flynn had no desire to become involved in a family fight. He thanked Cissy for the compliment, but pointed out that he could not see the logic of his becoming her heir.

Flynn, however, promised to do everything he could to help.

He would arrange for trustees and try to find a practical solution to her problem. First, he did a rough calculation and estimated there would be insufficient assets to pay the taxes on her estate—hence, either the *Times-Herald* or the stock would have to be sold, which is exactly the way things worked out. Then he suggested that she consult Kirkland, Green, Fleming, Martin and Ellis, the distinguished law firm retained by the Chicago *Tribune*, but she said she would have nothing to do with a firm that represented her cousin.

Flynn's resistance to becoming an heir gave him a halo in Cissy's eyes.

"You are an honest man," she told him. "I've checked up on everything you've told me and it was all straight. Some of my fellows are always giving me double-talk . . . but you're honest, and it's going to get you in trouble."

She then showed Flynn the list of seven executives to whom she planned to give the *Times-Herald* under her 1946 will. Flynn looked over the names and remarked frankly that he could not foresee the mixed bag working together harmoniously enough to get out a newspaper. A mischievous glint appeared in Cissy's eyes, and Flynn suspected that she was enjoying this prospect. Smiling, she predicted that under those conditions the wily Shelton would probably end up owning the paper.

"But what do I care?" she added. "I'll be dead."

Several times Flynn pointed out that the logical chief heir was Cissy's daughter. Cissy would not hear of it. Well, then, pursued Flynn, why not leave the estate to another member of the family, her talented niece, Alicia? Cissy replied that she didn't like Alicia's husband, but that she might leave the *Times-Herald* to Alicia anyway.

Strangely enough, Flynn was not the only person to whom she had offered the *Times-Herald*—and been refused. The other was Walter Trohan, Washington bureau chief of the Chicago *Tribune*. At first, back in 1945, Cissy had wanted Trohan to become her managing editor, at $35,000 a year, but he had stead-

fastly declined on the grounds that they were not temperamen-
tally attuned. Once, when they were visiting at Dower House,
Cissy became upset over the banner line in the first edition and
telephoned Managing Editor De Witt in a fury.

"She could dial a telephone like no one else," Trohan recalls.
"She could make it swear. You could almost see the smoke coming out."

Cissy chewed out De Witt in purple language, while Trohan
listened. When she hung up, he remarked, "That, Mrs. Patterson,
is why I wouldn't be your managing editor. You'd bawl me out
that way just once, and I'd quit."

Cissy then told Trohan she would like to leave the paper to
him in her will, but he foresaw the difficulties of running a newspaper without operating capital. Like Flynn, he suggested that
she leave it to someone within the family or set up a trust which
would keep it going.

Trohan stopped in to see Cissy a week before she died, and
again she casually offered to leave him her paper. "I don't like
this will," she said, referring to the last one she had signed.

Trohan suggested that she ought to discuss it with her old
friend, former Senator Burton K. Wheeler, who was on a legal
retainer with the *Times-Herald*.

Cissy had taken Flynn's advice to retain her own lawyer and
retained George Bruce Brooks, a Wall Street lawyer, to work on
the will. He was a brother of Joe Brooks, Alicia's former husband, whom Cissy liked. Indeed, she is said to have once told
Alicia that if she would divorce Guggenheim and remarry
Brooks she would leave her everything.

On second thought, she also took Flynn's advice and asked a
member of the Kirkland firm for help. She ruminated aloud
about a new will all spring and at one point gave the servants the
impression that she had one ready to be signed, though actually
it was not yet drafted. Finally, on Wednesday, July 21, she telephoned Wheeler and asked him to come to Dower House on the

following Monday to discuss her will. But on Friday night she died.

All the evidence indicates that in the new will Cissy would have made a major shift and left her newspaper to Alicia.

Of Joe Patterson's three daughters, Alicia was the most like himself and Cissy. Yet, she was a creative personality in her own right. (The other two Patterson daughters are Josephine Albright, who is married to the Chicago painter, Ivan Albright, and Elinor, now Mrs. Donald Baker, of Greenwich, Connecticut, who had a fling as a professional actress, appearing in *The White Sister* and *The Miracle*.)

Alicia was even more adventuresome than her aunt. She had hunted big game in Africa and was a record-breaking airplane pilot. In her early days in Chicago, one of her beaux had been Adlai Stevenson, and the friendship lasted a lifetime. Her first husband was James Simpson, Jr., a director of Marshall Field & Co.; her second husband, Brooks, had been an all-American football player at Colgate in 1911 and an officer in the Rainbow Division in France in World War I.

Alicia's third husband, Harry Guggenheim, an heir to millions in mining and minerals, was U.S. ambassador to Cuba from 1929 to 1933. After their marriage in 1939, they lived in Guggenheim's showplace estate near Cissy's house on Long Island. In 1940 they became founders and co-owners of *Newsday;* under Alicia's editorship, it became the fastest-growing and most profitable new daily in the United States.

Like the *Daily News* created by her father (with whom she was very close), Alicia's *Newsday* was bright, breezy, irreverent and editorially hard-hitting; but it was also a new kind of tabloid, tailored not for subway straphangers but for the more sophisticated young couples swarming out into the New Suburbia, in this case on Long Island. Also, whereas the *News* had grown more conservative politically, *Newsday* backed the liberals in both major parties on foreign and domestic issues.

While she herself warred with the liberals, Cissy recognized

that this next-generation Patterson was the best hope for continuing the *Times-Herald* as an independent and militant organ. For
Alicia had spunk and flair.

In the months before she died, Cissy talked openly about her
new will. She told Eve Borowik, her personal maid, that she
would leave her enough to start a dress shop on Connecticut
Avenue. To the Holloways at dinner the night she died she had
referred several times to the "great changes" that were in this
will.

Rumors that another will was in existence on the night of
Cissy's sudden death were enough to inspire speculation that
there had been foul play. Some of the circumstances of the death
did seem to have been borrowed from an Agatha Christie thriller:
the hot, opaque summer night deep in the wooded countryside;
the millionaire dowager alone in her bedroom in the old English
country house; the absent night watchman; the dog howling a
dirge; and the odd position of the body, belatedly discovered by
the butler.

Presumably, there was motivation too—among those who
would have been disinherited by a new will. But which of the
characters who stood to gain was ready, willing and able to commit murder? None of them was anywhere near Dower House on
the night of July 23. The thriller plot had another hole: There
was no evidence that Cissy died of anything but heart trouble.

There are, however, people in Washington who persist to this
day in believing that Cissy's death was somehow sinister. It has
become part of the legend.

After all, it had not seemed right for all the theatrics to end
abruptly when the curtain came down on Cissy's life. Drama did
indeed take a curtain call, but not until several weeks after the
funeral. One can almost hear the ghostly chuckle offstage. For
there is reason to believe that Cissy had foreseen that controversy
would cling to her even in death, and relished the thought. She
had remarked in the presence of her chauffeur, "They'll have a
damned good fight when I'm gone. I've fixed that!"

The fight began when the seven sudden "millionaires" moved for admission of the will to probate. Under the law the will could not be admitted without the assent of the sole heir-at-law and next-of-kin—Felicia. This assent Felicia refused to give, and the fat was in the fire.

Filing a formal notice of a contest, Felicia claimed title to the whole estate on the grounds that at the time the will was executed her mother was of "unsound mind" and was the victim of persons exerting an "undue influence." She also contended it was not the last will her mother made.

Felicia was doing battle with an imposing array of attorneys, including Randolph Paul, former general counsel of the Treasury Department; William A. Roberts, former people's counsel for the District of Columbia; and Harold A. Kertz, Washington lawyer.

Felicia's suit was of course very bad news for the seven executives and the two other principal heirs, Evie Robert and Ann Bowie Smith. If the 1946 will was ruled invalid, the court might go back to the next previous will—which would benefit only four of the nine principal heirs in the 1946 will. Or the entire estate—being then calculated roughly at more than $16,000,000—might go to Felicia.

The Patterson will was a good newspaper story, however you chose to see it—woman against seven men, or daughter against dead mother. Two events followed on the heels of Felicia's suit which permitted the story to be sensationalized in the news magazines and in the old left-wing New York *Star*, which had baited Cissy when she lived.

First, Betty Hines, who had received nothing in the will, was found dead in her bathroom, an empty bottle of sleeping pills nearby. Her brother said she had been despondent because Mrs. Patterson had promised to clear the mortgage on her home in her will. It is not clear how Felicia's suit could have motivated Miss Hines to commit suicide. In any event, the coroner certified after an autopsy that she had died of natural causes, a heart attack.

The other touch of melodrama had some elements in common
with an early Alfred Hitchcock movie. Later on the afternoon
of September 14, the day after Felicia filed her suit, the *Times-
Herald* news ticker carried a flash which electrified the city
room—and jarred the seven heirs. Charles B. Porter had been
found dead in Clarksburg, West Virginia. Porter had been a
financial adviser to Mrs. Patterson for fifteen years, and everyone knew that until the previous year he had been the eighth
member of the group that was to inherit the newspaper. According to the news flash, he had inexplicably plunged to the sidewalk
from his sixth-floor hotel room. The police had found in his
room three suitcases containing "writings."

At the moment, Washington was rife with rumors about hidden evidence that might support Felicia's suit. What did Porter
leave behind that might throw light on the soundness of her
mother's mind? He had been intimately associated with her in
her business affairs and was believed to have assembled a mass of
documents and notes for a sensational biography of her.

Managing Editor Mason Peters immediately assigned Sidney
Epstein, a crack reporter and rewrite man, to get to Clarksburg
as fast as he could. With him went Jack Barber, acting treasurer
of the *Times-Herald*. In the old hell-for-leather *Herald* style,
Epstein was to come back with everything he could lay his hands
on. He and Barber chartered a plane and flew to Pittsburgh,
where they hired another aircraft to fly them into the smaller
Clarksburg airfield.

Porter was one of the more unusual members of the cast of
characters affected by Cissy's will. A Scottish-born, fifty-two-
year-old financial wizard, he was educated and cultivated. He
held a philosophy degree in criminology from Edinburgh University and was a lawyer. Porter had first gone to work for Cissy
back in 1931 and they had clashed frequently—but he came to
know more about her finances than she did. He was fired three
times; after one of his dismissals, in May 1947, Cissy had added

a codicil to her will deleting his name from the executives who were to inherit her newspaper and leaving him only $5000.

Porter had been sacked for the last time early in 1948 and had since become increasingly neurotic. Only shortly before her death, though, Cissy had asked him to come back and he had declined. He decided to go home to Scotland for a rest, booked passage to sail August 5, and then abruptly canceled it. He told a friend he was sure detectives were shadowing him in order to learn the location of his secret files dealing with Mrs. Patterson's life.

On September 6, Porter put his three suitcases in a taxi and told the driver to take him 140 miles to Keyser, West Virginia. Three days later he checked into the Waldo Hotel in Clarksburg and attracted attention by his furtive, frightened manner. He was in touch only with a male friend, Roland de Corneille, a twenty-one-year-old divinity student. On September 14, a boy on the sidewalk saw Porter shatter the screen of his hotel room window, stand on the ledge for a moment, and then dive to his death.

In Porter's room police found a holographic will scrawled hastily on hotel stationery. In it he named Mrs. Sibilla Campbell, Cissy's former housekeeper, as his executrix. Other articles in the room were a bottle of sleeping pills, a nearly empty bottle of sherry, a steamship ticket to Scotland, a copy of Dale Carnegie's *How to Stop Worrying and Start Living*, and the three suitcases.

Epstein and Barber landed at the Clarksburg airport, which was not normally used after dark, in a chartered DC-3 at 2:15 A.M. At the police station they produced a "release" from Mrs. Campbell and asked for possession of the suitcases. The police obligingly turned the bags over to them—after removing a suit of clothes which would be needed for Porter's burial.

Epstein telephoned Peters and was told to return to Washington at once. He and Barber landed there just before dawn. They were met by Peters, who told them that Epstein's fiancée, Mary

Albritton, had agreed to let them use her apartment for the surreptitious examination of the contents of the bags. When they reached his fiancée's apartment, Epstein was somewhat surprised to be met by a majority of the seven heirs, all looking anxious. They were soon relieved to find that the bags contained nothing that apparently could be used to help Felicia break the will.

But the mystery of Porter's death, and the significance of what he knew, was due for more thorough exploitation. His death was ruled a suicide by the coroner, but Drew Pearson immediately got into the act on behalf of his ex-wife, Felicia. He inspired a new string of headlines by hinting that Porter might have been murdered. Pearson said Porter had been told that certain people had been trying to force him to return to Scotland because they believed he knew too much and would be a star witness in Felicia's suit.

Time magazine quoted Pearson and also reported a rumor that Porter had been offered a $50,000 bribe if he would support a phony $500,000 claim against Mrs. Patterson's estate. Shelton and Waldrop wrote *Time* on behalf of the seven heirs, charging that the statement implying that any of the seven were guilty of murder or bribery was "untrue." Glad to head off a possible libel suit, *Time* printed the letter and added: "After reviewing the facts, *Time* agrees that its account was unfair to Readers Shelton, Waldrop & Friends, regrets that it reported this 'eye-popping tale.'"

Felicia and her attorneys sought access to Porter's complete private papers, which were in an army locker trunk kept in storage. C. F. R. Ogilby, collector for the Porter estate, was directed by the court to produce the contents of the trunk and answer questions at a pretrial hearing.

Porter was said to have been preparing a lurid book. His folders of notes and other material divided up the more flamboyant aspects of Cissy's life. They bore such titles as "Cissy and Her Employees," "Cissy's Gifts to Me," "Cissy and Her Pensioners," "Cissy and Felicia," "Cissy and Alcohol," "Cissy and

AntiVivisection," "Cissy and the British," "Cissy and Barney Baruch," and "Cissy and Sex—Kinsey Report."

One folder was entitled simply "$1,000,000 check." It contained a canceled check for that amount, and Ogilby said he assumed it was signed by Mrs. Patterson. He did not disclose the recipient. There was also a folder titled *"Times-Herald Seven Shining Lights,"* presumably in reference to the seven executive heirs. More eloquent than any other item was a *Collier's* magazine article clipping headed, "Does Your Job Make You Sick?"

But Porter's files, juicy as they might seem at first glance, did nothing for Felicia. Like his suitcases, they became a footnote to the dragged-out will contest that seemed to be heading nowhere.

Meanwhile, Felicia's lawyers insisted their efforts to press the suit were hampered by cloak-and-dagger tactics. Early on the morning of October 17, Felicia told New York police that her apartment at 117 East 35th Street had been forcibly entered and ransacked. Afterward, she said, private detectives informed her there was evidence that wire-tapping equipment had been installed prior to the time of entry, and then hurriedly removed. A month later, Ogilby had reported that his law offices had been burgled. He said his desk had been searched, his files opened, and a small amount of cash and stamps stolen. No vital Porter documents had been taken, though.

All these bizarre developments kept the will story alive in the press, but no connection was ever established between them and the "seven dwarfs," or their lawyers. The fact remained that Felicia was making no progress in proving that her mother was mentally unsound and that unnamed persons had exerted "undue influence" on her when she made the will. Indeed, the thought of anyone pressuring Cissy into doing something she didn't want to do was startling to those who had known her well.

Charles C. Lattin, a *Times-Herald* trouble-shooter for Cissy, was one of the three witnesses to the will. He was in shirtsleeves on the afternoon of June 21, 1946, when he was suddenly summoned to Mrs. Patterson's private office. There he was seated on a green-leather davenport with two other men—A. A. Howard, a Washington, D.C., salesman, and George R. Titus, another *Times-Herald* employee. The only other person present besides Mrs. Patterson was a lawyer, Willis D. Nance. Lattin recalls her saying briskly: "Thank you for coming, gentlemen, this is my last will and testament, and I would like you to be witnesses to my signature."

"Following her death," Lattin comments, "there were legal proceedings which intimated Mrs. Patterson was coerced; unstable mentally; under duress, etc. Well, Eleanor Patterson was never coerced or under duress, and any mental instability was certainly the lot of her critics rather than herself. Her mind was always razor sharp and quick as a flash."

After many delays, the trial was set to open February 9, 1949. Felicia obviously had a hard case to prove, but she had that dogged determination of the Pattersons and was encouraged by the fact that many people in Washington felt that her mother had treated her shabbily in the will despite their past differences. As for the seven newspaper heirs, they were confident they could win the suit but quailed at the prospect of a long, bitter, costly court contest that was bound to air dirty linen, jangle their nerves, and continue to provide the national capital with the best free show it had had in years.

The situation seemed ripe for an out-of-court settlement. Suddenly, on January 30, 1949, a compromise was announced: Felicia agreed to accept a $400,000 lump-sum, tax-free payment in lieu of the $25,000 a year, tax-free, for life, left her in the will. She would still receive the corollary bequests, which were not inconsiderable—the Long Island and North Dakota properties and jewelry, paintings, clothes, and other personal property.

One might wonder why Felicia, approaching her forty-fourth birthday, figured she was better off with $400,000 than $25,000 a year for life. But, as her attorney, William Roberts noted, the lump-sum payment was equal to $25,000 a year until she would be sixty, without taking the interest into consideration. With interest figured at 3 percent, he said, it would equal $25,000 yearly until she was seventy-eight.

There was another, more important, motivation for Felicia's compromise. It had to do with the peculiar problems of the will, the estate and taxes. For tax purposes, Cissy's estate had finally been valued in the following way: The *Times-Herald,* $4.5 million; her stock in the family newspaper holdings, $9.5 million; other stocks and bonds, $1,563,715; household possessions, $160,-196. The total tax bite was figured at $10.5 million. And this posed some problems.

The will specified that the $25,000 a year to be paid to Felicia was to come out of the "residual estate," that is, what was left after the taxes were paid. She feared that, once the taxes were paid and all other estate administrative costs and expenses paid out, there just might not be enough left to assure her of $25,000 a year for life. In any case, she would rather not place her financial dependence for life on the wisdom of the trustees in handling the estate. And as a money-conscious Patterson, she was inclined to believe that a bird in the hand is worth two in the bush.

To make this cash settlement, the seven executives scurried around and raised a total of $377,500. The rest of the $400,000 was put up by the other two heirs who had cause to be concerned by the suit, Evie Robert ($15,000) and Ann Bowie Smith ($7500). Under the agreement, the $25,000 annual income which Felicia was to have received under the will goes to the seven executives for as long as she lives.

A statement issued through her attorneys said that Felicia "believed that the will did not represent her mother's true desire to fairly provide for her future welfare, especially in view of the more favorable provisions for her contained in earlier wills. She felt that she owed it to her mother, to herself, and to her daughter to inquire into all the circumstances surrounding the making of all the wills, including the circumstances surrounding the preparation of a new will upon which her mother was engaged shortly prior to her death . . ."

In view of the compromise settlement reached out of court, federal district Judge Alexander Holtzoff instructed the jury to bring in a verdict holding that the will was properly executed, that Mrs. Patterson was of sound mind and that no fraud, deceit or undue influence had been practiced.

The will brought to light the fact that Cissy had a secret list of seventeen friends whom she had been paying weekly and monthly stipends, for it directed that these payments continue to be made from her estate. A mixed assortment, they included Lady Marjorie Broderick, of Dublin, Ireland, widow of the late Sir John Joyce Broderick, onetime commercial counselor of the British Embassy; Cissy Patterson Smith, namesake daughter of Ann Smith; Cal Carrington, her old cowboy friend; Forney Cole, the foreman of her Wyoming ranch; and Count Wladislaw Tyszkiewicz, a Pole who had once lived in a fifty-room palace in Warsaw and now was reduced to an apartment in the Latin Quarter in Quebec.

Wherever she was, Cissy probably enjoyed the proceedings, because it was a fight and a good story, but she must have been disgusted with the tastelessness of a scene which occurred in April 1949. Felicia, having inherited her mother's overwhelming wardrobe, had sold it with the understanding that it would be disposed of in a dignified fashion in some sort of thrift shop. To her great embarrassment, she discovered that her mother's clothes were to be auctioned off. And the auction was to take place in, of all places, the stately old family residence on Du Pont Circle.

On the block went the wonderful items Cissy, a lifelong packrat, had collected over the years and hated to throw out long after they were obsolete—150 evening dresses dating back to the flapper era; 100 pairs of shoes, including high-button styles; gilded evening slippers; 20 pairs of assorted riding boots; and no less than 300 sets of lounging pajamas and slacks. The pajamas ranged from heavy velvets and satins to the finest silk.

Several hundred Washington women who had read about Cissy over the years, plus some who had known her, swarmed into the auction and tried to elbow one another aside in order to stare and scavenge. Their cackling almost drowned out the plea of the auctioneer—"Ladies, ladies, there are plenty of dresses and shoes for all of you, so let's have it quieter!" Tongue in cheek, he noted that some of the ladies might not fit into garments made for Cissy's svelte figure, but that their daughters might find them useful.

The sale lasted five hours, and few of the buxom buyers left empty-handed. One woman, making off with an elaborate white-satin dinner gown for twenty dollars, claimed that the buttons on the dress were worth twice what she paid for it.

Once the seven executives had finally inherited the *Times-Herald*, they considered the problems that faced them. The paper had succeeded as the vibrant voice of one woman. Could it survive as the expression of a committee? And could the committee itself survive the situation? First of all, they lacked one vital asset: operating capital. The major revenue on a newspaper is advertising, but advertisers do not necessarily pay up on a monthly basis. The "seven dwarfs" soon found themselves frantically borrowing money to meet the weekly payroll.

"She left us a gold mine," one of them lamented, "and forgot to give us a shovel."

Actually, things were not that bad. The paper's credit was good—it had been making a profit of $500,000 a year after taxes. The seven-man ownership could have arranged to pay their bills indefinitely, but they had internal problems: Four of the seven favored selling the paper, and some of them had sound reasons. Three, Flynn, Belt and Robinson, were over sixty years old and had to think about the liquidity of their own estates. Two of the others were executors of Cissy's estate, and they had to be concerned about the tax problem: If the *Times-Herald* was not sold before the end of the first tax year, the government could assess its worth at anything it chose (since the *Times-Herald*, having never been sold, had no fair market value of record). Suppose the government assessed the value of the paper at $8,000,000, which was not inconceivable. This would be disastrous to the residual estate, out of which the taxes had to come. And the executors were duty bound to conserve the residual estate as best they could; many other heirs had a stake in it.

The seven had a loose agreement that no one would pull out his share without notifying the others. But no one could be sure that this arrangement would hold indefinitely. There was always the future possibility that a purchaser could secretly buy out four of the seven, one by one, leaving the others at his mercy. No wonder the atmosphere was one of uneasiness.

Under the circumstances, a sale seemed inevitable before the end of the tax year. But to whom? The man who obviously stood to benefit the most was Eugene Meyer, publisher of the rival *Post*. If he purchased the *Times-Herald* and closed it up, he would wipe out his competition and insure a profit for his own paper for the first time since he acquired it back in 1933. But Meyer was cagey. He knew that buyers for a newspaper are not standing on every street corner and that the seven needed a rich uncle. It is probable that, if there had been no other buyer, the seven would have sold to him. Whether they could ever have faced their old colleagues again is another matter.

Fortunately, there was another buyer, none other than the last surviving member of the family newspaper triumvirate, Colonel McCormick. To the executors there was an additional advantage in selling to him. Cissy's $9.5 million worth of Chicago *Tribune*-New York *News* stock had to be sold to pay the taxes on the estate, but it was not that simple. These stockholdings were exceedingly nonliquid. Strictly speaking, they were not stockholdings at all. Like her cousin and her brother, Cissy was not a stockholder in the Tribune Company as such, but a beneficiary of the McCormick-Patterson trust.

To understand Cissy's financial position, one must understand how the trust worked. It holds a 51 percent controlling stock interest in the Tribune Company of Illinois, which owns the Chicago *Tribune,* New York *News,* and other multiple interests and has been a remarkably close-held corporation since it was chartered back in 1861. After Medill's death, the family purse strings were held by his daughters, Katherine and Elinor, until they died in 1932 and 1933, respectively. A trust for McCormick and the two Pattersons was then formed. Until this trust was formed, all three were dependent on allowances from their mothers, even to the point of making major expenditures on their newspapers.

To be sure, these were generous allowances by any standard, but Cissy lived on an extremely high scale prior to 1933, and she might have had to scrimp if she had not held some lucrative other stocks and bonds as well. Also, she actually owned more of the Tribune Company than her brother and cousin, for Joseph Medill had made her an outright gift of ten shares of that stock simply because she was his beloved granddaughter.

At the same time, it must be pointed out that Cissy's income prior to 1933 was not as great as many of her friends thought it was. She did not, as Arthur Brisbane had written, have an income of $1,000,000 a year. This was a fiction. In the twenties her income was closer to $600,000 a year. Even after her mother's death in 1933, Cissy was not as rich as was supposed. In an interview for a *Saturday Evening Post* article in 1939, she amused Stanley Walker by scoffing at reports of her million-a-year income.

"Why, that's the most ridiculous thing I ever heard," she said. "The best year I ever had I didn't get more than $800,000!"

Open-market investors in the McCormick-Patterson trust are hard to come by because there are no regular and certified reports of company operations and financial status, and units are of a fairly large dollar size—valued at $35,000 at the time of Cissy's death. Colonel McCormick gallantly rode to the rescue. He offered to do two things—to buy the *Times-Herald* for $4.5 million, and also to arrange to form a syndicate which would purchase all 272½ McCormick-Patterson trust units held by his sister's estate.

It turned out that the seven "overnight millionaires" were not quite that. But they wound up with $680,000 each as a result of Cissy's will, and no one need weep for them.

Thus, within a year of her death, the newspaper which was her *raison d'être* had passed into the hands of the cousin with whom she had battled out the last year of her life. But the crowning irony was still to come. Colonel McCormick, attempting to operate a Washington newspaper from Chicago, was unsuccessful. Also, he was growing old and wanted to be rid of financial headaches. Six years later, on St. Patrick's Day 1954, he stunned the newspaper world and Washington by selling the *Times-Herald* to, of all people, Eugene Meyer, the man Cissy had prevented from acquiring it since 1936. Meyer promptly shut down the *Times-Herald* after incorporating into his *Post* its best features and staff members.

The sinking of this last vestige of Cissy Patterson was sad. Washington knew it would miss this brassy counterpoint to the *Post* as much as it missed Cissy herself. The *Times-Herald* staff members virtually went into shock at the sudden loss of their bread-and-butter and their home-away-from-home. They formed an alumni association, and for ten years its members met every St. Patrick's night to toast the good old days and the extraordinary woman who had made them possible. It was a remarkably lasting testimonial to a dead newspaper.

The death of the roaring "voice" she had nursed to bouncing health marked Cissy's final posthumous tragedy. Had she succeeded in leaving her paper to Alicia Guggenheim, perhaps it would have survived her longer in a viable form, but Alicia herself was to die, when she was only fifty-six years old, in 1963. Then the problem of extending the dynasty into another generation would have to be faced all over again.

Cissy's death had shocked her friends and public, because no one had thought of this vital natural force dying suddenly and quietly. Yet, looked at in perspective, she died at the right time. She was not emotionally ready for the nuclear age.

Despite her disappointments, Cissy should not have judged herself a failure. She had added excitement to the lives of many, many people, and she had always fought for what she believed in. She ranked as the ultimate in personal journalism; indeed, she was one of the last of this vanishing breed. What had that accomplished? For twenty-four years, through her *Herald*, and then her *Times-Herald*, she had kept Washington from becoming a morning-monopoly newspaper town. If she had frequently used her newspaper for her own whims, she had nonetheless at the same time provided the capital of a great democracy with another vigorous voice, often of dissent.

With all her basic insecurity and often poignant human relationships, Cissy on the whole had had a rousing time. She was an American duchess, a product of her times, personifying in her many lives a whole succession of romanticized heroines—little sister of the rich, innocent heiress abroad, western sportswoman, Washington hostess, feuding editor and swashbuckling boss.

Taking it all together, she was unique. To try to imagine a Cissy Patterson flowering in a European or Asiatic culture, or at any other time, is difficult. Only in America could she have originated and flourished, and even in America she has had no exact counterpart. It is probably safe to say she never will.

INDEX